Louis Kahn's Situated Modernism

YALE UNIVERSITY PRESS NEW HAVEN & LONDON

SARAH WILLIAMS GOLDHAGEN

Louis Kahn's
Situated Modernism

Published with assistance from the Louis Stern
Memorial Fund.

The author and publisher wish to thank the Louis I. Kahn
Collection for providing many of the illustrations in this
book. The formal credit line for these images, "© 1977
Louis I. Kahn Collection, University of Pennsylvania and
Pennsylvania Historical and Museum Commission,"
is abbreviated in the captions after the first reference
(fig. 1.5) as "Kahn Collection."

Designed by Richard Hendel
Set in Bodoni and Meta type by Amy Storm
Printed in Italy by Conti Tipocolor

Library of Congress Cataloging-in-Publication Data
Goldhagen, Sarah Williams.
Louis Kahn's situated modernism / Sarah Williams
Goldhagen.
    p. cm.
Includes bibliographical references and index.
ISBN 0-300-07786-6 (alk. paper)
1. Kahn, Louis I., 1901–1974 – Criticism and
interpretation. 2. Architecture, Modern – 20th century –
United States. 3. Kahn, Louis I., 1901–1974 – Political and
social views. I. Kahn, Louis I., 1901–1974. II. Title.

NA737.K32 G65 2001
720'.92 – DC21
00-043677

A catalogue record for this book is available from the
British Library.

The paper in this book meets the guidelines for permanence
and durability of the Committee on Production Guidelines for
Book Longevity of the Council on Library Resources.

10 9 8 7 6 5 4 3 2 1

In memory of my father,

NORMAN WILLIAMS, JR.,

city planner and activist for

social justice

CONTENTS

Color plates follow page 40.

INTRODUCTION

Take Louis Kahn's Salk Institute in La Jolla, California. Here are two low-lying slab blocks: the external facades are monolithic and concrete, the internal ones woody and angular, scientists' offices craning their necks to look upon the sea (Plate 1). The central axis between the buildings is a marble-paved void with a single watery line drawing the eye to the ocean beyond. This is a composition of sublime poetic force, curiously difficult to describe without resort to the rhapsodic strains that Kahn liked to employ at the end of his life when speaking about his architecture. Or take the library at Exeter Academy in Exeter, New Hampshire, a great brick packing crate of a building that is dominated inside by geometries of circles inscribed in squares; natural light pours in around an improbably heavy **X**-shaped cross high above (Plate 2). Kahn's work can easily be seen as a formalist, quasi-mystical shaping of Platonic archetypes derived from historical references. Salk, Exeter—indeed, Kahn's architecture in general—are often described as an expression of the elemental, the transcendental, and the eternal.[1]

Other readings of these buildings, however, both are more powerful and better reflect Kahn's intentions. The Salk Institute's monolithic concrete periphery demarcates a strong boundary to the building, reinforcing the imagistic quality that makes the complex stick in the mind. It is self-consciously monumental without overawing the user, because its monumentality is mitigated by careful detailing that sustains a human scale. On the opposite, internal facades, the casual angularity of the scientists' offices, windows over every desk, speaks of human use. Between exterior and interior facades a dialectic is established between public and private, communal and individual. Had Kahn and his client, Jonas Salk, succeeded in raising the funds to build the meeting house and the temporary dwellings that were to have sat on opposing sand bluff crests, a hierarchy from private to public would have been created, with small office spaces accommodating the solitary activity of research and focused thought, townhouses for the small nucleus of the family, laboratories as the forum for common work, and a meeting house meant to foster the atmosphere of a polis.

One can certainly portray the Salk Institute as invoking elemental law and order. A better interpretation, though, would see it as an institute for a community of scientists, a monumental symbol proposing a society different from that which existed in the United States in 1962, a society in which people's pursuit of personal satisfaction did not overwhelm their capacity to participate in their community. In the Salk Institute's orientation of the laboratories to the ocean, one can infer references to the eternal, but one could better consider how these heavy buildings simultaneously work within and register the site's topography, views, and natural features, impressing on the viewer that she is standing in this and no other place, at this and no other time. Similarly, instead of seeing in the library at Exeter idealist geometries recalling past architectural traditions, one could better concentrate on the raw mass of brick surrounding a concrete core, and contemplate the social vision implied in placing a grand and richly detailed common space at the heart of a building where privileged teenagers come to do their math.

The standard accounts of the Salk Institute and the Exeter Library do not differ substantially from conventional readings of Kahn's other major buildings, most of which are structured by a number of disparate myths. These myths are so insistently repeated that many have acquired canonical status, governing interpretations of Kahn's architecture. Those even casually acquainted with Kahn's work will recognize these myths in the following brief accounts:

Myth: Kahn is a conservative, mystical thinker who sought to discover or create geometric archetypes of universal significance. A latter-day neo-Platonist, he believed it was the architect's job to "discover" ideal forms and then re-embody these archetypes in a new architectural language. Kahn himself encouraged this vision of his agenda, particularly toward the end of life when, under the influence of spiritually minded architects, mostly from the Indian subcontinent, he retroactively described his architectural agenda in the obfuscatory and transcendentalizing terms for which he is well known. In reality, however, Kahn laid this imaginative, otherworldly language on top of a "this-worldly" architectural vocabulary that had decidedly non-transcendental origins and intentions, and which was already well developed when he started designing his major buildings. The question for this book, then, is not whether Kahn's buildings touch upon something like universal archetypes, but how Kahn came to his elemental geometries, and what social and architectural ends he believed they served.

Myth: Kahn had been a social activist during and immediately after the Great Depression. As he developed his mature architecture, he became apolitical. It is true that as Kahn matured he became less politically active in the conventional sense. However, he remained politically engaged. As he matured, Kahn sought to embody his social vision directly into his architecture: his buildings and projects became his politics. He believed that the only good society was a genuinely democratic one, and that architecture could, indeed must, sustain and nourish democratic values. His vision of democracy was not sophisticated, but it was deeply felt. The question, then, is not whether Kahn was political, but what were his politics, what was his social vision, and how did they inform his architectural ideals and practice.

Myth: Kahn was the most important mid-twentieth-century practitioner of structural rationalism, an ideology of design that was first comprehensively articulated by the great nineteenth-century theorist Eugène-Emmanuel Viollet-le-Duc. Although Kahn repeatedly declared his interest in expressing the materials and processes by which a building was made, structure per se was not the overarching focus of his design. He did not hesitate to dissimulate the structure of his buildings when doing so served his broader agenda: the look of the ceilings of the Art Gallery at Yale in New Haven and the Kimbell Art Museum in Fort Worth obscures their structural properties; the concrete X-shaped cross below the skylit ceiling at the Exeter Library is grossly exaggerated for dramatic effect. The question, then, is not whether or not Kahn's insistence on materials and structure made him a structural rationalist, but what his attitude was toward the tectonics of a building, and whether these ideas fit into an overall agenda.

Myth: Kahn's career fell into two parts. From the 1930s to the late 1940s he was a competent if unremarkable practitioner of early modernism. From the early 1950s, when he was resident architect at the American Academy in Rome, until his death in 1974, Kahn increasingly broke from modernism toward the historically informed, Beaux-Arts-influenced vocabulary of his "great" mature architecture. The truth is that while Kahn was abroad, he principally explored abstraction and materiality, aesthetic issues that he had started to examine several years earlier. When he returned home, he embraced a mode of design, spearheaded by R. Buckminster Fuller, that had no use for historic precedents at all. As in other periods, Kahn's artistic development in the early 1950s, like life itself, was complex, fluid, and progressed only incrementally. The question, then, is not when and where came the putative epiphany, or even epiphanies, that led Kahn to his mature architecture, but how he gradually developed his ideas from early modernism, why they took the directions that they did, and why he adopted the vocabularies that he did to realize his architectural vision.

Myth: Kahn was the founding father of American historicist postmodernism: Robert Venturi, Charles Moore, Robert A. M. Stern, and others are his direct descendants. Kahn mentored both Venturi and Moore, but this tells us little about Kahn's own work. We cannot impute the aspirations of Venturi and Moore to Kahn; indeed, these younger architects used historical precedents with intentions and manifestations vastly different from Kahn's. The question, then, is not whether Kahn employed historical precedents, but how he used them, why he began to adapt them, and whether and how he integrated them into his overall agenda.

Myth: Kahn was a heroic genius, a slightly disheveled if charming Old World character toiling late into the night, walking out of step with the mainstream of American architectural culture. In fact, Kahn was gregarious, community ori-

ented, and dependent on friends, colleagues, and students for intellectual stim-
ulation, critiques, and ideas on architecture and society. Once asked how he
approached a new project, Kahn answered that his first step was to "talk to people . . . you can't wrap yourself up in yourself."[2] The question, then, is not
whether Kahn was a genius, but when, how, and what he learned from other
people, and how his social and architectural vision was influenced by the social
and cultural developments of his time.

These myths exaggerate selected aspects of Kahn's ideas and architecture while
downplaying or overlooking others. Some patently misrepresent his agenda and
his worldview. By simplifying and stylizing, they collectively belie the complexity of Kahn's development and his vision. We do not, then, yet have a complete,
or even an accurate, view of Kahn or his work. He is not seen as the moral actor
that he understood himself to be. His political and social vision is lost. The
social manner in which he developed his ideas is denied. The meanings he
intended for central elements of his vocabulary are misconstrued.

These myths may have persisted in spite of several important, archivally
grounded accounts of Kahn's career and of selected themes in his artistic oeuvre, because there has been, until now, no integrated interpretive study of his
intellectual and artistic development and his practice.[3] This book, adopting in
many ways a substantially different approach to him and his work, is such a
study. It presents a detailed analysis of the gradual evolution of his ideas and his
architecture from the late 1930s to the mid-1960s, the years in which he developed his mature architecture. It sets this development in the necessary context
of American architectural culture and social trends. In doing so, it situates and
rethinks Kahn's ideas and work, and his contribution to modern architecture.

During his entire professional life, Kahn concentrated on building institutions that might advance the public good. He completed only a small number of
private houses and even fewer commercial commissions. In the 1930s and
1940s he designed a number of low-cost housing projects; from the 1950s until
his death in 1974, he focused on public building for the arts, educational institutions, religious communities, and governments. The connection between
these two phases of his practice has not been systematically examined, yet it is
in their continuity that the heart of his lifelong enterprise can be discerned.

Kahn, throughout his career, sought to create a socially transformative architecture. The Salk Institute and the library at Exeter were not exceptions. Underlying the dramatic stylistic shifts that led Kahn from the early modernism of his
public housing projects to the mature idiom of buildings like the National
Assembly complex in Dhaka, Bangladesh, and the Salk Institute was a highly
specific social agenda, driven by Kahn's belief that architecture had to encourage a more humane and socially beneficial way of life—must, as he once put it,
"make man a different kind of man."[4] Kahn, like Le Corbusier and Walter

Gropius (two architects whom he much admired), always felt that the architect's mission was to better society by transforming its people and its institutions. "Did Mozart ask society what he should compose?" he once asked. "Of course not. He composed, and society became a different thing. The architect makes a work which inspires society to take a different turn."[5]

To elicit Kahn's vision of this "different thing," of how architecture could be marshaled to improve society, and of what architectural language would best advance this aim, this book operates on methodological, historical, empirical, interpretive, and theoretical levels. Methodologically, it begins with the assertion that human agency, though real, is dramatically constrained by a person's inevitable engagement in what Michel Foucault calls discourse, and what Pierre Bourdieu more generally describes as a field.[6] Kahn's self-descriptions are often cues to, or echoes of, larger debates on a variety of issues that troubled American architects, intellectuals, and social critics in the two decades after World War II. Kahn's civic and religious buildings, analyzed in light of these discussions, are not texts but intertexts situated, as Bourdieu would have it, "within the space" of other contemporary works. Kahn—sometimes consciously, sometimes unconsciously—"oriented" his work toward the perceived demands of his audiences: his buildings were powerful aesthetic propositions to debates that preoccupied many.[7]

This methodological premise necessitates a historical approach different from that conventionally employed in monographic art historical studies. Monographs typically focus principally on their subjects, providing a social or intellectual context for the work only occasionally and along the way. This study, by contrast, systematically shifts back and forth between discourse and subject, between field and agent. It does so in order to reconstruct the discursive communities, the "other half" of the discussions in which Kahn participated and his ideas were enmeshed. To analyze these, this book examines the work of his students at the schools of architecture where he principally taught— Yale, Princeton, and the University of Pennsylvania—as well as the course syllabi, studio projects, and published writings of his most important teaching colleagues. From these materials, combined with a comprehensive reading of the architectural periodicals to which Kahn subscribed, emerges not an ethereal "climate of the times" argument, but a precise elucidation of the series of overlapping microclimates of sociocritical and architectural discourses in which he was successively participating.

Most chapters, while casting new light on Kahn's ideas, depict and analyze an issue or issues central to American intellectual and architectural culture in the two decades in which Kahn was developing his mature architecture. Chapter 1, on selected essays, projects, and low-cost housing projects by Kahn in the 1940s, examines the convergence, in the United States, of the modern movement with the preexisting movement in public housing, and analyzes the debates within and outside the Congrès Internationaux d'Architecture Moderne (CIAM) on monumentality and modernism. Chapter 2, on Kahn's Art Gallery at Yale University, explores the interaction between artists and architects in the arts programs at Yale, and delineates some of the central issues in American abstract art in the early postwar years. Chapter 3, on Kahn and Anne Griswold Tyng's project for City Tower and on Kahn's AFL Medical Services in Philadelphia, offers a detailed account of one major attempt to reinvigorate the modern movement in the 1950s: Fuller's techno-organic movement in space frames. Chapter 4, on the Adath Jeshurun project for a synagogue in Elkins Park, Pennsylvania, examines how progressive American architects framed their ideas on religious buildings around the debates on monumentality. Chapter 5, on Kahn's Jewish Community Center and Bathhouse in Trenton, New Jersey, and his Philadelphia Civic Center plan, analyzes why, in the 1950s, progressive American architects turned toward an architecture that evoked historic precedent. Chapter 6, on the First Unitarian Church in Rochester, New York, outlines the Cold War–generated discourse among architects, mainly at the University of Pennsylvania, on the need for a public idiom that encouraged the democratic values of free choice and individual expression. Chapter 7, on the National Assembly complex in Dhaka, investigates the phenomenon of American architects working in developing countries. The chapter explores what they took from the cultures of their patrons and how they, and Kahn, brought their own cultural assumptions and social agendas to the governments and institutions for which they worked.

This book provides, then, a series of discrete analyses of the successive and sometimes overlapping themes central to American architectural culture in the twenty years after World War II. The principal way in which these cultural moments are linked is that Kahn moved through each one as each one moved him. Collectively, what emerges is a narrative of postwar architecture turning on a dual axis: architects' and intellectuals' evolving attitudes toward the potential of mass production and technology to effect positive social change, and architects' and intellectuals' responses to mass culture. These two themes underlay Kahn's ideas on topics as various as the future of the modern movement, the nature of monumentality and its relationship to modernism, architecture's role in advancing personal revelation and people's cognizance of the specificity of place, and the proper constitution of a democratic community.

Although this book is a critique of the conventional art historical study, in which the free agency of the individual is overly emphasized, it is also a critique of the kind of theoretical writing on art in which human agency, and the physical objects that people create, disappear. Such writing implicitly or explicitly argues that one must abandon the individual to focus instead only on discourse – Bourdieu dismisses the biography as a legitimate form of inquiry, and Foucault argues that "the theme of the founding subject permits us to elide the reality of discourse."[8] Here, a wealth of new information on Kahn is integrated into a more full-bodied picture of his ideas, showing how he recombined, changed, and interpreted the ideas to which he was exposed in order to devise a singular vocabulary.

Empirically, this study analyzes all kinds of new information on Kahn himself and on the discursive communities in which he was involved. For example, Kahn's little-studied entry for a Jefferson National Expansion Memorial in St. Louis, a commission that went to Eero Saarinen, is revealed as an important developmental link in Kahn's ideas about monumentality in the late 1940s. Kahn's paintings, sketches, and studio assignments at Yale show him to be more deeply involved in contemporary art than has been previously understood. Correspondence between him and Tyng, his collaborator and personal companion during a critical period in his development, discloses that her influence on his ideas was even more profound than has been assumed. Other correspondence, Kahn's notes on drawings and in his calendars, his journal entries, and his lectures reveal the wide network of Kahn's intellectual community, which included such visionaries as Fuller, such architects as Philip Johnson and Alison and Peter Smithson, such landscape architects as Ian McHarg, such social critics as John Keats and William H. Whyte. His slide collection, which until now had been only incompletely studied, confirms the depth of the impact of Tyng's ideas on Kahn's own. It also provides an excellent indicator of when and under what circumstances he began working consciously with natural light. A set of previously unknown drawings for his First Unitarian Church in Rochester illuminates critical aspects of early schemes for that project which emerged directly out of discussions about mass culture at the University of Pennsylvania, ideas that were later realized in his National Assembly complex in Dhaka.

The different methodological and historical approaches, together with new evidence and a rereading of known evidence, produces here new interpretations of Kahn's moral and political agenda, and of buildings and projects central to any assessment of Kahn and his career. This book treats in depth many of his most important buildings and projects, such as the Yale Art Gallery, the Adath Jeshurun synagogue project, the First Unitarian Church in Rochester, and the National Assembly complex in Dhaka. It also focuses on some usually neglected works to the exclusion of some familiar ones. Many interpreters, for example, have assumed that City Tower (1952–1957) was primarily Tyng's project, but a close analysis of correspondence between Kahn and Tyng reveals that, at least in the early years of its inception, the project was as much Kahn's as Tyng's— and this, in turn, suggests that in these years he was examining quite different issues than has been commonly recognized. By the same token, the Richards Medical Center in Philadelphia (1956–1965), which consolidated Kahn's international reputation and is usually considered to be central among his works, is deemed less important than previously assumed. Having been the product of a collaboration between Kahn and Auguste Komendant, his structural engineer, the Richards Medical Center, in its focus on an innovative, prefabricated structural system, is less indicative of Kahn's evolving thought in the mid-to-late 1950s than is the contemporaneous, but unbuilt, Jewish Community Center in Trenton. In the concluding chapter, I indicate how this understanding of the architectural vision that Kahn developed as he was shaping his mature architecture illuminates other major works in his oeuvre, such as the Salk Institute, the Yale Center for British Art, and the Kimbell Art Museum.

The methodological and historical approaches employed here have inspired a theoretical inquiry into the transformation of the modern movement in the years after World War II, which I am undertaking mainly in other work.[9] This broader inquiry, together with the findings and the new interpretations presented here of Kahn's work, has made it clear that Kahn's architecture needs to be theorized anew.

Much has been written on early modernism in the past three decades that has called into question the monolithic image of a teleological, progressive movement with a unified point of view that flourished in the second and third decades of the twentieth century, the image presented by such first-generation theorists as Sigfried Giedion and Sir Nikolaus Pevsner. We have learned of the ideological fissures in CIAM between Le Corbusier and those espousing a *Neue Sachlichkeit*, of Le Corbusier's opportunism and shifting political alliances and of his flirtations with the French Right; of Ludwig Mies van der Rohe's acceptance of the status quo; of Mies and Le Corbusier's deep entrenchment in historical precedents despite claims that they had created a style exquisitely tailored to the new social and cultural conditions of modern life. We have learned of the multiple irrationalities that were paraded as structural and functional rationalism. We have been challenged to think of a more inclusive modernism that might encompass Alvar Aalto, Hugo Häring, and Frank Lloyd Wright along with the canonical triad of Gropius, Le Corbusier, and Mies.[10]

Our image of the postwar period, by contrast, remains more or less one-dimensional. The conventional story is a bifurcated one. Early modernism ossified into the high modernist, corporate idiom of the International Style and into the ghetto style of high-rise public housing. At the same time, a group of younger architects in Europe (mainly Italy) and the United States spearheaded a historically informed approach to design in which typology and urban context were privileged. This movement, which came by the mid-1960s to be called postmodernism, led to the eventual collapse of modernism as a viable idiom.[11]

Just because early modernism was more multifaceted than its self-description allowed does not mean that the movement did not exist, if perhaps only as a family of resemblances. And just because the straw-man vision of early modernism has been picked apart does not mean that many architects did not continue to grapple with, build on, and reformulate their complex modernist heritage. The history of architecture in the postwar period is far richer and more complex than the one-eyed, curiously teleological narrative that posits post-modernism as its apotheosis.

Kahn was one of the architects who struggled with, rather than against, modernism. He reshaped the idiom of East Coast American modernism, which was in essential ways different from either its West Coast or its European counterparts, to adapt it both to the new social circumstances and new cultural concerns of his discursive communities and to his own moral and political agenda. To comprehend what this struggle wrought, this book's concluding chapter theorizes the character and elements of Kahn's original contribution to architecture, his situated modernism.

In the ten years of working on this book, I have spoken about Louis Kahn's architecture with many architects, architectural historians, and theorists. Many of them profess a great appreciation for Kahn's achievement and comment regretfully that they have little to say about the greatest architect of the postwar period. Kahn's work *is* difficult to talk about. My hope is that this study provides an analytical framework and a descriptive language that will help people to understand his intentions for his work, and to understand why his buildings effectuate the experiences that they do.

KAHN AND AMERICAN MODERNISM

THE SEARCH FOR COMMUNITY AND THE
TURN TOWARD MONUMENTALITY

1

Where is your school?
Where do your children play?
Where does your wife shop?
Where does your husband meet his friends?
Where do you find recreation?
Is it a "Neighborhood"?
—Louis Kahn and Oscar Stonorov, Why City Planning Is Your Responsibility

In the early 1930s, the conservative, Beaux-Arts-dominated American architectural community in which Louis Isadore Kahn moved was being challenged by a new movement that was largely an import from Europe. Modernism, or simply modern architecture, as its practitioners called it, celebrated industrial technology by employing imagery from factories, ocean liners, and grain silos; its leitmotifs were clean lines, flat roofs, the separation of a building's structure from its perimeter facades, and compositions of volumetric forms, irregularly disposed to reflect open plans within. Proponents of the modern movement insisted that architecture be determined not by considering such rigid, formalizing compositional elements as symmetry, hierarchy, or axial organization of spaces, but instead by making the structure of the building visible, and by planning internal spaces in a "functional" or "rational" manner that accommodated the needs of a building's users. Propelling this new style were architects' idealistic convictions that modern architecture might facilitate the quick, efficient mass production of buildings. Buildings produced in the way that automobiles were manufactured could improve the standard of living in two manners. Better housing would become more affordable, and therefore within the reach of many more people. And, by transferring the symbolic language of technology into more familiar settings like the home, mass-produced buildings could enable people to better cope with the alienation and anxieties caused by an accelerated, technologized modern life.

Such progressive-minded American architects as Kahn became familiar with these ideas through books, periodicals, and exhibitions. The most famous were Le Corbusier's *Towards a New Architecture*, which appeared in English in the

United States in 1927, and Henry-Russell Hitchcock and Philip Johnson's exhibition and catalogue of 1932, *The International Style*, which featured private houses, housing projects, and a few larger public buildings by an array of modern architects from countries ranging from Finland to Italy, from Spain to Russia. Modernist buildings, too, began to appear on American soil, some by natives influenced by these new trends, others by immigrants from Europe. Around Chicago and later in California, Frank Lloyd Wright built dramatic, low-slung houses; also in California, Viennese immigrants Richard Neutra and Rudolph Schindler constructed related but starker projects. In the Northeast, the first modernist skyscraper, the Philadelphia Savings and Fund Society, was finished in 1932 by William Lescaze and George Howe, the second being Kahn's mentor, and later his architectural partner.[1]

Modernism in the United States, at least in the circles in which Kahn traveled, had a somewhat different, and narrower, ideological edge than it did in Europe. Many European modernists were committed to social housing, and many believed that one of the new architecture's social tasks was to reinforce those bonds that created communal identity: this was especially evident in German public housing projects such as Bruno Taut's Berlin-Britz Hufeisensiedlung of 1925–1930. The focus of European architects on communal identity was, however, just one point in a social program to improve middle-class living standards by rationalizing building processes and promoting mass production. Kahn's colleagues in the Northeast, by contrast, fused convictions from the modern movement in Europe with tenets from the American public housing movement, which also sought to reinforce communal identity. While the "problem" of community had been one among many for European modernists, for many avant-garde American architects on the East Coast, it was often the social agenda that determined what it meant to be a modernist.

In the years that Kahn began practicing in earnest, he became involved in shaping American modernism around the question of how architecture and city planning might be used to reinforce and promote people's feelings of communal identification. Underlying this quest was an axiomatic conviction, which Kahn shared with his colleagues, that the architect's main responsibility was to change society for the better. When, in the 1940s, he began to think about these issues in reference to a monumental architectural idiom in addition to public housing, Kahn considered how his buildings might not only spatially facilitate the making of a community but also reinforce communal sentiment by creating symbols of public identity. The first he addressed in his public housing projects and essays, some of which were collaborative projects with his partners Oscar Stonorov and Howe; he combined the first with the second in his essay on monumentality in 1944 and in his 1947 entry for the Jefferson National Expansion Memorial in St. Louis.

That bringing people together in domestic or public collective settings would engender social good was an assumption so deeply ingrained in Kahn's worldview that it formed part of what Pierre Bourdieu calls a *habitus:* "embodied history, internalized as second nature and so forgotten as history."[2] The origin of Kahn's appreciation of a vital communal life lay in his experiences growing up in the immigrant ghettos of Philadelphia. Born in 1901 to Jewish parents in a small village in Estonia, his family immigrated to the United States in 1905, where Kahn's father, Leopold, kept a small shop and his mother, Bertha, made clothing samples for local manufacturers.[3] Kahn often described the city where he lived his entire life as a friendly place, later remembering that his father's shop had never been financially successful because if a customer longed for an item for which he could not pay, Leopold Kahn would offer it for free.[4] This was an environment where neighbors and family helped each other through the relentless pressures of poverty.

Kahn's parents strongly believed that immigrants to the United States were obliged to adapt themselves to the ways of their adopted country. Years later, he wrote that one of the deepest influences of his life had been "my mother's faith in America 200%."[5] His wife, Esther, a native Philadelphian and a Jew whom he married in 1930, similarly believed that immigrants should assimilate themselves into the American melting pot; as a girl, she attended a Protestant Sunday school because her father decided that the Jewish synagogue was too far from their neighborhood and that he preferred her to befriend children who were geographically proximate, no matter their background.[6] Kahn's experience of poverty in the ghetto, and his immigrant's conviction that one could find commonality with people of any ethnicity or religion, encouraged his assumption that the public welfare was advanced when individuals acted in concert to further the interests of a collectivity that was delimited not by class or religion but by culture, political convictions, or citizenship.

His personality also predisposed him to emphasize the social value of communing with others. By his own admission, Kahn was a man who relied on others to advance his architectural ideas and his personal growth. He was known for his gregariousness. He loved speaking in public, and often preferred spending leisure time either at his office or at the school where he happened to be teaching.[7] He relied on the company of students and professional colleagues not only for personal companionship but also for critical reactions to his outpourings of ideas.[8] Admitting as much in 1962, he answered a television interviewer's question as to how he got started on a project: "The exhilaration of getting the assignment of course makes you want to talk to people, you can't just sit back and merely wrap yourself up with yourself . . . from talking to people you get a sense of their radar about this problem and from that a sense of beginning for yourself."[9]

Kahn's childhood experiences and his personality inclined him to assume that communication with others could reap social as well as personal rewards. Assumptions were transformed into convictions when Kahn became associated with a group of architects, city planners, and social activists in the American public housing movement, an association that began in the 1930s and deepened through his partnership with Stonorov, the German immigrant architect with whom he worked from 1941 to 1947. Kahn's involvement in public housing was integral to his identity as a modernist: he was immersed in the city's small, close-knit community of architects, a center both of discussions about trends in European avant-garde architecture and of the movement to improve public housing through a national program.[10] Many, including Kahn, contributed to the modernist-inclined *T-Square Club Journal of Philadelphia*, which was funded by Howe until it was taken over in 1932 by R. Buckminster Fuller and renamed *Shelter*, at which point Howe withdrew funding, which led to the journal's demise.[11] In the wake of the construction industry's collapse in the early Depression years, Kahn kept himself busy with the Architectural Research Group, an activist organization that he had founded in 1931, devoted to promoting modern design.[12]

Kahn's social convictions were evident in the public housing developments and in unbuilt projects of these years. Among the projects of the 1930s, the most celebrated was the Jersey Homesteads (Fig. 1.1), which he designed while working as assistant architect to Alfred Kastner, an architect based in Washington, D.C.[13] Located near Hightstown, New Jersey, and ultimately built under the supervision of the federal Resettlement Administration for Jewish garment workers in New York City and Philadelphia, the Jersey Homesteads was the brainchild of a Ukrainian-born immigrant named Benjamin Brown. It was to include 250 homes on 1,200 acres of farmland, and was described by local papers as "one of the first government-sponsored attempts to induce workers of a centralized industry to desert the congestion of a large city for more favorable living conditions."[14] Residents of the project would till their own land and would perform larger-scale farming and manufacturing collectively. The Jersey Homesteads was, in essence, an American kibbutz; the radicalism of the ideas that underlay the project was not lost on one contemporary critic who bewailed the new "commune" built by (referring to Brown) "a little Russian-born Stalin."[15]

For Kahn and Kastner, this project was as much a test case for developing methods of architectural prefabrication as an experiment in social organization. The architectural avant-garde in Europe was exploring new techniques of prefabrication, and it seems that it was in this arena that Kahn and Kastner sought to make their mark as innovators. Kahn, in a report on the project in 1936, described his and Kastner's desire to "produce prefabricated building units with a definite advance in the lowering of construction costs for medium price housing." They wanted, he continued, to "sum up advances made by industry," and to that end, they focused on innovative uses of lightweight concrete and steel.[16]

1.1 Alfred Kastner and Louis I. Kahn, Jersey Homesteads, Hightstown, New Jersey, 1935–1937. Photo: E. Teitelman.

15

KAHN AND AMERICAN MODERNISM

By the 1940s, Kahn began to focus more on the social implications of his architectural designs as he became involved in a discursive community in Philadelphia that included Kastner, Stonorov, Catherine Bauer, Lewis Mumford, and Paul and Percival Goodman. In 1941 he and Howe began to collaborate with Stonorov, who remained politically allied with leftist causes throughout his career.[17] Before coming to the United States and settling in Philadelphia in 1931, Stonorov had lived in Paris, where he had edited the first volume of Le Corbusier's *Oeuvre complète* and worked for the Marxist architect André Lurçat. Like Lurçat's, Stonorov's commitment to the modern movement was founded less on stylistic than on ideological convictions. He believed that the architect should work not simply for those who hired him but for the greater social good. Specifically, though, Stonorov emphasized the importance of communal identity. Housing and urban planning were the means; concerning housing, it was not "so much a question of naked shelter only," he wrote in 1932, "it is the demand for reorganization of rotten communities into stable, sane, and healthy societies."[18]

If Stonorov's determination to "reorganize rotten communities" was inspired by Marxist ideas from Europe, it was reinforced by his exposure to a discourse developing in the United States among such social activists as his friend Catherine Bauer, whom he had met in 1932. Bauer had become a housing activist in the late 1920s; her study of new European public housing, *Modern Housing* (1934), established her as a leading authority in the field.[19] Stonorov met Bauer while he was working for Kastner on the Carl Mackley Houses in Philadelphia (1932–1935; Fig. 1.2), the first federally funded project of the Public Works Authority; together, the three of them worked on the Mackley Houses' design.[20] Stonorov and Bauer became friends: he secured a first job for her in Philadelphia, as surveyor of company towns in Pennsylvania,[21] and later Bauer, when she became director of the United States Housing Authority in 1941, set up her office in a corner of the space occupied by the firm Howe, Stonorov, and Kahn.[22]

Bauer's ideas on public housing had been shaped partly by her studies of German *Siedlung* projects abroad and partly by the sociopolitical ideas of Lewis Mumford, with whom she began a romantic and professional association in

1.2 Oscar Stonorov and Alfred Kastner, Carl Mackley Houses, Philadelphia, 1932–1935. Photo: E. Teitelman.

1931.[23] Bauer believed in the importance of collective action as a means of counteracting the impersonal power of the state under industrial capitalism. Such local action, she argued, could be encouraged by architects and city planners who designed according to what she called the "neighborhood unit concept." The resulting benefits of the communal identity would accrue to all members of society, Bauer argued: "All kinds of research on social disorganization and maladjustment tend to come down to the fact that we have lost a community base, at a level where personal participation, identification of individual and family with group and society, are possible."[24]

Mumford had insisted on the importance of "civil life" as early as 1919. Civil life, he wrote, meant "association . . . with the family, the trade union, the grange, the chamber of commerce, the professional institute, the church, the theater and the forum intermediating between the life of the individual and his life as the member of the . . . state."[25] By 1934, in *Technics and Civilization* (a book for which Bauer had been a research assistant), Mumford was specifically arguing that collectivism was a corrective and a cure to the "anarchic" individualism of the contemporary capitalist "paleotechnic" age, which was destroying communities and cities.[26] Both Bauer and Mumford upheld this ideology of communal association in their writings on the design of public housing, emphasizing the importance of communally oriented design and abundant public facilities.[27]

The design of the Mackley Houses was surely inspired by the Siedlung projects that Bauer had studied while abroad. Yet they were also a critique of such German *Zeilenbau* as the Siemensstadt development in Berlin, which was characterized by a repetitive, slab-block design in which the overwhelming considerations were efficiency and sun orientation. Both Bauer and Stonorov repudiated the slab-block designs of Germany, arguing that they undermined a sense of communal identity; in 1939, Stonorov attacked the German Siedlung as "sanitary barracks" that provided "no substitute for communal life."[28] Many years later Bauer attributed the failure of the public housing movement to her and her colleagues' emphasis on what she called "collectivism," which, she implied, went against the American individualistic grain.[29] The site plan, plans, and programming of the Mackley Houses, by contrast with the Siedlung developments in Germany, wove private apartments into a tight, neighborhood-like setting.[30] The repetitive, rectangular slab blocks of Ernst May's developments were replaced by notched plans so that housing blocks look onto and enclose playgrounds, lawns, an auditorium, and a pool. Each flat shares a balcony with its neighbor. Roofs become communal areas with not only laundry rooms but also nursery facilities, play areas, and a "women's club."

Bauer's ideal of collectivism originated in Mumford's response to the Great Depression, which he and other left-leaning intellectuals in the 1920s interpreted as proof that capitalism untrammeled brought little social good.[31] In the years after World War II, despite unequaled prosperity, a new generation of American practitioners and architectural commentators continued to espouse Mumfordian ideas. José Luis Sert, under Mumford's influence, proposed the topic of community as the focal point of the first postwar conference of CIAM, held in Bridgewater, England, in 1947.[32] Such themes were also central to Paul and Percival Goodman's *Communitas*, which appeared in 1947 and continued to be widely read through the 1960s.[33] The Goodmans, like Mumford, argued that American capitalism's overemphasis on the preservation of private interests had caused such massive social dislocation that the very legitimacy of the system should be rethought. Above people's drive for private pleasure, they argued, should be a sense of social responsibility: with the privilege of citizenship came obligations to one's neighbors.[34]

In effect, the pronouncements of Mumford, Stonorov, Bauer, and the Goodmans continued the debate on the ideals of communitarianism versus those of classical liberalism that had originated before World War I in the writings of such philosophers as John Dewey. In the interwar period Mumford was a major proponent of communitarianism, a philosophy rooted in an ethical critique of the every-man-out-for-himself culture that capitalism seemed naturally to promote, and which the politics of liberal individualism justified.[35] This, combined with the depredations caused by the Depression, led many to demand that the political system be changed. Among architectural thinkers, though, visions of the economic or political system by which capitalism might be supplanted were varied and often vague. The Goodmans argued that democracy should be replaced with a kind of decentralized, anarchic regionalism;[36] Mumford supported a less radical mix of regionalism and democracy. Always, however, the common ground was the hope of a society populated by citizens who were more active and aware.

Their models of social organization were the New England village and, in the case of the Goodmans and Sert, the polis of ancient Greece. Mumford recalled the New England town hall meeting as an emblem of the public realm, the architectural space where citizens gathered to discuss affairs of mutual concern, where every voice was heard.[37] The Goodmans argued for a model of political change driven by free and active citizens—a notion they traced back to the Athenian agora (Figs. 1.3 and 1.4). Citing the social changes effected by the growing technology of electronic communication, the changing form of cities, and other conditions of modern life, the Goodmans mused, "Perhaps there are no longer real occasions for social congregation in the square. . . . If this is so, it is a grievous and irreparable loss. There is no substitute for the spontaneous social conflux whose atoms unite, precisely, as citizens of a city." Subsequently they urged their readers to "take a lesson from the Greeks, who spent most of their time in public places," such as the agora and gymnasia.[38]

Of course Mumford, Sert, and the Goodmans idealized the models they invoked. Cooperation, tolerance, and the democratic process did characterize the New England town meeting and the Athenian agora, but only within extremely restricted parameters. It has often been pointed out that in Athens voting citizens constituted a very small percentage of the total population: with slaves and women excluded, only male property owners came to the agora to discuss public affairs.[39] Similarly, most residents of New England villages shared religious affiliation and ethnicity. Such homogeneity promoted a firm sense of community because pluralism and dissent generally stayed within tolerable bounds. Furthermore, both the New England village and Periclean Athens had under 5,000 inhabitants. The relevance of these models to a pluralistic and more democratic society or to larger urban conglomerations was questionable.

STONOROV AND KAHN AND THE BUILDING OF COMMUNITY

Perhaps it was the non-specificity of Mumford and Bauer's social ideals that made them so appealing to Kahn and others; in any case, Kahn's deep involve-

1.3 "A Busy Square," the contemporary version of the Athenian agora. From Paul and Percival Goodman, *Communitas: Means of Livelihood and Ways of Life* (Chicago: University of Chicago Press, 1947). © 1960 Sally and Percival Goodman. Reprinted by permission of the publisher.

ment in the neighborhood planning movement and his own account of his activities in these years confirm that his activism was deeply felt.[40] Years later, when asked about his collaborations with Stonorov, he specifically recalled how his colleague had mobilized him to social action. "When Oscar came to Philadelphia," he recounted, "he brought with him the certainty that housing guided by social concern was operative. We thought we had to invent this. Oscar knew it was operative and real because he had seen it in Europe. He brought with him a certainty that reassured us."[41] Kahn's political convictions led him to join many progressive activist organizations in the early 1940s, including Philadelphia's Citizen's Council on City Planning and the newly founded American Society of Planners and Architects, modeled on CIAM.[42]

Bauer, Mumford, and Stonorov's tandem ideals of collectivism and social activism were manifest in the collaborative projects that Kahn and Stonorov completed in the 1940s. Their Carver Court development in Coatesville, Pennsylvania; their two pamphlets on city planning for Revere Copper and Brass entitled *Why City Planning Is Your Responsibility* (1943) and *You and Your Neighborhood* (1944); and their proposal for a hotel for "194X" (which was solicited by *Architectural Forum* in 1943) all show that their sociopolitical ideals dominated their written and architectural projects in city planning and low-cost housing.

Carver Court, which was designed by Howe, Stonorov, and Kahn, was a 100-unit development for black steelworkers on a rural site, formerly a racetrack, located outside Coatesville, Pennsylvania (Figs. 1.5 and 1.6).[43] The architects' activist aims guided both its site plan and the design of the dwellings. They arranged small multiple dwellings in a loop that followed the previous configuration of the site. In an irregular oval arrangement, the architects knitted all homes into a single neighborhood unit and so reinforced the communal

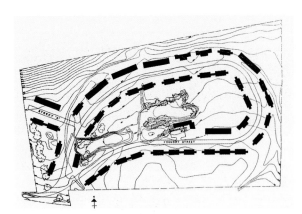

1.5 George Howe, Oscar Stonorov, and Louis I. Kahn, site plan for Carver Court with community building in center, Chester County, Pennsylvania, 1941–1943. © 1977. From the Louis I. Kahn Collection, University of Pennsylvania and Pennsylvania Historical and Museum Commission (hereafter Kahn Collection). Photo: Gottscho-Schleisner.

aspects of the complex while de-emphasizing privacy and individual identity. They further manifested such aims by locating, at the bottom of a slight slope, a small "community building" in the center of the complex (Fig. 1.7).

Howe, Stonorov, and Kahn elevated their dwelling units on slabs that recalled Le Corbusier's piloti, in what they maintained was an explicit critique of capitalist culture. In an essay they wrote on the project, entitled "'Standards' Versus Essential Space," they argued that their houses, with "basements" on the ground, provided "essential" space that was more efficient than the "standard" underground solution found in developer-built housing. In the standard solution, they claimed, it was not practical considerations but solely profit that guided developers in land-poor inner cities.[44]

Kahn and Stonorov's belief that individuals should identify with, and take responsibility for, their community was the principal topic of *Why City Planning Is Your Responsibility* (1943) and *You and Your Neighborhood* (1944). The epigraph for *You and Your Neighborhood* was taken from Mumford's *Faith for Living* (1940); it read "The final test of an economic system is not in the tons of iron, the tanks of oil, or the miles of textiles it produces: the final test lies in its ultimate products—the sort of men and women it nurtures and the order and beauty and sanity of their communities."[45] Kahn and Stonorov entreated citizens to envision different areas of the city as extensions of their own houses: "The plan of a city is like the plan of a house. . . . Dad's room is his office and his study. The city has its administration buildings, its museums, libraries, and places of education" (Fig. 1.8).[46] The authors emphasized the importance of community centers, writing that "the neighborhood house is the neighborhood club, the get-together place of the people in your area. . . . It is the center of social growth and neighborly cohesion. . . . We believe it is an essential building to stabilize the neighborhood." Once a proper neighborhood environment was created, they declared, "your task will not be done. Because . . . NEIGHBOR-HOODS are related to a COMMUNITY" (Fig. 1.9). With such claims Kahn and

1.6 Howe, Stonorov, and Kahn, Carver Court, Chester County, Pennsylvania, 1941–1943. From the Kahn Collection.

1.7 Howe, Stonorov, and Kahn, community building, Carver Court, Chester County, Pennsylvania, 1941–1943. From the Kahn Collection.

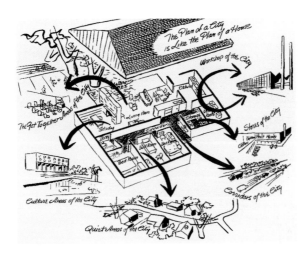

1.8 "The Plan of the City Is Like the Plan of a House." From Oscar Stonorov and Louis I. Kahn, *You and Your Neighborhood: A Primer for Neighborhood Planning* (New York: Revere Copper and Brass, 1944). Courtesy of the Architectural Archives of the University of Pennsylvania.

Stonorov tried to convince their readers that a well-planned built environment could help create a healthy community.

In both *Why City Planning* and *You and Your Neighborhood*, Kahn and Stonorov encouraged local citizens to involve themselves directly in the city-planning process by establishing planning councils, as if to resuscitate the democracy of the New England town hall or the Greek agora. "Alone you are powerless," they warned. "As an individual your power lies in citizen organization. The basic idea of the New England town meeting is citizen participation. Neighborhoods must recreate the town."

In 1944 Stonorov wrote to Howard Myers, the editor of *Architectural Forum*, that these ideas "correspond . . . to what happens in our town [Philadelphia] due to the activities of the Citizen's Council on City Planning."[47] This organization, to which both Kahn and Stonorov belonged, had been founded in Philadelphia in 1941 by local activists including Thomas Gutes, the president of the University of Pennsylvania, and G. Holmes Perkins, who would later become dean of the university's Graduate School of Fine Arts.[48] Based on the idea, described by Stonorov, that "it is up to the citizens to become vocal if they want things to happen in their community,"[49] the Citizen's Council held New England–style town meetings that included all who wanted to participate in the planning process. Edmund Bacon, later executive director of the Philadelphia City Planning Commission, and others argued that such democratic procedures differentiated their ambitious city plans from the authoritarianism driving the great urban schemes of the past.[50]

This notion—that citizens should participate in New England–style town meetings to create city and neighborhood plans that accommodated the interests of the community—was a logical extension of the community-centered designs that Kahn had helped to create in the Jersey Homesteads and Carver Court. In text and buildings, he was giving form to the idea that it was the architect's responsibility to combat the privatizing focus of American capitalism and

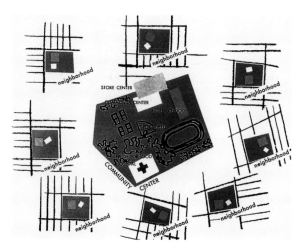

1.9 "NEIGHBORHOODS are related to a COMMUNITY." From Stonorov and Kahn, *You and Your Neighborhood*. Courtesy of the Architectural Archives of the University of Pennsylvania.

23

KAHN AND AMERICAN MODERNISM

political culture, and to shape spaces that would reinforce a sense of communal identity, thereby encouraging citizens to participate more actively in the public realm. In the 1940s, he explored social housing and city planning as the principal means to achieve these ends; in the progressive circles in which Kahn traveled, he earned a reputation as a solid designer of public housing and an aspiring urban planner. In his and Stonorov's hotel for "194X," a project published in 1943, Kahn also suggested another approach to promoting communal identity: the architects, declaring their intention to use a private commercial building to establish a communal symbol, explicitly stated their conviction that the public interest had to take precedence over private affairs (Figs. 1.10 and 1.11).

Architectural Forum, the leading architectural magazine of Kahn's generation, had been sponsoring an occasional series on "postwar design trends," and the editors invited leading architects to design "a variety of commercial and public buildings" for a hypothetical Main Street in a mid-sized city. Their model was a redevelopment plan then under way for Syracuse, New York.[51] Stonorov and Kahn transformed their assignment for a commercial hotel into a civic facility. "The hotel is the number one advertisement of a city," they wrote, "therefore it should be something of a community enterprise . . . presenting a challenge to the modern architect who has become conscious of his role as planner and engineer of civic expression."[52] Mies van der Rohe, who published his "Museum for a Small City" in the same issue, similarly claimed that his project would "create a noble background for the civic and cultural life of the whole community."[53] But whereas Mies made little attempt to have his museum spatially enact its civic role, Stonorov and Kahn designed their hotel as a "tie" between a visitor and city. The hotel, they argued, had to "fit the bill for the townspeople as well as for its out-of-town guests." They sited it so that traffic did not interfere with the access to a pedestrian mall that led to public institutions and shopping nearby. Extensive ground-floor public facilities would be housed, Corbusian style, in two interlocking rectangular spaces, to include a lounge called Peacock Alley, a drugstore, a cafeteria, a bar, and a restaurant. In order to create an up-to-date image for the whole, they proposed that guest rooms be housed in a slab-block, welded-steel tower faced with both marble and plastic veneers. An isolated, large-scale monumental building would consolidate communal identity with a plan that encouraged cooperative activity, and a highly visible form that provoked users and viewers to remember it as a symbol.

Kahn and Stonorov's 1943 hotel for "194X" is the first indication of a turn in Kahn's thinking toward combining spatial and planning gestures to facilitate the making of a community with a kind of monumentality that he believed could reinforce communal identity. In the mid-1940s, Kahn, working without Stonorov, began to contemplate the relationship of community to monumentality. This was the question to which he would repeatedly return during his career. In 1944, he contributed to a published symposium entitled *New Architecture and City Planning* with an essay on monumentality.[54] Three years later, Kahn submitted an entry for the Jefferson National Expansion Memorial competition, which Eero Saarinen would eventually win. The prospectus proposed a site on the banks of the Mississippi River in St. Louis and called for a public complex of buildings, challenging architects to address the problem of monumentality head on.

MONUMENTALITY 1944

In the early 1940s progressive architects and writers, European and American, began questioning if and how the modern approach to design—which they

1.10 Oscar Stonorov and Louis I. Kahn, Perspective of a hotel for "194X." From the Kahn Collection.

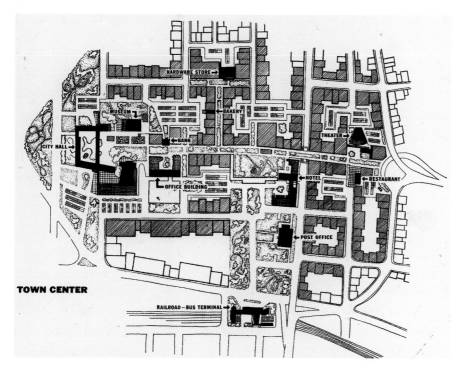

1.11 "194X": site plan for a medium-size postwar city (based on Syracuse, New York). The hotel by Stonorov and Kahn is above the post office in the center right; Charles Eames's city hall is on the far left; to its immediate right is Mies van der Rohe's Museum for a Small City. From *Architectural Forum* 78 (May 1943).

characterized as minimalist, rationalist, functional, and oriented toward the dwelling—suited the design of major monumental buildings and building complexes. Kahn and Stonorov's hero, Mumford, addressed this issue many times.[55] So did the secretary-general of CIAM, Sigfried Giedion, who wrote both alone and in collaboration with Sert and the French painter Fernand Léger. Others known to Kahn who wrote on the topic were Howe; Johnson and Elizabeth Mock of New York City's Museum of Modern Art; Jean Labatut, the leader of Princeton University's architecture program; and Joseph Hudnut, of the Graduate School of Design at Harvard.[56] Kahn's essay "Monumentality" appeared in 1944, and discussions continued thereafter: in 1948 a prominent symposium entitled "The Search for a New Monumentality" appeared in the *Architectural Review*, with Walter Gropius and Hitchcock among the contributors. The CIAM conferences of 1947 (in Bridgewater, England) and 1951 (in Hoddesdon, England) both addressed the theme.[57]

Architectural theorists' concern with monumentality had two immediate origins. One was the anticipated need for war memorials at the close of World War II.[58] At the end of World War I towns and villages in the United States had built, in place of "useless" memorials to the fallen, "living memorials" in the form of schools, community centers, public libraries, museums, and the like.[59] Expecting a revival of this trend, Johnson and Hudnut engaged in a lively debate on the relative merits of monuments that were purely symbolic versus institutional structures that could enhance their country's ideals by encouraging citizens to enact the principles of democratic life.

The debate revolved mainly around the question of which type of memorial more effectively reinforces communal identity. In 1944, the journal *The American City* ran an eight-part series in favor of living memorials, in which one author argued that "living and working together fruitfully . . . is above all a community task," and readers should work to "create memorials that will bring our people together in common understanding, affection, and purpose."[60] Hudnut reiterated these ideas: democratically minded architects should focus their energies not on symbolic monuments but on living memorials, he argued, even at the expense of the memory of the dead. "Our soldiers will understand our faith," he consoled. "They fought for it."[61]

A second source propelling the increased interest in monumentality, intimated in Hudnut's comments, was a response to the monumental architecture of totalitarian regimes. Throughout the 1930s the architects of Nazi Germany, Fascist Italy, and the Soviet Union employed an overblown academic Beaux-Arts vocabulary for their public architecture, images of which appeared regularly in the Western architectural press. As totalitarianism was increasingly associated with academicism, architectural writers in democratic countries correctly surmised that when postwar building began, practitioners from the modern movement would be called on to provide built symbols of local and national identity.

Even the most vocal proponents of the avant-garde, such as Giedion, wondered if the functionalist vocabulary they championed—so apparently hostile to grandeur—was up to the task. Traditionally, monumental architecture, reliant on the principles of academic design, favored expensive materials, the privileging of style over function, and the use of historical references to create stateliness by association. The modern tenets of functionalism rejected such techniques. This is why only a few early modernist theorists and architects had been interested in monumentality: Peter Behrens and Theo van Doesburg both wrote on the topic, and Le Corbusier's League of Nations and Palace of the Soviets projects would have been, if built, quite monumental. The editors of the *Architectural Review* asserted several years later that "functionalism can express little except utilitarian ideas."[62] Functionalism also blurred building typologies, because what was serviceable for the neighborhood elementary school potentially could be adequate for City Hall. A stringently functionalist approach produced buildings that were short on symbolic expression.

By the early 1940s such progressive architects as Alvar Aalto, in his Villa Mairea, and Le Corbusier, in his plans for Algiers, had already begun to address these shortcomings and to develop a more expressive vocabulary. Why, then, did the writers who discussed monumentality attack functionalism as vigorously as they did? The probable explanation is that, although functionalism was no longer considered "enough" (even "the heroes of the modern movement" had known that it was only a first, cleansing phase, claimed the *Review* several years later),[63] no coherent ideology had as yet emerged to replace it.

Architects working in the United States were even more prone to equate modernism with functionalism, because the avant-garde movement was younger than it was abroad.[64] In 1944 George Nelson summarized the predicament of American architects: "The contemporary architect, cut off from symbols, ornament and meaningful elaborations of structural forms . . . has desperately chased every functional requirement, every change in site or orientation, every technical improvement, to provide some basis for starting his work. Where the limitations were most rigorous, as for example in a factory . . . the designers were happiest and the results were most satisfying. But let a religious belief or a social ideal replace cubic foot costs or radiation losses, and nothing happened. There is not a single modern church in the entire country that is comparable to a first-rate cafeteria."[65] Which architectural vocabulary best symbolized American political identity was a question as old as the United States itself.[66] Now, as global tensions became manifested in debates on architectural style, the avant-garde's ambivalent attitude toward monumentality became a topic of sustained discussion.

Whereas in 1938 Mumford asserted simply that "if it is a monument it is not modern; if it is modern it cannot be a monument,"[67] only several years later Howe and Mock entreated architects to consider the possibilities for a modern, "democratic" monumentality. Howe cited Wright's Unity Church (1904) in Oak Park, Illinois; Mock looked to Saarinen, Saarinen, and Swanson's competition entry for the new Smithsonian Gallery (1939) in Washington, D.C.[68] Giedion's essays addressing this problem, appearing in the early 1940s, became the best known of many such tracts on the problem of monumentality. In his "Nine Points on Monumentality" (1943) and "The Need for a New Monumentality" (1944), he dismissed academic architecture as "pseudo-monumentality" and argued that the avant-garde must find a competing means of expression because "periods of real cultural life had always the capacity to project creatively their own image of society" in monumental architecture and urban squares.[69]

Giedion and others considered it axiomatic that monumental public architecture reinforced sentiments of communal identity. Monumentality was, as one writer described it, a "visible expression of [people's] collective consciousness."[70] Giedion, voicing the same anxiety that Stonorov and the Goodmans had expressed, feared that monumentality might be difficult to create because capitalist democracy itself, he believed, eroded people's sense of communal identity. Another German emigré writer, Walter Curt Behrendt, expressed this worry in 1938, and Hitchcock later repeated it in the *Architectural Review* symposium of 1948, stating that "to build monumentally requires faith."[71] Giedion predicted that true civic centers "will originate when cities are not regarded as mere agglomerations of jobs and traffic lights. They will arise when men become aware of the isolation in which they live amidst a kicking crowd, and when the demand for a fuller life, which means community life, becomes irresistible."[72] Expressing sentiments similar to the Goodmans', Giedion somewhat plaintively asked, "Where are the community centers? *Neither radio nor television can replace the personal contact which alone can develop community life.*"[73] He hoped, as did the Goodmans, and Kahn and Stonorov in their text accompanying the hotel for "194X," that great urban spaces and public architecture could revive this endangered communal realm.

Giedion proposed two architectural means to this symbolic end, each of which became important in Kahn's contribution to this debate. One could, he suggested, use new materials in ways that were simultaneously ornamental and structural. "Modern materials and new techniques are at hand," he declared, heralding "light metal structures; curved, laminated wooden arches; panels of different textures, colors, and sizes; light elements . . . that can be suspended from big trusses covering practically unlimited spans."[74] Giedion probably owed the inspiration for this last vision to Le Corbusier's proposal for the Palace of the Soviets, from which he likely extrapolated an inventory of possibilities.

Giedion also suggested collaborations between architects, painters, and sculptors, in what he called a "synthesis of the arts." His notion of artistic collaborations came from Le Corbusier,[75] although Giedion took it in a somewhat different direction. He envisioned new architectural forms allowing the projection of colored lights onto the surfaces of buildings at night: "Color and forms can be projected onto vast surfaces. Such displays could be projected upon buildings for purposes of publicity or propaganda. These buildings would have large plane surfaces planned for that purpose, surfaces which are non-existent today."[76]

Two sources underlay Giedion's vision of a light-based, dematerialized monumentality, and embedded in each of these sources was the assumption or assertion that such a monumentality would generate communal sentiment. Bruno Taut, in *Alpine Architecture* (1919), had proposed that colored lights be projected onto crystalline, mountaintop monuments to create an ecstatic symbol of a new, non-urban communal life. In the 1930s Giedion had written dismissively of Taut's ideas, but by 1943 he had assimilated them into his own search for a new monumentality.[77] Equally important were Giedion's own revelatory experiences at two world's fairs in the late 1930s, the 1937 exposition in Paris and the 1939 world's fair in New York City. Giedion recounted how he stood in a Parisian crowd on the Trocadero, where he was swept into a joyous "collective emotional event" while watching Beaudouin and Lods's "Light and Sound at the River Seine" water-and-fireworks spectacle in 1937 (Fig. 1.12). Labatut's "The Spirit of George Washington" display at the 1939 world's fair, which Giedion illustrated in his text, aroused similar feelings of collective solidarity.[78]

Kahn's essay on monumentality appeared with one of Giedion's, in a collection edited by architect Paul Zucker. It remains unclear why Zucker asked Kahn to contribute to a section called "The Problem of a New Monumentality," as Kahn was known primarily for his work in public housing.[79] Most of the other contributors to the section were more obvious choices: Nelson, Giedion, and Philip Goodwin, the co-architect with Edward Durrell Stone of the recently completed Museum of Modern Art in New York (1939). It is, however, clear why Kahn would be interested in addressing such a theme, because at the heart of the "problem of a new monumentality" was the question of how civic architecture could be marshaled to reinforce communal life.

Kahn placed himself squarely within the architectural community's debates on monumentality's relationship to modernism, and on the potential solution for a modernist monumentality, a synthesis of the arts.[80] Kahn's essay suggests that he was familiar with Giedion's ideas.[81] Kahn would have known Howe's ideas directly from Howe; he also knew and was corresponding with Hudnut and was connected to Mock through dealings with the Museum of Modern Art.[82]

Although Kahn did not draw on Giedion's call for spectacle, his essay echoed the ideas of the Swiss critic in most other significant ways. He rejected the pessimistic assertions of Hudnut and Behrendt that monumentality would be impossible for architects to create because contemporary society had no common image of itself to which architects could refer. "Some argue that we are living in an unbalanced state of relativity which cannot be expressed with a single intensity of purpose," Kahn began. "It is for this reason, I feel, that many of our confreres do not believe we are psychologically constituted to convey a quality of monumentality to our buildings."[83] He countered this pessimism by arguing for living memorials, which he called "social" monuments such as "the school, the community or culture center"; these, he contended, were the harbingers of a

1.12 Sigfried Giedion's model for a new monumentality: water-and-fireworks spectacle at the 1937 World's Exposition in Paris, by Beaudouin and Lods. From Paul Zucker, ed., *New Architecture and City Planning* (New York: Philosophical Library, 1944).

new civilization. If architects focused on these building types, he believed, they could exhume common ideals now buried under modernist anomie.[84]

His vision was resolutely reformist, just as were his and Stonorov's housing and urban planning projects, conceived in the same years. "What social or political phenomenon shall we yet experience?" Kahn asked, suggesting that new forms of collective organization could be symbolized in architecture even before they had been instituted as fact.[85] Later in the essay, he made explicit the parallels between his ideas on civic spaces and those on housing and city planning. Still discussing monumentality, Kahn wrote, "This generation is looking forward to its duty and its benefit to build for the masses with its problems of housing and health . . . the nation has adopted the beginnings of social reform."[86] In the context of the essay as a whole, the sentence initially seems a non sequitur. But upon reflection, the connection is clear: Kahn believed that the social revolution of housing reform would find its symbolic equivalent in a new monumentality.

He told the story of "the citizens of a metropolitan area of a city" who organized a committee in the manner he and Stonorov had recommended in *Why City Planning Is Your Responsibility*. This fictional committee formulated the program for a cultural center "endorsed by the national educational center." It was a communal project in inception, and would be a communal symbol in realization: "Its progress was the concern of many."[87] The cultural center would be a "synthesis of the arts," a total composition that embraced landscaping, architecture, and visual art (Fig. 1.13). Kahn, a painter himself (in these years he was executing many more paintings than buildings), suggested that tectonic architectural compositions would contain "new wall products of transparent, translucent, and opaque material with exciting textures and color . . . suspended . . . [from] the minor [structural] members. Slabs of paintings articulate the circulation in the vast sheltered space. Sculpture graces its interior." Like Giedion, Kahn wanted to use color, envisioning here sunlight refracting through "an undulating series of prismatic glass domes."[88]

As for the design of the cultural center, Kahn proposed using new materials to create a structurally derived idiom that symbolized the best achievements of his generation by employing the most advanced technologies of the age. Referring to the precedent of the Gothic cathedral, he asserted that monumentality was often the consequence of architects' drive for structural innovation. He reiterated the modern movement's injunction against direct historical reference and explicitly stated that it was the structural principles, not the forms, of the Gothic cathedral that inspired him: "Nostalgic yearning for the ways of the past will find but few ineffectual supporters," he warned; "no architect can rebuild a cathedral of another epoch."[89]

For this new, postwar era, Kahn argued, architects should explore the possibilities presented by new steel alloys. Plastics were also compelling, "so vast in their potentialities that already numerous journals and periodicals devoted

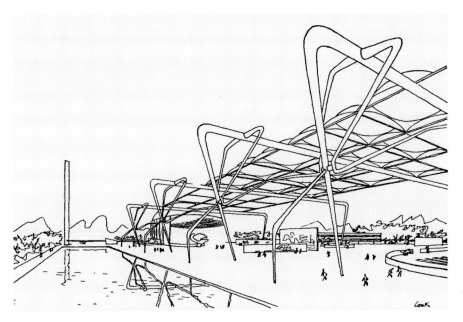

1.13 View of an arcade leading to a cultural center, with murals and sculpture in the midground. From Louis I. Kahn, "Monumentality" (1944), in Zucker, ed., *New Architecture and City Planning*.

solely to their many outlets are read with interest and hope." [90] Kahn also urged others to investigate the uses of laminated woods (which Giedion, probably inspired by Aalto, also mentioned), glass, asbestos, and rubber.

As many have pointed out, Kahn's argument fell within the structural rationalist tradition that Eugène-Emmanuel Viollet-le-Duc forged in the mid-nineteenth century and most of the pioneers of the modern movement espoused. Kahn may or may not have absorbed Viollet's ideas through his teacher Paul Cret, but he had certainly studied Le Corbusier's *Vers une architecture*, which reiterates many dictums derived from Viollet. [91] Even if Kahn had not been entirely aware of the sources of these ideas as he wrote his essay in 1944, they had become part of his habitus, his worldview.

Equally important, a more immediate discourse reinforced Kahn's engagement with the French structural rationalist tradition. [92] During the war, American intellectuals began entertaining, in a quasi-utopian manner, the notion that if wartime advances in technology were properly harnessed they could lead to a society that was dramatically improved. [93] Even Mumford, who criticized the social consequences that technology had wrought under capitalism, looked with hope toward a "neotechnic" age in which technology and communitarian society could work in tandem. [94] That Kahn had fallen under the sway of such optimistic notions was especially apparent in the monumentality essay's passages on plastics, an industry that was growing enormously in the 1940s, inspiring such magazines as *Newsweek* to announce a "new era in plastics" and *House Beautiful* to promise that plastics would lead the "way to a better more carefree life." [95] (Kahn continued to consider the architectural potential of plastics for several more years, assigning a studio problem at Yale in 1948 entitled "An Idea Center for Plastics," an entire building to be devoted to the display of the material's many potential uses. [96]) This technological utopianism, intimated in his essay on monumentality, was to escalate in the early 1950s, when Kahn embraced the social vision that his friend Fuller proposed.

Although Kahn explicitly rejected historical allusion as a means to a new monumentality, he published with his essay a series of lyrical drawings of light, vaulted, Gothic-inspired arcades leading to a projected urban cultural center (Fig. 1.14). Next to one sketch he copied Auguste Choisy's analysis of a bay of Beauvais Cathedral, famous since the Middle Ages as the building that was pushed too far toward lightness and collapsed. "Beauvais Cathedral needed the steel we have," Kahn wrote. [97]

The contradiction between what he drew in these sketches and what he stated in his text—"must the cathedral, the culture center . . . be built to resemble Chartres?"—revealed two aspects of his sensibility that would later come into tension with one another. On the one hand, he wished his architecture to have symbolic resonance, and one means of achieving this was through references to known buildings. On the other hand, he sought an idiom that gained conceptual force primarily from the discrete presence of its material articulation. In subsequent years, as Kahn's ideas and architecture evolved, he shaped this approach to material in a manner that mandated an abstract approach to form. The resulting tension between symbolism (or representation) and

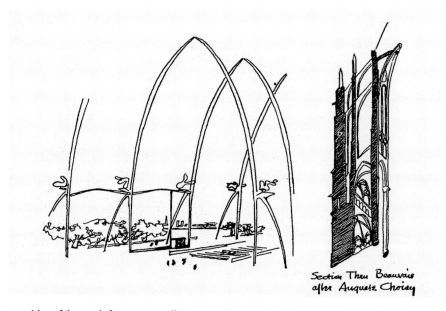

Section Thru Beauvais
after Auguste Choisy

1.14 A bay of the arcade for monumentality compared to a structural bay of Beauvais Cathedral. From Kahn, "Monumentality."

abstraction would take many different forms, but it would underlie Kahn's search for a new monumentality for the rest of his career.

Much of Kahn's essay was dominated by a technical discussion of various engineering issues. He argued that new technologies should be liberated from the shackles of profit-making and governmental regulation. The I-beam section was much heavier than necessary, owing to the exigencies of standardization and overly conservative building codes. According to Kahn, such practices stifled "the creation of the more graceful forms which the stress diagrams" might indicate. He argued for ever greater efficiency in other steel forms: "A bar of a certain area of cross section rolled into a tube of the same area of cross section (consequently of larger diameter) would possess a strength enormously greater than the bar." Common joint construction made "connections . . . complex and ugly," a situation exacerbated by stringent regulations on welding, in which "it was required to make loading tests for every joint."[98]

Such contentions closely paralleled the argument made several years earlier in the "'Standards' Versus Essential Space" essay. There Kahn, Stonorov, and Howe criticized profit-driven solutions for housing, arguing in favor of ones that were not only more pragmatic but more elegant. Here Kahn suggested that if society gave free rein to the architect and engineer so that he could explore the structural potential of his materials – not delimiting creativity in the interest of profit or industry – a new aesthetic of monumentality might emerge.

In this and other arguments, Kahn's essay illustrates how his reformist ideals could be extended to the problem of monumental civic architecture. His "culture center" program accommodated new, community-oriented social forms; this program would be developed by citizens working in collaboration with each other under a national organization that itself was devoted to the public interest. The aesthetic he envisioned relied on creative uses of new technologies, uses that were being stifled by the profit-making apparatus of capitalism. The aesthetic would symbolize both the Zeitgeist and the potential social progress that such technologies, if used properly, might advance.

MONUMENTALITY 1947: THE JEFFERSON NATIONAL EXPANSION MEMORIAL COMPETITION

In 1944 Kahn explored mainly in words how his social ideals might shape a civic idiom; by 1947, with his entry to the Jefferson National Expansion Memorial competition, these concepts began to acquire a tentative visual form (Fig. 1.15). As a total composition, the project is weak and derivative, and judging by formal criteria alone, it has been justly ignored. Even Kahn later admitted to Saarinen that he had "developed it rather poorly by injecting too many ideas [making] nothing particularly strong."[99] It did not survive beyond the competition's first stage. Yet the entry provides a map of Kahn's community-oriented objectives in these years. His selection of building programs, his site plan, and

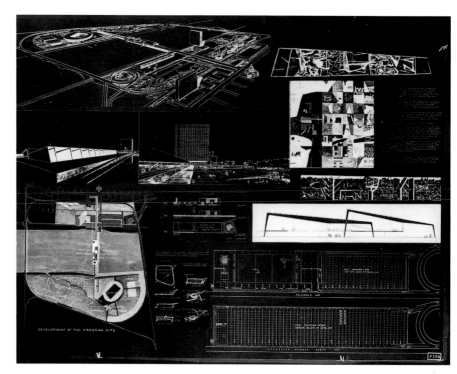

1.15 Jefferson National Expansion Memorial competition board, 1947, with sketches of a sculpted mural in the top right, a painted mural below it, a perspective of the Laboratory of Education in the center, an aerial perspective on the upper left, and a section of the UNESCO National Center on the center left. National Park Service, Jefferson National Expansion Memorial, JNEMA Records, Image Number V105-180.

his sketchy architectural images were all directed toward symbolizing and shaping a realizable utopia of communal participation.

The competition was an appropriately grand opportunity for Kahn and his colleagues to explore ideas of a modern monumentality. One hundred seventy-one firms entered this open contest to build on an eighty-eight-acre sloping site in downtown St. Louis along the Mississippi River, with the historic Eads Bridge in the distance.[100] Howe was the competition director, and among the jurors were other prominent modernists such as Neutra and William Wurster, then dean of the School of Architecture at the Massachusetts Institute of Technology. Many features in Howe's prospectus recalled his own ideas on "democratic" monuments and commemorative works of art. He called for a combination of memorial, public park, and cultural center, all to celebrate Thomas Jefferson's foresight in negotiating the Louisiana Purchase, which gave "ever greater opportunities" to people to improve "their lot under democracy." He suggested a monument or monuments dedicated to various critical moments in westward expansion and a "living memorial" to Jefferson. Also to be commemorated were the Lewis and Clark expedition, the trappers and fur traders "who channeled the wealth of the Western forests and streams through Old St. Louis," and the "Pioneer Movement in general."[101] Recalling Giedion's ideas on

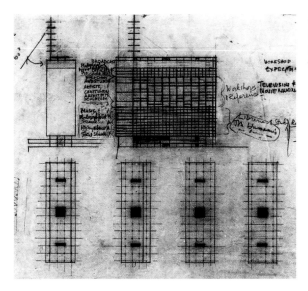

1.16 Laboratory of Education with brise-soleil, Jefferson National Expansion Memorial, 1947. From the Kahn Collection.

35

K A H N   A N D   A M E R I C A N   M O D E R N I S M

a synthesis of the arts, Howe recommended that entrants associate themselves with landscape architects, sculptors, and painters.

In his entry, Kahn's interest in social monuments and living memorials as well as Howe's prospectus led him to envision a massive "culture center" rather than a "useless" symbolic monument as the focus of his scheme. (In terms of how he fared with the jurors, that was his first mistake. Most of the entries chosen to proceed to the second stage were dominated by some grand symbolic gesture; later, Kahn wrote to Saarinen in frustration, "I forgot physical monumentality—I felt that the force should be the *kind* of work [not the buildings].")[102] Bordering one end of a central plaza along the Mississippi River stood a skyscraper, a "Laboratory of Education," with a brise-soleil-like, highly textured surface (Fig. 1.16). Opposite the tower at the other end of the plaza was a low-slung, long-span steel-and-glass exhibition hall that consisted of two lithe, tilting, and interlaced spanning elements containing a vast open area, with auditoriums and exhibition spaces suspended from the ceiling (Fig. 1.17). This was the national branch of United Nations Educational, Scientific, and Cultural Organization (UNESCO). Smooth, transparent, and structure oriented, it was a vehicle for Kahn to explore ideas he had first advanced in the essay "Monumentality," where he envisioned thinning and lightening the steel frame until it became, as he wrote in a journal entry, "insect-like."[103] Thus in the two principal buildings proposed for the site, Kahn worked in the two dominant modernist idioms of American architecture in the 1940s, with the Laboratory recalling Le Corbusier's skin-oriented, monumentalizing skyscraper projects for Algiers and UNESCO echoing the transparent, minimalist structures of Mies.

Also recalling Le Corbusier was the plaza-slab combination, similar to the Swiss architect's highly acclaimed proposed center for St. Dié.[104] Between the

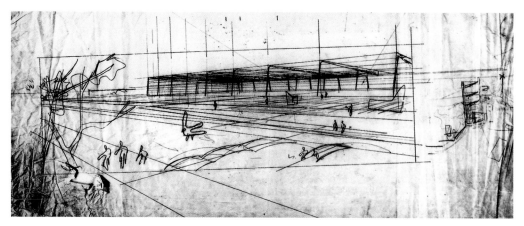

1.17 UNESCO National Center, Jefferson National Expansion Memorial, 1947. From the Kahn Collection.

Laboratory of Education and the UNESCO Center would be a multilevel terraced agora, with its riverside space a glazed, elevated pedestrian spine that accommodated changing exhibitions while maximizing views of the river (Fig. 1.18). The benefits for the community of such urban plazas had been acclaimed by members of CIAM, including Sert, as well as by Mumford and the Goodmans. In Kahn's people-filled agora, the citizens of St. Louis could meet; a sculptural composition of ramps and bridges provided a central spot where local children might play. This idea of a plaza bordered and defined by multilevel circulation was similar to Kahn's contemporary scheme for a cultural center in his Triangle plan for Philadelphia, and both explicitly recalled New York City's recently completed and widely admired Rockefeller Center.

About communal gathering was the theme of the two large figurative murals, one painted and one sculpted, that he set within the square. The effect of incorporating large-scale painting and sculpture into architecture would have been similar to that of Carlos Raoul Villanueva's contemporaneous University City in Caracas,[105] but unlike Villanueva, Kahn relied on representational imagery's narrative potential to convey surprisingly activist messages. For St. Louis—a segregated city—he proposed a painted mural that would champion the achievements not only of whites but of Native Americans and African Americans (Fig. 1.19). Its subject, he wrote, was "the influence of the many races on American education, science, and culture," to be symbolized by one red, one black, and one white man "working together in building a structure which symbolizes the forces of cooperation."[106]

About his second, sculpted mural, "Life and Traffic on the Mississippi," Kahn rhapsodized that it would be constructed according to the principles of community participation that he and Stonorov had developed. Under the direction of a "master artist," he wrote, "community groups, groups of school children and students, and prominent individuals may take part in the laying of the individual

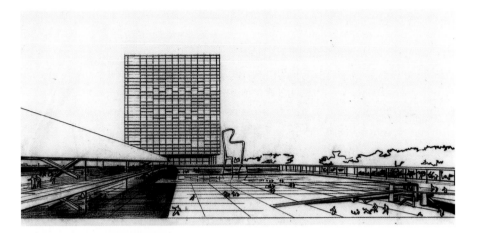

1.18 Public square looking toward the Laboratory of Education from the UNESCO National Center, with a pedestrian spine to the left showing views to the river beyond, Jefferson National Expansion Memorial, 1947. From the Kahn Collection.

1.19 Jefferson National Expansion Memorial, competition board with scheme for painted murals, 1947. National Park Service, Jefferson National Expansion Memorial, JNEMA Records, Image Number V105-180.

stones [that will serve to record] . . . these acts of participation." The sculpted mural, like the painting, could be read as small, individual panels up close, and "as a single monolithic expression from the east bank and from vantage points on the Mississippi." Such a visual experience would be analogous to the kind of community that Kahn and his colleagues championed, in which each individual could maintain personal identity while contributing to the public interest.

In site plan, architectural aesthetic, programming, and visual art, Kahn's Jefferson Memorial entry elaborated on and gave visual form to ideas he had proposed in his essay on monumentality. It encouraged the people of St. Louis to recognize themselves as—indeed, to act as—members of a community. The two major civic buildings he projected embodied a new, more international agenda that drew on his previous ideas. The Laboratory of Education tower would house not only an office for a local branch of the Citizen's Council on City Planning but also the major institutions of communication known in 1947: a public library, radio and television broadcasting stations, a newspaper office, and a film studio. To emphasize the Laboratory's symbolic role, Kahn considered a monumental flèche on its roof that would also serve as a broadcasting transmitter.

Kahn's low-slung "culture center" to the north, which would house the national branch of UNESCO, represented the same tendency to reach beyond the immediate, local community. UNESCO was founded as part of the United Nations charter in 1945 to promote world peace by facilitating international cultural exchange. What the organization meant to Kahn is apparent in a written prospectus he gave to his students at Yale in the fall following his submission to the competition in St. Louis. He assigned a problem that duplicated the central issues Howe had set forth for the Jefferson Memorial: architects, painters, and sculptors would collaborate on a UNESCO center that would be a "vast" flexible space created by a long-span structure that relied on "the most advanced engineering knowledge and skill." [107] Quoting from a UNESCO report that stressed the potential of new communications technologies to facilitate a world community, Kahn's handout read: "A technological development of revolutionary importance and incalculable potentialities for good or evil has taken place in the press, radio, the motion picture. . . . It is now, for the first time, possible to conceive of culture in planetary terms because it is now, for the first time, possible to communicate on a planetary scale."

That Kahn might have wanted to expand his ideal of communal cooperation beyond the confines of the neighborhood is unsurprising, and his new preoccupation with "planetary culture" was propelled by the same inclination toward social critique that had inspired his earlier ideas. In 1947 Kahn wrote to Myers that he believed "intensely" in the United Nations. Indeed, he so ardently hoped that he might be chosen to design the new complex that he simultaneously arranged for himself an introduction to its chief architect, Wallace K. Harrison, and signed a petition calling for Harrison's dismissal from the post.[108]

Such fervor, or bad judgment, should be viewed in light of the causes that Kahn supported these same years. In 1946, he attended meetings of an organization dedicated to replacing each nation's legislative autonomy with a single world government, and collected copies of the organization's monthly bulletin, the *World Government News* (Fig. 1.20).[109] The next year, Kahn joined the Progressive Citizens of America, a leftist political party founded by President Harry Truman's former secretary of agriculture, Henry Wallace (Fig. 1.21).[110]

The United Nations, the Progressive Citizens, and the advocates for world government championed very different causes, but all were united in their support of internationalist cooperation as a countermeasure to nationalist sentiment. Wallace had been fired from Truman's cabinet for publicly declaring that the president was creating tension between the superpowers with his suspicions of the USSR in the wake of the Soviet explosion of an atom bomb and its increased presence in Eastern Europe. He specifically formulated his party's platform as a critique of Truman's foreign policy, denouncing the nationalist flames stoked at the onset of the Cold War.[111]

World Government
NEWS

A MONTHLY REPORT OF TRENDS AND EVENTS LEADING TO WORLD FEDERATION

The World Government News Award

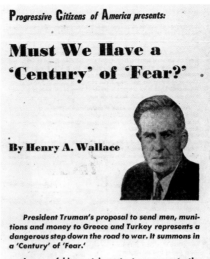

Progressive **C**itizens of **A**merica presents:

Must We Have a 'Century' of 'Fear?'

By Henry A. Wallace

*President Truman's proposal to send men, muni-
tions and money to Greece and Turkey represents a
dangerous step down the road to war. It summons in
a 'Century' of 'Fear.'*

*In one of his most important messages to the
American people, Henry Wallace replies to the Pres-
ident's proposals, points the way to a Century of
Peace and Plenty, calls for the people to SPEAK UP ...*

1.20 Kahn's signature (upper right) on an issue
of *World Government News*. From the Kahn
Collection.

1.21 Progressive Citizens of America brochure from
Kahn's files. From the Kahn Collection.

Declaring his candidacy for the 1948 presidential election, Wallace gained support among "dissident liberals, trade unionists, veteran Communists, and Hollywood artists"; indeed, the party was influenced by Marxist ideas and goals.[112] Kahn became an active member sometime in early 1947. He telegrammed statements for meetings, wrote platform proposals for the party's Building Industry Division, and carefully kept in touch with its base in New York City.[113] The party platform included many items Kahn would have found appealing, such as an active public housing program and increased federal spending for education and health care. But the PCA's main objective was to convince mainstream members of the Democratic Party to defuse the coming Cold War by supporting a strong, independent United Nations.

Kahn's social critique, just as it had earlier led him to focus on more locally oriented ideals, now, with the changed international and domestic political environment, led him to consider the prospect of an international community. His hope for a community that transcended local and even national boundaries extended the scope of his earlier convictions: his ideal, on a small scale, would be Bauer's neighborhood unit concept; and on an international scale it would be world harmony achieved through world government, sustained by organizations like the United Nations and its cultural branch, UNESCO. In both cases, Kahn's preoccupation with how architecture could encourage communal identity through monumental buildings and urban spaces emerged from the modernism in which his architecture was firmly rooted. From his knowledge of early modernism in Europe and his involvement in city planning and social housing in the United States came his interest in architecture's potential to consolidate community; from wartime and early postwar debates within CIAM came his related interest in monumentality.

In the coming years, Kahn would no longer rely exclusively on two-dimensional visual narratives or a judicious choice of building programs to communicate his ideas. He would seek to develop an architectural vocabulary that symbolically embodied these convictions through style, and thereby to integrate all aspects of architecture into a forceful tool for implementing his social agenda. His first such attempt was in his Yale Art Gallery of 1951–1953, where he fused his ideas on modernism and monumentality with a new ideal—authenticity. Subsequent, different kinds of attempts were made in his and Tyng's City Tower project and in his AFL Medical Services of 1955–1957, in which Kahn joined his interest in modernism and monumentality with a technological utopianism, influenced by the maverick engineer and social theorist Buckminster Fuller.

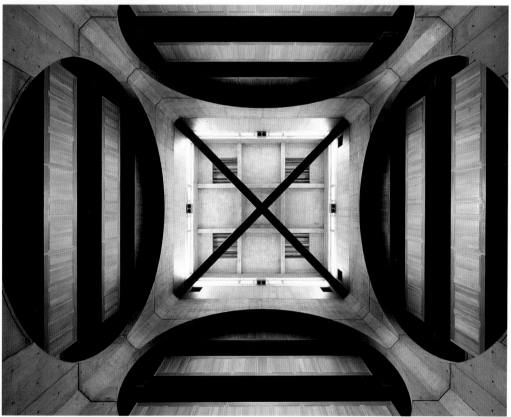

PLATE 2
Library, Phillips Exeter Academy, Exeter, New Hampshire, 1965–1972.
Photo: Grant Mudford.

PLATE 4
Gallery looking toward the stair "silo" of poured concrete, with textures from wooden formwork,
Yale University Art Gallery, New Haven, Connecticut, 1951–1954.
Photo: Grant Mudford.

(opposite) **PLATE 3**
Entrance to the Yale University Art Gallery, with contrasting brick
and glazed walls and concrete drip courses coinciding with floor levels,
New Haven, Connecticut, 1951–1954.
Photo: Grant Mudford.

PLATE 5
An expressionistic sketch of Saint Mark's, Venice, 1951. Private collection.

PLATE 6
Pyramids, Giza, Egypt, 1951. Private collection.

PLATE 7
AFL Medical Services, Philadelphia, 1954–1957.
Photo: E. Teitelman.

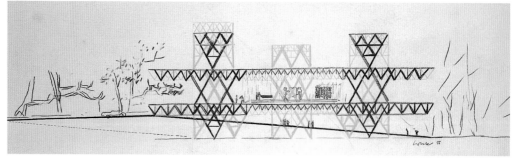

PLATE 8
Section study for the Adath Jeshurun synagogue and school, 1954. From the Kahn Collection.

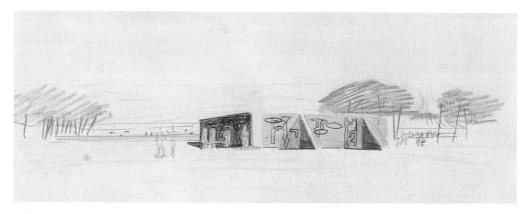

PLATE 9
Elevation of an intermediate scheme for the Bathhouse, 1955. From the Kahn Collection.

PLATE 10
Site plan for the Jewish Community Center, with the Bathhouse and pool in center left, adjacent to the modular buildings in the dark band in center, 1956. From the Kahn Collection.

PLATE 11
Perspective of the gymnasium, Jewish Commmunity Center, 1957. From the Kahn Collection.

PLATE 12
First Unitarian Church of Rochester, Rochester, New York, 1959–1962.

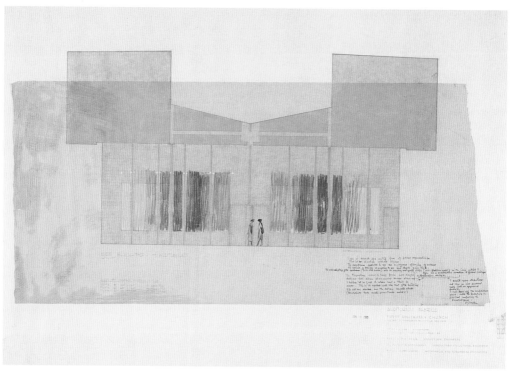

PLATE 13
Kahn's sketch of a tapestry for the First Unitarian Church.
From the collection of the First Unitarian Church in Rochester.

PLATE 14
Interior photograph of a light-study model of the First Unitarian Church of Rochester, ca. 1960.
From the Kahn Collection.

PLATE 15
Drawing of the elevation of the First Unitarian Church of Rochester, ca. 1960.
From the collection of the First Unitarian Church in Rochester.

PLATE 16
Sanctuary with light falling from corner lightwells and tapestries designed by Kahn,
First Unitarian Church of Rochester, Rochester, New York, 1959–1962.

PLATE 17
National Assembly Building with prayer hall in center flanked by office blocks on either side, and
the dome of the assembly chamber projecting above, Sher-e-Bangla Nagar, Dhaka, Bangladesh,
1962–1983. Photo: David B. Brownlee.

PLATE 18
Ambulatory of the National Assembly Building, Sher-e-Bangla Nagar,
Dhaka, Bangladesh, 1962–1983. Photo: Kazi Khaleed Ashraf.

PLATE 19
View of the National Assembly Building, Sher-e-Bangla Nagar, Dhaka, Bangladesh, 1962–1983.

PLATE 20
The National Assembly Building with reflections in surrounding lakes, Sher-e-Bangla Nagar, Dhaka, Bangladesh, 1962–1983. Photo © Shahidul Alam/Drik Picture Library, Ltd., Bangladesh.

PLATE 21
Ambulatory of the National Assembly Building with layers of space, dramatically shifting scales, and a swathe of sunlight falling in late afternoon, Sher-e-Bangla Nagar, Dhaka, Bangladesh, 1962–1983.

PLATE 23
Prayer hall with light flooding in from "hollow columns," National Assembly Building,
Sher-e-Bangla Nagar, Dhaka, Bangladesh, 1962–1983. Photo © Shahidul Alam/Drik Picture
Library, Ltd., Bangladesh.

(opposite) **PLATE 22**
The Salk Institute for Biological Studies' "dichotomous space": study towers with offices in front,
laboratories behind, La Jolla, California, 1959–1965. Photo: Grant Mudford.

PLATE 24
Ambulatory in midday with light falling directly from above, National Assembly Building,
Sher-e-Bangla Nagar, Dhaka, Bangladesh, 1962–1983. Photo: Kazi Khaleed Ashraf.

THE QUEST FOR AUTHENTICITY

THE ART GALLERY AT YALE

2

One might feel that only persons who are in flight from themselves,
who need plaster and wallpaper for their emotional security, can be
uncomfortable in this building. Its planes speak of Being and Truth.
—Louis I. Kahn, "Order and Form: Yale Art Gallery and Design Center"

I believe in frank architecture. A building is a struggle, not a miracle,
and the architect should acknowledge this.
—Louis I. Kahn, in "The Architect Speaks"

Before Louis Kahn was awarded the commission to design a major
addition to the Yale University Art Gallery in New Haven in 1951 (Plate 3), he
had been exploring his progressive, community-oriented social agenda mainly
through the use of representational murals and urban plans. Not yet focused on
how these ideas could be embodied in architectural form, Kahn for the Art
Gallery temporarily shifted his attention away from social activism onto an
inquiry that was more strictly architectural. In this, his first major commission,
Kahn designed a building thick with high modernist tropes: an open plan; the
restrained minimalism of Walter Gropius and Ludwig Mies van der Rohe; the
materials of industrial technology (steel, glass, and reinforced concrete); a pre-
tense toward tectonic expression. Yet the Art Gallery addition simultaneously
constituted a powerful critique of contemporary high modernist monuments as
being too insubstantial, too cool and too machined, qualities apparent to varying degrees in Gropius' contemporaneous Harkness Commons at Harvard University (1948), Gordon Bunshaft's Lever House on Park Avenue in New York
City (1952), or Mies's Alumni Memorial Hall at the Illinois Institute of Technology in Chicago (1945), all of which were widely lauded upon their completion.
Kahn designed and built the Yale Art Gallery with tough love and blunt honesty.
The structure and services of this self-consciously primitivistic building are
insistently manifested. It is made of everyday materials, which are combined in
a manner that stresses process over finish, leaving traces of the human hand in
the making of the building. Materiality, substance, and weight prevail.[1]

This was a new aesthetic, which Kahn developed by transmuting into architectural form ideas he had assimilated from disparate sources. Most important
were movements in contemporary painting to which he was exposed principally

2.1 Ludwig Mies van der Rohe, Alumni Memorial Hall, Illinois Institute of Technology, 1945.

through his teaching at Yale's School of Fine Arts, where he became a visiting critic in 1947 and was later chief critic in advanced design. Also influential were new trends in modern architecture, particularly in the work of Mies and Le Corbusier, which reinforced concepts that Kahn developed at Yale. Of some significance, too, were his travels abroad in the months preceding his Art Gallery design. Underlying and unifying these various strains of experience and influence were the thematics of Existentialist philosophy, which in these years formed the intellectual ethos of many architects, artists, and intellectuals in Kahn's discursive community. Kahn's Art Gallery can best be described and understood with terms drawn from Existentialism.

AN INTERNAL CRITIQUE OF HIGH MODERNISM

Kahn's Art Gallery uses the techniques and materials conventionally associated with modernism while critiquing some of the basic precepts of the modern movement. This is evident if one examines his building in relation to one of the quintessential monuments of early postwar American modernism, Mies's Alumni Memorial Hall at the Illinois Institute of Technology (1945; Fig. 2.1). These two buildings look alike: they are rectangular, made of steel, glass, and blond brick, with parts meticulously articulated. Their designers have carefully revealed the non-load-bearing quality of brick walls in the detailing of their corners — at IIT by the frame of steel, at Yale by the transparent lateral facades or slips of concrete pier that suggest another form of support within. Predominating in each is a minimalism of detail and articulation, a quiet restraint, and an exquisite sense of proportion that keeps the human figure a close if absent presence.

Yet Kahn's building breaks from the precedent to which it owes a debt. On the exterior of the Mies building one sees a careful balancing act of brick and glass planes knit together with dark metallic lines. All compositional gestures defer to the grid, reminding the viewer of the steel supports that control the building in a tight, imageable whole. In Kahn's Art Gallery, by contrast, all one initially confronts on the street facade is two walls, one smaller stepped behind a larger: two blank, looming, four-story brick walls, broken only by four concrete "drip courses" marking levels between each floor (Fig. 2.2). By their transparent adjacent facades and abutting concrete piers, these walls are

2.2 The brick Chapel Street facade of the Yale University Art Gallery, New Haven, Connecticut, 1951–1954.

2.3 Glazed walls with a pattern of prominent window mullions on the High Street facade, Yale University Art Gallery, New Haven, Connecticut, 1951–1954.

silently marked as non-supporting. The viewer registers how this building is put together, but the focus is more insistently on the materiality of the wall, its texture, the pattern of its brick. Even in the glazed portions of the elevations, the viewer's eye is prevented from traveling into deep space by a network of prominently extruding black mullions (Fig. 2.3). Kahn turned up the volume on Mies, having made of a vocabulary that stresses its own substance a building that is

determinedly, obstinately about substantiality and texture. That the rear elevation opens so gently onto an enclosed, terraced courtyard makes the tactile
boldness of those two solid street walls more pronounced (Fig. 2.4).

The plans and interiors of the Mies and Kahn buildings make the forcefulness
of Kahn's, in opposition to the refined elegance of Mies's, still more apparent. The
Alumni Memorial Hall plan is a sophisticated arrangement of point supports
enclosed by the brick-and-glass frame; no element escapes the taut discipline of
the grid. Kahn's Art Gallery plan is dumber, less refined: one small rectangle, the
transition to the original building, abuts a larger one, with the entrance asymmetrically placed near the intersection of the two (Fig. 2.5). A service band containing
stairway, elevator, and bathrooms inelegantly bifurcates the main gallery space.

The materiality intimated on the outside becomes nearly overbearing within,
with loft-like spaces dominated by two heavily sculpted gestures: a poured concrete, tetrahedral ceiling, which at nearly three feet deep seems hand carved out
of light and shade (Fig. 2.6), and a blank concrete stair silo that shoots on axis
from the entrance through the rectangular plan (Plate 4). There is little of the
early modernist emphasis on sequence and movement through space. Volumes
are simply there. The eye goes again to materials: here, all is rough concrete
texture and weight. Carved and incised into the unfinished concrete in the stair
silo and supporting piers are patterns left from the narrow wooden shuttering:
deeply shadowed circular plug holes, swirling surface patterns, lively vertical
striations, and the occasional wooden splinter. Square piers and the circular
staircase play against the grainy concrete tetrahedral ceiling, which is variegated
in hue because of the oils that bled from the shuttering as the concrete dried.

This building manifests uncompromising honesty, a principle that also gov-
erns the manner in which the building's services are treated. Kahn laid into the
ceiling at Yale all electrical wiring, outlets, lighting fixtures, and ductwork, making them visible when one looks straight up. This had previously been done
only in factories or warehouses, not in such a refined institution as an art
museum. Additional larger ducts are laid in the service zone between the two
tetrahedral slabs and are shielded only by a mesh metal screen. The heating
registers are visible inside a lightweight black mesh casing (Fig. 2.7).

In its revelation of structure, its abstraction, its lack of ornamentation, its
restraint, its use of steel, glass, and reinforced concrete, and its open plan, the
Yale Art Gallery addition is firmly within the tradition of the modern movement.
But Kahn challenged some of the principal leitmotifs of early modernist architecture, among them its tendency toward lightness and transparency, its
reliance on machine metaphors, and its emphasis on volumes of space. He generated this new aesthetic principally by selectively adopting certain stylistic
aspects of early modernism and fusing them with ideas he had assimilated from
outside the discipline of architecture, namely, in contemporary art and, more
distantly, philosophy. Combining threads of various and interwoven cultural

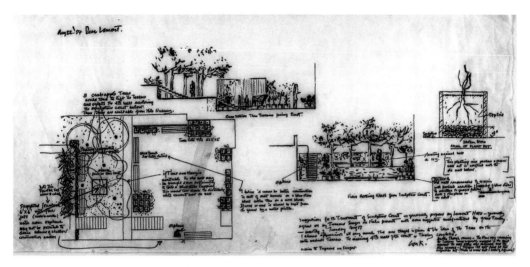

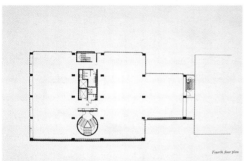

2.4 Landscaping for rear courtyard, Yale University Art Gallery, New Haven, Connecticut, 1951–1954. From the Kahn Collection.

2.5 Plan, Yale University Art Gallery, New Haven, Connecticut, 1951–1954. From the Kahn Collection.

discourses into a new aesthetic language, Kahn aimed to create at Yale an architecture of autonomous and forceful presence.

"PRESENTATIONAL ART": EXPRESSION AND MATERIALITY AT YALE

The motivation driving Kahn's new aesthetic—thus, ultimately, its meaning, at least for Kahn—cannot be even minimally comprehended without an appreciation for the intellectual atmosphere at Yale's Department of Fine Arts, which, in 1950, became the Department of Architecture and Design. Until Kahn started teaching at Yale several months after he finished his submission for the Jefferson National Expansion Memorial in 1947, he had spent all his life in the same city, professionally unaffiliated with any university. Now, suddenly, his intellectual world expanded dramatically.[2] Under the influence of Josef Albers and other contemporary artists to whose work he was exposed, Kahn learned to value abstract art that used the basic elements of its composition—whether color, material, line, or plane—to create objects that were presented not as representations of something else, windows on a world, but rather as presences in and of themselves. This would be achieved through a variety of artistic techniques that Kahn imported into architectural praxis.

The impact of Kahn's tenure at Yale on his ideas has long been recognized;

2.6 Detail of tetrahedral ceiling, showing variations in the color of the concrete, Yale University Art Gallery, New Haven, Connecticut, 1951–1954.

2.7 Heating register wrapped in black metal mesh, Yale University Art Gallery, New Haven, Connecticut, 1951–1954.

even at the time, his young employees noticed how excited he was upon return-ing from New Haven each week.[3] His appointment was part of a general reor-ganization that would extricate Yale from a Beaux-Arts system of education, a response to the growing strength of the modern movement.[4] Hired as steward for this task was Charles Sawyer, the former director of the Worcester Museum of Fine Arts, who had an expressed commitment to modernism.[5] Sawyer's charge was to develop a program distinct from the Bauhaus-style modernism then dom-inant at Harvard's Graduate School of Design, where collaborations between the Departments of Architecture, Landscape Architecture, and Urban Planning were institutionalized. Sawyer developed a more artistically oriented program that paralleled the vision Sigfried Giedion offered for a new monumentality, in which architects, sculptors, and painters would collaborate as a means to a new art and a new architecture.[6]

To this end Sawyer recruited Albers, the former Bauhaus teacher who, since his arrival in the United States in 1933, had been heading the arts program at Black Mountain College in North Carolina.[7] Albers first came to Yale as visiting critic in 1948, a year after Kahn, and in 1950 joined the faculty as chairman of the program in fine arts. Kahn helped to bring Albers to the school, and they soon became close friends.[8] Albers, a leader in color theory who was interested in Gestalt psychology, completely reshaped the program, abolishing all remnants of the Beaux-Arts system to make abstraction the foundation of the school's artistic philosophy.[9] He instituted a first-year program much like the Bauhaus' *Vorkors*, which stressed the fundamental principles of vision. The task of the instructors was to teach the students to *see*. They explicitly prohibited pupils from the study of historical models, and trained them to think formally through a sequence of explorations into first line, then volume, and then form.[10] In a curriculum committee memo of 1948, Albers urged that students first study only "the basic elements of visual expression," and recommended that much of the first year of training should consist of manipulating ordinary materials and textures in various lights. Light, "being the means whereby all seeing is done," was primogenitor of form; students studied light first from direct sources, natural and artificial, then from reflective surfaces like paper, wood, metal, plastics, and glass. In all cases, teachers encouraged the students to identify and study the structural and visual properties intrinsic to each material, and to make artworks revealing that material, reflecting in its forms its physical properties, and making visible the process by which it had been shaped.

The emphasis, then, was on stripping the creative process down to its principles: the most basic forms of vision; common, everyday materials ("There is no extraordinary without the ordinary," Albers asserted);[11] and what could be made with the artist's hand. Although little documentation survives of Albers' thoughts on architecture while at Yale, he published an essay four years before he first came to Yale that articulated a set of architectural ideas. Appearing in 1944 in the same collection that contained Kahn's essay on monumentality, *New Architecture and City Planning*, Albers' piece was entitled "The Educational Value of Manual Work and Handicraft in Relation to Architecture."[12] Challenging early modernism's infatuation with technology and mass production, Albers wrote that "in an industrial age, when machines dominate production, it seems significant that building, considered as a key industry, depends to a large extent on work by hand." Modernist ideology belied the reality that for most constructions "manual work . . . will remain a necessity as long as individual needs in housing are recognized"; most buildings were "handmade."[13] Students should confront reality and focus on craftsmanship. They should learn the time-honored, even archaic methods of manipulating materials. "If student and teacher do not overlook . . . the more basic and perennial constructions," Albers contended, "technically and educationally, the old time-tested joints in wood, metal and stone still hold good."[14]

Albers' focus on materials, on simple forms of making and seeing, on craftsmanship and the human hand, were evident in the pedagogical program he formulated at Yale, in this essay on architecture, and also in his art. In his early years at Yale Albers worked on a series of black paintings etched with white-lined geometric figures; in these, ambiguous perspectival relationships dominate as Albers tested the eye's Gestalt tendency toward order (Fig. 2.8). He also began working on a series entitled "Homage to the Square," which consist of small, square, colored canvases onto which he superimposed one or two other squares, centrally located and progressively diminishing in size (Fig. 2.9). In this series Albers' central preoccupation was color: how colors changed in relation to each other, how the eye perceived pure hue. An uncompromising "truth to materials" philosophy propelled the artistic process. He applied pure colors by palette knife directly from the tube to the canvas—no mixing—in one primary coat "without under or over painting, without any correction. No painting medium [was] used." [15] The message in Albers' own work, as in his teaching and in his recommendations to architects, was that the artist should choose simple materials, examine them carefully, use them truthfully, play no tricks, focus on making and craft.

Albers called his "Homage to the Square" series "presentational" painting. He rejected the word "abstract" because the shadow of a figure was still present in the word: abstract bore meaning only in its sense of "being abstracted from." "Non-representational" was too negative, because Albers' wish was to create something positive, which "had its own discrete presence" and could be "directly . . . apprehended by the mind." [16] He sought meaning that emanated from the canvas to the senses, representing nothing. In the catalogue to an exhibition on Albers' work at the Yale Art Gallery in 1949, Sawyer called this quality "intrinsic significance." [17]

A palpable tension in Albers' paintings emanates from his contradictory impulses toward an expression of the shaping hand, on the one hand, and the abstract anonymity of geometric restraint, on the other. Critics at the time, most notably Clement Greenberg and Elaine de Kooning, commented on this. In a review of a gallery exhibition in New York City of early 1949, Greenberg wrote that Albers was a "sensuous, even original" colorist, but lamented that in adhering "to the dogma of the straight line" the work became too cold: "One has to regret that Albers has so rarely allowed the warmth and true plastic feeling we see in his color to dissolve the ruled rectangles in which all these potential virtues are imprisoned." [18] De Kooning wryly commented on this tension as well, affectionately undercutting Albers' claim that his work contained "no personal handwriting" [19] and simply explored "actual, mathematical relationships" [20] by recounting Albers' delight in the sticky texture of paint found in a tube left uncovered for days. Albers' paintings, she concluded, could not have been painted "except by Albers himself." [21]

It was perhaps this tension in his own sensibility that drew Albers to the very different painting of de Kooning's husband, Willem. Albers had brought Willem de Kooning to Black Mountain College in the late 1940s, and the first appointment Albers made at Yale, for the academic year 1950–1951, went to the Dutch artist, who taught a studio that Albers called "the genius shop." [22] These were the years when de Kooning produced the series that established his career. Collectively entitled "Woman," these large paintings depict distorted, disturbing

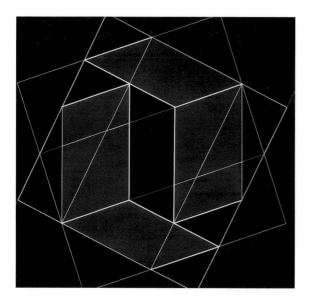

2.8 Josef Albers' exploration of ambiguous perspectival relationships, *Structural Constellation: Transformation of Scheme No. 12*, 1950. © 2000 The Josef and Anni Albers Foundation/ Artists Rights Society (ARS), New York.

faces and bodies quickly sketched with the strokes of the hand or brush left visible, and with paint alternately applied in heavy impastos and thin washes (Fig. 2.10). For de Kooning, artistic process was paramount, and he left etched across his completed canvases traces of paintings that might have been.[23] Painting was struggle, man against canvas. Material, paint, reigned supreme: "I like a nice, juicy, greasy surface," said de Kooning in 1953.[24]

KAHN AND THE PRESENTATIONAL AESTHETIC

The artistic ethos Albers forged at the School of Fine Arts at Yale championed an aesthetic of abstraction that demanded — through the rigorously honest use of everyday materials — intense, focused seeing. From Albers came an emphasis on simple, geometric forms, on the self-conscious articulation of making, and on materials and artistic process. The repressed sensuality in Albers' own canvases was incarnated in the gestural paintings of de Kooning, who insistently, even defiantly, revealed the hand of the creator. Both these leading artists aimed to create painting that was beyond representation, paintings that were things, not signs.

This ideology of creation changed Kahn's work. He could hardly have avoided these ideas: his personal friendship with Albers aside, contemporary art pervaded the intellectual climate of the school. Students and faculty had access to many of the principal shapers of the New York contemporary art world,[25] including James Johnson Sweeney and Thomas Hess, both of whom had associations with the Museum of Modern Art; Aline Loucheim, an art critic who later married Eero Saarinen; and Henry-Russell Hitchcock, who was writing a catalogue of the Miller corporation's collection of architecture-related contemporary art, published in 1952 as *Painting Toward Architecture*.[26] These

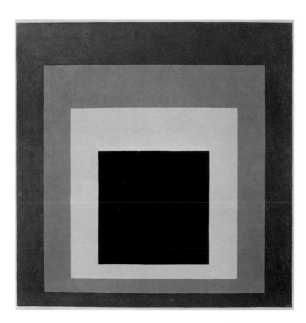

2.9 Josef Albers' investigations into color and process, *Homage to the Square*, 1955. © 2000 The Josef and Anni Albers Foundation / Artists Rights Society (ARS), New York.

and other art world figures lectured in a yearly series sponsored by the Yale Art Gallery, which was housed in the same building as the Department of Fine Arts; hence the Art Gallery was not only Kahn's client but also one of the largest rooms in his new intellectual home. After 1941, when Katherine Dreier bequeathed more than six hundred paintings and sculptures she had assembled in collaboration with Marcel Duchamp, the Art Gallery was known to have the best university collection of contemporary art in the country.[27]

Kahn had been interested in Giedion's ideas on a synthesis of the arts before he came to Yale, as evidenced by his entry to the Jefferson National Expansion Memorial competition. At Yale, breathing the cultural air of his environment, Kahn concentrated his energy on thinking about modern painting and about the relationship between painting and architecture. This is evident in the studios he taught, the books he read, the sketches he drew and exhibited, and the paintings he painted. In these years, he added to his library recently published monographs of many artists featured in major exhibitions, including Pierre Bonnard, Paul Cézanne, Raoul Dufy, Pablo Picasso, and, a little later, Jean Dubuffet.[28] In 1952 and 1955 he exhibited his conceptual sketches in a show in Philadelphia entitled *Creative Parallels*, which included work by architects, sculptors, and painters.[29] Already in 1948, when the dean of the School of Fine Arts, Harold Hauf, asked Kahn to indicate the kind of courses he would like to teach, Kahn wrote back that the Rome collaborative—a project sponsored by the American Academy in Rome to encourage collaboration between painters, sculptors, and architects—was of particular interest.[30] That same year he borrowed from the Yale library an article from the *RIBA Journal* on collaborations

2.10 Willem de Kooning's abstract
expressionist emphasis on the distortion
of features, gesture, and artistic process,
Woman, 1950. From the Museum of Modern
Art, New York.

51

AUTHENTICITY AND THE ART GALLERY AT YALE

between artists and architects.[31] Between 1948 and 1950 he chose to teach two studios in which students in painting, sculpture, and architecture collaborated.

For his first studio at Yale, Kahn assigned a national center for UNESCO (which he had proposed in his entry to the Jefferson National Expansion Memorial only months before), in which architects would design long-span structures, sculptors the "vertical circulation element," and painters the monumental artworks to go around the building and inside.[32] He co-taught another studio the following year with the newly arrived Albers and the designer Elliot Noyes, an architect from Harvard who had recently curated the exhibition *Plastics in Art and Industry*. This studio, entitled an "Idea Center for Plastics," was meant to redress the failings of the UNESCO studio, which Kahn believed had been insufficiently collaborative because the architecture students had designed the buildings by themselves, and the artists had merely decorated the sheds.[33] Kahn was principally responsible for conceptualizing the studio problem in which students would seek better designs for a material that was omnipresent but often visually unappealing. They were instructed to design "a showroom demonstrating to consumers potential uses of this new material"—namely, plastic—" in varying environmental circumstances." Kahn, synthesizing Albers' ideas, wrote in his prospectus that an abstract aesthetic should prevail, in which students would explore the inherent qualities of different kinds and colors of plastic in changeable light. In a distinctly Albersian directive, Kahn instructed his students that the "principals [*sic*] of optics are of primary importance."[34]

Albers' and de Kooning's influences on Kahn also transformed his paintings and sketches of these years. From 1948 onward his signal interests were abstract, simple forms, and optical tendencies in ambiguous or shifting perspectives or in changed conditions of light.[35] In one series of paintings and sketches, Kahn explored simple, hard-edged, abstract shapes with light and shade as their defining features. Variations of light and dark complicate normal solid-to-void relationships, as if Kahn had embarked on a Gestalt-inspired quest to test the eye's compulsion toward order (Fig. 2.11). Another familiar motif in both his paintings and drawings is the open-ended cube with its perspective distorted; sometimes an apparently transparent slab is superimposed, sometimes the cube is interlocked with another similarly distorted, open-ended cube (Fig. 2.12). In other drawings, Kahn layered floating slabs punctuated by a flight of stairs. These drawings, in their emphasis on solid-void and figure-ground relationships, bear obvious affinities with Albers' work of the same period. Several of Kahn's sketches suggest that he also absorbed de Kooning's interest in the unfinished and in the expression of the artistic process, first indirectly and then later from de Kooning himself. In a triad of self-portraits from approximately 1949 (before de Kooning arrived to teach at Yale), Kahn explored a progressive distortion of features and altered his drawing medium and the pressure exerted as he held down his pencil (Figs. 2.13, 2.14, and 2.15).

When Kahn went abroad—to the American Academy in Rome in December 1950 and traveling through Italy, Egypt, and Greece in 1951—he continued his dual-pronged investigation into Albersian abstraction and Abstract Expressionism. The few drawings he made in Rome indicate that he used the city to continue his explorations of simple geometric solids in light (Fig. 2.16). Joseph Amisano, an architect who was at the American Academy with Kahn, remembered that "the effects of light preoccupied Louis and fascinated him; the deliberateness of the detailed forms; some carved like deep wounds with shadows deepening into reaches."[36] Kahn also continued his forays into a more expressionistic vocabulary in several experiments with quick, scrawl-like lines and lurid colors (Plate 5). At Giza in Egypt, where he traveled with Amisano that February, he focused on making numerous sketches of the elementary forms of the pyramids (Plate 6), exploring how the triangular shadow coming off one side of a pyramid distorted one's perception of its regularity, an idea he had broached in his abstract line drawings for several years. Impressed by the monumentality and simplicity of forms, he wrote home of "incomparable Acropolis," asserting, "I now know that Greece and Egypt are musts."[37]

He was drawn to Italian architecture's texture, materiality, and weight, seeing in them architectural analogues to the kinds of preoccupations that the faculty and student painters at Yale explored in two dimensions. "I finally realize that the architecture of Italy will remain as the inspirational source of the works of the future," Kahn wrote his office employees. "Those who don't see it that way

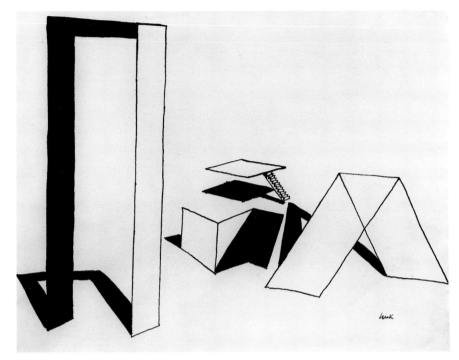

2.11 *Abstract of Planes and Steps*, 1948–1950. Private collection.

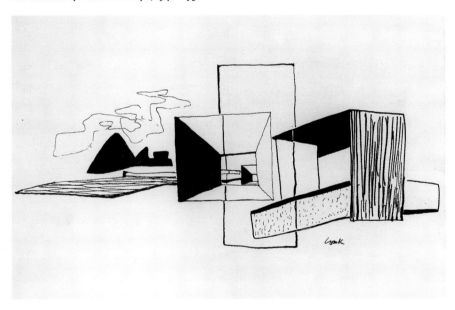

2.12 *Transparency #1*, 1948–1950. Private collection.

2.13 *Self-Portrait*, ca. 1949. Pencil on paper. Private collection.

2.14 *Self-Portrait*, ca. 1949. Charcoal on paper. Private collection.

ought to look again. Our stuff looks tinny compared to it."[38] An affectionate letter to Kahn from Howe, who had been instrumental in getting his former partner the fellowship, read: "I always knew Rome was your dish. Yes, brick and stone are wonderful. We have spoken often of the pitiful ruin America will present when the archaeologists dig it up 5000 years from now."[39] Kahn's travels abroad, taken at the height of his receptivity to the new ideas about painting

2.15 *Self-Portrait* with distorted features, 1949. Charcoal on paper. Private collection.

55

A U T H E N T I C I T Y   A N D   T H E   A R T   G A L L E R Y   A T   Y A L E

and creating that he learned at Yale, led him to consider how one might transmute an artistic aesthetic into a new architecture.

THE YALE ART GALLERY

While a resident at the American Academy, Kahn received the commission for a major addition to the Yale University Art Gallery, a neo-romanesque building from 1928 located on Chapel Street at the southern border of the Yale campus. The new building would house the growing collection; more important, it would symbolize the university's commitment to the art and architecture of the twentieth century. A traditional-style building was never considered.[40] The program called for gallery space, classrooms, art and architecture studios, and departmental offices for the School of Architecture and Design, all arranged flexibly enough so that at some indeterminate date the art gallery could take over the entire building (as it subsequently did). In designing the building, Kahn was associated with a local architect, Douglas Orr, and dealt with Sawyer, who represented the university as the client.

Kahn's examination of Albers' paintings and recent buildings by Mies reinforced his already-established propensity for simple geometries: for the Art Gallery he chose a simple rectilinear shape. Philip Johnson, Mies's disciple, had used a circle inside a rectangle in his house in New Canaan (1950), a motif that Kahn repeated in his concrete cylindrical staircase. The resulting "vertical circulation element" was as plastic as those he had hoped to elicit from his sculpture students in his UNESCO studio several years before.

2.16 *Roman Wall*, Rome-Ostia, Italy, 1951.
From the collection of M. Louis Goodman.

Considerations of surface, texture, and materiality drove many of the later stages of the design. Kahn projected a masonry facade on Chapel Street from the start. For adjacent elevations, he initially considered a nearly complete transparency, only later adding the latticed network of black mullions that keeps the eye traveling across exterior planes (Fig. 2.17). For the ceiling, Kahn first envisioned smooth, shallow barrel vaults; Tyng convinced him to use a modified space-frame motif instead.[41]

Kahn hardly understood the structural aspects of the space frame, which was receiving much critical attention in the early 1950s because R. Buckminster Fuller had recently invented the geodesic dome. The strength of the geodesic dome, a new form of vaulting based on a section of a sphere configured to cover the largest area with the least material, derived from its three-dimensional triangulation of small, repetitive parts; it could be built quickly and inexpensively in a variety of materials, including aluminum, steel, and wood; its parts were demountable and therefore extremely flexible. Kahn never considered constructing the Art Gallery ceiling in light or demountable materials, and he never cared much about an economic use of materials—efficiency, in the engineering sense—or about the expression of structural forces.[42] This is evident in the manifold structural unclarities and inefficiencies of the Art Gallery's celebrated ceiling. The ceiling is made of reinforced concrete—itself a tectonically ambiguous material, because its tensile strength derives from reinforcing rods that are invisible—and is a slab-and-beam structure far heavier than it needs to be, because it is configured to resemble a space frame.[43] What Kahn sought was not a rational approach to structure but a sincerity in the making and in the expression of a material's intrinsic properties. He liked his concrete "space frame" because of its monumental, aggressively textured surface and because the deep ceiling's voided pockets obviated the need for further acoustical treatment that might mask the building innards.

Many other aspects of the design were also shaped by this honest approach to the materials and elements that constitute a modern building. Into the

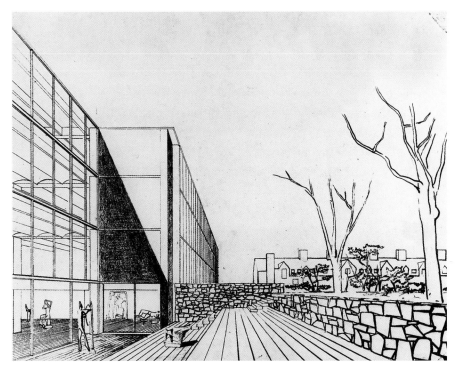

2.17 Early sketch for the rear facade of the Yale University Art Gallery, with transparent glazed facades. From the Kahn Collection.

unfinished concrete tetrahedrons, in which structural and non-structural elements are immediately visible, Kahn laid electrical wiring and lighting fixtures, heating and ventilation ducts. "We should try more to devise structures which can harbor the mechanical needs of rooms and spaces and require no covering," Kahn exhorted in a lecture in 1953. Even if these mechanicals are unattractive, "the pasting on of lighting and acoustical material, the burying of tortured unwanted ducts, conduits, and pipelines . . . [is] intolerable." [44] This moral aesthetic of tough veracity drove both Albers and de Kooning (for Albers, no medium, no varnish, just the viewer and a couple of unmixed colors; for de Kooning, the ugly, aggressive sexuality of "Woman"), and it must have made a potent impression on Kahn. Yet Kahn's decision to take these ideas in the direction of exposing services was inspired by Alison and Peter Smithson's exposed ductwork and electrical lines in the Hunstanton Elementary School in England (1949–1954), drawings of which were published in 1949. It is likely that Kahn saw the project only when it was widely published upon its completion in 1954, but perhaps he assimilated, even without his knowledge, the British architects' ideas through Douglas Haskell, the editor of *Architectural Forum*, with whom Kahn served on a jury at Yale in May 1951, at a time when Haskell was strongly advocating that services be exposed. [45]

Albers recommended that students start from everyday matter and make the ordinary extraordinary. Kahn constructed with brick, glass, and plain black metal on the outside; concrete block, poured concrete, and simple pine within. Through his unexpected use of such materials Kahn wished to confront his viewers with the imminent qualities of the materials themselves. The unusual configuration of the ceilings prods the viewer out of passivity into active observation.

As Kahn worked out the construction details of the Art Gallery addition, he developed a language in keeping with the Yale program's aesthetic, one that emanated from artistic process; in Kahn's case, from the process of construction. He left the Art Gallery addition's concrete unfinished and frankly exposed. In 1953, as he was finishing his Art Gallery design, Kahn admitted to an infatuation with process and intimated that contemporary art had inspired it. In architecture, he declared, "as in all art, the artist instinctively keeps the marks which reveal how a thing was done."[46] An architect should show "how [the building] was done, how it works. . . . The feeling that our present-day architecture needs embellishment stems in part from our tendency to fair [sic] joints out of existence — in other words, to conceal how parts are put together. If we were to train ourselves to draw as we build, from the bottom up, stopping our pencils at the joints of pouring or erecting, ornament would evolve out of our love for the perfection of construction."[47] Draw as we build: Kahn stressed the transposition from three to two dimensions, as if he were searching for analogues to ideas he had seen in another medium. He drew from architectural sources as well, admiring Le Corbusier's recently completed apartment block in Marseilles, which he had not seen in person but which had been widely published. Of the lack of finish in the Art Gallery's staircase cylinder, Kahn proudly stated: "We didn't smooth off the impression left by the mould we poured the concrete into. Why bother to deny how it was made? We're proud of it. Le Corbusier, in his Marseilles apartments, even left the wooden splinters."[48]

Kahn's wrenching of an aesthetic language out of the processes of construction conveyed not only the sense of inartificiality but also that the making of architecture was a series of human acts. This approach accorded with Albers' dictum that architects should candidly admit that their buildings were in large part hand- rather than machine-made. It also explicitly rejected metaphors of mass production and industrial technology that had been central to early modernism. Kahn instead stressed the humanity of making. Sounding very much like de Kooning, Kahn explained to a journalist when the Yale Art Gallery was completed: "I believe in a frank architecture. A building is a struggle, not a miracle, and the architecture should acknowledge this."[49]

Like Abstract Expressionism, the aesthetic Kahn was shaping was self-consciously heroic. He reintroduced the subject as the maker of architecture in a manner that acknowledged that human capacities were both creative and limited. This emphatic shift of focus onto the humanity of making a building went hand in hand with Kahn's sensitivity, in the Art Gallery and in all his subsequent buildings, to human scale. The Art Gallery, in spite of the brashness of some of its gestures, is a building acutely attuned to the proportions of its users. On the exterior the "drip course" at sidewalk level gives the facade a scaling device; inside, the ceiling appears lower, more scaled to the human body than it is, because of its highly animated surfaces. In discussing his decision to expose the structure and services, Kahn specifically stated that "ceilings with structure furred in tend to erase the scale." [50]

Kahn's humanism, if one might call it that, is not the Renaissance humanism of elegance, comfort, and balance. It is a humanism that offsets sensitivity to the scale of the human body with an aggressive, unfamiliar use of materials and language. Viewers feel unsettled by the building, an effect that made Kahn especially proud. Few in Kahn's circles were interested in beauty, a classical concept that was understood to rely on eye-soothing formulas and familiar motifs. On at least three separate occasions from 1954 to 1955, Kahn explicitly rejected beauty as an essential artistic pursuit, declaring in a lecture at Tulane University in December 1954 that "architecture need not necessarily be beautiful." [51] More important, he suggested, was fidelity to the spirit of the thing: "The same order created the dwarf and the Adonis." Even objects or people that might appear ugly according to normal conventions could have integrity: "Beauty will evolve." In November 1955, Kahn stated flatly: "Beauty cannot be built into architecture by design. Beauty evolves from acceptance and love." Better to aim for the awkward but true, even if those expecting plaster and wallpaper would turn away. Speaking of the Art Gallery addition, Kahn later proudly recalled that "on alumni visiting day, the year the gallery was being completed, a bewildered old grad came over to the old student drafting room and said, 'I was just over in the basement of the new art gallery next door, looking around. Then I went upstairs to the first floor—but I was still in the basement!'" [52]

AUTHENTICITY

As Kahn himself recognized, the ideas he developed in the Art Gallery addition at Yale resonated with the work of several other architects, most notably Le Corbusier, who shaped a heavier, more primitivizing aesthetic in his built work of the late 1940s and early 1950s, such as the Unité d'habitation in Marseilles (1949) and the Maisons Jaoul in Neuilly-sur-Seine (1956). The Smithsons worked in a more Miesian but similarly rough-edged manner. The propinquity of these continentally disjoined ideas led Reyner Banham in the early 1950s to collect these and other buildings together under the rubric of a new movement, which he, following the Smithsons, dubbed the New Brutalism. [53]

Banham described Brutalism in formal terms, writing, for example, that Le Corbusier's central postwar realization was that "concrete starts life as a messy soup of suspended dusts, grits, and slumpy aggregate, mixed and poured under conditions subject to the vagaries of weather and human fallibility." [54] But he described the movement's underlying principles with language that contained a heavy dose of Existentialism. Banham's reliance on such philosophical ideas is well known,[55] provoked in part by the sources of his subjects, given that Le Corbusier's stylistic turn was inspired in part by Camus's writings, and the Smithsons were profoundly influenced by Sartrean ideas.[56]

The fortunes of Existentialism were no less happy in the United States, especially in New York, where Sartre became a celebrity intellectual in the years 1946–1951, owing to his increasing influence abroad and the appearance of his play *No Exit*, which was widely reviewed with puzzled acclaim.[57] Long profiles and articles on Sartre specifically, and on Existentialism more generally, appeared in the *New Yorker* (two in 1946–1947), the *New York Times Magazine* (two in 1946–1949), the *Saturday Review*, and *Time*.[58] The new philosophical movement was often discussed in the New York art world, and probably influenced American Abstract Expressionism, a movement that, of course, includes de Kooning.[59]

At Kahn's home away from home, Yale, many of his colleagues were discussing Existentialist ideas. Among them was Vincent Scully, whose early writings about Kahn's work were saturated with the Existentialist romanticization of the primitive and the Sartrean idea of authenticity. Scully described the Yale Art Gallery as an "archaic universe," and maintained that new stylistic trends evident in the work of Kahn and others, and also apparent in contemporary painting, indicated "the yearning of a complex age for direct and simple experience, deeply felt and presented as general truth, without rhetoric."[60] Scully may have drawn this concept from Giedion, still the most important critic and historian in the 1950s, who in an article published in 1952 heralded an architecture that reflected "a new stage of civilization" in formation in which "the human being as such—the bare and naked man—will find a direct means of expression." Quoting Sartre, Giedion advised that "we need today signs and symbols which spring directly to the senses."[61] Kahn sat on a jury in which Paul Weiss, a philosopher at Yale who frequented the School of Architecture as a good friend of Howe's, discussed the Sartrean concept of authenticity. Howe, in 1954, declared that "our present philosophy is sort of an imposed existential philosophy" demanding deep contemplation of the moral implications of human freedom.[62]

It is all but certain that Kahn did not read Sartre: Kahn was not a reader, did not take well to philosophy, and tended toward the visual rather than the literary. Existentialist ideas, however, were prevalent both in East Coast intellectual culture and in the work of European artists and architects who directly or indirectly influenced Kahn. It should not be surprising, then, that the Art Gallery addition at Yale bore strong overtones of an Existentialist aesthetic.

The best term to describe Kahn's aspirations in the New Haven gallery is "authenticity," a concept introduced into twentieth-century philosophy by Martin Heidegger and later popularized by Sartre.[63] In *Nausea* and other works,

Sartre's characters long for the sensation of authenticity that springs from a person's courageous confrontation with life's meaninglessness, and her consequent shouldering of responsibility for shaping her own destiny even in defiance of social convention. Living authentically requires that one extricate oneself from the habit of constructing one's identity as a representation or set of representations dictated by social convention.[64] Antoine Roquentin, the main character in *Nausea*, observes derisively, "People who live in society have learned how to see themselves in mirrors as they appear to their friends."[65] Instead, the goal is to construct one's own inner rules—although Sartre acknowledges that this is nearly impossible to achieve.[66] Even if one succeeds in such a quest, the cost is estrangement from others. In challenging social convention, one might appear ugly, abnormal, strange. Sitting in a cafe, Roquentin suffers from the isolation his quest for authenticity imposes: "I am alone in the midst of these happy, reasonable voices. All these creatures spend their time explaining, realizing happily that they agree with each other."[67]

Authenticity is more than simply self-realization: it is an ethic and a mode of action. Sartre also suggests a shape for its aesthetics. To live authentically, one has to strive for a heightened awareness not only of oneself but also of one's place in a specific historical moment and place. This requires acute perception of one's social and physical environment, which is difficult because a person tends to apprehend the objects and buildings that surround her as instruments, and in instrumentalizing the world, she is prohibited from really *seeing* it in the plenitude of its own character. The virtue of experiencing an object in its own discreteness is that a person feels more situated in historical time; reflecting upon her surroundings might compel her to comprehend her existential situatedness. That realization in turn reminds a person of her freedom and responsibility to question the social norms and rituals enacted in, around, and through such spaces.

Art, then, must press upon one an intense awareness of the immediate and the everyday. One must see one's surroundings in all their complexity, and experience everyday objects in the fulsomeness of their own qualities—their shape, their texture, their materiality—rather than as representations of objects already known. Art can effect such experiences *if* artists eschew the conventional means of achieving artistry and beauty in order to fashion objects that might, according to artistic convention, be ugly. Artists must choose their subject matter from the stuff of the world around them, and use compositional techniques to subvert the viewer's expectations so that she focuses not on the instrumentality of the everyday world but rather on an object's shape, texture, and materiality.

In *Nausea*, Sartre intimates that this might be done by fixing one's attention on touch instead of sight.[68] Roquentin's epiphanic moments occur mainly when he perceives not through his eyes but through his skin: "A little while ago, just as I was coming into my room, I stopped short because I felt in my hand a cold object which held my attention. . . . I opened my hand, I looked: I was simply holding the doorknob." Roquentin subsequently notices that the self-taught man's hand felt "like a fat white worm in my own."[69] In another passage Sartre writes of how he can perceive objects in the plenitude of their own character, and that it frightens him: "You use [objects], put them back in place, you live among them: they are useful, nothing more. But [objects] touch me, it is unbearable. I am afraid of being in contact with them, as though they were living beasts."[70]

The proximity of Kahn's Yale Art Gallery to an Existentialist aesthetic is striking. Unexpected transformations of modernist tropes are marshaled toward the unsettling effects that Sartre envisioned. The monumental street facade is blank. The ceiling is unusually shaped and an active presence. The celebratory staircase is a secret sharer, hidden inside an opaque cylinder. Because these compositional gestures do not match the viewer's expectations, she focuses more intently on the building, on its materiality and its presence as a singular object. The Existentialist emphasis on human choice is given architectural form in the techniques Kahn employed to expose the act of building, the pouring of slumpy aggregate into this tetrahedronal shuttering. Kahn shunned Mies's emphasis on the diaphanous and the transparent so that he could press the viewer up against materiality, substance, and weight. The building's massiveness, abstraction, and process-oriented aesthetic confer the impression that this architecture is non-referential in spite of its resemblances to Mies's buildings at IIT or the Smithsons' school at Hunstanton. Kahn aimed for an architecture that conveys the sensation of being solidly *there*.

It is no coincidence that the Sartrean idea of authenticity best describes Kahn's achievement in the Yale Art Gallery. The principal sources from which Kahn drew in developing this new aesthetic were, directly or indirectly, touched by this new philosophy. Although Albers appears not to have been interested in Existentialism per se, his notion of a presentational aesthetic bore affinities to the Existentialist reification of "presence" instantiated within an object rather than represented from without. Albers' and de Kooning's common ideals were honesty, tactility, and (to some extent) materiality, and these qualities also appeared in the Existentialist-influenced avant-garde architecture from abroad of which Kahn was aware. The emphasis on process over finish conveyed the authentic quality of immediacy, which was esteemed by many artists and architects whom Kahn knew. The eschewal of social convention evident in such gestures as exposing ductwork and electrical fixtures, the delight in designing a public institution synonymous with beauty and refinement that the untrained viewer might confuse with a basement—all point to Kahn's quest for an architecture of authenticity.

In the Art Gallery addition Kahn began to shape a new aesthetic language, both of early modernism and beyond it. It was a language of apparently simple, almost dumb geometric forms that were animated by tactile and plastic surfaces in an emerging dialectic of intellectual restraint and sensual expressiveness. It was also a language of primitivizing weight, a language that reified the notion of presence. He achieved these qualities by combining various specific techniques such as the evident use of ordinary materials, an emphasis on visible structure and the process of construction, and the use of compositional gestures that undermine the viewer's assumptions about what she will see.

Yet this was only a beginning, for Kahn's success at the Yale Art Gallery was only partial. The aesthetic impact of the composition derives largely from a ceiling that is overwrought, indeed, ridiculously heavy. His triangulated geometric system for the ceiling is so rigid that the vertical support system could not be visually integrated into the ceiling plane, something that Kahn tried to correct in such later projects as the design for the Adath Jeshurun synagogue in 1954.[71] Most important, there is an unsettling disjuncture — an incoherence, really — between the muscularity of the building's planes and masses and the unmolded airy openness of spaces that are a product of the open plan. The building's surfaces connote stasis, while its spaces demand flow.

As Kahn developed in the coming years into a mature artist, he would retain some aspects of this new aesthetic, transform others, and abandon some altogether. His immediate concern in the early 1950s was to find a way to harness this aesthetic to his moral conviction that architecture should perform the specific social role of symbolizing and reinforcing communal identity. He needed to move to an idiom that merged the authentic with the monumental and the symbolic. This was the task he set himself in the design of two projects for downtown Philadelphia, a projected new city hall and a medical center for the American Federation of Labor.

3

TECHNO-ORGANIC SYMBOLS
OF COMMUNITY

A NEW CITY HALL FOR PHILADELPHIA
AND THE AFL MEDICAL SERVICES

I studied at the University of Pennsylvania, and although I can still feel the
spiritual aspects of that training, I have spent all my time since graduation
unlearning what I learned.
—Louis I. Kahn, speech at Princeton University

Architects . . . envision the release of pent-up potentialities in structures and
processes of integration resulting in more naturally evolved forms and spaces. To
this end the explorations now barely beginning in . . . space frames . . . could lead
to a more encompassing expression of our time.
—Louis I. Kahn, lecture at North Carolina State College

Even while Louis Kahn was preoccupied with the design of the Yale Art
Gallery, he began to consider how he might marshal his emerging interest in
authenticity into a new civic architecture. From 1952 to 1957 he worked on two
projects that were to house institutions which were central to the well-being of a
society run on the principle of public participation. With Anne Tyng he designed
City Tower, a project that he first proposed as a new city hall and then hoped that
the City of Philadelphia might construct as a much-needed major annex to the
existing city hall (Fig. 3.1). It was never built. In 1954 Kahn began work on a
commission for a medical services building for the American Federation of
Labor (AFL), the largest labor union in the region; the building was completed
in 1957 and demolished in 1973 (Plate 7). These projects constitute Kahn's first
attempt to give architectural form to his belief that public buildings should
become symbols of communal identity and membership while spatially enabling
the kinds of interactions that fostered communal participation. But what this
form would be could not have been predicted by looking at his previous work.
Sheepishly admitting in 1952 that he was "constantly in a formative stage, being
influenced by many diverse things,"[1] Kahn, for these projects, chose a new
vocabulary derived from space frames, which he believed consistent with both
his modernist social and design agenda and his aesthetic of authenticity.

Gothic times, architects built in solid stones. Now we can build with hollow stones. The spaces defined by the members of
structure are as important as the members. These spaces range in scale from the voids of an insulation panel, voids for air,
heating and heat to circulate, to spaces big enough to walk through or live in.
: desire to express voids positively in the design of structure is evidenced by the growing interest and work in the develop-
nt of space frames. The forms being experimented with come from a closer knowledge of nature and the outgrowth of the
stant search for order. Design habits leading to the concealment of structure have no place in this implied order. Such hab-
retard the development of an art. I believe that in architecture, as in all art, the artist instinctively keeps the marks which re-
l how a thing was done. The feeling that our present day architecture needs embellishment stems in part from our tendency
air joints out of sight, to conceal how parts are put together. Structures should be devised which can harbor the mechanical
ds of rooms and spaces. Ceilings with structure furred in tend to erase scale. If we were to train ourselves to draw as we build,
m the bottom up, when we do, stopping our pencil to make a mark at the joints of pouring or erecting, ornament would
w out of our love for the expression of method. It would follow that the pasting over the construction of lighting and acous-
l material, the burying of tortured unwanted ducts, conduits and pipe lines, would become intolerable. The desire to express
v it is done would filter through the entire society of building, to architect, engineer, builder and craftsman.

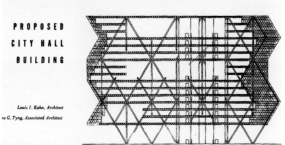

3.1 City Tower as Louis I. Kahn
and Anne Tyng's "Proposed City
Hall Building." From "Toward a
Plan for Midtown Philadelphia,"
Perspecta 2 (August 1953).

MODERNISM, TECHNOLOGY, ORGANICISM

Kahn's involvement in, and responses to, the intellectual discourse attending space-frame design reveal why he adopted space frames and the meanings he assigned to these forms. When, in mid-1951, he decided on a "space frame" for the ceiling of the Yale Art Gallery, he had only recently been introduced to these structures by Tyng, and knew little about their structural properties.[2] In the ensuing several years, space frames became the object of cult-like attention within the East Coast architectural community and beyond. Proponents championed them as a means of reinvigorating the language of modernism because they were inexpensive to mass-produce and structurally expressive, thereby seeming the natural successors to the technologically derived forms of the early modern movement. By assigning to space frames a surprising array of mystical meanings that are not self-evidently intrinsic to the forms, the theorists and designers around Kahn claimed for space frames an almost messianic social role. Kahn became embroiled in these discussions: discovering that space frames harbored connotations consistent with his preexisting aesthetic and social ideals, he embraced these forms more directly, and by mid-1953 had developed a new philosophy of design.

He soon began discussing space frames with R. Buckminster Fuller, who had inspired Tyng's interest in these forms. Kahn had known Fuller since the 1930s, and Fuller taught at Yale in the years that he developed his geodesic dome. He and Kahn commuted to New Haven together, with Kahn boarding the train in Philadelphia and Fuller getting on in New York City.[3] Fuller claimed to have "regaled Louis" on these train rides with the principles underlying his combinations of tetrahedra, octahedra, and spheres that he called Energetic-Synergetic geometry,[4] and indeed, as if to corroborate Fuller's claim, Kahn kept in his personal collection slides of Fuller's students constructing a cardboard geodesic (Fig. 3.2).[5] The escalating influence of Fuller's ideas on Kahn was reinforced by William Huff, the Yale student closest to Kahn from 1950 to 1952, who intensively studied geometry in space-frame design.[6] Moreover, Fuller offered studios at many universities and colleges in the early 1950s—a peripatetic preacher, he delivered his epiphanic message and left a version of the geodesic dome behind—and his stops included Princeton, where Kahn lectured in 1953 and frequently served as a visiting critic, and North Carolina State, a center for advanced thought on architectural structure in the early 1950s, where Kahn spoke in early 1953 and had many friends.[7]

Through Tyng, Kahn also came to know the work of the French structural engineer Robert Le Ricolais.[8] Le Ricolais, like Fuller, used small structural units configured into three-dimensional triangulated forms, but he argued that Fuller's use of the sphere was structurally inefficient because it did not account for the problem of deflection. His own work used flat spans instead.[9] Le Ricolais was introduced by mail to Kahn in March 1953, and the two had developed a warm relationship by the time they met in person in early 1954, when Le Ricolais was a visiting professor at North Carolina State.[10] By 1952 Kahn also knew of the work of Felix Samuely, the British structural engineer who designed the space-frame roof for the Pavilion of Transport at the Festival of Britain in 1951 (Fig. 3.3);[11] in 1953, Kahn invited Samuely to Yale. When Samuely arrived in April 1954, Kahn shepherded him through his days at Yale and hosted him at his Philadelphia office the following week.[12]

Fuller's, Le Ricolais', and Samuely's ideas were so popular among students that space frames became the locus of a veritable new movement that generated much excitement in the mainstream architectural press.[13] No fewer than ten articles on space frames appeared from 1951 to 1954 in *Architectural Forum* alone. When Douglas Haskell looked into his "crystal ball" in 1951, it was space frames that he saw in architecture's future.[14] "Is This Tomorrow's Structure?" asked the editors of *Forum* in 1953, reprinting the text of a 1951 lecture by Samuely, which optimistically proclaimed that "hundreds of years hence, people will look back on this time as the one when constructions changed over from 'plane' to 'space' and saw the birth of a new architecture."[15] Samuely's text was accompanied by comments from Fuller, Walter Gropius, Paul Rudolph, Le Ricolais, and Konrad Wachsmann, who was teaching with Mies at the Illinois Institute of Technology.[16] Mies also grappled with these ideas for long-span

3.2 Kahn's slide of Yale students constructing a cardboard geodesic, Buckminster Fuller studio, 1952. From the Kahn Collection.

3.3 Felix Samuely, space-frame ceiling for the Pavilion of Transport, Festival of Britain, London, 1951. From Samuely, "Space Frames and Stressed Skin Construction," *Royal Institute of British Architects Journal* 59 (March 1952).

structures, designing in 1953 a project for a convention center in Chicago that contained a huge span created by a lattice of interwoven trusses.

Although participants in the emerging movement in space frames diverged on the finer points of engineering, they shared a core of beliefs and collectively shaped a narrative that assigned social meanings to these forms. Space frames were so inexpensive and structurally efficient that, properly harnessed, they could effect radical change not only in commercial architecture but also in housing and public buildings.[17] Fuller declared in 1951 that his geodesic structures were "the only architectural revolution," and later wrote that they were part of his "transcendental world design plan . . . [for] a whole new world industry concerned with man's unavoidable needs and implementation of his inherent freedoms." Haskell predicted that space frames (as well as related new uses of technology) would lead toward "a new order of construction . . . a vast new industrial creation."[18]

In using these structural and technological innovations, Haskell implied, architects could breathe fresh air into a modern movement that was beginning to decline. As late as 1940, modernism bore the imprimatur of the avant-garde, but by the early 1950s it was no longer new. Hudnut complained in early 1953 that the idiom had become "arid," and at a conference early the following year, Sert disparaged functionalism as having produced works of "appalling poverty" while Rudolph groused that "modern architecture's range of expression is from A to B."[19] To redress this trend, structurally innovative work was often proposed, and such journals as *Architectural Forum* and *Progressive Architecture* published an abundance of articles on the work of such structurally oriented archi-tects and structural engineers as Eduardo Catalano, Eduardo Torroja, and Matthew Nowicki.[20] Henry-Russell Hitchcock, a frequent juror at Yale in these years, celebrated London's Festival of Britain by curating an exhibition in 1951 on the Crystal Palace which highlighted the building's structural features (the show was accompanied by a catalogue, a copy of which Kahn owned).[21]

Because space frames incorporated technological advances made during World War II, they also exemplified the kind of technological transfer from the military to the civilian sphere that the post–World War I founders of modernism had made their ideal. Fuller and Haskell reasoned that while scientific and technological discovery had necessarily been used to destructive ends, society's task now was to employ it for social good; this conviction was famously espoused by President Dwight D. Eisenhower in his "Atoms for Peace" speech of December 1953.[22] Fuller wrote,

> God says
> observe the paradox
> of man's creative potentials
> and his destructive tactics . . .
> We have the plenty, we have . . .
> the ability.
> Let us start the mechanism to creative account;
> not to vaster and vaster destructive means.[23]

Echoing Fuller's ideas, Haskell wrote that atomic energy was "the negative side of a tremendous power opportunity"; space frames, as well as associated uses of new technology, were the "positive side," the obverse of the coin.[24]

Space frames, then, were imbued with symbolic implications that made them appealing to those who, like Kahn, believed in the continuing validity of the modern movement. With their tectonic expression and use of mass production techniques, space frames offered a way to adhere to the underlying precepts of the modern movement while reinvigorating its forms.[25] Using space frames was also perceived as consistent with modernism's social agenda, for Fuller and Haskell implied that such technological transfer, in offering better, cheaper buildings for all, would advance the cause of social equality. Such technological optimism was common after World War II: as Roland Marchand, a cultural his-torian, writes, "Wartime discourse resonated with acclamations of equality and promises of the coming of a better, technologically wondrous life for all. . . . Americans emerged from the war confident of a snowballing trend toward eco-nomic democraticization and a classless culture."[26] So technology became asso-ciated (or indeed, continued its pre–World War II association) with the progress of democracy.

The space frame's coupling with progressive social ideas was also manifested in a more oblique way. Le Ricolais, Tyng, and Fuller, among others, based their unusual forms on scientific studies of geometry in nature. Their interest in the geometric structure underlying organic and inorganic forms was sparked largely by an exhibition at the Institute of Contemporary Art (ICA) in London in 1951, mounted in honor of D'Arcy Thompson, whose 1917 *On Growth and Form* became widely read by architects after its reprint of 1942.[27] The popularity of *On Growth and Form* inspired space-frame enthusiasts to seek out similar studies, which led them to the H.M.S. *Challenger* report of 1874 by German biologist and philosopher Ernst Haeckel. The *Challenger* report contained a series of carefully wrought drawings revealing the geometric structure of various underwater organisms. Le Ricolais extolled "this stupendous vocabulary of forms," and in 1953 used a Haeckel drawing of a radiolarian on the cover of a North Carolina State journal devoted to his work (Fig. 3.4).[28]

Thompson's and Haeckel's findings were augmented by discoveries made possible by the electron microscope, which became commercially available in the mid-1930s. With the electron microscope, scientists found that tetrahedra, octahedra, hexagons, and triangles recurred not only in protozoa, crystals, and soap bubbles but also in a huge array of forms including diatoms and chemical compounds (Figs. 3.5 and 3.6). For Le Ricolais, Tyng, and Fuller, the very ubiquity of these geometric figures in nature confirmed their inherent structural efficiency. Such beliefs were reiterated by Gyorgy Kepes, a former member of the Bauhaus and a painter based at MIT, who was already examining organic geometries when he served on a jury with Kahn at Yale in May 1951, before Kahn took up these ideas.[29] Kepes curated an exhibition at MIT in 1953, entitled *The New Landscape in Art and Science*, which included many photographs taken under the electron microscope.[30]

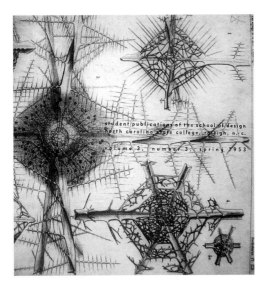

3.4 Radiolarians in a plate from Ernst Haeckel's *The Voyage of H.M.S. Challenger* (1853), on the cover of a special issue on the work of Robert Le Ricolais, *North Carolina State College Student Publication of the School of Design* 3 (Spring 1953).

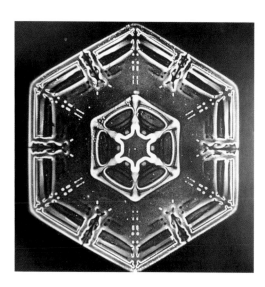

3.5 Magnified view of a hexagonal form in a snowflake. From Gyorgy Kepes, *The New Landscape in Art and Science* (Chicago: Paul Theobald, 1956).

Le Ricolais, Tyng, and Fuller associated space frames with a progressive social agenda in two ways. The first was their proposition, familiar to supporters of the modern movement, that technology properly used would create a better world. The second was more mystical. Space frames, in their reliance on nature's geometries, revealed that underneath the apparent chaos and randomness of structures and forms in contemporary life was an order of almost mystical simplicity. Referring in 1940 to geometries in natural forms, Fuller wrote that "these wondrous actualities were always *there*, inherent in the universe of a god of meaning," in a poem that was reprinted in 1953 in North Carolina State's *Student Publications of the School of Design*. He suggested that God was not a static, transcendental presence but "a verb, the most active, connoting the vast harmonic reordering of the universe . . . and there is born unheralded," he predicted, "a great natural peace."[31] Kepes contrasted the "old world of sense experiences" with the "confident and vigorous unifying force" of scientific discovery.[32] Tyng, Kepes, Fuller, and others assumed that if people could only harness the logic that science had uncovered, the lack of fit that people felt with their world could be redressed.[33]

Space frames, through the "universal" geometries they employed, could ameliorate alienation. This was the implication of the argument advanced in bits and pieces by Fuller, Kepes, and Tyng, and it became a central part of the narrative surrounding space frames. Important to this narrative were the writings of Lancelot Law Whyte, an eccentric British science commentator on whose work Kepes and, especially, Tyng relied.[34] Whyte had edited the ICA catalogue on D'Arcy Thompson, and his earlier book, *The Next Development in Man* (1948), was a kind of cult classic among architects in the early 1950s. Kahn knew of it almost immediately upon its publication.[35]

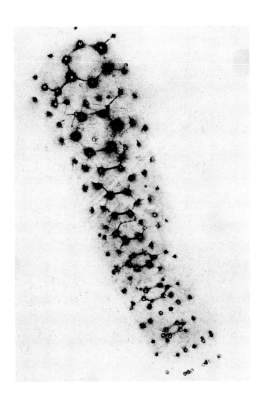

3.6 Magnified view of hexagonal forms in a chemical compound. From Kepes, *The New Landscape in Art and Science.*

Whyte's writing surpassed even the utopian rhetoric of Fuller and Kepes. Fuller believed that better uses of technology would make of the world a "one-town community"; Tyng espoused similar ideas, emphasizing the commonality of human experience, which she believed was subject to a complex system of natural laws "from microcosm to macrocosm." [36] Whyte took such claims further, explaining that his aim was "the development of a world community," which would occur when contemporary man "understood himself" through proper comprehension of recent discoveries in science. Literature, art, politics, economics – all other cultural forms had failed to bring about these ends. Whyte argued that the only solution was for man to reorganize his "knowledge of nature so that he may recognize himself as part of the system of nature." [37]

Whyte and Tyng believed that artistic references to the structure of nature might bring people together by making them recognize the universality of their experience. In non-political terms, this agenda resonated with Kahn's previous desire to promote a "world community" through political and social means, which he had hoped to advance in such projects as the Laboratory for Education and the UNESCO headquarters in his Jefferson National Expansion Memorial entry. In the work of Fuller and others, Kahn had found an idiom whereby such an agenda might be advanced directly in symbolic architectural form. That this idiom harmonized with other aspects of his architectural aesthetic made its appeal still that much greater.

"A RENAISSANCE OF ART AND SCIENCE"

The call to use recent scientific and technological discoveries to find a new architecture had an identifiable, and escalating, impact on Kahn's thought. He embraced and reconfigured the techno-organic movement's forms and its social vision. He began to study crystallography and bought a copy of Louis Figuier's studies on organic structure.[38] He collected photographs of radiolarians, of the bones of vultures' wings, and of plates from Haeckel's *Challenger* report, filing them with his drawings and sketches (Fig. 3.7). More telling, he began making proclamations, suffused with the language of his sources, that architecture, through science, could promote and exemplify a new order that had been revealed. (In this respect 1953 was a crucial year, for Kahn spoke at North Carolina State College in February and at Princeton in December; in June and July he worked on his first major article of the decade, for *Perspecta*, "Toward a Plan for Midtown Philadelphia.")[39] Kahn was developing an organic ideology of design that assimilated the ideas of Tyng, Le Ricolais, Samuely, Fuller, Kepes, and Whyte, not only in their substance but in their prophetic tones.

Kahn asserted in his article for *Perspecta* that space frames came from "a closer knowledge of nature and the outgrowth of a constant search for order."[40] Order became one of Kahn's key theoretical concepts, and he repeated it as if repetition itself would make the notion clear. By December, order had been transformed from a quality to a form: something to be discovered, not constructed. Kahn wrote to Tyng that he believed order, such as that underlying crystals and radiolarians, "is mostly structure. The structural idea harboring embodying [*sic*] the needs of air, light, quiet, noise, etc. It is embodying what makes the structure grow into a life of fibre *It is the seed it is integration.*"[41] Kahn wrote to another friend that he was beginning to distinguish between order and design; a few days earlier he had asserted that order was "consistent"; design was "circumstantial," the fulfilling of mechanical and material demands.[42] Kahn's concept of order paralleled the double experience of nature that Fuller and Kepes had admired: chaotic and incidental in appearance, structured and consistent at its core.

Kahn predicted "a renaissance of art and science" that space frames would ignite, writing that "architects concerned with the search for an order envision the release of pent up potentialities in structures and processes of integration resulting in more naturally evolved forms and spaces. To this end the explorations now barely beginning in . . . space frames . . . could lead to a more encompassing expression of our time."[43] Echoing Kahn's sentiments, Le Ricolais wrote (in halting English), "I pretend that to day it would be more profitable for a young Architect to spend six months in a cristallographer [*sic*] laboratory than to go to Rome to make some beautiful rendus of ancient monuments."[44] At the conference at Princeton in December 1953, Kahn lamented architects' reliance on past architectural styles. He unequivocally stated, "I studied at the University of

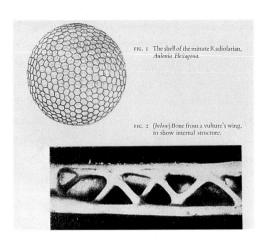

FIG. 1 The shell of the minute Radiolarian, *Aulonia Hexagona*.

FIG. 2 (*below*) Bone from a vulture's wing, to show internal structure.

3.7 Kahn's slides of a radiolarian with hexagonal forms and a bone from a vulture's wing showing triangulated forms. From the Kahn Collection.

Pennsylvania [where he received a Beaux-Arts training under Paul Cret], and although I can still feel the spiritual aspects of that training, I have spent all my time since graduation unlearning what I learned."[45]

Kahn also became preoccupied with a notion he called integration, which he had begun to develop while designing the Yale Art Gallery; by it, he meant that structural, mechanical, and programmatic demands would be approached as one. As was evident in his design for the Yale Art Gallery, this desire to integrate all aspects of a building into a conceptual whole was concordant with the exigencies of authenticity, which demanded that the essential elements of a building be foregrounded, made present. Kahn now added an organic dimension to this conviction: the architect should aspire to make his building *grow* into a living whole — an approach that he predicted "will improve with the recognition of the methods of science."[46]

Kahn began to call space frames "structures of hollow stones," stating, as if a prophet declaring a new age, that "in gothic times, architects built in solid stones. Now we can build with hollow stones."[47] He believed that space frames were analogous to Gothic buildings because the forms of both were determined by the dictates of structural efficiency; in each, aesthetic and structure were one. Here is the same championing of tectonic expression that Kahn lauded in his essay on monumentality and claimed to seek in his design (but in practice ignored in the building) of the Yale Art Gallery, to which he now added an organic dimension. For him, "hollow stones" meant the steel or aluminum cylinders used in space-frame construction, which Le Ricolais compared to the siliceous tubes of a radiolarian or the stem of a leaf.[48]

Order, integration, hollow stones: these new concepts signaled the profound effect on Kahn of the techno-organic movement in space frames. Like his contemporaries, he sought an architectural expression of a geometric order which was veiled by manifest reality. Like them, he believed that this expression would emerge from innovative uses of technology and materials. Like them, he predicted that the adoption of these new forms would lead to a renaissance; a rebirth, a new architecture for an era in which all humanity joined in recognition of the universal laws of science.

The hazy notion of a world of users joined together in recognition of their union with nature was intrinsic to the discourse on space frames: such meanings came packaged in these forms. The quasi-mystical union of humanity that Fuller, Tyng, and Whyte envisioned was certainly not as overtly political as the "world community" that Kahn entertained in the 1940s, which had been based on his support for such actually existing institutions as the organization for world government and the United Nations. Still, the impulses were on the same continuum. Moreover, Kahn found in the techno-organic movement in space frames something that his more direct political involvements had not offered him: a clear architectural direction.

Space frames relied on the simple geometries to which Kahn had previously been attracted through his affiliations with the modern movement and through his teachings at Yale, although the system that space frames employed was more rigid and more controlling. Still, they could be designed and constructed in a manner consistent with his aesthetic of authenticity. For Kahn, they promised to reinvigorate a modern movement beginning to decline, and they suggested a universalizing means to symbolize the cause of community. That is why in the mid-1950s Kahn employed this language in his two principal civic projects for his hometown of Philadelphia: a new city hall and a medical center for the most powerful local labor union in town.

CITY TOWER AS PHILADELPHIA'S NEW CITY HALL

A shifting, awkward skyscraper based on hexagonal plans and three-dimensionally triangulated sections, City Tower appears to be a purely formal exercise: it looks eminently unbuildable, or at least ungainly were it built.[49] The building lists as it rises, with no level directly above the last, so that dramatic and odd sectional shifts shape the profiles of the facades. Three abutting hexagons compose each main floor, the hexagon being a standard, almost paradigmatic form in the natural phenomena that Kahn and Tyng were studying, itself composed of an even more basic geometric figure, the triangle.[50] These floors are laced into a tower eighteen stories high, including six principal levels with mezzanines sandwiched between.

Kahn held the highest civic aspirations for the project, first, with Tyng, envisioning it as a new city hall for Philadelphia (Fig. 3.8), and then, on his own initiative, proposing that it be considered for an annex to the old city hall on Market Street, on a nearby site, Reyburn Plaza (Fig. 3.9). City Tower had a double origin, one in Kahn's city-planning schemes of the early 1950s, another in the conceptual work of Tyng. Since the 1940s, Kahn had been involved in various organizations charged with replanning Philadelphia's downtown. One nagging

3.8 Perspective showing City Tower on the Schuylkill River site with a hexagonal plan and triangulated sections. From "Toward a Plan for Midtown Philadelphia." Photo from the Kahn Collection.

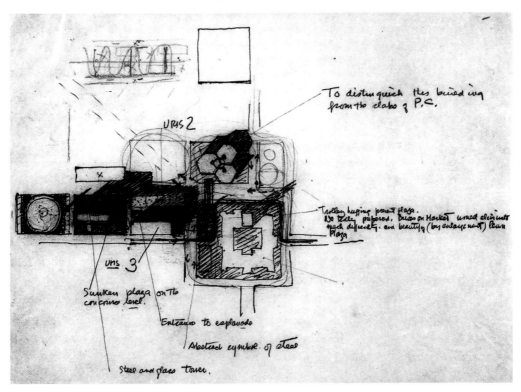

3.9 Sketches of City Tower for the Reyburn Plaza site next to Philadelphia's city hall, ca. 1954. From the Kahn Collection.

problem was the old city hall, built in 1872. The town's administrative functions had outgrown the space available in the Second Empire building, which was functionally flawed and costly to maintain; in addition, its siting contributed to the increasingly severe problem of traffic congestion because it broke the axis of the city's main thoroughfare, Market Street, deflecting vehicles to either its north or its south side.[51] In late 1951, Kahn proposed to a local chapter of the American Institute of Architects a new civic center, with a new city hall, along the east side of the Schuylkill River.[52] A triangular slab rendered in the abstracted vocabulary he had developed in the late 1940s and early 1950s, it would be surrounded by a long, low arcade with several structures located within. Yet the Committee on Municipal Improvements rejected the proposal out of hand.[53] Shortly thereafter, sometime in 1952, Tyng started working on City Tower, a project that explored the implications of extending a space frame into a multistoried structure. Tyng envisioned a tetrahedral space frame with a plan of gently bowed triangles and three-dimensionally triangulated structural supports.[54] When Kahn started to collaborate with Tyng on this project in 1953, they drew up a new version of City Tower as Philadelphia's new city hall. They sited it at the prow of a civic center by the Schuylkill River, an urban redevelopment scheme then under way under the direction of Edmund Bacon, the executive director of the City Planning Commission (Fig. 3.10).[55]

In early 1954, when municipal authorities relinquished the idea of building a new civic center by the Schuylkill, deciding instead to construct an annex to the old city hall on Reyburn Plaza, Kahn, on his own, actively lobbied for the chance to bring his and Tyng's proposal to fruition.[56] Finding that he had supporters on the board of the Redevelopment Authority, which was responsible for choosing an architect for the site, Kahn analyzed the Reyburn Plaza problem in depth, taking photographs and making sketches of the old building (Fig. 3.11) and of the sight lines from Reyburn Plaza back to city hall (Fig. 3.12).[57] Kahn wrote Tyng that for reasons of efficiency he might change City Tower's configuration to two squares. "Of course," he continued, "we could build two of these hexagons instead of three. What do you think?" he asked, ending, "I wish we had the commission."[58]

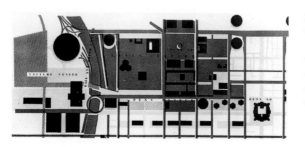

3.10 Plan for a new civic center development by the Schuylkill River in downtown Philadelphia, with the clustered hexagons of City Tower in the upper left-hand quadrant. From "Toward a Plan for Midtown Philadelphia."

3.11 Sketch of Philadelphia's old city hall, probably done while Kahn was teaching a studio on the proposed city hall annex at the University of Pennsylvania, 1954. From the Kahn Collection.

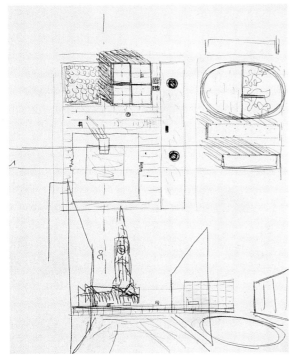

3.12 Sketches of sight lines from Reyburn Plaza back to City Hall and a version of City Tower with a plan of four abutting squares, 1954. From the Kahn Collection.

In the design for City Tower Kahn and Tyng integrated the themes of authenticity and community in a techno-organic monumentality. Oddly listing walls and windows formed a defamiliarizing gesture still more potent than the Yale Art Gallery's looming walls; they would surprise the viewer into focusing on the materiality of the object, and would also serve to evoke other floors and other users, so that those inside the building would be reminded constantly of their membership in a collectivity. Kahn wrote that he designed the tower's open volumes and public spaces to be "nondirectional," implying democratic accessibility, and he and Tyng tried to promote public participation by setting aside the entire ground floor of the building for exhibitions and events that the general public would attend (Fig. 3.13).[59]

They envisioned exposed concrete interiors similar to the Yale Art Gallery, preferring concrete over the space frame's usual metal framework both because of its heaviness and because a skyscraper of reinforced concrete required no fireproofing that would mask the building's structure. Because the project was never built, it is not known how Kahn would have articulated the process of construction; still, it is fair to assume that he would have used the same techniques to create a sense of materiality that he had employed in the building at Yale. Other design elements also came from Yale: the tetrahedronal ceiling with air ducts laid up inside it; a network of aluminum mesh (like that under the handrail edging the staircase in New Haven) that stretches across the south and west facades to provide shade from the sun (Fig. 3.14).

City Tower emerged in part from dissatisfactions Kahn felt with the Art Gallery addition, especially with the integration of the vertical and horizontal support systems. He reflected that at Yale "the order could have been more developed to include a vertical control system integrated with the columnar system,"[60] and he drew an ex post facto scheme in which the "columns" would be three-dimensionally triangulated lattices woven into the tetrahedral ceiling (Fig. 3.15). Yet in City Tower, Kahn no more succeeded in making strides in architectural structure than he had in the Art Gallery at Yale. He erroneously discussed the project in tectonic terms, justifying City Tower's form by arguing that it best expressed buttressing against wind stresses: "The mind envisions a construction of a building growing from a base crossing its members as it rises against the forces of the wind."[61] Yet neither Tyng nor Kahn checked their wind-stress argument with a structural engineer, who would have told them that because of the forces of gravity, a tower rising in a more-or-less straight vertical is dramatically more efficient.[62] Moreover, problems of compression would have made the project fantastically inefficient to build. Other problems are also evident: glazing would have been difficult; an aluminum-mesh sun screen would

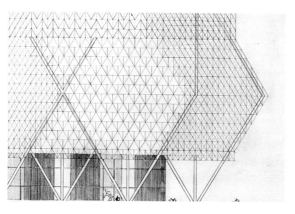

3.13 Detail of City Tower with its double-height ground floor that opens into the city for public use. From the Kahn Collection.

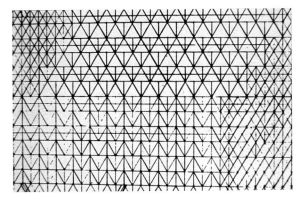

3.14 Detail of wire mesh (recalling the wire mesh used under the banisters and around the heating registers at the Yale Art Gallery) on a sketch of the facade of City Tower. From "Toward a Plan for Midtown Philadelphia."

3.15 Reconceptualization of vertical supports for the Yale Art Gallery, ca. 1954. From the Kahn Collection.

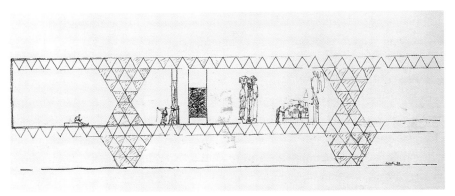

have conducted heat even as it provided bits of shade. The structural members that ran through the entire building on diagonals would have made situating service cores and partitions a daunting proposition.

Some of his assertions notwithstanding, Kahn's concerns in the design of City Tower were not structural: they were aesthetic, symbolic, and social. He conceived of the building within the context of his preoccupation with communal life. He envisioned an urban monument that, by its visibility and the way it met the street, might mobilize local users to participate as members of the urban community. Through its techno-organic imagery, it simultaneously symbolized the possibility of world community. Kahn's larger aspirations for the project were apparent in a lecture that he gave at Tulane only months after submitting his proposal for the Reyburn Plaza site. Repeating themes that originated in his work on public housing and city planning, he lamented that city halls in contemporary society had lost the symbolic and functional roles of consolidating communal identity. "If you think of civic," he asked a group of students in December 1954, "what do you think of? You think of city hall, you think of the firehouse, the post office. . . . Actually, the present tendency is not for us to meet in the city hall to discuss problems. We are not really a participating part of any meeting house, which was at one time held in what we call 'city hall.'"[63]

Kahn returned to the proposal in 1956; symbolically and literally, his own

"city hall" would be a "meeting house" that would encourage people to "participate," to shoulder their responsibility as members of a democratic community.
He predicted that his and Tyng's triangulated, space-frame skyscraper would
"reveal itself as a new Philadelphia landmark," implying that people would
eventually embrace the clunky, odd building, intuiting the meanings embedded
within.[64] Like other space frames, City Tower symbolically reenacted the hidden
order underlying nature, and because the project was based on geometries
found in organic and inorganic form, it would be more universally accessible
than the Beaux-Arts city hall nearby, which relied on cultural precedents and so
implied a more restricted audience that was familiar with them. In its realization the project would manifest the aesthetic of authenticity; in its symbolism
and planning, it would set forth a civic idiom for all by representing the commonality of humanity in nature, from microcosm to macrocosm.

THE AFL MEDICAL SERVICES

While City Tower was confined to the imagination, Kahn turned to work on
his AFL Medical Services, a four-story, granite- and glass-paneled square block
of a building in downtown Philadelphia. Here the complex nexus of themes—
authenticity, monumentality, techno-organicism, community—took built form.
In the AFL, Kahn sought to create a public building that, through both spatial
and symbolic means, would remind users of their role as participants in the collectivity of their organization and in the larger public realm, while conferring
the potent impression of monumentality and authenticity.[65]

The site was at the edge of Center City, on Vine Street; the program was for a
facility that would provide free health care to seventy thousand members of one
of the largest labor unions in the country. Kahn explained that because his clients
"were working people, I had to make this as close as possible to a palace,"[66]
thereby evoking precedents like the Maisons du Peuple built in Europe by a previous generation of modern architects. Although the AFL was too circumspect a
design to command the street presence that City Tower might have had, Kahn
enhanced the masonry monumentality of the building by alternating polished
granite slabs with transparent planes of glass. To impart nobility was especially
important, he argued, because in the very act of joining, union members had
"expressed their faith" in the power of collective action.[67] Kahn conceived of the
AFL in terms drawn from his work in city planning with Stonorov in the 1940s: a
labor union embodied his ideal of individual empowerment and greater social
good achieved by individual participation in a collectivity.

In the design of the AFL Medical Services building, Kahn accommodated
both the individual user and the collectivity to which that user belonged. Stone
and glass panels were oriented vertically, referring to the standing human figure
and thereby drawing the individual user into a phenomenological relationship
to the building. Kahn put a rectangular ground floor into a relatively small,

nearly square building (devoting the remainder of the ground floor to parking). Users entered on the long axis in an entry sequence that maximized the grandeur by which Kahn's "working people," the users of the building, would process inside (Fig. 3.16). At the same time, Kahn insisted upon establishing a relationship between the AFL and other civic institutions of Philadelphia. In an early sketch of the AFL he faintly drew the mansarded tower of the old city hall, although the Vine Street site was at the periphery of Center City (Fig. 3.17). This same sketch, like Kahn and Tyng's plan for a new city hall, depicted the building with a double-height glazed waiting area that opens onto the city beyond.

Kahn wanted to establish the AFL's larger role within the civic institutions of the city: this is revealed in the developmental stages of the project and in the final scheme. Early on, he explored a misguided idea that would have diminished the monumentality of the entrance sequence, envisioning the granite panels of the upper stories on the ground floor. To highlight the transitions from the street to the semi-public waiting rooms, he pulled these panels off the facade to create a small enclosed area (Fig. 3.18). In the final conception, he constructed instead a glassy wall, emphasizing the transparency of the semi-public waiting room by pulling back the two corner columns within. The double-height, airy, light-filled area imparted a sense of dignity to the place where union members waited; it also forced their sight lines outward and south toward views of the city beyond, as if to remind them that their small community was a microcosm, and a constituent part, of the larger community of the city itself.

Architects working in Kahn's office report that he considered the monumental, four-foot-deep Vierendeel truss he used here equivalent to the tetrahedral

3.16 Entrance lobby showing, on left, a Vierendeel truss sliding past a supporting post, AFL Medical Services, Philadelphia, 1954–1957. Photo: E. Teitelman.

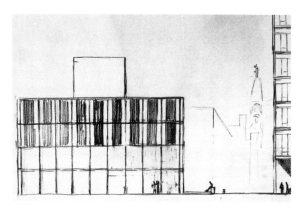

3.17 Elevation study of the AFL Medical Services, with Philadelphia's old city hall lightly sketched to the right in the background, ca. 1954. From the Kahn Collection.

3.18 Perspective of an early scheme for the AFL Medical Services, with vertical slabs of ground-floor facade continued to right to create an outdoor entry courtyard, ca. 1954. Photo: E. Teitelman.

3.19 Detail of Vierendeel trusses, AFL Medical Services, Philadelphia, 1954–1957. Photo: E. Teitelman.

concrete ceiling at Yale, but more usable, because services could be threaded easily through apertures more than two feet high (Fig. 3.19).[68] The heavy, awkward Vierendeel is called a truss but acts like a perforated beam; like the poured concrete tetrahedronal ceiling at Yale, it is not an especially efficient structural form. But the Vierendeel truss, like the space frame, is particular to the twentieth century. It was invented by a Belgian structural engineer in 1898 and could be constructed only in reinforced concrete or steel, materials that, for many architects, symbolized modernity.[69] Like tetrahedral forms, the open lattice-like form of the Vierendeel could be traced to organic precedents (Fig. 3.20). Rarely had the Vierendeel been used architecturally; almost never had it been exposed.[70] In adopting it, Kahn returned to the search, begun with the Yale Art Gallery addition and continued with City Tower, for unusual forms that conferred the impression of a raw monumentality while bearing the patina of structural advance.

That Kahn perceived the AFL's structure as part of his project of creating authenticity while "searching for an [organic] order" is apparent in his use of materials, his articulation of the spaces within, and his use of geometry in the plan. Using a still starker combination of materials than he had at Yale — poured concrete, brick, metal, and concrete block (here unrelieved by the warmth of wood) — Kahn was even more relentless in his expression of the building's material presence. He confronted the viewer with the dumb, insistent gridded skeleton of the building, bones inside a transparent skin, framing outdoor spaces and

3.20 Kahn's photograph of a plate illustrating radiolarians from Ernst Haeckel's *The Voyage of the H.M.S. Challenger* (1853), with shapes similar to those in the Vierendeel trusses used in the AFL Medical Services. From the Kahn Collection.

3.21 Open parking garage with a Vierendeel truss, AFL Medical Services, Philadelphia, 1954–1957. Photo: E. Teitelman.

all the rooms (Fig. 3.21). The enclosed part of the ground floor held only the waiting area, a telegraph office, and a reception desk; to be seen by a doctor, a person had to ascend to the floor above. In the stairwell through which all traffic passed, a Vierendeel reappeared, now embedded in brick (Fig. 3.22): this manifested the transition between floor levels and also signaled the organic interrelatedness of the whole. Once upstairs, she was again facing her fellow union members and the city before turning 180 degrees and proceeding to examination rooms behind (Fig. 3.23).

Le Ricolais and Samuely believed that cubic forms were part of nature's repertoire. Kahn had briefly considered them for City Tower, but in the AFL plan they take on a central role. Essentially, the plan is a nine square, but with one slip added to take the building to the edge of the property line. Geometric order controlled the whole, with the dimensions of the slip equaling the dimensions of the partitions marking rooms inside (Fig. 3.24). The central square, the heart, was the service core that shoots up out of the building in a design decision that Kahn later regretted and tried to change in two intermediary schemes. The square motif was carried into the smallest details, such as the shape of the columns supporting the Vierendeels.

An ordered articulation of parts ran through Kahn's handling of the AFL structure from large to small. The Vierendeel of the main facade, for example, was not joined to vertical members but instead slid by them, each beam maintaining its discreet integrity (see Fig. 3.16). Similarly, for the banisters in the stairwells Kahn came up with two designs; in each, the tubular handrail was one straight piece of metal that slid by, rather than curved into, the rail for the level below. This emphasis on the discrete integrity of a building's fundamental

3.22 Staircase with an embedded Vierendeel truss, AFL Medical Services, Philadelphia, 1954–1957. Photo: E. Teitelman.

85

TECHNO-ORGANIC SYMBOLS OF COMMUNITY

structural elements not only alluded to the dictates of space-frame design but also conferred upon the AFL the same kind of primitivizing quality with which Kahn imbued the Yale Art Gallery.

The AFL Medical Services building was more "integrated" than the design for the Art Gallery at Yale; it was more practical than the scheme he imagined for City Tower. In the AFL Kahn used a technologically progressive structure as a figurative analogue for a program embodying the conviction that communal participation could lead to social change. As with City Tower, Kahn designed the building in a language potentially accessible to all users: organic tropes press themselves upon attempts to describe its forms: skeleton, skin, veins, heart.

A TENTATIVE ARCHITECTURAL SYNTHESIS

In his entry for the Jefferson National Expansion Memorial, Kahn had focused on finding monumental urban and artistic forms for his social agenda of fostering communal participation; he then, with the Yale Art Gallery, temporarily abandoned such explorations to concentrate on the development of an architectural aesthetic. In the space-frame-inspired City Tower and AFL Medical Services, Kahn brought together his two heretofore disjoined architectural inquiries, symbolizing and monumentalizing his aspirations for communal participation, and furthering his project of authenticity. Through weight, mass, and the revelation of structure and of the processes of construction, these buildings

3.23 Balcony overlooking the double-height entry space, AFL Medical Services, Philadelphia, 1954–1957. From the Charles Moore Archive, University of Texas.

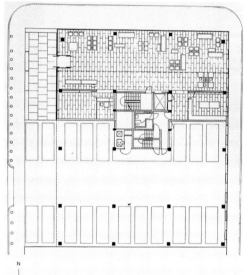

3.24 Ground-floor plan, AFL Medical Services, 1954–1957. From the Kahn Collection.

N

conveyed (or promised to convey) the same kind of presence that the Art Gallery at Yale did: they emphasized honesty over beauty by using everyday materials in compositions that made structure apparent, and, in juxtaposing unusual, defamiliarizing forms with controlling geometries, they were animated by the same tension between expressivity and restraint that surfaces in the Art Gallery at Yale. At the same time, these space frames advanced Kahn's social agenda. They did so by establishing or projecting an open relation to the street and a non-hierarchical circulation system through the open plan. They also symbolized people's commonality in nature through the techno-organic symbolism they employed.

Whereas City Tower and the AFL Medical Services building proved to be the first attempt at a synthesis of Kahn's disparate inquiries, it was problematic. His and Tyng's idea of projecting Fuller's spanning systems into three-dimensional forms promised visually interesting but, from an engineering point of view, unworkable forms; the highly monumental City Tower would have been difficult to build, and the more restrained but buildable AFL did not command the street presence Kahn would later achieve in his civic architecture. Furthermore, the geometries of space frames were unforgivingly rigid, and the symbolism underlying them would have been apparent only to users who were aware of the organic forms to which they referred.

Kahn's search for a monumental idiom that would create symbols of civic identity lay unresolved. Moreover, Kahn's concept of organic order contradicted his aesthetic of authenticity in two important ways. First was the idiomatic use of representation: space frames were laden with intricate symbolic references to organic forms; the search for authenticity, by contrast, required the bypassing of representation in favor of "direct" communication.[71] The second contradiction touched on the differences between space-frame theorists and Existentialist aestheticians' respective worldviews: space frames, in their use of "organic" geometries, referred to an idealist world constituted of basic geometric forms, whereas authenticity was a profoundly anti-idealist aspiration, meant to provoke heightened awareness of this moment only. Kahn's ideas were moving in partly contradictory directions: simultaneously toward idealism and authenticity, simultaneously toward representation and abstraction.

With the addition to the Art Gallery at Yale, City Tower, and the AFL Medical Services Kahn synthesized his ideas about modernism, monumentality, and community by combining the aesthetic of authenticity with the style of the techno-organic movement in space frames. A few years later, he would partially resolve the problems this stylistic synthesis presented by adopting a new idiom that would bring him to his mature architecture. In the meantime, however, he faced a different challenge. He began to consider his social and aesthetic goals in the context of religious identity. This he did with a synagogue project he began in 1954.

4

GATHERING PEOPLE INTO A COMMUNITY

THE ADATH JESHURUN "SYNAGOGUE FOR COMMUNICATION"

Religion is a form of communication. As a matter of fact, a meeting house at one time was a form of communication, and we don't use that any more . . . .
—Louis I. Kahn, "This Business of Architecture"

In early 1954, members of the Adath Jeshurun synagogue asked Louis Kahn to design their new building for a large, pastoral site in Elkins Park, a wealthy suburb of Philadelphia (Plate 8). Kahn, a Jewish architect confronting his first major synagogue commission, made no exploration of the specific contours of Jewish identity in the scheme; instead, he expanded upon his and Tyng's architectural explorations in projects like City Tower, designing a tetrahedral space-frame structure from which he deliberately edited out all references that could be read as explicitly Judaic. He surveyed his religion's history until he found those elements that resonated with his earlier search for a modern, monumental architecture that consolidated communal participation; in doing so, he conceptualized his synagogue not as a space for spiritual transcendence but as an indoor-outdoor "meeting house," or town hall, where people would gather to discuss significant matters of social and political concern.[1] In this vision of the modern synagogue, Kahn recalled ancient, more than modern, rituals of Jewish worship, while simultaneously pushing his tetrahedral, organically derived vocabulary toward more explicitly symbolic forms.

ARCHITECTURE AND THE RELIGIOUS REVIVAL IN THE UNITED STATES

In coming to his conception and design of the Adath Jeshurun synagogue, Kahn simultaneously expressed his own understanding of the essence of religion and grappled with developments in postwar American religious culture and architecture. The postwar period saw a marked religious revival in America: in a Gallup poll after the war, 94 percent of Americans said that they believed in God, while a poll from the *Ladies' Home Journal* indicated that 87 percent were "absolutely certain of God's existence."[2] More significantly, attendance at churches and synagogues across the country was rising rapidly. Church membership rose from 64.5 million in 1940 to 114.5 million in 1960.[3] One Protestant parishioner from the South remembered that his church's "Sunday school was becoming as crowded as the local public school system,"[4] and by 1950, enrollments in Protestant and Jewish seminaries across the country were twice what they had been before World War II, as students flocked for training to fill the increased demand for ministers and rabbis.[5]

Along with this rise in actual participation in religious institutions came an apparent dissipation of religious faith; contemporary social critics noted that the cultural boundaries demarcating religious from social and even civic life were becoming less distinct. Will Herberg, in the widely read study *Protestant–Catholic–Jew* of 1955, condemned Americans for the superficiality of their religious sentiments, citing statistics reporting that whereas nearly 90 percent of adults claimed that they believed in God, almost 50 percent could not name even one of the four gospels.[6] Another writer commented in January 1953 that President Dwight D. Eisenhower, "like many Americans, is a very fervent believer in a very vague religion"; this was prompted by the president's famous remark of December 1952 that "our government makes no sense unless it is founded in a deeply felt religious faith–and I don't care what [faith] it is."[7] William H. Whyte, in his popular book *The Organization Man* (1956), reiterated that the increase in religious participation in the early 1950s was accompanied by a definition of faith that was ever more indeterminate.[8] Whyte acknowledged that churches had always served as neighborhood social condensers, but now churchgoers were motivated by interests far more communal than spiritual, and their pastors followed suit by stressing themes of social intercourse over those of faith. "Is it a church," Whyte asked bluntly, "or is it a social center?"[9]

This postwar "religious" awakening was partly political in character, effecting "a mutually accommodative role between religion and state."[10] A writer commenting on increased synagogue attendance, in an article that appeared in the *National Jewish Welfare Board Circle* of 1955, observed disapprovingly: "The Synagogue has become the beneficiary of a religious revival with patriotic overtones; it is now almost essential that a good American should belong to a church or a synagogue. He would belong, even if he doesn't attend too often. His children must go to religious school, even if they may not learn too much."[11] President Eisenhower repeatedly stressed that religion distinguished democratic from communist living, that piety confirmed one's American identity.

Whereas the major religions and denominations differed in many important respects, all struggled to define spirituality so that personal fulfillment would be balanced with a collective identity that was sympathetic to the principles of American democracy. Many theologians thought that spiritual fellowship was strengthened by balancing individual needs with participation in social and civic affairs.[12] This attempt to foster both personal fulfillment and social participation recalled the search Kahn undertook in his housing projects of the 1930s and 1940s, in which he sought to encourage communal participation to bring equilibrium to a society that overemphasized the principles of individualism.

Swelling congregations, and unmet needs that had been deferred because of the Depression and two world wars, escalated religious building construction to astronomical numbers. At the same time, architects, like pastors and churchgoers, contemplated the social role of religious institutions, seeing in them a means to bind people to a larger community. Although statistics for all types of construction reached new highs in this decade, religious architecture was consistently one of the largest areas of expansion, jumping 24.2 percent in 1953 alone.[13] After the American involvement in the Korean War wound to a close that same year, and restrictions on many essential building materials were lifted, the yearly figures continued to rise.[14]

With the soaring pace of religious institutional construction, cultural critics noted the fluid boundaries demarcating the social and religious spheres. This inspired the architectural community to again take up the issue of modern architecture's perceived incapacity for monumental expression. In the debates on monumentality in the 1940s, ecclesiastical architecture was little discussed: Kahn and Joseph Hudnut had focused their ideas on such "social" monuments as schools and community centers, whereas Henry-Russell Hitchcock and Gregor Paulsson discussed religious monuments in relation to the past but not the present.[15]

As the architectural community struggled to find an appropriate language for religious institutions in these new social roles, the rise in religious building in the 1950s unmoored the problem of monumentality from the early postwar anchor of the civic-social sphere. Architects who approached religious commissions as new opportunities to investigate the problem of monumentality also blurred the typological boundaries between political, cultural, and religious institutions. When the editors of *Architectural Forum* commended Eero Saarinen's model for a non-denominational chapel at the Massachusetts Institute of Technology, they employed the rhetoric of previous discussions on monumentality: "Civilizations of the past seem to have placed a greater, almost spiritual value on architecture . . . is it not possible that architecture may, some day, play this higher role again?"[16] Philip Johnson used similar language, justifying the domed foyer of his Kneses Tifreth Synagogue (1954) as "an ordering feature for the purpose of monumentality and symmetry, symbolizing a non-utilitarian building—a strong feature criticized for introduction of extra-structural and extra-functional values."[17]

In these discussions on monumentality and religious architecture, as in the debates on monumentality itself, architects questioned whether monumentality required an explicitly symbolic vocabulary that might compromise, or even obviate, the abstraction of early modernism. Successful modernist ecclesiastical spaces appeared in the postwar years, of which Eliel Saarinen's First Christian Church in Columbus, Indiana (1942), was the best example. Some critics were nevertheless troubled by the illegibility of buildings like Mies's small chapel at the Illinois Institute of Technology, which, on the face of it, alarmingly resembled the campus boiler house. Several prominent architects, grappling with the question of an appropriate form for religious space, turned to a historicizing vocabulary that explicitly recalled older architectural forms. Saarinen's round brick chapel at MIT recalled early Christian baptisteries, and Johnson's Kneses Tifreth leaned heavily on stylistic gestures drawn from the work of the eighteenth-century British architect John Soane. As American worshipers and their architects emphasized the social functions of religious institutions, the question of which aesthetic bore a religiously appropriate gravitas, symbolic or abstract, weighed on architects' minds.

KAHN ON RELIGION

Kahn fused his feelings about his own Jewishness with his response to contemporary trends in American religious culture to arrive at an explicitly nontranscendental religious ideal, which extended his conviction that each individual should participate in a community as a means to a richer, more responsive polis. He blurred the definitional boundaries between religious and public institutions, approaching the Adath Jeshurun commission on fundamentally social and civic terms.[18] (Later, in the early 1960s, his equation of religious sanctuaries with political meeting places became even more pronounced, as he transposed his early ideas for a Unitarian Church in Rochester into his drawings for the National Assembly Building in Dhaka, Bangladesh.) Considerations of architectural distribution certainly facilitated his approach, because the programs for ecclesiastical and parliamentary spaces were compatible, differing mainly in scale: they demanded one large, prominent meeting hall, an array of mid-size conference rooms or classrooms, and a group of offices. Augmenting the typological logic was Kahn's freewheeling approach to religion, which permitted him to conceive of religious and civic spaces as of the same genus.

Kahn's attitude toward things Jewish was distinctly de-Judaized: he was not an observant Jew, nor was he well informed about the particularities of devotional ritual. His stance toward his heritage resembled that of many immigrants, including many Jewish ones: assimilation without denying one's ethnic roots.[19] He spoke no Hebrew, probably never had a bar mitzvah, and knew little of the character of and practice in the congregations of Philadelphia. He proudly differentiated himself from other Jews by employing ethnic stereotypes, once joking to engineer Auguste Komendant that he was "the only Jew who didn't care about money."[20] His wife, Esther, of German-Jewish lineage, emphasized the similarities between Jews and other groups rather than their differences. When Kahn's daughter, Sue Ann, was growing up, she composed Christmas carols that the Kahn family sent to their friends in lieu of holiday greeting cards.[21] Although the family library was filled with books on Jewish topics, Kahn had "absolutely no interest" in them, according to his wife; most of them were hers, and the rest were gifts from friends.[22]

Still, Kahn felt some sense of belonging and collective ties. Before he became well known, he was involved in a few local Jewish organizations, the most important having been the building bureau of the National Jewish Welfare Board, which he joined in 1946, becoming a member of its executive committee several years later.[23] Though not a Zionist, he traveled under the National Jewish Welfare Board's auspices to Israel in April 1949 to offer advice on the housing crisis. Like a good modernist, he proposed using mass production techniques to build lightweight, low-cost permanent dwellings — suggestions that the Israelis ignored, deciding to build temporary shelters instead. His journal from this trip records no reaction to being in the newly established Jewish homeland. His only identifiable sketch from Israel depicts a mosque.[24]

THE ADATH JESHURUN DESIGN: A SPACE FOR WORSHIPING UNDER TREES

When Kahn began to work with the Adath Jeshurun congregation in May 1954, he conceptualized the problem of synagogue design within a cultural and personal matrix influenced by trends in American building and architectural discourse, by his response to the institution his client represented, and by his convictions about democracy and community. His design for the Adath Jeshurun reflected this: he proposed a glass-encased sanctuary supported by open vertical clusters of reinforced concrete columns, a gathering space that he hoped would evoke the earliest, outdoor forms of Jewish worship, which he had discovered echoed his ideal of democratic communal participation.

The Adath Jeshurun congregation had been located in downtown Philadelphia, in an area undergoing the kind of demographic transition common to Center City neighborhoods after the war.[25] Many inhabitants of the neighborhood, once solidly Jewish and middle class, were fleeing to the suburbs as African Americans arrived. The congregation was also outgrowing its present quarters, and it began losing membership to competing synagogues that could accommodate the rising demand for facilities that had access to secular-religious spaces like community centers and schools.[26]

In 1951, the synagogue's leaders purchased a large polygonal site in Elkins Park, where many of its members were moving. The short end of the lot faced a major thoroughfare, and the remainder sloped back into a more pastoral setting that was bisected diagonally by a small stream (Fig. 4.1). A building committee was not formed until 1953, two years after the site was purchased; it included Benjamin Weiss, a contractor, and Morris Dembrowitz, a young rabbi who urged his colleagues to select a progressive architect. Although the Adath Jeshurun congregation was Conservative in name, its practices leaned more toward reform than tradition: men wore no prayer shawls; services were mostly in English, not Hebrew; and the board of directors was proud of its "beautiful organ," which would have been anathema in a more Conservative setting.[27] Dembrowitz was responsible for convincing other members of the committee that they

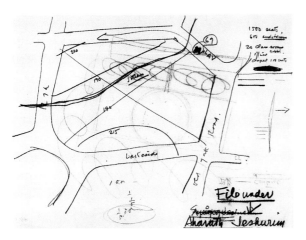

should find a prominent architect who could express the character of their congregation — part Reform, part Conservative.

The building committee in any case felt pressure to produce a landmark that could compete with Frank Lloyd Wright's recently announced Temple Beth Shalom (1954–1959), to be constructed on a site less than five miles up the road. Wright, choosing an explicitly symbolic vocabulary, flamboyantly envisioned his synagogue as a giant "pyramid of light" that he claimed would evoke memories of the sacred Mount Sinai. Wright's striking design was already attracting new members to Beth Shalom.[28] Members of the Adath Jeshurun congregation knew they needed as forceful a building to attract worshipers and students, and they hoped that their school, once completed, would "numerically and educationally, [be] one of the finest . . . in the community."[29]

Over the years, Kahn had been employed by many Jewish clients for whom he had built mainly private houses (and one unremarkable synagogue, the Ahavath Israel, in Philadelphia in 1937). Through this work he had acquired a reputation as a sort of idiot savant, an excellent architect who had sense of neither budgets nor schedules ("Louis Kahn was great if you had a printing press for money," Dembrowitz later fondly recalled).[30] The building committee decided to take its chances,[31] and in May, Kahn received an inquiry from Benjamin Weiss, asking if he would be interested in their commission.[32]

Kahn still may have been hoping to build the City Hall annex, but the office was quiet and he was anxious for work. Reviews of the Yale Art Gallery were just coming out, and Kahn excitedly wrote to Tyng in Italy, reporting his prospects for this important new commission.[33] In an ex post facto sketch for the Yale Art Gallery, Kahn revisited the techno-organic geometries he had used extensively in City Tower and the AFL Medical Services, depicting the same poured-concrete tetrahedral "space-frame" ceiling extending into lattice-like, open, triangulated concrete columns. This sketch became the starting point that June for his work on the Adath Jeshurun. Using the same hexagonal plan he had used for City Tower, Kahn envisioned two reinforced concrete slabs, enclosed by floor-to-ceiling glass panes and supported by tetrahedral space-frame "columns" that flared inward from the floor to a narrow point and then flared back out toward the space-slab ceiling.[34]

Kahn compared such hollowed columns to "the stem of a leaf or the trunk of a tree,"[35] an idea he persistently repeated throughout the short-lived design development of the Adath Jeshurun. Once he compared his columns to "great hollow tree trunk[s]"; once he explained that they "thus spread, grip[ping] the floor and roof structure like outspread fingers."[36] These evocative descriptions indicate that he was deeply wedded to Fuller's, Le Ricolais', and Tyng's notions of organic design; they further reveal the specific *parti* underlying his conception for the Adath Jeshurun.

A synagogue, Kahn insisted, was "a great center of communion . . . a space to assemble under a tree." Kahn intended to make this metaphor literal: this design would symbolically express a group of trees, under which people would congregate.[37] The sanctuary would be perched above ground, with school and ancillary spaces on the first floor below, and the sweeping interior space opening onto the pastoral site outside. This interest in transparency also appeared in the contemporaneous AFL Medical Services, although the metaphoric connotations with which Kahn worked here were new. Worshipers would sit inside a sweeping, dramatic elevated space that seemed outside, nestled between and protected by spreading concrete "trees" and appreciating, as Kahn put it, "Nature's designs."[38]

Why would Kahn want to create a synagogue that would metaphorically enact the event of people assembled under trees? He told Rabbi Dembrowitz that he wanted to evoke the earliest forms of Jewish worship. He learned more about such beginnings by consulting a book entitled *Churches and Temples* (1954), one of whose co-authors was his friend Henry Kamphoefner, dean of the School of Design at North Carolina State. Kahn carefully studied this survey of historical and contemporary synagogue and church design, marking many of its plates.[39] Kamphoefner and his co-authors introduced the section on synagogues by writing, "Since Israelites were both a nomadic and an agricultural people, it is thought their religious meetings were first held out of doors."[40] Kahn must have fused this idea of outdoor worship with his experience of the Adath Jeshurun site, which contained many large, old trees.

About these early religious gatherings, what Kamphoefner emphasized was not their spiritual but their social—indeed, their political—character. Surely this appealed to Kahn. Kahn emphasized the synagogue's communal functions, never mentioning worship or faith.[41] Kamphoefner and his co-authors explained that because these early nomadic Jewish communities were "deprived of the leadership of kings and priests," what resulted was "in today's terms, a grassroots, democratic form springing from, and encouraging, individual initiative and responsibility based on common understanding."[42]

That ideal faultlessly echoed the social vision that Kahn had expressed earlier, in his essay on monumentality and his entry to the Jefferson National Expansion Memorial competition, and then, in more abstracted language, in his civic projects of the early 1950s. Kahn was trying to produce in a synagogue the atmosphere of a New England meeting house or a town hall. He explained: both "religion" and "a meeting house" were forms of "communication"[43]—in other words, of individual participation in a communal gathering, and for the common good. In the Adath Jeshurun, Kahn reframed his and Stonorov's veneration for the New England meeting house into the more archaized form of nomadic worship, bringing his ideal of communal participation back to its earliest, non-conventionalized forms.

In rejecting institutionalized rituals of worship in favor of a more spontaneous mode of communing, Kahn revealed his ongoing quest for an architecture of authenticity, an architecture that forced people to consider the socially derived assumptions they held as they moved through the world and chose how to live and act. That Kahn sought an authentic aesthetic is not as apparent in the Adath Jeshurun as it is in his other, built works, because the aesthetic of authenticity relies so heavily on the choice and handling of materials, and on the expression of the processes of construction, none of which were present in this project, which was aborted at an early stage. That he wanted to create the experience of authenticity is evident, however, in the way he handled his guiding metaphor of an architecture that would make people feel as if they were sitting under trees. The "trees" that he wanted were abstracted, hollow, and capped by skylights similar to one over the Yale Art Gallery staircase. This was an elaboration of the "hollow column" he initially conceived for City Tower. Kahn wrote to Tyng: "My latest idea is that the area of support of each column is the area for the control of light and air so that we can say that we have evolved from the Greek completely. The order of [sketch of a Greek temple front] is no more but it is the proof of a magnificence of its order since it has persisted so long. *Now* the column must be hollow," he explained, again invoking natural imagery like the trunk of a tree.[44] He was particularly excited that here—as he had done in other ways at the Art Gallery at Yale and in the City Tower—he could subvert the viewer's expectations of a column as a solid, thereby transforming the unfamiliar—an idea that became a foundational element of his later, mature architecture.

Kahn continued to employ one of the canonical stylistic elements of early modernism, choosing for the Adath Jeshurun an open plan. He also sought once again to make his mark with a dramatic, if not coherent, structural innovation, predicting that the lattice-like, tetrahedral support system could result in longer clear spans, for "the cantilever possibilities of the deep construction combined with the wider shear head of the hollow column would create a system of fewer columns."[45] Such a configuration for the support system also served a functional purpose, for it addressed one of the major challenges in the design of any religious space that was particularly perplexing in modern synagogues: the huge variability in attendance. On the High Holidays, it was not unusual for larger congregations to host 1,500 or even 2,000 worshipers. At weekly services during the rest of the year, attendance was small. The architect needed to accommodate the seasonal crowds while still providing an intimate devotional space for the regular worshipers. Originally, the Adath Jeshurun program called for a large sanctuary with 1,500 seats and a small sanctuary with 100; its other major requirements were an auditorium with 600 seats and a school with twenty classrooms.[46] Kahn decided to fuse the small weekly devotional space with the large sanctuary, using a hexagonal plan that arranged two concentric rings around an inner core (Fig. 4.2). For the weekly services, partitions would enclose this inner core to give the necessary feeling of intimacy for a small congregation. On the High Holidays, all screens would be removed (Fig. 4.3).

The building committee was enthusiastic about Kahn's ideas, directing him sometime in the summer of 1954 to gather preliminary estimates and bids. When he returned to the committee in August 1954 to deliver the requested information, he brought with him a different design.[47] He now presented drawings showing a triangular sanctuary inscribed in a sloping circular embankment with a rectangular school coming off one of the triangle's points (Fig. 4.4). He had dropped as too complex the idea of triangulated columns while retaining his concept of evoking worship under trees. He arranged circular or triangular columns in three loose clusters of nine, each "harbor[ing] a stairway as though captured in a great hollow tree trunk" (Fig. 4.5).[48]

This new scheme had the pragmatic advantage of separating the noisy areas of the school from the quiet realm of the sanctuary, with classrooms and offices facing onto an interior courtyard. Despite Kahn's claims to the contrary, however, it had a disadvantage: the new, more buildable support system compro-

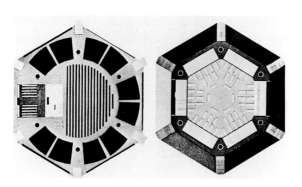

4.2 **Studies of a hexagonal plan, first scheme, Adath Jeshurun synagogue, 1954. From the Kahn Collection.**

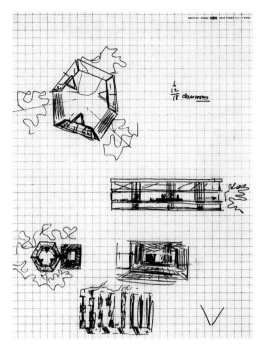

4.3 Sketch (center right) with transparent sanctuary, Adath Jeshurun synagogue, 1954. From the Kahn Collection.

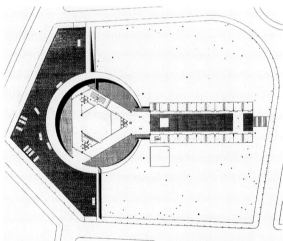

4.4 Plan, second scheme, with a triangular synagogue appended to a rectangular school, Adath Jeshurun synagogue, 1954. From the Kahn Collection.

mised the design's symbolism. These new columns did not spread upward, so no longer would the viewer sit under columns that elicited an association with trees. Kahn's attempt to conjure up the concept of three groves of trees with light filtering through their leaves would likely be lost on the viewer in a large space that was simply flat, unarticulated, and loft-like. The principal geometric statement, the triangular shape, would have been almost indiscernible from within, especially with partitions in place. Similarly, the effect of the sloping embankment encircling the triangular structure, so monumental in plan, would be virtually imperceptible in elevation.

Notwithstanding his efforts to create a more realistic structural system, Kahn

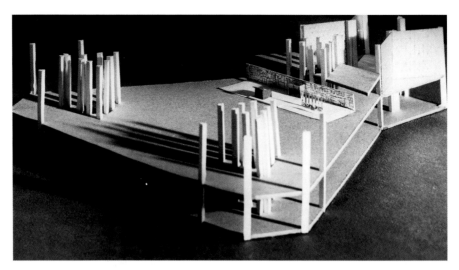

4.5 Model of the second scheme with clustered supports at corners meant to evoke groves of trees, Adath Jeshurun synagogue, 1954. From the Kahn Collection.

must not have intended this scheme to be built as envisioned. Sketches and plans were published between March and May 1955 in *Perspecta* in which he ignored the site's topography, both its sloping incline and the stream. Nevertheless, he carefully presented to the building committee different versions of the design, each a scaled-down iteration of the last, in an attempt to accommodate the financial limitations of the congregation (Fig. 4.6).[49] The building committee initially accepted these revised plans, intending to exhibit them to the congregation that September.[50]

In the meantime, Dembrowitz, Weiss, and others began to fear that they would waste money and time while Kahn endlessly revised his design; that worry was fueled by what they had already heard of his reputation. By December, they were negotiating with another architect, although no available documents indicate that they had discussed their doubts with Kahn.[51] Only in April 1955 did Weiss dismiss Kahn, writing to him that his design was "out of spirit with the type of building wanted by the Board."[52] That was a cover for their real reason, Dembrowitz maintains; they thought that Kahn would be less hurt if he had been branded too avant-garde than if he had been deemed impractical.[53]

Why did Kahn switch to this second scheme? Although Wright's Beth Shalom plan, also a modified hexagon, may have motivated Kahn to change his design, according to Tyng the more important factor was Kahn's wish to avoid all literal references to Jewish symbolism.[54] In a six-sided plan, people would almost certainly see an allusion to the six-pointed Star of David, even though Kahn had chosen the hexagon because of his work with organic geometries. Kahn's aversion to literal symbols of Jewish worship was also apparent in his queries to Rabbi Dembrowitz about the history of Jewish temples, in which he

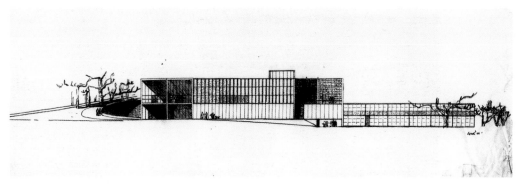

4.6 Elevation study, second scheme, with a rectangular school to the right of a triangular sanctuary, Adath Jeshurun synagogue, 1954. From the Kahn Collection.

focused on abstract data like the number of steps leading to the main entrance of the Temple of Solomon rather than on literal imagery.[55] Yet he gave a different explanation to the building committee, that he switched from a hexagon to a triangle to simplify the building's form.[56] Perhaps he had decided that the exterior envelope of his first plan would have been insufficiently monumental or overly complex; certainly the designs he had marked in *Churches and Temples* were all much simpler.

A succession of scholars, in continued attempts to impute a historicism to Kahn's work of the early 1950s, have pointed out the similarity of this second scheme to Claude-Nicolas Ledoux's 1780 project for an inn in the Faubourg St.-Marceau, Paris. Kahn reinterpreted Ledoux's plan, so the hypothesis goes, which he had probably seen in Emil Kaufmann's popular book *Three Revolutionary Architects: Boullée, Ledoux, Lequeu,* published in Philadelphia in 1952.[57] This may well be so, for one of Kahn's drawings shows that sometime in the early 1950s, Kahn sketched Ledoux's plan.[58] Still, the existence of an image does not render it significant: Kahn's second Adath Jeshurun scheme was different from Ledoux's plan in one determinative respect, namely, in Ledoux's plan the points at which the triangle joined the circle were marked by smaller circles. Kahn carefully included this aspect of Ledoux's design in his own sketch but not in the Adath Jeshurun plan, suggesting that he explicitly avoided referring directly to this historical source. More important still, Kahn had previously adopted the motif of a triangle inscribed in a circle, using it both in his hotel design of 1952 and in the staircase of the Yale Art Gallery.[59] Furthermore, one of Kahn's favorite students, William Huff, was using similar geometries in his bachelor's thesis project of 1952 for an urban church, designing a triangular courtyard enclosing a circular building (Fig. 4.7). If Kahn was attracted to Ledoux's plan, then, it was because it used in simplified form motifs that he had already made his own. Letters, lectures, journal entries, and the designs themselves provide powerful evidence that historical sources were not much on his mind in these years—and this is in striking contrast to his public and private

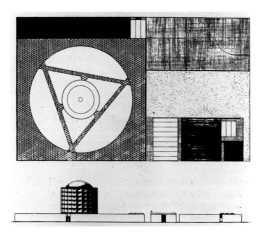

4.7 William Huff, design for an urban church, 1954. From *Oppositions* 4 (October 1974). Courtesy MIT Press.

ruminations several years later, when he repeatedly invoked history and tradition in discussing his architectural vision.[60]

In consonance with Kahn's own working out of his modernist aesthetic, he stated explicitly that with the Adath Jeshurun he wanted *not* to evoke memories of the past but rather to suggest something unfamiliar. Describing his ideas for the Adath Jeshurun in a review of a new book on synagogues in November 1955, after he had lost the commission, Kahn wrote that it was "free from a single traditional plan, free from a space everyone remembers as typical and bound to no continued association with a powerful style."[61] Unlike Saarinen in his allusion to early Christian architecture, Kahn followed the stated aims of the modern movement in the abstraction of the Adath Jeshurun's forms. He sought symbolic resonance of another kind by pushing his techno-organic vocabulary toward a representation of nature's forms, both visible and invisible.

Kahn wanted the Adath Jeshurun synagogue to represent people's connection to each other in a community. To that end, he combined the oblique symbolism of organically resonant geometries, which he had used in other projects, with the more transparent symbolism of a synagogue that visibly represented "a place to meet under a tree."[62] However, he also wanted his architecture and the people who used it to eschew ritualized interactions in favor of direct communication that would be facilitated by authentic, integrated design. The resulting tension, between representational symbolism and abstraction, had already surfaced in Kahn's essay on monumentality and in his ongoing work on City Tower. Now it resurfaced as Kahn tried to create a monumental religious building with a vocabulary that was abstract but which bore the emotional resonances of a techno-organic representational symbolism that would advance his social agenda. Like the irresolution between the expressionism of de Kooning and the restraint of Albers, which the Yale Art Gallery made particularly apparent, in the coming years this tension between representation and abstraction would change configurations without ever reaching a resolution: it would work dialectically to animate Kahn's work rather than diminish it.

In this unbuilt and incipiently designed project, Kahn developed a conception of religious spaces that was informed by his personal relationship to religion and his ongoing and active response to discussions in American religious culture and in American architecture. The Adath Jeshurun project was important to Kahn's development of an architectural aesthetic for several reasons. In it, he first extended his social agenda into the arena of religious spaces. He conflated civic and ecclesiastical typologies in a manner that would became central to his conceptualization of later projects like the Unitarian Church in Rochester and the National Assembly Building in Dhaka. He also advanced his search for an aesthetic of authenticity by recalling ancient forms of Jewish worship with stylistic gestures that would subvert the viewer's expectations, hoping that this would elicit non-ritualized, and non-routinized, forms of human action.

5

STRUGGLING FOR A NEW IDIOM

THE TRENTON JEWISH COMMUNITY CENTER AND BATHHOUSE, AND THE PHILADELPHIA CIVIC CENTER PLAN

Our architectural concepts should be much greater, much more telling, they should be something that you see from a distance by the car, and recognize it by its image, not only a modification of little sensitive designs of another way of doing what somebody else has done before, changing only some plaster chintz. The images are not powerful enough.
—Louis I. Kahn, lecture entitled "City Planning for the Year 2000"

In the mid-1950s Kahn worked on a number of important projects. Two in particular show that in these years he reached a juncture in his intellectual and artistic development: the Trenton Jewish Community Center and Bathhouse (1955–1959; Figs. 5.1, 5.2, and 5.3), and the Civic Center plan for downtown Philadelphia of 1956–1957 (Fig. 5.4).[1] The Trenton Bathhouse was constructed the year it was commissioned, in 1955. The Community Center was never built. Because he worked on the Community Center design off and on until 1959, changes in its design map critical aspects of Kahn's intellectual trajectory during this five-year period. The Philadelphia Civic Center plan marks the fulcrum of a paradigmatic shift in Kahn's thought, a shift that he subsequently elaborated upon in later designs for the Community Center. To understand Kahn's intellectual evolution in this period, one needs to first analyze the Trenton Bathhouse and the early schemes for the Community Center, then move to a comprehensive explication of the Philadelphia Civic Center plan, and only then return to Kahn's later schemes for the Trenton Jewish Community Center.

Kahn's projects of the early 1950s are animated by the tension between the abstraction that emerged in part from his interest in authenticity and the representation of techno-organicism. This dialectic of abstraction and representation continued as Kahn worked on the Trenton Bathhouse and Jewish Community Center and on the Philadelphia Civic Center plan, but in the middle of this period one of its factors changed. Kahn dropped techno-organicism and began to explore a different symbolic language, loosely drawn from history. He moved to a historically informed vocabulary partly because he came to a dead end with techno-organicism and partly because he developed a means of using

5.1 Elevation study, Jewish Community Center, 1956. From the Kahn Collection.

5.2 Elevation study, Jewish Community Center, 1958. From the Kahn Collection.

historical precedents that was consistent with, and even advanced, his social and formal agenda.

TRENTON'S JEWISH COMMUNITY CENTER: AN INSTITUTION IN SEARCH OF AN IDENTITY

When the board members of the Jewish Community Center of Trenton decided to hire Kahn, the identity of their institution was in flux.[2] Trenton's Jewish Community Center had been founded at the turn of the century as one in a growing network of centers that were opening around the country to welcome the multitudes of Jewish immigrants arriving from Eastern Europe.[3] Providing the same recreational and meeting facilities for young people as a YMCA, these centers became focal points for immigrant neighborhoods. They were also indispensable for their "Americanization programs," which coached immigrants on the prevailing social mores and taught them English.[4]

After World War II, fewer users were recent immigrants, so the need for Americanization had diminished.[5] Community centers in general, and Trenton in particular, having lost their assimilating mission, became more complex social institutions, defined as much by what they were not as by what they were.[6] American Jews were riven by denominational divisions among Reform, Conservative, and Orthodox congregations, and, at least in the early postwar years, over the ques-

5.3 Bathhouse, Ewing Township, New Jersey, 1955. From the Kahn Collection.

tion of Zionism.[7] By then, Jewish Community Centers had become the one neutral arena in which all factions of the Jewish community could congregate. The Trenton Jewish Community Center admitted in 1954 that "more and more the community looks to the Center as the only place where Jewish people of varying shades of opinion and various affiliations can have a common meeting ground."[8]

As Trenton's Jews moved to the suburbs, the membership rolls of the Jewish Community Center undoubtedly shifted substantially, which likely further complicated the social relations within it and therefore the institution's identity.[9] The Trenton Jewish Community Center served two distinct factions: people from the less privileged sector of the Jewish community and the area's ruling elite, some of whom lived not in Trenton but closer to nearby, upper-class Princeton.[10] At times, tensions between these two groups ran high over the kind of building that each deemed appropriate.

The changing function of a Jewish Community Center, a rapidly changing membership, and battles between its factions produced indecision about the institution's identity. Not surprisingly, throughout the nearly five-year-long collaboration, the building committee never managed to communicate to Kahn a clear image of its institution, relaying only specific programmatic demands.[11] This absence of a strong client identity had far-reaching consequences for the commission. It was partly responsible for the unstable architect-client relations throughout the duration of the commission. Kahn did not consistently have a strong committee responding to, or forcing him to rethink, his ideas, except insofar as the budget was concerned.

These circumstances allowed Kahn to pursue his own interests. In 1944, Kahn had singled out community centers as the typology most amenable to becoming vehicles for a new, non-authoritarian monumentality.[12] He approached this commission not as a Jewish project but as an opportunity to further his previous explorations into monumentality and authenticity. From an ignoble program calling for poolside changing rooms and a recreational building housing a basketball court, locker rooms, meeting spaces, and a nursery

5.4 Sketch for the Philadelphia Civic Center project, with the old city hall (upper left), City Tower, and a large truncated pyramid (right center) 1956–1957. From the Museum of Modern Art, New York.

school, Kahn tried to create a complex that might buttress communal identity and symbolically link the community's members to the dominant culture from which they stood somewhat apart.

THE BATHHOUSE

The Trenton Bathhouse, a four-room, partially enclosed shelter of concrete block, holds a foundational place in the development of Kahn's aesthetic and in the history of postwar modern architecture. Designed and constructed in four months in the beginning of 1955, the Bathhouse is the most successful synthesis of the leitmotifs of Kahn's preoccupations of the early 1950s; techno-organic geometries are modeled with structure and materials that convey the impression of authenticity. In large part, Kahn achieved this forceful melding of his two strains of inquiry because he was searching for solutions to the architectural community's dissatisfaction with the open plan as it was being deployed in International Style postwar buildings.

Kahn worked on the Jewish Community Center and Bathhouse with Anne Tyng, who returned from Italy in December 1954 and rejoined the office. First he quickly laid a grid over the forty-seven-acre parcel, conceiving of the Community Center as a series of square pavilions punctuated with several internal courtyards. The square cell was part of R. Buckminster Fuller's repertoire. Kahn had used it previously, in a version of City Tower on the Reyburn Plaza site and in many domestic plans of these years, like the houses for the Adlers and the De Vores.

The executive committee decided to build the pool and Bathhouse first, so that they would be ready for summer. In February 1955 Kahn left off on site planning to work on these designs.[13] Early drawings for the Bathhouse indicate a long, rectilinear structure with men's changing rooms on one side of a wall and women's on the other. An inverted, T-shaped wall was extended out of the partition on the central axis, creating two entrances that also would serve as shielding elements, obviating the need for doors. A later drawing shows the Bathhouse as a square (Fig. 5.5 and Plate 9), perhaps to make it connect visually with Kahn's new schemes for the Community Center, in which he sought a proper relationship of open courtyards, top-lit pavilions, and fully enclosed spaces. In March, the plan and roofing of the square Bathhouse were still being worked out.[14]

Tyng has long claimed credit for the final Bathhouse plan (Fig. 5.6).[15] This was confirmed by Tim Vreeland, a leading designer in the office in these years who had been a student of Kahn's at Yale and had come to Philadelphia in early 1955. Vreeland described the Bathhouse's next design phase: "Anne, Lou, and I were working late in the office one night, and it was around midnight. Lou was over with me, working on my [square] scheme for the Bathhouse, which he just hated. Suddenly, Anne said, Lou, come here. We went over to her drawing board, and there on it was the plan for the Trenton Bathhouse, the scheme that subsequently dictated the ideas for the Community Center as a whole."[16] Incorporating several of Vreeland's ideas, including the use of walls as baffle spaces in order to avoid doors, Tyng's plan called for four interlocking squares arranged around an open courtyard. At the points where the pavilions interlock, they form a smaller square with a voided internal face, a more successful version of the "hollow columns" that Kahn had started working with in his design for the Adath Jeshurun synagogue project. On the central axis of these hollow columns, a freestanding wall made the baffle spaces that would serve as entrances. These squares, following the geometry of the design, repeat on the pavilion's external corners, providing areas for storage and for bathrooms. The tops of these hollow columns serve as point supports for the roof.

In its clear separation of principal rooms from ancillary areas, the Bathhouse plan provoked Kahn to distinguish clearly between what he came to call

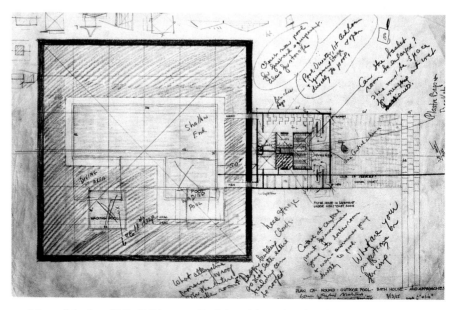

5.5 Intermediate plan with the Bathhouse on the right and the pool on the left. From the Kahn Collection.

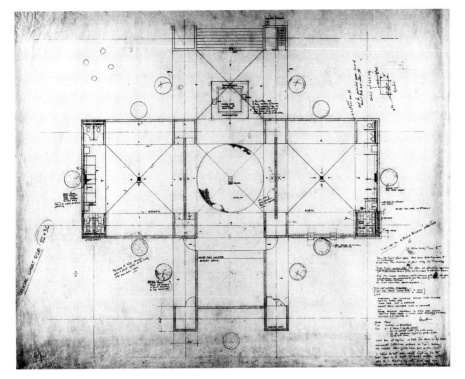

5.6 **Final plan for the Bathhouse. From the Kahn Collection.**

"served" and "servant" spaces, a model that shaped several important subse-quent projects, most notably the Richards Medical Center (1957–1965).[17] Kahn later recalled how working on the Bathhouse had led him to conceive of the served-servant paradigm: in designing the building "I discovered a very simple thing. I discovered that certain spaces are very unimportant and some spaces are the real raison d'être for doing what you're doing. But the small spaces were contributing to the strength of the larger spaces. They were serving them."[18]

In overall configuration, the Bathhouse recalls a Greek cross plan, although Tyng and Kahn still conceptualized the design in terms of techno-organicism. Tyng, unlike Kahn, was to remain focused on the implications of Fuller's ideas throughout her professional career. Direct appropriation of a Renaissance motif, in the Bathhouse or in any other project, would have been anathema to her, because in her view an idealizing organicism does not suffer the contin-gencies and limitations that history inevitably does.[19] The Bathhouse plan, in its centrality and its overall configuration, may echo central-plan churches of the Italian Renaissance. Yet Kahn and Tyng's primary focus in conceiving the Bath-house plan was to continue their exploration of the architectonic possibilities of techno-organicism.

Fleshing out the Bathhouse design, Kahn and Tyng endowed organicism with authenticity, designing a building that was less a technological celebration of

Fuller-like geometries than a reinterpreted primitive hut. Budgetary constraints led them to use plain concrete block. That suited Kahn, who, following Albers' dictum that "there can be no extraordinary without the ordinary," had sought a transformation of the commonplace in all his designs since the Yale Art Gallery. As in the interior of the Yale Art Gallery, Kahn made no effort here to hide the gray, off-the-yard blocks. These concrete blocks emerge from the ground uninterrupted, into walls and piers, articulating the basic geometric figures they inscribe. Because of the building's adherence to a rigid geometric scheme, the entrance is dissimulated and the circulation scheme is circumambulatory.

Here is heavy, imageable architecture: the Bathhouse elicits the impression of primal monumentality despite its small scale. Openings are defined only when walls end; walls are only walls, voids only voids. Kahn and Tyng, in their handling of the building's four roofs, reinforced this parsing of the elements of architecture: low, hipped wooden structures with oculi in each center are perched above enclosing walls to highlight their identity as a separate unit of building. Because these roofs do not lie directly on top of the concrete walls that they cover, natural light falls between wall and roof and from the oculi.

Four opaque pavilions around a single "pavilion" void: the Bathhouse manifests the basic condition of architecture as shelter and the definition of space. This is different from Kahn's, or Kahn and Tyng's, projects of the early 1950s, such as City Tower, the AFL Medical Services, and the Adath Jeshurun synagogue, each of which employed some form of the open plan. In the Bathhouse, Kahn and Tyng built rooms. Where did this idea come from, and what did it mean?

In a journal entry of early 1955, perhaps written while he was working on the Bathhouse, Kahn mused on the inadequacies of the open plan: "Space made by a dome then divided by walls is not the same space. . . . A room should be a constructed entity or—an ordered segment of a construction system. Rooms divided off from a single larger space must read as a completed space."[20] Kahn determined that the important elements enclosing a space must be immediately apprehensible, from structure to surface. For this the open plan was inadequate because partitions, which were customarily used to mark off spaces, masked a concentrated perception of the building as a "constructed entity."

Kahn's new determination to make "compartmented spaces" advanced his search for an architectural language of authenticity, since in a "constructed" room the viewer saw exactly and only that which constituted the essence of the building. In a space constructed from an open plan, by contrast, a viewer could acquire a full sense of the building's tectonics only if he or she moved through and around its partitions. Kahn envisioned a viewer who lingered, standing still. Rooms would be immediately, bluntly apparent. With this unstated assumption of a viewer in stasis, Kahn challenged Sigfried Giedion's definition of modern architecture as defined by the quintessentially twentieth-century experience of "space-time." Dynamic motion and fluid spaces, designed by Le Corbusier,

Ludwig Mies van der Rohe, and other early twentieth-century modernists, gave way with Kahn to constructed spaces that pushed the viewer into a heightened but static perception of the physical.

This turn toward stasis and tectonically bound spaces emerged in part because it was consistent with Kahn's search for authenticity, and in part because, as high modernism became the prevailing idiom of corporate America, many progressive American architects were then challenging the dominance of the open plan. In the 1940s, architects and critics singled out expression as the Achilles' heel of functionalism. By the 1950s, they also discussed the problem of human scale, because the success of the modern movement (known by then principally as the International Style) produced a dramatic increase in the size of its monuments. Arthur Drexler discussed this problem in 1957, writing of Eero Saarinen's Technical Research Center for General Motors and Minoru Yamasaki's Lambert Airport in St. Louis: "When the building is finished it often looks as if the model maker has gone mad and built the final model in full scale. It is this air of plastic and tinfoil unreality which so often discomforts European visitors."[21]

The open plan created unprecedented dynamism in smaller-scale buildings, but all too often it laid out an undifferentiated ocean of space in larger ones. Drexler and others elaborated on the ensuing sacrifices. Scully wrote in 1954, describing the architecture of Philip Johnson, Paul Rudolph, Paul Schweiker, and Kahn, that "vaults and domes have reappeared . . . space no longer necessarily 'flows.'"[22] Architecture as *shelter* was the new ideal. Rudolph, in an especially Existentialist-suffused dictum, insisted on conceptualizing building as stasis and dwelling: "Architectural space is related to a room . . . we have too many goldfish bowls, too few caves."[23] Colin Rowe wrote that John Johanson's Goodyear House and Eero Saarinen's MIT chapel, both of 1953, betrayed a "hankering for something comfortably womb-like yet seeming to belong to the future."[24]

By the mid-1950s, the desire for "something womb-like" had already produced a number of projects shaped by some sort of articulated room, not necessarily enclosed. Rudolph used structure to mold small-scale spaces in domestic projects in Florida (Fig. 5.7).[25] Johnson explored the room in a Wrightian plan composed entirely of circles of different sizes (Fig. 5.8).[26] In part, these developments reflected American architects' assimilation of Le Corbusier's Maisons Jaoul, in which enclosed spaces are created with a repeating rhythm of Catalan vaults (Fig. 5.9).

Kahn and Tyng surely knew of these developments. Kahn watched Le Corbusier's work closely, Rudolph's houses were widely published, and Kahn and Johnson had known each other since the mid-1940s.[27] Kahn and Tyng had already employed modules to articulate small-scale spaces in domestic projects in 1954, working on an idea that had emerged from the model of an organic accretion of cells.[28] Walter Gropius and Alfred Clauss, the latter a Philadelphia designer

5.7 Paul Rudolph, house in Siesta Key, Florida, 1953. From *The Architect's Journal* 118 (1953).

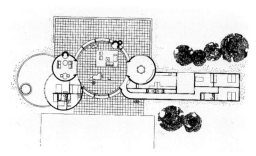

5.8 Philip Johnson, house with circular rooms, 1953. From *Philip Johnson: Architecture, 1949–1965*, 2nd ed. (London: Thames and Hudson, 1970).

of some repute, were also exploring modular plans, and the exact configuration of the Bathhouse, designed in late March or early April 1955, may have been partly inspired by their work. In the October 1954 issue of *Progressive Architecture*, Gropius' Architects' Collaborative presented a prototype elementary school consisting of square pavilions, top-lit by oculi, arranged in Greek cross formations (Fig. 5.10; Tyng, it may be remembered, had been a student under Gropius at Harvard).[29] In *Progressive Architecture* in January 1955, the Greek cross pavilion plan appeared again, in Clauss's project for a home for the indigent that had won first prize in a citywide competition in Philadelphia (Fig. 5.11).[30]

The Bathhouse design differs from these immediate precedents, first in that the four squares composing the plan interlock to create "hollow columns," and second in that the building's structure is integrated with its form, thereby making the spaces much more restricted. Nevertheless, the Bathhouse plan is proximate to the contemporaneous designs of these other architects; indeed, it was simply one, albeit powerful, proposal to reintroduce the room into a modern building while maintaining the structural integrity of a design.

As built, the Bathhouse employs many of the design techniques that eventually defined Kahn's mature idiom. Simple geometric forms in plan are made perceptible three-dimensionally. A controlling geometry is rigorously adhered to—so much so that here, as in later buildings, Kahn neglected to exaggerate the entrance in any way, making it difficult to discern. Spaces are bound, static, and centralized. The parts of a building are stringently articulated. Masonry is explicitly used. Blank exterior walls create monumentality, the impression of a

primal integrity; monumentality is humanized by an exquisite sense of human proportion. Natural light is sculpted into an active interior presence.

Although the inception of the Bathhouse at Trenton emerged from Kahn's synthesis of techno-organicism and primitivizing authenticity, its "constructed entity" rooms also looked to a more sophisticated tradition of architecture in its allusion to a Renaissance Greek cross plan. The Bathhouse, in short, pointed the way toward a new stylistic synthesis, this time of authenticity with a modernist use of historical motifs. Kahn may have realized this in a journal entry he wrote sometime in 1955, which he entitled "Palladian Plan." He wrote, "I have discovered what everyone else has found[,] that a bay system is a room system. A room is a defined space—defined by the way it is made."[31] But Kahn was not yet committed to expanding on the historical aspects of his "Palladian plan." He still concentrated on the cellular, techno-organic implications of the Bathhouse for one more year. He attempted to push the Bathhouse's cellular plan during late 1955 and early 1956 into a community center for Trenton's Jews. Only then did he find that his techno-organic vocabulary solved few problems when applied to a complex program with competing demands.

THE LIMITS OF TECHNO-ORGANICISM: EARLY SCHEMES
FOR THE JEWISH COMMUNITY CENTER

The first comprehensive scheme for the Trenton Jewish Community Center has been widely published, though little analyzed. Those who focus on the Bathhouse's centralized and seemingly historicizing qualities have perhaps been puzzled by Kahn's apparent reversion to cellular forms in this design. But if one accepts that the inception of the Bathhouse is continuous with Kahn's earlier ideas on nature-based geometries and on authenticity, this scheme for the Community Center not only makes sense but becomes important for under-

5.10 Walter Gropius and The Architect's Collaborative, prototype elementary school, 1954. From *Progressive Architecture* 35 (October 1954).

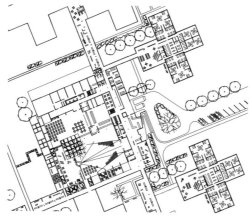

5.11 Alfred Clauss, home for the indigent with modular spaces and Greek cross plans, 1955. From *Progressive Architecture* 36 (January 1955). © *Progressive Architecture* 1955.

standing Kahn in the mid-1950s. In it, he was further developing his ideas of the past several years.

As Kahn turned to work on the Community Center, he sought to integrate his ideas on compartmented spaces and served-servant spaces into a large-scale design (Plate 10). Rotating the Bathhouse's square pavilion forty-five degrees, he sketched out a new plan for the Community Center consisting of octagonal cells bounded on four of their eight sides by small squares, in which the smaller modules could house what he called the servant functions. This sketch became the datum for a series of more developed plans, culminating in the often-published elevation study of March 1956 (see Fig. 5.1). Scholars have long sought to attribute this design in full or in part to Tyng.[32] But just as the plan of the Bathhouse, thought to be Kahn's, was by Tyng; so this octahedral scheme for the Community Center, often thought to be Tyng's, is by Kahn. All the drawings that bear the trace of any hand are clearly not by Tyng but by Kahn; and Tyng, who is anxious to receive credit when deserving, firmly attributes this scheme to Kahn alone.[33]

Kahn's authorship of this octahedral scheme for the Community Center further demonstrates that, well after the Bathhouse's completion, he was still thinking primarily in organic terms. This is confirmed by his lectures and letters of mid-1955 to mid-1956. In September 1955, only two months before the first dated drawing for the octahedral scheme, he delivered a lecture in Philadelphia entitled "Nature, Order, and Design"; although no text of the lecture survives, the title itself bears testimony that he was still investigating the ideas of the past several years.[34] His correspondence points to the same conclusion. Sometime in December 1955, Rowe and the painter Robert Slutsky visited Kahn at his office; in the following months the letters they exchanged confirm that Kahn had presented his work entirely in organic terms. Rowe described their conversation as one in which he had been for the old Beaux-Arts design strategy of "composition" while Kahn had argued for "growth," with all the organic implications the term implied. Slutsky, in a separate letter, also mentioned that Kahn spoke of "growing a skyscraper"—obviously a reference to City Tower—and distinctly remembered Kahn speaking of his work in organic terms.[35]

In the subsequent revisions of the octahedral scheme for the Community Center, Kahn worked on siting and tried to straighten out circulation patterns in a complex system of enclosed and voided octahedrons (Fig. 5.12). Schemes dated March 1956, which he probably presented to board members that June, showed a compact octahedral composition.[36] An open loggia marked the entrance, and the gymnasium was embedded within. Kahn clarified circulation patterns by combining octagons with squares, with one diagonal and one L-shaped axis projecting from an asymmetrically placed entrance foyer. This move, though pragmatically advantageous, compromised the principle of small servant spaces doing duty for the larger served ones, for now the large units were also employed for "service" uses. The elevation study depicted a building eleven octahedrons long, with cells piled three stories high above the gymnasium. Each octahedron, like each pavilion of the Bathhouse, had a hipped roof, with the glazed triangular panels creating clerestory-like skylights.

It is, in all, an extremely awkward design. The repetitiveness of the cellular structure, with each element resembling the others, made it impossible for

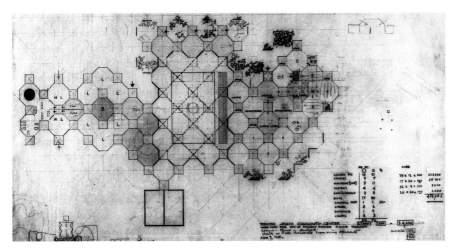

5.12 Modular plan of the second scheme of the Jewish Community Center with alternating octagonal (served) and square (servant) spaces, 1956. From the Kahn Collection.

Kahn to design a climax into the building and thereby achieve the primal monumentality that he and Tyng built into the Bathhouse. He also found it nearly impossible to create any sense of hierarchy inside, a Beaux-Arts concept that he first used the following year while preparing a description of a later version of the project for publication in 1957.[37] The design suffered from technical problems as well, for in its rigidity it wasted both space and structure; if built in wood, as Tyng reported Kahn intended, the structure would have required much craftsmanship for the upper levels, which would have contributed little to the building's usefulness.[38] Tectonic clarity was compromised because Kahn stretched small-scale modules over the long span of the gymnasium. Finally, the design harbored conceptual ambiguities: Kahn's concept of served and servant spaces, so well etched into the Bathhouse, was illegible. Kahn surely recognized these inconsistencies and inadequacies. During or after the preparation of this second, octahedral scheme for the Community Center, he must have realized that he could not conjoin his techno-organic vocabulary to his concept of the constructed room. Coming to the end of the road with his cellular vocabulary, he was working an unworkable idea.

ABSTRACTED HISTORY AS MODERNISM: THE CIVIC CENTER PLAN FOR PHILADELPHIA

Reference to a historical plan was only an incipient theme in the Bathhouse, emerging in the form of a Greek cross plan because it dovetailed with techno-organic geometries and with Kahn and Tyng's search for the articulated room. In mid-1956, around the time that Kahn grappled with the cellular plan for the Community Center, he began a theoretical scheme for downtown Philadelphia, which he called Civic Center (see Fig. 5.4).[39] In this plan he revived his explorations into monumentality and urban symbolism as a means to consolidate communal identity. These aspirations, with him at least since his essay on monumentality and his submission to the Jefferson National Expansion Memorial in the mid-1940s, had been precluded from his architecture during his infatuation with the inflexible geometric cell.

In his Philadelphia Civic Center plan, Kahn liberated himself from the problems underlying the Trenton Jewish Community Center scheme to address a different set of themes concerning the urban core and the large-scale civic institution. Here Kahn drew on architecture's monumental tradition. However, this was not an unreflective bow to the authority of tradition, in the manner that early modernists had deplored. It was also not a direct appropriation of historical motifs, as American architects of a younger generation would employ only a decade later. Kahn used historical references in a manner consistent with the modernist project and with the abstract, geometricizing sensibility that he had employed with techno-organicism. He abstracted a few select formal qualities of historic monuments, specifically their large scale and their imageable shapes, and subsumed them under his modernist social and political agenda.

Kahn's Civic Center plans were for a site on Market Street between City Hall and Independence Hall called Market East, which the Philadelphia City Planning Commission was studying.[40] He had no expectation of earning a commission for this project. The City Planning Commission had turned the adjacent Penn Center into an agglomeration of commercial skyscrapers. For this site they intended to gather together the more civic and public functions of a city, including a sports arena, transportation and "amusement" centers, and a convention hall. Kahn had already been, and would continue to be, deeply occupied with the question of a civic center's proper form, assigning the problem to his students at Yale and Penn several times in the mid-to-late 1950s.[41]

His civic center studio for his students recalled the monumentality debates of the mid-to-late 1940s. In many ways Kahn's own Civic Center plan responded directly to ideas propounded in the CIAM Hoddesdon conference of 1951 entitled "Heart of the City," proceedings of which were published in 1952.[42] Contemplating CIAM's emphasis on the piazza as a means of reinvigorating the core, Kahn asked in a journal entry of mid-1955, "What activities what desires and needs now call for the open space, as compared with reason for the open spaces of the Romans and the Italians." He continued, "Our urban life does not associate the square or the piazza with a need," by which he meant that the piazza accommodated older, pedestrian societies better than contemporary, motorized ones. He rejected the Italian square as any kind of model for open space in the contemporary city, asserting that "since the era of the piazza, towns have grown linearly—a phenomenon which does not suggest the square. Even in the building of new areas in Europe the square seems artificial."[43]

In its layout, Kahn's Market East drew from Le Corbusier's urban plans and N. A. Milyutin's "linear city" plan of 1930, in lining civic spaces and buildings along the ten-block-long axis of Market Street in a multi-leveled spine that separated automotive transportation at the street level from the civic buildings and pedestrian walkways located on a platform one story above (Fig. 5.13). Le Corbusier, in his earliest urban plans, proposed such a separation of pedestrian and mechanized transportation systems, and Kahn in the mid-1950s acknowledged the debt, writing, "Corbu as always is the prophet."[44] Rectangular cutaways in the pedestrian platform would allow natural light to penetrate to the street level—and, unremarked on by Kahn, they would vent automotive exhaust onto the pedestrian walkways above. Linking all on the pedestrian level was a moving sidewalk; Kahn explained when he published the project in 1957 that this "extends the area" of the village green of old.[45]

Although he believed it misguided to think of Italian piazzas as models for contemporary urban spaces, Kahn did think that the scale of historic buildings

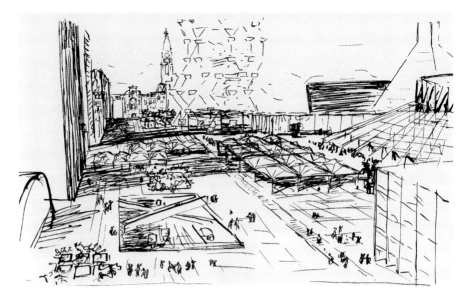

5.13 Civic Center plan showing separation of pedestrian and automotive traffic and "lampshade" covered arena, 1956–1957. From the Kahn Collection, Architectural Archives of the University of Pennsylvania. Gift of Richard Saul Wurman.

could be a guide to civic grandeur. He hardly can be said to have designed architecture for this plan, yet he drew images that revealed a new interest in dramatic, almost theatrical, large-scale edifices with striking and often simple profiles. An arena, covered with a lampshade-like roof, was pulled back from the facade line to open a covered courtyard.[46] City Tower, now twice as high, was relocated to the east rather than the north of the existing City Hall.

Market Street would be terminated by a colossal truncated pyramid recalling the pyramids he saw in Giza years before (Fig. 5.14). The circular automobile "docks," which formed a ring around this projected civic core, would be large enough to house 1,500 cars (Fig. 5.15).[47] Medieval fortifications inspired the ring of towers around the Civic Center core, providing a model for defense against the privatizing tendencies of the automobile: "Carcassonne was designed from an order of defense. A modern city will renew itself from its order-concept of movement which is a defense against its destruction by the automobile."[48] The whole Civic Center complex, he wrote, would be "a Forum not unlike the Roman Forum but more."[49] Most of the sketchy buildings in the Civic Center scheme are static and monumental. They reveal a vision radically different from the repetitive "organic" architecture that Kahn had spent the past several years engrossed in inventing.

Kahn was attempting yet again to find forms that would best allow architecture to enhance social and political life. Discussing the Civic Center project, he repeatedly insisted that the public institutions of a city be collected into a single, monumental core. Only buildings of overwhelming monumentality, he contended, could serve as bastions protecting against the moneyed interests that

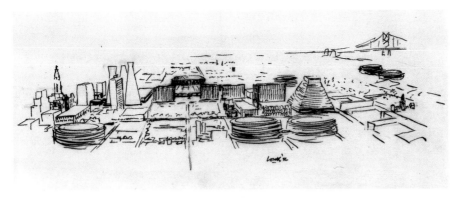

5.14 Philadelphia Civic Center with monumental axis from City Hall to truncated pyramid, 1956–1957. From the Kahn Collection.

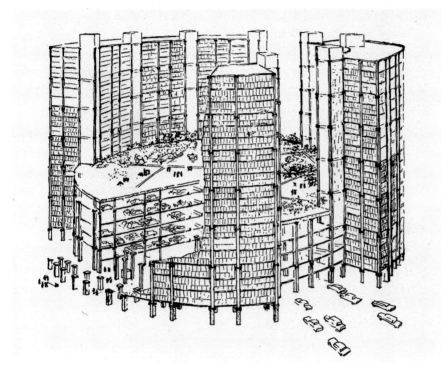

5.15 Parking dock: for scale, look at figures on lower left. From the Kahn Collection, Architectural Archives of the University of Pennsylvania. Gift of Richard Saul Wurman.

were destroying the dignity of the urban center. This is evident in his proposal for a highly publicized development in Boston, which later became the Prudential Center.[50] Envisioning the same enormous truncated pyramid that appeared on his Civic Center drawings, he argued:

> I believe the consolidation of immense large building projects is important and . . . can't be chewed apart by developers. If you know in Boston in the Back Bay Center, a project which was a beautifully conceived, balanced architectural center . . . [it] is now being broken apart into little pieces. . . . It

was conceived so delicately that it's falling apart. What it should have been, probably, was a great pyramid, one building . . . that would have been economical, and you couldn't destroy it. . . . our architectural concepts should be much greater, much more telling, they should be something that you see from a distance by the car, and recognize it by its image, not only a modification of little sensitive designs of another way of doing what somebody else has done before, changing only some plaster chintz. The images are not powerful enough.[51]

Discussing a city's most heraldic, civic spaces, Kahn applied the same anti-capitalist sentiments that he had expressed with Oscar Stonorov and George Howe in "'Standards' Versus Essential Space," their essay on housing of 1942, where they critiqued developers who minimized their costs rather than maximizing the space of habitable, affordable dwellings. Kahn believed that he found in traditional monuments — not in their specific forms but in their large scale and imageability — an insuperable means of protecting against the debasement of American cities by private developers.

Kahn did not come on his own to this view of past architecture's potential to provide models that might help save the embattled city. His Beaux-Arts training under Cret notwithstanding, it was not until a contemporary architectural discourse in which he participated had laid the groundwork that Kahn's interest in monumental architectural precedents flourished. During these years, many architects and architectural writers were discussing the perceived rapid deterioration of the American urban and suburban landscape. Some proposed that the use of historical precedents in architecture and city planning might play an important ameliorative role. Kahn participated in these politicized debates on the future of the American city, and through them, he developed his conviction that civic institutions could anchor communities if they could encourage people to recollect cultures past.

THE SPECTER OF MASS CULTURE

Kahn's view that the device of abstracted historical allusion might further his social and architectural aims grew out of his reaction to a complex interweaving of social trends and shifting associations in American architectural culture of the 1950s. At the core of these trends was the explosion of consumerism generally and suburbanization specifically, which generated a reaction among intellectuals against "mass culture," which for architects, came to be symbolized by mass production and the use of advanced technologies. Thus, whereas progressive architects previously had believed that technology and mass production could be both a facilitator of and a symbol for the modern movement's social agenda, increasingly they viewed them with hostility.

An economic boom and concomitant consumerist explosion dramatically reconfigured the landscape of the United States in the 1950s.[52] The changes in American society in these years were enormous: between 1945 and 1960, the gross national product rose 250 percent.[53] In 1920, before the Depression, 30 percent of Americans were middle class. By the mid-1950s, the number had doubled to 60 percent.[54] As the middle class expanded, so did consumption; initiates appointed their households with the trappings of their upward mobility: refrigerators, dishwashers, linoleum counters, barbecues, televisions, cars.

Amid all this buying, acquiring of a home was the quintessential purchase that enabled many others.[55] Suburban developments cropped up everywhere, prompting John Keats, author of a widely read book entitled *The Crack in the Picture Window*, to complain that America was building "fresh-air slums around the edges of America's cities."[56] The growth of the construction industry was astonishing: by 1960, expenditures on new construction were nine times what they had been in 1945.[57] Between 1950 and 1960, 18 million people moved to the suburbs, whereas the country's total population increase was only 28 million.[58]

Few argued that prosperity was undesirable, yet architects and urbanists assessed the architectural and urbanistic consequences, such as suburban tract-house developments, in largely negative terms. Their critiques were part of a broader debate on mass culture.[59] In this debate the suburb, as constructed embodiment of mass culture, became a symbol for its evils. Keats, in *Crack in the Picture Window*, wrote: "The typical postwar development operator was a man who figured how many houses he could possibly cram onto a piece of land and have the local zoning board still hold for it. Then he whistled up the bulldozers to knock down all the trees, bat the lumps off the terrain, and level the ensuing desolation. Then up went the houses . . . the result was a little box on a cold concrete slab containing two bedrooms, bath, and an eating space the size of a broom closet. . . . There was a sheet of plate glass in the living-room wall. That, the builder said, was the picture window. The picture it framed was of the box across the treeless street."[60]

William H. Whyte, who won national fame with *The Organization Man*, also turned his journalistic diatribes in the mid-1950s to suburban development.[61] Architectural journalists joined in. In 1957 the preeminent journal *Architectural Forum* ran an article typical of the time, by Mary Mix Foley, that reproduced Margaret Bourke White's famous aerial photograph of Levittown and railed against "the raucous ugliness taking over our land."[62] Suburban developments were homogenizing the American landscape, eradicating physical and demographic differences. (Keats acidly assured his reader, "You can be certain that all other houses will be precisely like yours."[63]) Culture, it was feared, might descend to the lowest common denominator: Foley entitled her article "The Debacle of Popular Taste" and quoted freely from José Ortega y Gasset's *The Revolt of the Masses*, an anti-mass-culture tract from 1930 arguing that all humanity had become subject to "the brutal empire of the masses"—or to "barbarism."[64]

At the University of Pennsylvania, where Kahn began to teach full time in 1955, the intellectual environment was much more politicized than at Yale. Many faculty members grappled with this perceived crisis in the American city and suburb. G. Holmes Perkins, whom Kahn knew from his involvement in the 1940s in the American Society of Planners and Architects, had taken over as dean of Penn's Graduate School of Fine Arts in January 1951, and had established a program that stressed the interaction of city planning and architecture to effect social change. As an indication of Perkins' left-leaning political inclinations, his first major appointment was Lewis Mumford, whose ideas in the 1940s had so profoundly shaped Kahn's.

Perkins and Mumford initiated a critique of suburbia that was echoed by the school's two prominent landscape architects, Karl Linn and Ian McHarg, who each worked on architectural projects for Kahn.[65] Linn and McHarg bewailed suburban development's deleterious consequences for older urban centers.[66] McHarg complained that "squalor and anarchy" best described the contemporary environment, a despoliation caused by "prevailing values [which] esteem the ephemeral consumer product over landscape and townscape."[67] Developers cared not for cities but for profit, making no attempt to create a sense of place. "The accretion of ugliness," McHarg concluded, was "the inevitable consequence."[68] This concern for the distinctiveness of a place echoed sentiments expressed in the architectural criticism: Foley bemoaned people's loss of connection to the natural environment; Keats lamented the leveling of hills and dales.

At Penn, the consensus on how to counteract the impending sameness of the American landscape was to strengthen the identity of the historic urban center into a bulwark of the public realm. Perkins described downtowns as "direly in need of surgery . . . [from] decay, obsolescence, and congestion."[69] What suburbs lacked, each city could provide: new commercial and especially monumental civic construction should be marshaled to serve the higher social purpose of revitalizing the urban core and reinforcing people's connections to their city. Two important sources shaping this discussion were Paul and Percival Goodman's *Communitas* and urban theorist Kevin Lynch's ideas on place, which, combined, proposed that a highly articulated urban center could protect the public realm. *Communitas* appeared on many course and studio syllabi at the Graduate School of Fine Arts from 1953 to 1965,[70] and Kahn's poetic assertion in his descriptions of his Civic Center scheme that "Center City is a place to go to—not to go through" was a reworking, conscious or unconscious, of a line from the Goodmans' text.[71] Although Lynch's *The Image of the City* appeared in 1960,[72] from the mid-1950s onward he was already disseminating his ideas on the importance of landmarks and urban monuments for "imageability."[73] Lynch's ideas also had a direct impact on Kahn.[74]

At the same time that the critique of suburbanization reached its shrillest tones, many of Kahn's colleagues and friends began to question the role of technology in progressive design. Perkins argued as early as 1952 that the modern movement had perhaps too unthinkingly worshiped at the "early altar of technocracy,"[75] and in 1961 Lawrence Anderson of MIT mused that many contemporary architects had grown "pessimistic and disillusioned about technology."[76] Interest in Fuller's ideas also began to wane, with only one or two short pieces appearing on him in the architectural press each year; in 1956, Johnson said that he had "nothing against [Fuller's] discontinuous domes, but for goodness sake let's not call it architecture."[77]

A substantial challenge was developing to the early modern movement's central tenet that the growth of industrial technology and the potential of mass production should be principal determinants of twentieth-century architectural form. This challenge emerged because these architects recognized that suburban development, which appeared to be eradicating all sense of individuated places, had been enabled by efficient uses of technology. To them, suburbanization proved that marrying mass production to architecture reaped not social profit but social doom.

Kahn's ambivalence about the virtues of capitalism predisposed him to anxiety about mass culture and its supposed erosion of the public sphere, and he could hardly avoid exposure to such notions, which reverberated down the many hallways of intellectual inquiry that he walked. For example, he subscribed to *Architectural Forum*, in which Foley's article appeared.[78] Whyte sent him a copy of his critique of tract developments, "Urban Sprawl," in 1957. Kahn's appreciative note of thanks shows that it made a deep impression: "I am inspired by your article. . . . It arouses a spirit of home beyond one's own. It arouses a spirit of patriotism and civic responsibility."[79] Both Whyte and Keats spoke at the Philadelphia chapter of the Citizen's Council on City Planning in the mid-1950s.[80]

Kahn actively participated in the discourse on suburbanization after he began teaching at Penn. Topical changes in his writings and a new design vocabulary suggest that his new set of colleagues and students markedly influenced his ideas.[81] The themes that first surfaced in Kahn's Civic Center scheme can be traced directly or indirectly to issues discussed in the architectural community at large and specifically by his colleagues at Penn. These include his rising concern for the preservation of the urban center and his forceful rejection of a culture dominated by consumerism.

Kahn's Civic Center plan is saturated with the ideas on the urban center that then prevailed at Penn. Decentralization, he wrote in the text accompanying the publication of the Civic Center plan, "disperses and destroys a city." From his civic center he evicted the most visible symbol of consumer culture, the automobile. He asserted that only "the consolidation of all centers—cultural, academic, commercial, athletic, health, and civic—into one Forum will inspire the renewal of the city."[82] In this way (as he had said before), the city "can't be chewed apart by developers." Kahn's drawings proposed a spatialization of what planners at Penn theorized. He consolidated the commercial, cultural, and civic functions into one small downtown area of Philadelphia's Center City to create buildings and an urban space that would engender a distinctive, imageable place.

Just as Kahn was becoming disenchanted with the ever more highly visible instruments of mass culture, so too was he becoming openly disaffected with celebrating new technologies for their own sake. He began to distance himself from Fuller's conviction that technology could save humanity; at the same time, Tyng's influence on him waned. In his pursuit of authenticity, Kahn had already betrayed an ambivalence toward the conventional equating of modern ideals with mass production, because the language of authenticity demanded that the architect stress the handcrafted over the machined in order to emphasize that the act of building was composed of a series of human decisions. But the discourse about mass culture and suburbia brought this ambivalence to a head. By 1957, Kahn openly rejected steel as a building material *specifically* because of its symbolic associations with high technology. "Concrete columns are better," Kahn told a journalist from *Architectural Forum* that summer. "They're real columns! Of course, steel is a marvelous material. You can do wonderful things with it, build great machines, but in architecture you're not building airplanes after all, are you?"[83] In 1956, Kahn complained to the journalist Ian MacAllum that "manufactured buildings dominate design"; the following year, Kahn's friend Peter Blake pointed out that although more than 1 million homes had been built since World War II, "the vast majority of them has ranged from bad to terrible . . . demonstrat[ing] the advantages and the drawbacks of mass production and mass consumption in a free enterprise society."[84] Along with architects' critique of suburbia came a loss of faith in the promise of architectural uses of technology as a means to social improvement.

THE TALISMAN OF TRADITION

Changes in the way Kahn spoke about architecture between 1956 and 1959 suggest that the central ideas in his Civic Center plan derived from the critique of suburbanization propounded by the architectural community at large, and by architects, urbanists, and landscape architects at Penn in particular. The cellular geometries that he had been using not only proved too inflexible but also symbolized aspirations that were no longer his. Now doubting that the union of high technology with organic geometries bore promise for future architectural form, Kahn instead focused on how to reverse urban decentralization and how to redress the contemporary city's perceived loss of a vital center, the anchor for any communal sense of place. These goals fused with his long-standing desire to create an architecture that would become a symbol of communal identity and encourage communal participation. His self-appointed task was to design

buildings and civic spaces that would revitalize what he perceived to be an
endangered public realm.

a tentative attempt to visualize an architecture that might achieve this
purpose, Kahn traced onto his Civic Center plan, next to an increasingly gos-
samer City Tower, buildings inspired by the grandeur of historic monuments.
Why was it in a project meant to compensate for the carnage that he believed
suburban development was visiting upon the American landscape that Kahn
first appropriated the techniques of historic monuments? Why would tradition
be the talisman protecting against the specter of mass culture?

Kahn's thinking about the use of historical referents in design before 1956
laid the groundwork for the position he took in the heated debates on history
among his colleagues and friends. The early modern movement had a
conflicted relationship with history. Gropius, Mies, and Le Corbusier avoided
literal tropes of academic design and Victorian eclecticism as they searched for
a style that expressed what they believed to be the essential social and economic transformation of the twentieth century, the growth of industrial technology. In the early years of his career Kahn's attitude toward historical references echoed that of the earlier modern masters. Although in his essay on
monumentality of 1944 he stressed that "the buildings of our future must, in
some sense, rely" on past monuments—just as Le Corbusier had stated that he
had "only one master" and that this was "the past"—Kahn argued against
explicit historical references, asking, "Must the cathedral, the culture center . . .
be built to resemble Chartres?"[85] But this did not mean that abstract allusions
to history were shunned: Le Corbusier had designed a ziggurat for his
Mundadeum project of the late 1920s; Kahn, for his culture center of 1944,
envisioned a kind of lattice-like, modernized Gothic arcade (see Fig. 1.13).[86]

Until the mid-1950s, however, Kahn had not given much thought to past architectural monuments as ongoing sources of inspiration for his designs. Now, with
the Civic Center, he did, and he did so because his colleagues in the architectural
community had begun to redefine a study of the past so that it was not woolly academicism—something he had to "unlearn," as he had stated in 1953—but was
instead a tool consistent with his social and political aspirations as a modernist.

Johnson was the first prominent American proponent of modernism to
employ overt historical references, in his Glass House in New Canaan, which
was published in September 1950.[87] Johnson turned to symbolism and history
in the 1940s while searching for a solution to the problem of a new monumentality, lauding the classicizing, geometrically clear architecture of Claude-Nicolas Ledoux and Mies.[88] In his publication of the Glass House, Johnson brazenly,
and in detail, outlined the heritage of his design decisions, recalling site-plan-
ning techniques from the Acropolis in Athens and Schinkel's Casino in
Glienicke Park in Potsdam (Fig. 5.16), and massing from Claude-Nicolas

STRUGGLING FOR A NEW IDIOM

Karl Friedrich Schinkel: Casino in Glienicke Park near Potsdam c. 1830.
Entrance façade.

*The site relation of my house is pure Neo-Classic Romantic—
more specifically, Schinkelesque. Like his Casino my house is
approached on dead-level and, like his, faces its principal (rear)
façade toward a sharp bluff.*

5.16 Karl Friedrich Schinkel, casino in Glienicke Park near Potsdam, entrance facade. "The site relation of my house is pure Neo-Classic Romantic — more specifically, Schinkelesque," claimed Philip Johnson in his description of his house in New Canaan, Connecticut. From *Architectural Review* (September 1950). Reproduced courtesy of the *Architectural Review*.

Ledoux's Gardener's House project and Mies's still unfinished Farnsworth House.[89] For the rest of the decade Johnson's interest in history quickened, and in various projects he drew from a wide array of sources that included the work of John Soane, Gian Lorenzo Bernini, Le Corbusier, and Mies. Other architects, such as Johanson, Schweiker (Fig. 5.17), Edward Durrell Stone, and Yamasaki followed Johnson's lead, producing in the middle of the decade a mini-revival of classicism, or formalism, as it was often termed.[90]

Johnson's proclamations on American architecture in the 1950s intimated the ideas underlying his use of historical references in design: the new formalism, he suggested, would express America's newfound stature as the world leader in democracy. As fascinating as the past, Johnson claimed, was "our [American] place in history in the middle of the century. Through my eyes it looks wonderful; through my eyes, it seems we are in the middle of a Golden Age—none more golden!"[91] He asserted, "It is up to my generation to . . . create the monuments which, like the buildings of other Golden Ages—Egypt, Rome, Byzantium—will act as beacons to the future, as physical reasons for remembering our times and our century."[92] Monuments would commemorate the greatness of American democracy, as the pyramids commemorated theocracy and the Roman Forum, the empire. At Yale, Howe also spoke often in the early 1950s of the responsibility of his students to lead the way toward what he called "a 'Great Style,'" which he claimed emanated from "a *great* culture."[93] These imperial sentiments appeared in the architectural press as well: *Architectural Forum*'s editors reminded readers that "the U.S. is embarked on the most exciting and ambitious project that it has ever undertaken: the creation of a more agreeable and attractive society, which is to say, the creation of a new civilization."[94] Underlying and shaping this rhetoric were the cultural politics of the Cold War: such statements cast the United States as the leader of the free world and as the country where the kind of democracy that Kahn had always supported would be freely exercised.[95]

5.17 Paul Schweiker, church in
Teaneck, N.J. © *Progressive
Architecture* 1955. Photo courtesy
Will Bruder.

125

STRUGGLING FOR A NEW IDIOM

The American architectural community's confident assumption of world cultural command was the flip side of their tortured critique of mass culture. The prevailing sentiments ran as follows: the United States, on the one hand, faces debasement and possible self-destruction from the pernicious effects of mass consumption. On the other hand, the promise of economic prosperity, combined with the moral virtue of democracy, could produce a great society, if this debasement could be forfended by an elite that protected and strengthened cultural traditions.[96] Although this constellation of anxieties and ambitions was never clearly mapped out, Johnson hinted of it to his biographer, Franz Schulze, when he told him that the text that "came closer than anything to explicating the world view he espoused" was an article entitled "Revolted by the Masses," which reviewed critiques of mass culture from Ortega y Gasset.[97] For Johnson, tradition was a bulwark against mass culture, because an understanding of history would, he thought, illuminate the transient meaninglessness of a life driven by consumption.

At the same time Johnson, Howe, and others were recasting the use of historical references to simultaneously protect American society against mass culture and represent its greatness, Kahn came upon a sustained discussion about the role of historical references in modern architecture among a group of students and faculty at Princeton, where he often participated in juries and conducted a studio in 1956.[98] At Princeton, the history of architecture was closely attended to, even during those years in which it played little role at competing universities, with the understanding having been that abstracted references to historical monuments were part of the modern project.[99] Jean Labatut, the chair of the program, who had trained at the Ecole des Beaux-Arts in Paris, considered an education in the history of architecture continuous with, rather than contradictory to, the principles of the modern movement.[100] Like some early modernists, Labatut encouraged students to employ historical analogies but to reject a direct appropriation of motifs from the past: "The past should be taken as a stimulant, not as a refuge," he wrote in 1941, a sentence he repeated verbatim again and again. "It is wise to step back, to take a better leap into the future only if one does not forget to jump [forward] after stepping back."[101]

The Princeton students whom Kahn knew took Labatut's words to heart. Kahn served on Robert Venturi's thesis jury in 1950 and was highly impressed by the younger architect's design for a church, for which he carefully outlined the formal precedents in the manner that Johnson had used for the Glass House only months before. Venturi illustrated the plan of the Mausoleum of Galla Placidia in Ravenna, the facade of Salisbury Cathedral, beams from Wright's Taliesin West, and shed roofs by Albert Kahn.[102]

Charles Moore, who was Kahn's teaching assistant in 1955–1956, was also deeply involved in thinking about tradition. Moore was indebted to Labatut and his studio critic, Enrico Peressutti, who was a principal in the Milan-based firm BBPR, which was designing the gothicizing Torre Velasca for a site next to the Milan cathedral.[103] Peressutti, like Labatut, believed that references to history did not represent "a drift away from the basic principles of modern architecture";[104] architecture, he insisted, "must be a living connection between the past and the future at a cultural level."[105] Peressutti's studio problem for Moore's class in 1955 was a tourist resort on a Mayan site called Hotel Mayaland; in preparation, the class traveled to the Yucatan to study the proposed sites at Chichén Itzá and Uxmal. Under Kahn's tutelage, Moore presented in June 1956 another historically oriented design, a museum of the Spanish and Mexican occupation of California (Figs. 5.18 and 5.19).[106]

For the intellectual substructure of such an approach, Moore and Venturi relied on literary sources that defined an artist's relationship to the past in explicitly modernist terms. Moore quoted Henry James's preface to *The Aspern Papers* and T. S. Eliot's "Tradition and the Individual Talent"; Venturi also used Eliot's essay in his 1966 publication *Complexity and Contradiction in Architecture*. Eliot protested that literary modernism (like some strains of its architectural counterpart) had so denigrated tradition that "seldom does the word appear except in a phrase of censure."[107] The best works of art, he countered, always contain "the historical sense," and the true artist perceives "not only the pastness of the past, but its presence." A writer's responsibility was to address the whole canon of Western art in his every work, for the canon was a "timeless" and self-sustaining entity—"the existing monuments form an ideal order among themselves"—and each "really new" work of art created by the individual talent modifies and alters "the whole."

The appeal of such assertions to Moore and Venturi is clear. Some architects of the early modern movement, including Gropius, claimed that they had rejected the appropriation of historical motifs in favor of a more functionally and technologically oriented approach to design. But Eliot's essay made an awareness of tradition seem an inevitable, and thus a legitimate, part of making

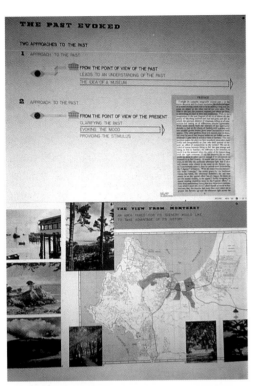

5.18 Charles Moore, project board for a Museum for the Spanish and Mexican Occupation in Monterey, California, with a quotation from Henry James's *The Aspern Papers*, Princeton University, 1956. From the Charles Moore Archive, University of Texas.

5.19 Charles Moore, project for a Museum for the Spanish and Mexican Occupation in Monterey, California, Princeton University, 1956. From the Charles Moore Archive, University of Texas.

great art. Eliot also suggested an approach to tradition that resembled Labatut's, one that transcended overt reference and so kept the spirit of early modernist abstraction. For them, a true artist used history not in mindless semantic repetition of past forms but to establish his creation as part of an ideal order.

Kahn's Philadelphia Civic Center project, with its explicit use of history, may have been directly inspired by working with Moore and serving on juries at Princeton. Moore's use of Eliot's ideas implied that only by using historical reference could an architect design the kinds of urban monuments that endured. Kahn was highly impressed with the surveys that Princeton students made of past monuments, even if he was not especially taken with their designs.[108] Only one year after he saw the Roman Colosseum in a student project at Princeton on monumentality did Kahn design a Colosseum-like parking "dock" for the Civic Center plan.

Discussions within the architectural community and at Princeton presented Kahn with the option of this new direction just when his experience at Penn, and his troubles with the Jewish Community Center plan, made him realize the limitations of an architecture based on the promise of technology and mass production. No longer would he avoid historical forms, from which he abstracted models for scale, definition, and monumentality — qualities that might countervail the dissipating urbanism of mass culture. Alluding to historic monuments also recalled past world powers, thereby advancing the search for a Great Style that would announce the United States to be the new empire: an empire of democracy.

Kahn's social agenda to consolidate a communal ethos could also benefit from abstracted allusions to historical precedents. By commemorating communal identity, historical references might foster a community's perpetuation. In 1966, the Italian architect Aldo Rossi wrote in *The Architecture of the City* that any "great" architectural "manifestation of social life" — by which he meant any monument — enables "the life of the collective" to survive.[109] For Kahn, modern buildings that echoed historical ones bound a viewer to a greater community of past users: "Modern space is really not different from Renaissance space," he said in 1959. "In many ways it is not. We still want domes, we still wants walls, we still want arches, arcades, and loggias of all kinds."[110] In embracing architectural precedents, Kahn reshaped his architectural language to reinforce the social bonds that make a community cohere.

Kahn was still expressing progressive, anti-capitalist proclivities, yet he now also espoused an architectural and social conservatism that was new. With his techno-organic vocabulary, he had proposed an architecture that was unfamiliar in the extreme; in turning toward tradition, he was developing an aesthetic that employed less jarring, more familiar forms. Kahn chose organically derived geometries in part because they symbolized all humanity's common origins in nature, which potentially appealed to a wide body of viewers and users. The audience for architecture shaped with reference to tradition was more limited, because culturally specific historical forms and motifs were apprehensible not to all humanity but only to those who share and know a common heritage.

Kahn thus began to look to architectural precedents in the mid-1950s because of a complex confluence of social and intellectual circumstances. Already during the 1940s he had believed that oblique historical allusions were consistent with the modernist enterprise. Yet this belief languished undeveloped as Kahn pursued other ideas. The specter of mass culture soured him on technology, now held responsible for urban blight, and turned him toward questions of how to reverse urban decentralization and to create a sense of place. Because of his dealings with architects and students at Princeton, and because he was anyway seeking a way out of the artistic dead end of techno-organicism, he began for the first time to act on his belief about architecture's relationship to history. In the Civic Center, Kahn drew abstracted allusions to historical precedent as one way toward a monumentality that would consolidate communal identity and sustain collective memory. Such allusions also expressed his unstated assumption—which he shared with Johnson, Howe, and certainly others—that America had assumed the mantle of world political and cultural leadership after World War II.

LATER SCHEMES FOR THE TRENTON JEWISH COMMUNITY CENTER

When Kahn resumed work on the Jewish Community Center sometime in late 1956, he combined his "constructed rooms," realized in the Bathhouse, with new considerations that he first explored in his Philadelphia Civic Center plan. He wanted to design a potent symbolic center for Trenton's Jewish community, which meant for him—as it had in his design for the Adath Jeshurun synagogue—a monument not to his clients' ethnicity or religion but to their commonality with American culture. To achieve this, Kahn sought to synthesize the symbolism of historical references with the abstraction of authenticity.

The board of the Community Center announced in December that Kahn would make his presentation of "the final drawings." The following May, he published a new scheme in *Architectural Review* (Figs. 5.20 and 5.21).[111] It must

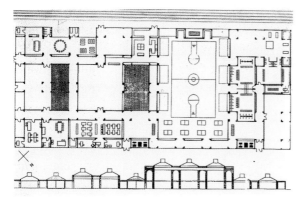

5.20 Model of the third scheme for the Jewish Community Center, with Roman brick arches, 1957. From the Kahn Collection.

5.21 Plan of the third scheme for the Jewish Community Center, 1957. From the Kahn Collection.

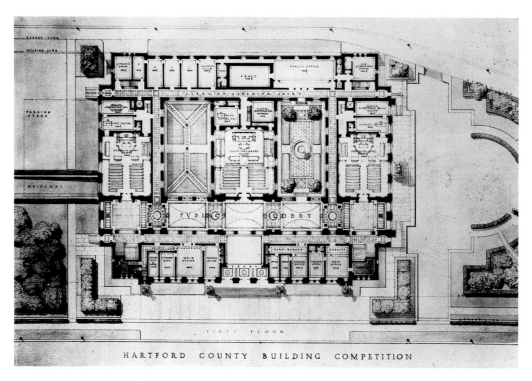

HARTFORD COUNTY BUILDING COMPETITION

5.22 Paul Cret, Hartford County Building, Hartford, Connecticut, 1926. From the Architectural Archives, University of Pennsylvania.

have been immediately evident to him that this new rectilinear scheme retained the modular system while solving all sorts of problems that the octahedrons had posed. The plan was much more flexible. It allowed for the use of internal point supports, so that interior spaces would not have been constrained by the insistent pattern of the octahedrons. Also, whereas the plan still articulated served and servant spaces, its "tartan grid" pattern lined up the servants one after another, making it possible to use them for circulation and allowing Kahn to develop the kind of hierarchy of spaces that he found so difficult to accomplish using the octahedrons. This new version was also preferable because its facades, simpler and flat, created a more monumental exterior, and the modular pavilions, relating visually to the Bathhouse, rendered all the buildings on the site a unified composition. Now the viewer, upon entering the complex, would see the small Bathhouse on axis and the larger related Community Center on the cross axis, as a monumental boundary to the site.

Certainly, formal and pragmatic pressures forced Kahn to metamorphose the mid-1956 octahedral plan into the rectilinear scheme designed between late 1956 and early 1957. Still, these cannot account for the newer plan's historical resonances.[112] Its similarities to, for example, Cret's Hartford County Building of 1926–1927 (Figs. 5.22 and 5.23) are evident. Both employ the tartan grid plan in

5.23 Paul Cret, Hartford County Building, Hartford, Connecticut, 1926. From the Architectural Archives, University of Pennsylvania.

which structural elements articulate a hierarchy of "constructed" rooms. The Bathhouse had made Kahn realize the Palladian qualities of his search for "compartmented containers,"[113] and his early background in Beaux-Arts design, combined with extensive exposure to the contemporary discourse on the use of historical precedents, encouraged him to adopt such a boldly allusive design.

In his new schemes for the Community Center, Kahn combined his Palladian rooms with a panoply of other historical techniques: constructed hierarchies of spaces; a monumental, masonry exterior; large scale. Kahn, acknowledging this new direction, added Roman arches to the now-brick facade (see Fig. 5.20) which coincided with the concrete beams that supported the gymnasium roof (during this period he was also considering arched windows for the Richards Medical Center). By no means a trailblazer, Kahn made this explicitly histori-cizing gesture on the facade years after Schweiker, Johnson, Rudolph, and Stone had already used arches in their designs.

Yet Kahn was not happy with such explicit references, and the arches disap-peared in subsequent versions of the Community Center. This back-and-forthing prefigured the tension between historical references and abstraction that would course through Kahn's work from then on. The Community Center design bespoke the past. Yet it also pulled historical models apart in the de-familiarizing manner that Kahn had developed through his search for authen-ticity, and with the same intention of forcing the viewer to notice the building in which he stood, rather than simply to use it as an instrument, without really looking. The oblong plan of the Community Center was proportionally longer than that of Cret's building, undermining a central emphasis. Kahn incorporated two main entrances but, unlike an academic designer, disposed them asymmetrically. The right door led to the "noisy areas" of the gymnasium and locker rooms, the left door to the "quieter areas" of the social hall and meeting rooms.[114] Cret's plan contains an axial arrangement, which reaches a climax in the superior court; by contrast, Kahn's circulation patterns were far more complex. Entering the left-hand entrance, one would face on one side a lobby with space bleeding toward the game room and gymnasium, and, directly ahead, the courtyard. The Community Center's two major spaces would be entered obliquely: the gymnasium would be penetrated at its corners, the social hall approached on a diagonal. Just as in the Bathhouse, where Kahn employed a Greek cross plan only to construct a circulation sequence that undercut its centrality, the sequences in the Community Center did not at all recall spaces constructed along academic principles.

The differences between Cret's and Kahn's elevations are also striking, for whereas Cret used the repetitive bay rhythm to unify his facade and shield the complexity of spaces behind, Kahn instead developed a scheme that forcefully, honestly conveyed the variety of spaces projected within. This he did by modulating the height and the configuration of the roof. In earlier designs, he had been disturbed that both major and minor spaces were spanned with the same repeating twenty-two-foot bay hipped roof. The constraints of the earlier, modular system, Kahn found, contradicted another of his design principles, that internal spaces be expressed on the exterior even if the results were aesthetically awkward. In his new design (which was probably prepared in collaboration with Auguste Komendant, a structural engineer specializing in reinforced concrete whom Kahn had met in 1956 and with whom he was then collaborating on the Richards Medical Center) spanning the Community Center's larger spaces became his primary focus.[115] In a lecture that May, Kahn asked, "Shouldn't there be little spans for little spaces and big spans for big spaces?"[116] Thus, in his revised design, the pavilions over the gymnasium disappeared. They would be supported with beams anyway, and so were replaced with a series of regularly spaced Vierendeel trusses (which, Kahn wrote, "will be excitingly painted"), which ran across the shorter dimension of the rectangle (Plate 11).[117] Above the "undulating" roofline, the beams supported bell-shaped skylights that brought natural light into the gymnasium during the day and supported the runners for electric lights. For the social hall, Kahn projected yet another span, which he described in a presentation to the building committee as "a ceiling of four high coffers or triangular domes," with skylights placed between triangular segments (Fig. 5.24).[118] The corresponding interior perspectives reveal a patent historicism. One drawing, from 1957, resembled nothing so much as the interior of a Pompeian villa, or perhaps a Roman bath (Fig. 5.25). Such imagery was suited to a community center, where people would come together for recreation and

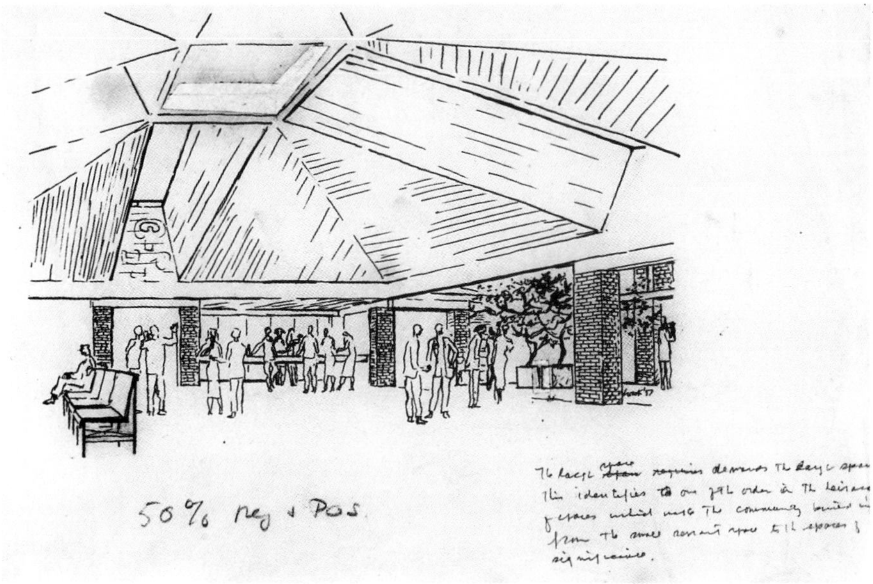

5.24 Perspective of the vaulted social hall, Jewish Community Center, 1957. From the Kahn Collection.

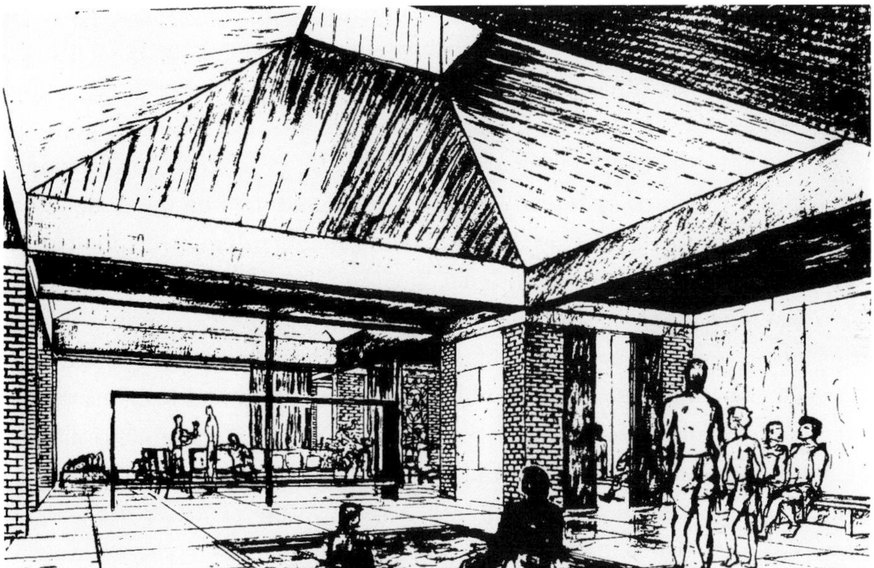

5.25 Perspective of the men's locker room, Jewish Community Center, 1957. From the Kahn Collection.

leisure. Such symbolism furthered Kahn's aim of expressing the projected users' commonality with Western culture as a whole.

The grandeur of these interiors would not have been matched in the elevations. The bizarre, disjunctive facade of the building compromised its obvious aspiration toward monumentality. It almost seems as if, on the interior, Kahn made references to historical tradition so explicit that he needed, on the exterior, to more decidedly undercut their referentiality. In doing so, however, he also undermined his aspiration to create an architectural monument. All later schemes of the Community Center were composed of disparate, barely related parts, with the gymnasium sporting one kind of profile, the social hall another. The composition faded away at the edges. Kahn, evidently attempting to pull the building into a strong, imageable composition, strung an arcade of pavilions along the front of the entire facade.

Neither Kahn nor the building committee was happy with these plans, and Community Center members turned to the National Jewish Welfare Board from New York City for advice.[119] Its experts pointed out that using a gymnasium as an auditorium "had not worked out well anywhere" and urged the Jewish Community Center to build two separate spaces. Moreover, they added, having "two main entrances with lobbies is a continuous headache and costly" and that "one entrance is preferable." Kahn again returned to the drawing board and devised yet another ill-fated scheme with an auditorium on one end, a gymnasium on the other, and all other ancillary spaces threaded between, now collected around a single internal courtyard. Dejectedly, he wrote to Nick Gianopolus, another structural engineer who had worked with him on the design, that "the job has proved to be a very costly and unprofitable affair. I still don't know where I am going to come out with my clients."[120] Negotiations lasted well into 1959. Kahn became increasingly frustrated with a building committee that was demanding more and more building for less and less money. The death of H. Harvey Saaz, a member of the building committee who had been a fulsome supporter of Kahn's project, contributed to increasingly acrimonious relations between client and architect.[121] Still, the building committee wanted Kahn to complete the structure,[122] asking him to redraw all the plans with their revisions. Kahn decided he had spent too much time and money on the job already, and asked for more money before he started afresh. The building committee refused, so Kahn withdrew from the commission.

Although Kahn never completed the Trenton Jewish Community Center design, this five-year-long project, in combination with the Bathhouse and his Civic Center plans, became defining moments in his artistic evolution. With these two projects, Kahn consolidated the role that he had begun to adopt with the Yale Art Gallery, City Tower, and the AFL Medical Services: that of a simultaneous critic and practitioner of the modernist tradition. This is the role he would maintain for the rest of his career. He challenged early modernism's emphasis on mass production and turned his back on the symbolic imagery of industrial technology, because he believed that mass production connoted or realized an architecture bearing little connection either to the place where it was built or to the community that it served. He also rejected modernism's transparency and open plan in favor of more heavily bound, anchoring spaces.

Yet he adhered to modernism's general conviction that architecture could change the life of a society, and to his own specific agenda that it could and should symbolize and enhance people's sense of communal identity. In the Trenton Jewish Community Center and Bathhouse he tried to create a large-scale, imageable, monumental complex. He rejected the use of ornament, constructed tectonically allusive spaces, and continued working in profoundly abstract, minimalist forms. When he chose to adopt abstracted historical references, he did so not against modernism but for it, as a subsidiary means to his modern ends in response to new developments in the social world.

The Jewish Community Center and Bathhouse is the first instance of what Kahn was gradually developing: an architecture that rethinks the fundamental features of the modern movement while adhering to its call for social engagement by reinforcing a user's sense of connection to her community and her place. The Jewish Community Center's hierarchical plan, historically derived symbolism, and overall imageability furthered this aim. But in this design he only partly succeeded: these aspirations would be better realized in the coming years.

Although there is no evidence of Kahn's response to the demise of the Community Center commission, he may have been relieved to put it behind him. Constant troubles with the building committee, changing square footage, the mutating profiles of the facade; such factors suggest that the Jewish Community Center for Trenton was, throughout, a transitional design. To push his ideas to a working synthesis, he needed to start afresh, with different programs, with building committees more sympathetic to his developing ideals. In the commissions for a Unitarian Church in Rochester, New York, and for a parliament building in Dhaka, Bangladesh, Kahn got that opportunity.

6

RETHINKING MODERNISM

AUTHENTICITY AND COMMUNITY IN THE
FIRST UNITARIAN CHURCH OF ROCHESTER

I have some ideas about the "existence will" re: our institutions with direct bearing
on architecture that will interest you.
—*Louis I. Kahn to Alison and Peter Smithson*

Louis Kahn's First Unitarian Church in Rochester is a faceted, compact, apparently windowless acropolis of dense red brick set on a flat, grassy site (Plate 12). At two stories with a footprint of 14,900 square feet, this small yet monumental building prefigured Kahn's first great works of the early 1960s, the Salk Institute in La Jolla, California, and the National Assembly complex in Dhaka, Bangladesh. The Unitarian Church was the first building Kahn built that gave an indication of his mature style, and it was recognized by Kahn's colleagues upon its completion as his best work yet.[1]

Kahn worked on the Unitarian Church for more than three years, from 1959 to 1962, progressively scaling back his ideas owing to a meager budget (an addition that nearly doubled the size of the building, designed by Kahn, was completed in 1969). In the early schemes he elaborated on a newly refined ideal of communal participation, which he developed partly in continuing response to the intellectual discourse at the University of Pennsylvania and partly as a consequence of his intense collaboration with members of the Unitarian Church, with whom Kahn developed a client-architect relationship so compatible that in 1961 he thanked the congregation and building committee alike "for the privilege they offered me to design the church."[2] In the final, built version, Kahn synthesized a compromised embodiment of his expanding social vision with new ideas on how to achieve an architecture of authenticity.

THE UNITARIAN CONGREGATION OF ROCHESTER

In late 1958, members of the Unitarian Church in Rochester faced an emergency decision, and their response perfectly characterized the liberal tenor of this congregation. For generations, they had worshiped in a downtown Gothic revival building designed in 1859 by Richard Upjohn and had held their Sunday school meetings in a building nearby. In late 1958, city officials notified them that their school was among the edifices designated for demolition in conjunction with the building of Midtown Plaza, the first urban redevelopment in the United States to include an all-pedestrian mall.[3] Municipal authorities offered them half a million dollars to vacate both buildings. Before the congregation responded, blasting in neighboring areas so shook the foundations of the church that it became structurally unsound.[4]

The Unitarian minister, David Williams, met with the church's board of trustees and distributed a memo outlining three possible courses of action: to build elsewhere in downtown Rochester, to build in the suburbs, or to try to hold on to the old church and find another way to house the school. Members of the church then broke down into discussion groups of twenty so that each voice could be heard. After the groups had met, the congregation gathered as a whole and voted. The majority decided that the congregation should sell and build anew on a site near the periphery of Rochester, where many members had moved. Williams disagreed with the decision, arguing that it was the duty of the church to stay downtown to serve the poor. But he accepted the democratic will.

Consensus achieved through a delicate balancing of individual expression and communal compromise was the Rochester Unitarians' highest ideal: they described themselves as intellectuals who rejected dogma and ritual in favor of an exploratory approach to faith. Many had left religions they deemed to be more conservative, such as Judaism and Catholicism; most were white-collar and upper-middle class, and many of them were affiliated with the University of Rochester or worked at Kodak, the major local industry. Their minister had little patience with ritual or the other comforts offered by the traditional congregations, as indicated by a memo of 1958 in which he pondered the question of why his congregation was growing so rapidly. Referring to the growing anxiety in the late 1950s that nuclear warfare with the Soviet Union might be imminent, he wrote that some had suggested the rise in church membership was a response "to the precarious times in which we live."[5] But this could not be so, Williams sternly averred: his brand of Unitarianism "offers no comfort" but "forces people to face the hard realities of the day." He concluded that the search by young, politically liberal parents for a church suitable to their needs was the factor most responsible for the congregation's growth.

Unitarianism had been founded in the early nineteenth century in reaction to the Calvinist doctrine of election. It emphasized "God's benevolence, humankind's free will, and the dignity rather than the depravity of human nature."[6] In the 1930s, the upper echelons of the church suffered a schism when one vocal and powerful faction of ministers denied that God existed at all. One member of the Rochester congregation thought that most of his fellow congregants "were either agnostics or atheists."[7]

Whatever the status of their faith, Unitarians historically emphasized social activism over the rituals of worship.[8] As with Unitarian fellowships nationwide, the congregation in Rochester had always been involved in politics. In the early twentieth century, it sponsored surveys on the city's housing conditions for the poor. It took an active role in the women's suffrage movement, and when Planned Parenthood set up shop in Rochester in 1934, its first home was on the premises of the Unitarian Church.[9] By the late 1950s, the church was more or less openly aligned with the Democratic Party.[10]

Given its emphasis on individual freedom and choice, it should hardly be surprising that, after voting to build in early 1959, the congregation began the process of selecting an architect by distributing questionnaires, asking its members to characterize Unitarianism and express their views on what a new building should be. Out of a list of twenty or so possible adjectives provided to describe their faith, the top five selected were "searching" (60 percent), "rational" (44 percent), "democratic" and "non-dogmatic" (both 43 percent), and "tolerant" (39 percent). Seventy-three percent wanted a building in "contemporary or modern" style "with a sparing use of symbols"; some members of the congregation expressed a preference for "stone or brick with glass and wood as secondary materials."[11]

A selection committee composed of two architects and one architectural historian drew up a list of out-of-town candidates for the commission. Their final list included Kahn along with Walter Gropius' TAC (The Architects' Collaborative), Carl Koch (a partner of Pietro Belluschi's), Hugh Stubbins, Eero Saarinen, and Paul Rudolph. The selection committee, rather than inviting each architect to Rochester to make a presentation, decided to take several weekends to travel to cities around the East Coast, interviewing the candidates and visiting their buildings.[12]

Kahn later said that initially he knew "nothing about Unitarianism," but the committee made at least the general tenor of their congregation known to him from the start. Jim Cunningham, the member of the selection committee who first inquired whether Kahn would be interested in the commission, wrote to him that "this committee feels that the liberal point of view . . . coupled with the talents of a leading architect could result in a most satisfying architectural achievement." Kahn wrote back two days later that he "should be pleased to work on a problem and with a building committee with your point of view."[13] Several members of the selection committee later remembered that their decision to recommend Kahn was based as much on his personality and his philosophy as on the buildings they saw, which included, in Philadelphia, the AFL Medical Services and the recently completed Richards Medical Center, and in New Haven, the Yale Art Gallery. Spending one day in May 1959 with Kahn convinced them that he was "a natural Unitarian."[14] They sent him the results of their questionnaires and invited him to Rochester to present his ideas for a congregation-wide vote.[15] He came in June, met with the twelve building committee members, and lectured before the whole congregation. They signed the contract in August.

The program for the Unitarian Church was similar to that for the Adath Jeshurun synagogue, except that it was smaller in scale: the building committee called for a sanctuary to seat five hundred, a school, offices, and a library.[16] Kahn's first drawings, perhaps from mid-summer 1959, did not reiterate the Adath Jeshurun's separation of the school from the sanctuary. Instead, Kahn drew a more complex version of the central plan that he had employed for the Trenton Bathhouse, concentrically arranged, in which a square seating area would be surrounded first by a circular ambulatory and then by subsidiary rooms (Fig. 6.1).[17] Beams supported a dome over the sanctuary, transferring weight to massive external buttresses (Fig. 6.2).

In subsequent designs Kahn slowly elaborated on the *parti* of concentric spaces surrounding, and leading to, a sanctuary; in December he presented his first formal scheme to the building committee, including a model and site plans.[18] He placed the large, three-story church (Fig. 6.3) beyond a garden at the far end of the site, on the crest of a slope, so that it would be only half visible from the road (Fig. 6.4).[19] It would rest on a flattened area circumscribed on three sides by a banked, rectangular terrace, and was thus similar to, but more monumental than, the circular embankment that he had envisioned for the later schemes of the Adath Jeshurun. The entrance was linked to the garden beyond by a bridge, slung as if over an empty moat.

Between the screened, square sanctuary and the fourteen-sided corridor leading to the peripheral rooms was the ambulatory that had appeared on the initial schemes; sections indicate that Kahn sank the sanctuary below the ambulatory. One would move from a garden, over a bridge, into a shady area between two blocks housing classrooms, into a dark corridor, and from there descend into the lighter space of gathering. Although many aspects of this

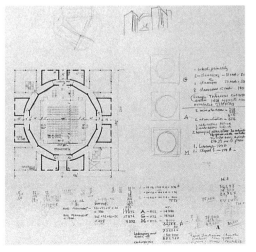

6.1 Plan for the first scheme of the First Unitarian Church of Rochester, 1959. From the collection of the First Unitarian Church in Rochester.

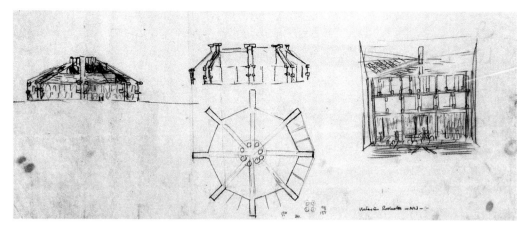

6.2 Early sketches for the first scheme of the First Unitarian Church of Rochester, showing massive external buttresses. From the Museum of Modern Art, New York.

6.3 Model of the first scheme of the First Unitarian Church of Rochester. From the Kahn Collection. Photo: William Porter.

scheme were eventually cut out, mainly for budgetary reasons, its principal motifs—concentric rings of space, a sequence from dark to light, a sanctuary illuminated by an unusual light source but without views to the outside—all appeared in the Unitarian Church as it was constructed.

Kahn's basic *parti*—a central room, ambulatory surrounding, and ancillary spaces and school around the ambulatory—cast off the last vestiges of the modular geometries of the mid-1950s in favor of overlays of much simpler forms. Why in this design did Kahn finally extricate himself from a modular form of organization? Why was this initial site plan so elaborate? Why did he include an ambulatory? This last question is particularly puzzling: historically, churches contained ambulatories so that worshipers could reach subsidiary chapels with-

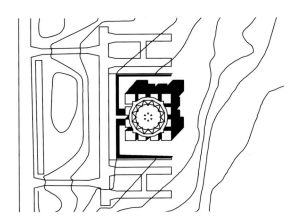

6.4 Site plan for the first scheme of the First Unitarian Church of Rochester showing "moat" surrounding three sides of building and (on right) bridge leading inside. From the collection of the First Unitarian Church in Rochester. Redrawn by Lan-Ying Ip.

out disturbing services in the nave, but Rochester's Unitarians had dispensed with all such rituals of worship, telling Kahn that they "envisage services entirely composed of such artistic communication as drama, dance, choral or instrumental music, or cinema."[20] Another puzzle is that Kahn used the clear historical precedent of the central-plan Renaissance church. What had a Renaissance church to do with the Rochester Unitarians? All these decisions embodied Kahn's explicit response to the liberal principles of Unitarianism, but none can be understood without examining the intellectual field in which Kahn conceived them.

THE AMBULATORY

People who attended Kahn's initial presentation to the Rochester congregation remember that even then, he envisioned their church encircled first by an ambulatory and then by the school.[21] Only months before he started working on the schematic drawings, he described his ideas for a religious space in his closing remarks to the CIAM conference in Otterlo, the Netherlands: "So, what is a chapel really? A chapel, to me, is a space that one can be in, but it must have an excess of space around it, so that you don't have to go in. That means, it must have an ambulatory, so that you don't have to go into the chapel; and the ambulatory must have an arcade outside, so that you don't have to go in to the ambulatory; and . . . outside is a garden so that you don't have to go into the arcade; and the garden has a wall, so that you can be inside or outside of it."[22] A curious concept for a church—to focus attention on those who do not want to be inside it. This idea did, however, reflect the convictions of the Rochester Unitarians by articulating various levels of communal involvement governed by the principle of free choice.

As much as this church plan was tailored to the catholicity of Unitarian ideals, Kahn had already devised this concept before the Rochester commission. Since September 1956, he had been assigning his students the design of a non-denominational chapel for the University of Pennsylvania, a program that

Kahn surely gleaned from Saarinen's non-denominational chapel at MIT and which was relevant to universities across the country during this period of enormous expansion. Initially Kahn co-taught the chapel studio with Holmes Perkins, in which they revived Sigfried Giedion's ideas for a synthesis of the arts, making it "a problem of architecture and parallels in the arts of sculpture and painting."[23] By mid-1957, two years before he received the commission for the Rochester Church, Kahn had formed his own ideas for a non-denominational chapel. They were inspired by his visit, years earlier, to the Leaning Tower of Pisa. He recounted this experience in a lecture in 1957, and again at Otterlo in 1959:[24] "When I first came to Pisa I went straight in the direction of the Piazza. Nearing it and seeing a distant glimpse of the Tower filled me so that I stopped short to enter a shop where I bought an ill-fitting English jacket. Not daring to enter the Piazza I diverted to other streets toward it but never allowed myself to arrive. The next day I went straight for the Tower touched its marble and that of the Duomo and Baptistery. The next day I boldly entered the buildings." Kahn continued, "So it is with a university chapel. Possibly a space protected by an ambulatory entered from an open arcade. . . . Space for those who never go there, those who must be near and don't enter and those who go in."[25] The walls surrounding the Campo Santo in Pisa had allowed Kahn to prolong his private experience of absorbing the meaning of the buildings, and to choose when first to enter the public arena of the complex, and then the buildings themselves. When Kahn received the Unitarian Church Commission, his preexisting ideas on church design meshed perfectly with the Unitarians' ideals.

THE PROBLEM OF THE INDIVIDUAL AND THE COLLECTIVE

That a concept Kahn had been working on for several years could so well suit the needs of his clients suggests that he was indeed a "natural Unitarian." His sensitivity to the tensions between free will and consensus was cultivated in Kahn by the discussions of the 1950s. In the architectural community at large and among Kahn's colleagues at Penn, the discourse on mass culture increasingly turned on the architect's responsibility to create a workable hierarchy between the individual and the collective that would make people aware of a public realm, separate and distinct from their private lives, in which they would be encouraged to exercise their obligation to participate.

In American intellectuals' rising reaction against mass culture in the 1950s, many feared that with the dramatic expansion of the middle class through consumerism came a diminution of social difference, that the culture of consumption would spawn an undifferentiated "mass" of buyers. In *The Crack in the Picture Window*, John Keats warned his imaginary audience of tract-house owners that they were to live in neighborhoods "inhabited by people whose age, income, number of children, problems, habits, conversation, dress, possessions and perhaps even blood type are precisely like yours."[26] Because of this homo-geneity, people would stop identifying themselves with the specific community where they lived, and this lack of identification would engender social apathy. By the end of the decade, litanies on the dangers of passive conformism could be heard on any college campus and read in popular magazines from *Fortune* to *Time.* This discussion originated in the early 1950s with the publication of *The Lonely Crowd* (1950), by David Riesman, Nathan Glazer, and Raul Denney. This influential book proposed that previous generations of Americans had been "inner-directed," guided by their own internal compasses, but that contempo-rary Americans were "other-directed," navigating their lives by the winds of social pressure blowing upon them from (middle-class) peers. William H. Whyte's best-selling *The Organization Man* of 1956 condemned the passivity of American middle-class employees working in the vastly expanding corporate bureaucracies, which he believed extended to the rest of their lives.[27]

For some writers explicitly (such as Eric Hoffer in *The True Believer* and Han-nah Arendt in *The Origins of Totalitarianism,* both 1951) and for others implicitly (such as Whyte and Riesman), a society in which citizens focused on personal fulfillment to the neglect of their communal obligations disintegrated the very foundations of democracy.[28] Such a people, willingly forfeiting control, could easily lose its personal freedom through manipulation from above. Underlying the con-cerns regarding the dangers of mass culture, then, were Cold War anxieties that mass culture might pave the way for totalitarian forces to undermine the American polity. Facilitating individual expression within a participatory community was seen as preventive medicine against the threat of communism.

By the middle of the decade the architectural community had assimilated this specific set of associations, including the idea that consumerism destroyed the communal identification which fostered citizen participation and that the ensuing apathy could open the path to the acceptance of authoritarian rule. In *Perspecta,* Paul Nelson wrote in 1956 that one of an architect's principal tasks was to create the means for democratic participation. He warned of "the extreme danger in a mass production society of absorbing the individual into a collective pattern of passive conformity" and urged that "means must be found to permit an individual to intervene, to participate, to express himself."[29] At least by 1961, perhaps before, Vincent Scully had also picked up such griev-ances, arguing in a symposium Kahn attended that "one trend as it can be per-ceived in American mass culture as a whole, is a growing lack of respect for action or accomplishment."[30]

At Penn, these ideas translated into an increasing conviction that architects should design urban, especially civic, monuments that nurture an individual's sense of obligation to participate in the life and governance of his community. Landscape architects Karl Linn and Ian McHarg voiced such directives, and so did members of the department of architecture such as Robert Geddes, Aldo Giurgola, and Tim Vreeland. Giurgola and Vreeland were among Kahn's closest associates.[31] Geddes and Vreeland began a studio program in 1956 with the statement "Let us assume, for the moment, that a sense of community is a desirable goal. And let us further assume that the design of the physical environment has an effect in creating a sense of community. . . . What can be done to improve the physical environment and create a greater sense of community?"[32]

Geddes, Vreeland, and Giurgola all insisted that such public buildings as the community center, courthouse, city hall, or library, when well designed, enabled individuals to identify with a larger social body and share in its ideals; Vreeland and Giurgola regularly assigned the problem of a courthouse for a smaller city outside Philadelphia, which Vreeland described as "the civic heart of the town."[33] Such monuments, they argued, commanded a sense of place.

The aims and concerns of the Penn faculty flowed from two sources: the social criticism by American writers discussed above, and the polemics of the loosely organized group of European architects and theorists known as Team Ten, who saw themselves as reconceptualizing modernism, especially city planning, so that it would reinforce existing communities rather than destroy them in order to build afresh. Alison and Peter Smithson introduced such issues at the CIAM conference in Aix-en-Provence in 1953, presenting themselves as both extending Le Corbusier's concerns for "the dialogue between the individual and the collective" (especially as manifested in the Unité d'habitation in Marseilles) and critiquing his Athens Charter's "four functions" of city form, which included traffic, housing, industry, and recreation.[34] In place of the four functions the Smithsons proposed a new system that, they argued, would lead to "urban re-identification" through emphasizing instead four levels of human "patterns of association": the house, the street, the district, and the city (Fig. 6.5).[35]

After 1956, Team Ten's ideas permeated discussions at Penn about the future of cities and architecture. Relations between the Graduate School of Fine Arts (GSFA) and the European, and particularly the British, community of architects

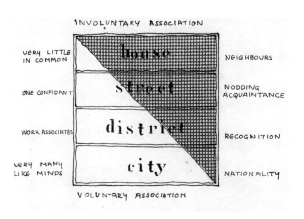

6.5 Alison and Peter Smithson, hierarchy of association, 1952. Courtesy Peter Smithson.

had been close since the arrival of Perkins as dean in 1951. (Richard Saul Wurman, an architect who worked with Kahn, remembered that when he was teaching at Penn in the late 1950s, "you got a job if you had a British accent.")[36] Perkins recalled the Smithsons' identity grid almost verbatim, often stating in lectures that a sense of community should be encouraged at all levels of social organization, "from the family to the city."[37] In 1957, the GSFA hosted an exhibition of projects presented at the tenth CIAM conference in Dubrovnik, Yugoslavia, where the work of Team Ten members was prominently represented.[38] Peter Smithson first came to the United States that same year; he lectured at Penn and spent enough time with Kahn to become his friend. The Smithsons' work was included in another exhibition at the GSFA in 1959, and it was Peter Smithson who was responsible for inviting Kahn to the CIAM conference at Otterlo that same year.[39]

Mainly, the Smithsons had been interested in the ideal relationship of the individual to the collective, and how it could be fostered. Those concerns were the foundation for, in 1952, their scheme for public housing called Golden Lane and, in 1964, their three-building Economist complex in London. As Team Ten ideas settled onto Philadelphia soil, however, they were transformed. European desires to create a workable hierarchy of public and private fused with the mounting American reaction against mass culture. Although the Smithsons after 1956 came to envision mass culture as potentially emancipatory, at Penn, "real" community was always presented in opposition to the perceived non-community of what American sociologist C. Wright Mills simply called the Mass.[40]

Through the 1950s Kahn came to value communal life even more than he had in previous years. Perhaps this was partly because during the decade he had learned much from his colleagues. Publicly he liked to deny that any other living person had ever inspired him, but his method of working suggests otherwise: when he received a new commission, he said, his first act was to talk to other people about his ideas.[41] The following year, he claimed, somewhat fatuously but self-revealingly, that "A city is where one comes to know oneself better, where [one] comes to meet and interact with others. No one ever wrote a great book in the country or in the sticks."[42]

Whereas Kahn had previously entertained the possibility that popular culture could itself provide the arena for people to come together, he had by 1961 emphatically changed his mind: "There is no so-called 'City-Place.' . . . A place where fountains play; a place where boy meets girl. Such places are given to you by commercial means? No. . . . The sense of patriotism of the city can be [achieved] by giving great places to the city instead of one stream of commercial enterprise all fighting for a place."[43] But a "City-Place" could happen only if the architect created a building that would encourage people, as they moved through its spaces, to enact his social ideals of individuals exercising their freedom in good faith to participate in the public realm.

Throughout the 1940s and early 1950s, Kahn was working with an amorphous, and therefore problematic, notion of community (or even, with his techno-organicism, a notion of world community), which ignored the need for irruptions of individuality. He was finding it difficult to inscribe his ideal of this homogeneous community into architectural form except through some form of symbolism, which (as in the case of techno-organicism) often proved opaque or even illegible to viewers. When Kahn turned to design the First Unitarian Church, he found that the discourses on cities among American social critics, at Penn, and among members of Team Ten — like his own earlier notions about church design — fortuitously coincided with Unitarian ideals. With this confluence of ideas as a foundation, Kahn was able to work out a more complex scheme for how his vision of community might be manifested in architectural form.

Kahn found that his newly refined social agenda could be directly embedded into the plans and site plans of his buildings. His multi-layered, concentric organizational concept elaborated on his idea for a university chapel, providing an arena that encouraged, through phenomenological means, free choice and communal participation, the hope having been that people would choose to work for the good of the community. He reinforced this new ideal of community by employing a new symbolic language that stressed an individual's relationship to a larger whole. This symbolism is especially evident in one early sketch for the Unitarian Church, on which he noted a source: a circle inside a square, with smaller circles in a ring inside the large. Kahn had made abstracted allusions to historic precedents in his later schemes for the Trenton Jewish Community Center; here, he directly transcribed an ideal church plan by Leonardo da Vinci (Fig. 6.6).[44] It was at this time that Kahn, when speaking in Otterlo in September, contended that modern and Renaissance spaces were similar.

Central-plan churches bore iconographic associations to humanism. Scully, contemplating new trends toward classicism in American architecture, unmasked associations to humanism that also underlay Renaissance forms. The classicizing overtones he saw in the work of Kahn and others suggested to him that "our fate in the present remains more wholly human than we had been led to believe and that the world as we know it is made up not only of nature, nor of machines . . . but of the blazing ardor of men. It may be that in the face of total challenge [from communism, or mass culture, or both] the values of humanist civilization, as not yet dead, call to us, and we take our stand."[45] In 1959, William Jordy similarly guessed that the motivation behind the "new formalism" was the "aura of humanism clinging to classicistic forms [that] automatically dilutes the sense of impersonality in the completed building."[46]

Renaissance models also referred to the individual through the proportional relationships they employ. Leonardo's centralized church plans recall the famous "Vitruvian man" inscribed in both a circle and a square, thereby repre-

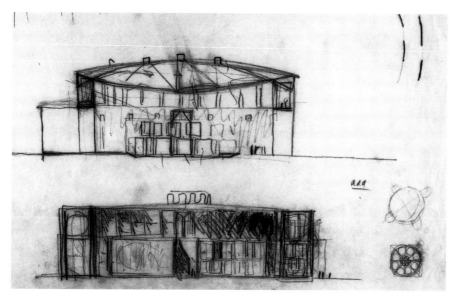

6.6 First scheme for the First Unitarian Church of Rochester (top), with Kahn's copy of Leonardo da Vinci's sketch for a central plan (bottom). From the Museum of Modern Art, New York.

senting man's individual place in a larger cosmic scheme.[47] Saarinen acknowledged in 1954, "The Renaissance was greatly concerned with the human response to proportions. . . . I begin to see its profound importance."[48] Scully, in 1957, also described the new classicizing tendencies apparent in the work of Saarinen and Johnson—"closed corners . . . central openings"—as "the result of a humanist search for clear, man-centered forms." He cited Geoffrey Scott's *The Architecture of Humanism* to argue that "the center of that [i.e., Renaissance] architecture was the human body."[49] Again and again, writers linked the geometries of Renaissance forms to human proportions, and further implied that users would intuit this relationship.

While designing the buildings at Trenton, Kahn had realized that Palladian architecture offered a "bay system" to challenge modernism's open plan. Now, in a total reversal of his techno-organic philosophy of the early 1950s, and again reflecting his involvement in contemporary discourse, he turned to geometries that connoted both human culture and the proportions of the human body. At Otterlo, Kahn insisted: "It is in the nature of art that it should be different from nature. Of this I am certain." Two years later he maintained, "You are not allowed to do things as nature does, if you try, nature will only laugh at you."[50] Instead, one should look at what "a man makes."[51] Kahn chose Renaissance forms specifically for the Rochester Unitarians, for clients who made clear to him that they put their emphasis on "the dignity rather than the depravity of man."

Into his first scheme for the Unitarian Church, Kahn embedded symbolic references to "humanist" Renaissance architecture and to the human body. The ensuing emphasis on the individual was reinforced with a plan that encouraged users to choose their manner of participation in communal gatherings. In designing a plan that accommodated such ideals, Kahn revealed that he was participating in the discourses on individualism and democratic communal participation, which had dominated American culture since the beginning of the postwar period, accelerating in the mid-1950s in dual response to the Cold War and to the ongoing explosion of consumer culture. Because this discourse of individual freedom and communal responsibility dovetailed with the ideals set forth by Kahn's clients, it is no surprise that upon finishing the church he spoke of the "friendship, which I deeply feel" with the Rochester Unitarians.[52]

THE ARCHITECTURE OF INSTITUTIONS

In what is probably his most famous lecture, "Form and Design," which he delivered in 1960, Kahn called this first scheme for the Unitarian Church the "form concept," meaning that whereas it did not delineate broom closets and bathrooms, it conveyed his essential concept for the design. In wrapping the children's Sunday school around the sanctuary, Kahn asserted that he had symbolized the Unitarian doctrine of question and search. The auditorium was a metaphor for a "question, and the school . . . was that which raised the question." For Unitarians, he explained, these two branches of inquiry were "inseparable" (Fig. 6.7).[53]

In making the essence of Unitarianism central to his first scheme for the Unitarian Church, Kahn conceptualized anew his process of design. He now contended that the architect must, initially, work from an approach that disregarded considerations of function and program. Abandoning one of the principal practices that the early modernists espoused to develop a new architecture, functionalism, which dictated that architectural form should be derived from a strict analysis of the client's program, Kahn asserted that "the program is nothing. The program is a hindrance."[54] What was important was that the architect ideate the social role of the institution he was to design, independent of the ideas of the client. Kahn first used the word "institution" in this sense the year he received the Rochester commission, writing to the Smithsons in March, "I have some ideas about the 'existence will' re: our institutions with direct bearing on architecture that will interest you."[55] By July 1959, he wrote an acquaintance that he had "come to realizations about architecture which now form the entire basis of my work. . . [which is] a result of interplay of desire and needs in relation to our Institution[s]."[56]

Kahn maintained that the architect should create a "form concept" neither by analyzing the changeable and small-minded functions with which clients littered their programs nor by taking recourse in some abstract, unchanging ideal. Instead, she should focus on what Kahn repeatedly referred to as a "way of life."[57] The epiphany of Form came only to the architect who worked as a cultural anthropologist: "The way of life in California," Kahn pointed out, "is very different from say Seattle or Hong Kong—or in a closed place like Vermont."[58]

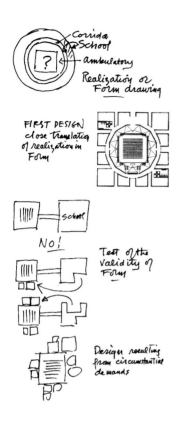

Corrida
School
ambulatory
Realization or Form drawing

FIRST DESIGN
close translation of realization in Form

School
NO!
Test of the Validity of Form

Design resulting from circumstantial demands

6.7 Plan diagrams for "Form and Design" illustrating the sanctuary as "a question" and the surrounding school as "that which raised the question," First Unitarian Church of Rochester, January 1961. From Jan Rowan, "Wanting to Be: The Philadelphia School," *Progressive Architecture* 42 (April 1961).

In this social definition of architecture, Kahn substituted the word "Form" for "Order." "Order," as he used it in the 1953 poem "Order and Design," referred to the pure geometric forms that he believed underlay all organic and inorganic matter. Form, by contrast—as in "Form and Design"—"characterizes a harmony of spaces that is good for a certain activity of man."[59]

Kahn had already been practicing such an approach since 1954, when he conceived of the Adath Jeshurun synagogue in a manner that recalled the earliest, nomadic forms of Jewish worship. Now, however, he conceptualized this practice and articulated an idea that became central to his mature architecture: the architect "should train his mind [to] lead him to realizations of new spaces, good for these institutions. He should fight the stock programs of spaces now destroying the entire sense from which institutions . . . took hold."[60] The architect, as guardian of the public realm, should maintain independence from the client's demands. Because clients were constrained by budget, self-interest, and, at times, the lack of a broad social vision, the responsibility fell to the architect to imagine a Form that was "good for man." The architect should be an activist, Kahn argued, giving society not the spaces it thought it needed but the spaces it *should* want. "I don't think that Mozart was a failure, do you?" Kahn asked an audience in 1966. "And don't you think Mozart makes a society? Did society make Mozart? No, it's the man, the man only, not a committee, not a mob—nothing makes anything but a single, single man."[61] This conviction, that an architect should design institutions that manifested an idealized conception of human interaction, heroized the architect as it conferred upon him a dignified social role. It was this conviction that became the linchpin of Kahn's mature philosophy, helping to guide the design for the Unitarian Church and most of his subsequent projects.

THE FINAL PLAN: FROM FORM TO DESIGN

In working out his initial conception for the Unitarian Church, Kahn, in order to suit the budget and accommodate the disaggregated needs that are intrinsic to any program, reduced the size and scale of his projected building, and moved from what he called Form to what he called Design.[62] In doing so, he structured a plan that better articulated his ideal of an institution that encouraged communal participation while allowing for individual freedom.

In the "Form and Design" lecture, Kahn recounted how he arrived at the final plan for the Unitarian Church. His first plan, he conceded, was "very rigid." As the design process continued, "every committee member began to eat away at the rigid geometry."[63] At one point the building committee, citing worries about traffic and internal noise, suggested that the school be severed from the sanctuary and put into a separate wing.[64] Then they realized the error of their ways, he explained in self-satisfied tones. Back went school and offices around the sanctuary. For Kahn, this confirmed the programmatic and symbolic wisdom of his initial *parti:* "the Form held."[65]

In this second plan, ancillary spaces took on a much looser configuration, related to one another not geometrically but according to their use (Fig. 6.8). As a result, the entry sequence radically departed from the Renaissance sources of the original plan. One entered a small, oblong room; on axis was the library-lounge, while diagonally to the right, situated entirely without ceremony, was the door to the sanctuary. This plan now followed the building committee's instructions exactly. They had requested that the library-lounge adjoin the lobby; that the kindergarten and nursery school not be located on opposite sides of the building but "be developed as a unit"; and that service and administration areas be grouped.[66]

This laying out of specific rooms Kahn dubbed Design, which, he maintained, was "a circumstantial act." Whereas Form emanated from the architect's conceptualization of a "way of life," Design "belongs to the designer." Dictated by "how much money there is available, the site, the client, the extent of knowledge," Design was the impingement of the everyday on the institutional ideal of the Form.[67] For the Unitarian Church in Rochester, the plan that resulted balanced a rigid, centralized shape with a more picturesque composition, which was configured to accommodate specific needs. This inclination toward more incidental arrangements of rooms had appeared in Kahn's work several years before he

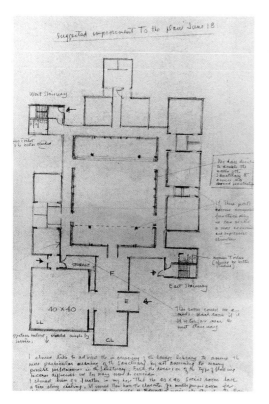

6.8 Second scheme, with spaces related according to use, First Unitarian Church of Rochester, June 1960. From the Kahn Collection.

151

RETHINKING MODERNISM

took up the Rochester commission. In the Morton Goldenberg House of 1957, he attempted to break out of his modular, geometric rigidity to accommodate the complex incidents of private life;[68] similarly, in the Trenton Jewish Community Center's small Day Camp, also of 1957 (the only part of the commission that he built besides the Bathhouse), a series of rectangular pavilions are irregularly arranged atop a circular concrete plate (1957).

The loosely composed, individuated cells of the final plan of the Unitarian Church grate against the rigid centrality of the sanctuary and the building's overall rectilinear footprint (Fig. 6.9). The resulting tension — call it a discordance between Design and Form — parallels the conflicting impulses of expressiveness and restraint that had already surfaced in Kahn's Yale Art Gallery and the AFL Medical Services. Both sets of discordances emerged from Kahn's movement toward an impersonal formalism, on the one hand, and a more individuated, gestural vocabulary, on the other. The balance of these conflicting impulses, now expressed in multiple ways, animates not only the Unitarian Church but also many of Kahn's most successful later civic and religious projects.

By elucidating and giving architectural expression to the difference between Form and Design, Kahn advanced his larger architectural agenda on both the social and the formal levels. In social terms, he schematized an ideal relationship between the free individual and the freely chosen community into a concentric plan. Smaller spaces are inflected with individual identities, then

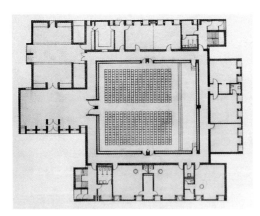

6.9 Final plan for the First Unitarian Church of Rochester, ca. June 1961. From the Kahn Collection.

arranged around a larger communal gathering space where all would feel welcome, where all was stasis and calm.

In formal terms, Kahn's final plan for the Unitarian Church undermines the
referentiality of his historicizing starting point in Leonardo's ideal plans.
Departing from his initial sources, Kahn reiterated one of the axioms shared by
early modernism and the Existentialist aesthetic of authenticity: the taking of
recognizable images and then defamiliarizing them in the service of an overriding abstraction. He liked to evoke past buildings—as in his equation, at Otterlo,
of modern space with Renaissance space—because sources drawn from history,
associated with high culture, were potential weapons in the battle against mass
culture.[69] But the references had to be oblique. "The worst kind of art," he said
to his students the same year he began to design the First Unitarian Church, "is
art that is trying to *represent* something." Later he advised that one "cannot
think of architecture representing anything."[70] Referring to Wright's description
of his Beth Shalom synagogue in Elkins Park as the built embodiment of Mount
Sinai, Kahn contended that one "can't do . . . an architecture school representing an Ionic column or a synagogue representing Mt. Sinai."[71]

Kahn continued to strive to create an architecture that was beyond rhetoric,
an architecture that, as Giedion had described several years earlier, "sprung
directly from the senses." He claimed that even his geometries, which in their
Euclidean simplicity so invited symbolic interpretation, were abstract. "I use
the square to begin my solutions because the square is a non-choice, really," he
insisted a few years after the completion of the Unitarian Church. "In the
course of development, I search for the forces that disprove the square."[72] When
designing the tapestries for the sanctuary several years after the completion of
the church, Kahn wrote of his determination to use an abstract idiom, and settled on a pattern of color bands representing daylight or light refracted through
a prism (Plate 13).

In their emphasis on abstraction, Kahn's new ideas on Form and Design resonated with his search for an architecture of authenticity. Also consonant with

the requisites of authenticity was his emphasis, in the Design part of his process of conceptualization, on the individual. Into the Rochester plan, Kahn inscribed (or believed he was inscribing) the needs of the user. His hope was that the individual would feel these spaces inflected toward her needs, which would heighten her awareness of her particular situation. That furthered Kahn's quest of making an architecture of authenticity, which would inspire the epiphanic experience of the living of life in the immediate moment and place.

LIGHT, COMPOSITION, MATERIALS: AUTHENTICITY IN THE FINAL DESIGN

As he completed the design, elevations, and internal spaces of the Unitarian Church, Kahn concentrated on manifesting the experience of authenticity that he had introduced into the final iteration of the plan. In his previous projects he acknowledged the tectonic realities of building, stressed materiality by emphasizing the process of construction, and allowed for a subtle lack of surface finish. In the Unitarian Church, he again employed these techniques, to which he added new (or newly matured) ones that powerfully furthered his aims.

Natural light now became one of Kahn's principal preoccupations, even an obsession. From his earliest sketches for the First Unitarian Church, he struggled with the problem of getting daylight to internal spaces, a problem that he contemplated in later designs for the Trenton Jewish Community Center. His first scheme for the church called for a fourteen-sided sanctuary, capped by a low-slung, flat-topped dome. An alternating ring of upside-down isosceles and right-side-up equilateral triangles would constitute the spring of the dome;[73] encircling and beneath it was a clerestory, an idea Kahn probably got from his recent visit to Le Corbusier's pilgrimage chapel at Ronchamp, France, where an apparently heavy roof floats on a band of light (Figs. 6.10 and 6.11).[74] Daylight would also fall from skylights, or lightwells, located at the apexes of the right-side-up triangles, and from an oculus at the dome's center.[75]

Many religious traditions draw an analogy between light and the presence of God. Still, as the history of Kahn's treatment of light shows, his preoccupation with it for the Unitarian Church was not, primarily, spiritually inspired. He had been experimenting with ways to bring natural light into his interiors since the early 1950s: the skylight at the top of the stairwell in the Yale Art Gallery, though not his earliest, was in 1960 still his most poetic exploration of this theme (Fig. 6.12).[76] For the Trenton Jewish Community Center he specified top-lit pavilions, an idea that would not be successful because direct, unshielded light would fall in staccato patterns throughout the building, creating what Kahn would later dismiss (in reference to Rudolph's Jewett Art Center at Wellesley) as "little pinpoints of glare."[77] This first version of the Unitarian Church sanctuary would have suffered similar problems.

In January 1960, Kahn left off designing the Unitarian Church design to travel to Luanda, Angola, in conjunction with his commission for a U.S. con-

6.10 Kahn's sketch of Le Corbusier's Notre-Dame-du-Haut, Ronchamp, France, 1959. From the Kahn Collection, Architectural Archives of the University of Pennsylvania, Gift of Richard Saul Wurman.

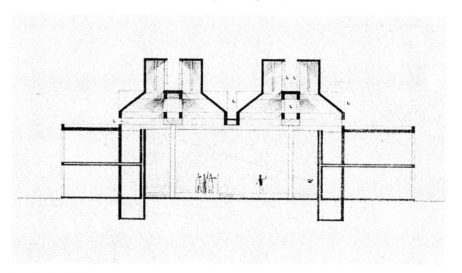

6.11 Section showing a Ronchamp-like separation between ceiling and walls. From the collection of the First Unitarian Church in Rochester.

6.12 Skylight at top of the staircase, Yale University Art Gallery, New Haven, Connecticut, 1951–1954. Photo: Grant Mudford.

sulate there. In Luanda, he realized that light—its quality, hue, and intensity— distinguished one place from another. Again and again in lectures of the early 1960s, Kahn described how tropical light was different from the northern light with which he was more familiar. In Luanda, he realized that he enjoyed natural light and disliked glare, saying that "the glare is killing." "Light is a needed thing, but still an enemy . . . the relentless sun above, the siesta comes over you like thunder. . . . You practically fall in the street.[78] Upon returning home, he redrew his designs for the Unitarian Church, orienting them around a problem that occupied him for the remainder of his career: how to bring natural light inside while diffusing glare.

When Kahn returned from Luanda, he focused on design development for the Unitarian Church, searching for ways to soften the light that would fall into the sanctuary. First he used four square lightwells with crossed beams supporting small extruding pavilions with thin slits on four sides (Fig. 6.13). Later he designed cross-shaped protruding elements that ended in skylights for more direct illumination. Still dissatisfied, Kahn, for the first time, directed his employees to make small cardboard study models of various ideas and take them to Fairmount Park to examine, and photograph, how light fell inside (Plate 14).

Kahn's growing propensity to sculpt light also appeared in his later designs for elevations, for which he developed faceted walls that—he claimed—shielded

6.13 Model of an intermediate version with clerestory windows at midpoints of cubic light towers, First Unitarian Church of Rochester, March 1960. From the Kahn Collection. Photo: William Porter.

6.14 Facade study of the First Unitarian Church of Rochester, January 1961. From the Museum of Modern Art, New York.

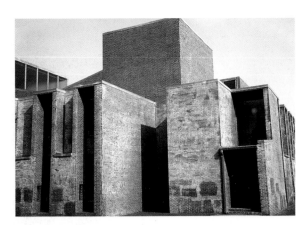

6.15 Facade detail showing, on left, the inset windows of the First Unitarian Church of Rochester, Rochester, New York, 1959–1962.

157

RETHINKING MODERNISM

windows from glare. But glare in Rochester was certainly not what it was in Luanda, and his justifiably famous, and lovingly executed, elevation studies betray that his real interest was to sculpt rhythms of light across the facade and create the impression of massiveness in order to increase the monumentality of what was by then a rather modest, two-story building (Fig. 6.14). With windows inset, the building's two major facades display an irregular pattern of solid walls and black, vertical voids (Fig. 6.15). Thirteen or fourteen feet from the ground, the solid walls are notched back, creating a contrapuntal rhythm of long, flat shadows interspersed with short polygonal ones. The result is a colonnade of shadows that supports neither lintel nor pediment, a kind of negative colonnade (Plate 15).

Inside the sanctuary, an inward-sloping, two-way folded concrete plate ceiling opens into four tower-like lightwells that are sliced on their internal faces and placed at the voided outer corners of the square room (Plate 16). One's first impression is of cool, pale colors and of light: not the red walls and black shadows of the exterior, but soft tones, gray and white. As jarring and heavy as the exterior is, so static, soothing, and light is the space of communal gathering. The eye travels first upward, then out toward the corners of the room: from these edges, daylight falls, although the light sources are nearly invisible. The sanctuary consolidates into poetic fruition all the conditions Kahn set himself for the design of the church.

Such careful manipulation of natural light, inside and out, helps to generate the sense that this building belongs to the site on which it stands. Kahn explained that his fascination with light came from its uniqueness to a place. "Artificial light is only a single little moment in light," he declared; natural light is changeable, registering not only the time of day but also the season. Bringing natural light inside connects a building to the forces of nature—"to the moon," Kahn said—"it just makes a difference."[79] Natural light was more humanistic: while he was designing the laboratories for the Salk Institute, he observed that "when I go talking to some of the underlings I soon found out that they were very unhappy without a window so that they . . . could tell whether there's a bird outside, or if it's snowing or raining."[80] Relying on the same anti-commercial logic whereby he proposed a massive pyramid for Philadelphia's Civic Center, Kahn ventured that his contemporaries were ignoring such basic human needs as daylight because it was cheaper that way. "A man isn't just an automaton sitting in a laboratory," he passionately insisted. "You cannot work in a space [without] . . . natural light. If you say you can, you [mean to] say that the management thinks you can."[81]

In the Unitarian Church, and in every other building that Kahn designed after 1960, spaces and elevations change with the hour, the season, the weather. He was still intently focused on the effects of light while he was designing the Yale Center for British Art in New Haven in 1969–1974, predicting that "on a gray day it will look like a moth; on a sunny day like a butterfly."[82] Because each day is unique in the way these forces combine, a building by Kahn becomes an instrument that exaggerates, and so heightens one's awareness of, nature's infinite variations. With this approach, Kahn promoted his aesthetic of authenticity, because he subtly prods his viewer toward a recognition of the contingent historical moment in which she lives, and of the contingent place on earth where she stands.

Compositional elements furthered the authenticity that is so potently established with Kahn's interior and exterior manipulation of natural light. The Unitarian Church's elevations provoke a viewer's focused gaze, because the proportions between the two-story "negative colonnade" and the four blank brick light towers are strange, with the towers awkwardly bulky and squat in relation to the refined rhythms below. Determined by an honest expression of internal volumes, this composition is awkward in the same manner as were later schemes for the Trenton Jewish Community Center. Yet what it loses in refined elegance, it gains in authenticity; as a single concentrated mass, it manages to be both gawky and resolved, a diminutive monolith of a building which one of Kahn's assistants described as "something odd and beautiful."[83]

The sequence into the sanctuary was finalized only after Kahn settled the structure of the sanctuary ceiling, a problem that was ultimately solved by Auguste Komendant, who suggested the folded plate.[84] To support the folded plate, Kahn and Komendant placed concrete posts at the central points of the plate, which landed one post right in the entrance to the sanctuary (see Fig. 6.9). As with the disjunctive proportions on the exterior, the placement of this post in the entrance into the main heraldic space was just the kind of overturning of traditional axioms—in this case, of the uninterrupted processional movement into a Renaissance church—on which Kahn would increasingly rely. The post became the juncture between two doors leading inside.

To finish the Unitarian Church, Kahn carefully chose materials for their richness and, in combining them, laid bare the process of construction, fashioning the impression of blunt honesty and emphasizing the presence of the human hand. Both were techniques he had employed since his design of the Art Gallery at Yale. In the Unitarian Church Kahn exerted greater control in putting together materials than he had in earlier buildings. Seeking a saturated red surface for the exterior, he demanded that brick samples be delivered to the Rochester site so that their color could be checked and irregular specimens discarded.[85] In the sanctuary, he carefully arranged the several shades of concrete block (Fig. 6.16). Before the folded plate ceiling was poured, he procured extralong wood so that there would be no horizontal seams from end to end, although he still exposed the patterns from the wooden planks that held the concrete pour.[86]

All these decisions indicate that, whereas he continued to strive for an aesthetic of authenticity in the late 1950s, Kahn had softened his vision. He still believed in a "frank architecture"—still thought that "a building is a struggle, not a miracle, and the architecture should acknowledge this"[87]—but he also tempered the quality of authenticity that he sought to achieve. No longer would he be proud if a user confused the main floor with the basement, as he once had been with the Yale Art Gallery.

In the Unitarian Church Kahn combined woodwork with concrete for the first time in his career, a combination that he subsequently used in the Salk Institute and in most of his other projects.[88] In another manifestation of his now-exaggerated dislike of the sleek products of mass production, Kahn, to make his woodwork look old-fashioned, assigned an office employee to spend months tracking down square-headed nails, which were almost out of production.[89] This warmer sensibility was a product of Kahn's emerging emphasis on people rather than on technologies of construction or on an obtuse symbolic vocabulary. This new orientation was evident in his conceptualization of the architecture of institutions as the embodiment of a "way of life," in his concentration on users' movements through and around his buildings and their surroundings, in his oblique references to Renaissance motifs that were believed to represent a kind of humanism, and in his heightened emphasis on the human hand in the process of construction. In the early 1950s, his theoretical statements on architecture were dominated by disembodied discussions of structure, technology, and techno-organicism. From now on he sought a softer, more refined, more human-centered aesthetic.

His picturesquely composed plan, his careful use of pedestrian materials, his jarring entry sequence, his unusually proportioned lightwells, his decision to open natural light only into the corners of the sanctuary, all made the design of the First Unitarian Church a radical departure from its initial historicizing

6.16 Detail of the sanctuary showing concrete blocks arranged according to shade, First Unitarian Church of Rochester, Rochester, New York, 1959–1962.

sources. Here Kahn's ideas on authenticity were simultaneously made more potent, and softened, with natural light, and with the innovative combination of brick, poured concrete, concrete block, and wood. Kahn's new approach to planning, which inflected rigid geometries to individuated needs, reinforced his emphasis on the user's phenomenological experience. This, in turn, reinforced the individuating agenda of authenticity.

Although the building in Rochester in many respects reflected Kahn's later aesthetic, its final Form did not embody his ideal of a "way of life" for a Unitarian Church. For budgetary reasons, Kahn was forced to excise central features of his initial scheme. Ambulatory, terracing, and garden were gone. There was no concentric hierarchy of spaces to allow various levels of communal participation. By virtue of its small size, it was unlikely that the church would become a symbolic anchor for any community larger than that of its own members.

Kahn believed that, in another way, the Unitarian Church as built still reflected the beliefs of his clients. Komendant related that Kahn delivered the sermon in Rochester to inaugurate the opening of the building in 1962, speaking of "the cathedrals, whose size and height was intended to show God's greatness and might and man's lowness, so that men would be frightened and obey His laws." For this small parish, Kahn "used atmosphere and beauty to create respect and understanding for God's aims, kindness, and forgiveness."[90] The raw sim-plicity of the sanctuary, combined with its intimate scale, generates a feeling of community in which no individual identity is disempowered or subsumed.

Emerging from Kahn's work on the Unitarian Church was a newly synthe-sized idiom in which his ideals for a monumentality that nurtured and synthe-sized community worked in tandem with his aesthetic of authenticity, which made each individual feel situated phenomenologically and aware that she existed only in a simple sequence of contingent moments. Creating an architec-ture that consolidated communal identity situated people socially by mooring them to the social body in which they lived their lives. Refining the respective languages he employed to further each of these two long-standing pursuits, Kahn brought them in alignment with each other. The First Unitarian Church heralded a new kind of modernism, a modernism oriented not around a sym-bolic or literal embrace of technology and mass production, but instead around the problem of locatedness, of place. To consummate these ideas, Kahn would have to travel halfway across the world to one of the poorest countries on earth. There he would build a corridor, and an ambulatory, and a terrace, and a gar-den, in the Muslim country of East Pakistan, later called Bangladesh.

7

SITUATING THE DEMOCRATIC
WAY OF LIFE

The National Assembly Building expresses the Majesty of the government of the
people working for the common good.
—Louis I. Kahn, "PAC Progress Booklet"

The National Assembly complex in Dhaka, Bangladesh, is not often
visited except by the most dedicated architectural enthusiasts. It remains
among the least understood of Louis Kahn's major projects (Plates 17 and 18).
Yet along with the Salk Institute in La Jolla, which was designed in the same
period, it constituted the first full realization of Kahn's mature architectural
vision. The National Assembly complex was conceived when Dhaka was the
capital city of East Pakistan. Many elements of its design—there were more than
10,000 drawings in all—were never built, and the complex was completed in
1983, nine years after he died. Still, even in what was executed, Kahn, having
the good fortune of creative freedom and an ample budget, succeeded in weav-
ing the various strands of his social and architectural agenda into a vital civic
monument that is perhaps the crowning achievement of his career.

Kahn received the commission for the National Assembly complex in late
1962—the commission from Jonas Salk came that same year—and he designed
it principally from 1963 to 1966, beginning just as the First Unitarian Church in
Rochester was nearing completion. The National Assembly complex, housing a
democratic parliament and associated functions, is the apotheosis of Kahn's
long search for a new kind of modernism that transforms monumentality into a
symbolic vehicle for the nurturing of a participatory community, and inter-
twines that monumentality with an authenticity that situates the self. The main
component of the Capitol Complex is a primitivizing, ten-story concrete and
marble prism that seems to reave straight from the earth and water, anchored at
two edges by the brick hostels stretching diagonally like arms across the vast,
flat site.[1] Kahn's ideas and intentions, embedded throughout these buildings,
can be best understood by tracing the design and construction process from the
client's conception for the project; to Kahn's reworking of that concept into
what he called the "Form"; to his first schemes for the National Assembly

Building, hostels, and the surrounding public gardens; to the design development of the site plan and of the National Assembly; to its final design and specifications for its construction. With each of these phases, another element of Kahn's situated modernism became apparent.

"BUILD A LADDER TO THE MOON AND HANG THE COST": AYUB KHAN, THE CLIENT

In August 1962, Kahn was asked whether he might like to design a new governmental complex in Dhaka, East Pakistan, an invitation he quickly accepted. A history of the inception of the commission and of how Kahn came upon it presaged the nature of his working relationship with his clients. Pakistan, a Muslim country, was created in 1947 by the partition of India. Its two sections, east and west, were divided by more than one thousand miles of India, and ethnic, social, and economic differences abounded between them. West Pakistanis spoke Urdu and were light-skinned, more Westernized, better educated, and richer. East Pakistanis spoke Bengali, were dark-skinned, and suffered from an unending round of natural catastrophes and from economic impoverishment. The seat of government was located in West Pakistan, first in Karachi (1947–1958), then in Rawalpindi (1958–1962), and finally in Islamabad. The multiple advantages of the western portion of the country combined with its geographic separation from the East meant that, politically, the less-privileged East Pakistanis were dramatically underrepresented, and their interests and needs were often ignored.[2] For these and other reasons, Pakistan suffered a series of political upheavals, and in a coup of 1958, the commander in chief of the army, Ayub Khan, took the reins of government, imposed martial law, and declared himself Supreme Commander.[3]

Ayub Khan pronounced himself committed to a political system that joined democracy with the Muslim faith. He began working on a constitution and instituted a number of land, educational, and health reforms.[4] Although he pushed through a new constitution in 1962, which established a 150-member National Assembly and a presidential term of five years, he retained the right to dissolve the parliament for any reason and, in practice, ran the country in collaboration with a small elite.[5]

In 1960, while martial law was still in place, Ayub Khan was "elected" to a five-year term. The new constitution of 1962 mandated that the first genuine democratic election be held in 1965. This sparked in Ayub Khan a concern for his own reelection, because he knew that winning the support of East Pakistanis would be essential to his political future. To convince East Pakistanis of his regard for their well-being, he determined that the National Assembly, which met twice a year, would convene not in Islamabad but in the former capital of East Bengal, Dhaka. This city had inherited a few governmental buildings from the days of British colonialism, but nothing outfitted with a large assembly chamber that could house parliamentary proceedings. Ayub Khan opted for the grand gesture of building a great governmental complex, hoping that if the East Pakistanis saw a lot of money spent on a monument to their importance, they would repay him with their votes. The commissioning of the Capitol Complex in Dhaka was, effectively, an election stunt.[6]

Initially, Khan's employees from the Pakistan Public Works Department (PWD) found a local architect for the job, a young, Yale-trained Bengali named Mazharul Islam, who had been working to establish a school of architecture in Dhaka.[7] Islam sketched a few designs before deciding that his experience and skills were not adequate to such a large task. He convinced officials at the PWD that Pakistan should hire a major Western practitioner instead, recommending three candidates: Le Corbusier, Alvar Aalto, and Kahn, the last of whom he knew from his studies at Yale. The PWD telegrammed each. Le Corbusier declined immediately. Aalto fell ill. Kahn got the commission partly by default.

As soon as Kahn was hired, the PWD in West Pakistan assumed responsibility for overseeing the design and construction of the complex. Appointed as the PWD's chief engineer for the project was Kafiluddin Ahmad, a Western-trained West Pakistani who quickly developed a reverential esteem for Kahn, despite the latter's disregard for schedules and deadlines. As work on the project progressed, Kahn, paradoxically, gained ever more control, for he was so slow to come up with a design that Ayub Khan grew desperate to get buildings out of the ground. Kahn should put up anything, as long as it went up. One of Kahn's employees telegrammed Philadelphia in late 1963 that Ayub Khan had demanded that Kafiluddin "start anything—build a shed."[8] The tenor of the client-architect relationship was perfectly characterized in a letter home from one of Kahn's savvier employees in 1964: "We've got a real political bull by the tail. . . . There is no union to fight with, only the PWD and right now they couldn't be happier if we told them to build a ladder to the moon and hang the cost. Kafiluddin told me confidentially that he will spend as much money as he must, disregarding the budget. He will justify it by having buildings to show."[9]

Kahn had a most unusual commission. His client cared little about the design and character of what he was buying—in Ayub Khan's lengthy, self-congratulatory autobiography, there is not a word about the building of the complex in Dhaka. Yet Kahn had access to a virtually unlimited flow of funding and worked with intermediaries whose respect for him was near total.[10] Such a constellation of circumstances allowed him the creative and economic freedom to design a complex equal to his ambitions.

DEMOCRACY AS A WAY OF LIFE: THE FORM

Kahn's philosophy of the "architecture of institutions," developed while designing the First Unitarian Church in Rochester, stipulated that the architect's first and highest duty was to develop an idealized vision of an institution's "way of life" and then to give that vision form—or, as he would have put it, Form. No institutions more occupied his thoughts and aspirations in these years than those housing democratic life, be they a city hall, a U.S. consulate, a civic center, or a parliament building. Kahn believed that underlying all such institutions was the common agenda of a government by and for the common citizens.

For years Kahn had yearned to build a governmental institution. His lobbying campaign in 1954 to earn the city hall annex contract in Philadelphia was only one such instance. In December 1959 Kahn managed to secure a governmental contract, commissioned by the U.S. State Department to design a consulate in Luanda, Angola.[11] But by 1962, the Luanda project ended unhappily, with Washington's bureaucrats unable to tolerate Kahn's dilatoriness or to comprehend his designs (which they insisted would produce a "cold and rather formidable" building "more appropriate to a mausoleum or a power substation than a modest office building or residence").[12] Although the State Department's official notification advised Kahn that political instability in Luanda had led to the project's cancellation, previous correspondence suggests that his slow working habits and intransigent responses to the design dictums of the Foreign Buildings Operations (FBO) might in any case have provoked his dismissal.[13]

The experience of working with the FBO in Washington must have compounded Kahn's ongoing frustration over his inability to secure work from the City of Philadelphia. In the early 1960s, in a letter he wrote soon after he was hired to design the complex in Dhaka, Kahn expressed palpable disappointment in being passed over for governmental commission after governmental commission, reflecting bitterly "on the fact that I have not as yet received a direct commission from the City of Philadelphia but have been asked to design the Second Capitol of Pakistan in Dacca. Someday I hope to build a building for Philadelphia and for the United States Government."[14] Even when hired, in 1960, merely to consult on the interior design of manned space capsules for travel to the moon, Kahn wrote that he felt "indeed honored" at having been called to serve his country.[15]

Kahn's political commitments underlay his yearning for a governmental commission: he believed in the virtue of democracy and of a vibrant public sphere. Although he and his colleagues, at Penn and in the architectural community at large, protested the depredations of untrammeled capitalism, they expressed little but patriotic pride in democracy. Lacing their rhetoric were the tensions of the Cold War: even Karl Linn, who was so critical of American consumerism, wrote in 1960 that "it is this very democracy and greater freedom that we yet enjoy [in contrast to the Soviet Union] which entitle and obligate the United States to world leadership."[16] Henry-Russell Hitchcock, in a memo on a radio show he was assembling for the Voice of America, revealed to Kahn a similarly consensual view of the American democratic system, writing that the point of the broadcast was to "stimulate among the intelligentsia behind the iron curtain an awareness of . . . patterns of thought . . . differing substantially from those to which they are currently restricted."[17]

But Kahn's fidelity to democracy and his ruminations on its nature were not merely an outgrowth of the Cold War. For nearly twenty-five years, he had been thinking about democracy's social and human constitution, about the way of life that democracy promoted and required for its sustenance. With his Jefferson National Expansion Memorial competition entry and his collaborations with Oscar Stonorov, Kahn advocated citizen participation in the public realm as essential to the health of a democracy. From the early 1950s, when he began to conceptualize a governmental function for City Tower, he began complaining that, in contemporary society, a city hall—the municipal equivalent of a parliament, after all—did little to foster citizen participation. Thinking perhaps of the granite pile that was the Philadelphia City Hall, Kahn protested that city halls generally had become "great quarries" where one went only when compelled to renew a driver's license or pay taxes. He exhorted architects to encourage "civic responsibility" with landmarks, which he took to calling "loyalties" because, he explained, they helped to "build patriotism," which he considered essential if citizens were to be active politically for the common good.[18] A typical lecture—this one in 1961 at the Cranbrook Academy in Bloomfield Hills, Michigan—began, "Our institutions should be given such spaces so that they will evoke a greater sense of dignity, greater sense of loyalty to . . . institutions which are really there as establishments of an inevitable responsibility to civic living."[19] City hall had "started with participation" but had lost its way; it should be a "place . . . where [the mayor] can invite the council instead of going to the Sheraton Hotel, where now the many organizations that make the backbone of our Democracy only report pitiful budgets in some out of the way place."[20]

For Kahn, the virtues of democracy were self-evident, although only deliberate action and constant struggle would construct the social and architectural building blocks of democratic virtue. In developing a "form-concept" for the National Assembly complex, Kahn acted on the modernist belief that the architect should be a social activist: the client's wishes were important only insofar as they concorded with the architect's ideal. Consciously overlooking Ayub Khan's authoritarian practices, of which he was well aware,[21] he instead took at face value his client's stated goal of creating a new democracy. (Ayub Khan told the U.S. Congress in 1961 that "our aim always was and always has been and always shall be to have representative institutions.")[22] Kahn's general approach to the Capitol Complex is apparent in a note that he wrote to himself in late 1963. "This is a new capitol in a new country. . . . [It] must be indicative of a new way of life."[23] The "way of life" that the Capitol Complex at Dhaka would "indicate" was that of a democracy.

In early 1963, Kahn traveled for the first time to Dhaka, where he was taken to see the expansive, flat site near a military airport outside the city. It contained little except a small agricultural school and a brick-making plant.[24] He was given a detailed program, which included offices and housing for assembly members, government ministers, and secretaries; single-family residences for the president, the speakers, and the secretary of the assembly; an assembly building; a mosque; and a prayer hall.[25] (By the final designs, the provisions for a separate mosque had been dropped, and only the prayer hall, which Kahn sometimes continued to call a mosque, was constructed.) The religious facilities were to be accessible from the parliament for daytime prayer, because most Pakistanis were Muslim. The provision for residences was extensive, because most of the members of the National Assembly would likely be coming from West Pakistan and would require accommodations during legislative session. At the same time that Kahn was given the principal program, he was also asked to develop a master plan for the entire site, envisioned to be between 800 and 1,000 acres, where the government eventually expected to build, for itself, a Supreme Court, offices, and additional residences, and for the public, markets, schools, a hospital, a library, a museum, and recreational areas.[26]

Following his principle that "the program is nothing," that it was the duty of the architect to interpret the client's perceived needs to conform with a higher ideal, Kahn immediately rearranged the priorities given him by the PWD. He sought to create an institution that evoked a "sense of loyalty," a sense of the "inevitable responsibility" of "civic living," wanting above all—as he had with such American institutions as the neighborhood community center, the city hall, the public park (as in the Jefferson National Expansion Memorial), and the local church—to encourage free individuals to participate actively in self-governance.

Kahn believed that the judicial branch of government, the safeguard of the rule of law before which all people are equal, was too important to a genuine democracy to be consigned to a few scratchy lines on a master plan. The PWD had designated the Supreme Court as part of a later building campaign, but Kahn, in his first site plan, transposed the Supreme Court from future projection to immediate need, drawing a unified composition for the parliament, mosque, Supreme Court, and the group residences, and arguing that these elements, "in their interplay psychologically," expressed "the nature of a government institution" (Fig. 7.1).[27] As part of his democratic reshuffling act, Kahn marginalized the individual residences for the president and speakers to the outer edge of the assembly site. In subsequent plans, he more or less ignored them (Fig. 7.2). The organization and plan of the complex at Dhaka expressed Kahn's political ideology no less than Le Corbusier's capitol complex at Chandigarh

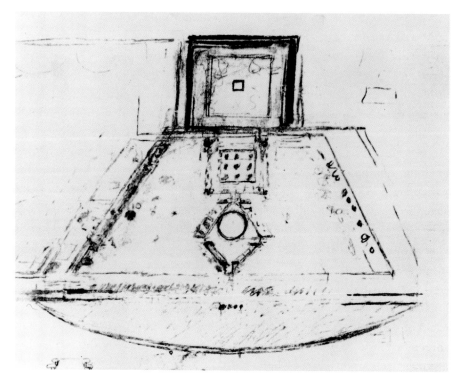

7.1 An early site plan of the National Assembly complex, with the National Assembly Building at the bottom center, the mosque (later called the prayer hall) in the center, the Supreme Court at the top, and hostels to each side, 1963. From *North Carolina State Student Publication of the School of Design* 14 (May 1964).

instantiated his. Le Corbusier, demonstrably supportive of authoritarian power,[28] placed the Governor's Palace at the apex of his design (Fig. 7.3). Kahn, the democrat, relegated the presidential residence to the margins and created the complex's focal point around the governmental branches representing the people and their laws.

Kahn presented this early site plan with mystical incantations: "On the night of the third day," he recalled in a lecture in 1966, "I fell out of bed with the idea which is still the prevailing idea of the plan. This came simply from the realization that assembly is of a transcendent nature. Men came to assemble not for personal gain, but to touch the spirit of commonness."[29] Yet under the wafting aura of transcendentalism was his hard-headed faith in this democratic, participatory institution: assembly was "of a transcendent nature" not because it contained a religious dimension but because it expressed people's higher moral instincts, in which self-interest was sacrificed to what he called "commonness." With this statement, Kahn also specifically justified the inclusion of a mosque in the Capitol Complex—perhaps difficult for one who had been schooled in the belief that a democracy entailed a separation of church and state.

In a democracy, each individual had a voice: "No matter what kind of a rogue you are," Kahn explained to students at Berkeley when presenting his design for the complex, "when you enter the assembly, your vote is a considered one."[30] In conceptualizing the institution as one into which any person can bring her concerns, Kahn simultaneously expanded on, and politicized, the vision that he had developed while working with the Unitarians in Rochester, which held communal participation to be a delicate balancing of individual expression and cooperation with a group. In Kahn's ideal society, free individuals would freely engage in a flourishing public realm.

For the plan of the National Assembly Building and the site plan of the complex, Kahn transposed not only his institutional vision but also his architectural ideas from his early scheme for the Unitarian Church in Rochester. Again he called for a central meeting space surrounded first by an ambulatory and then by blocks of smaller rooms. His early sketches of the complex placed a parliament and mosque on a plinth at the center of the enormous site: he insisted to the client that "this is a reservation . . . of important buildings in their garden" and "should clearly distance itself from the city" (Fig. 7.4).[31] Whereas the first scheme for the church at Rochester elongated the entry sequence by placing the sanctuary at the far end of the site, surrounded by a dry "moat" to be transversed by a bridge, Kahn envisioned an actual lake around the National Assembly Building, bound diagonally on east and west by two banks of hostels. On the south, the assembly would touch a road; south of the road would be a second, crescent-shaped lake. North of the assembly was first the mosque, then the Supreme Court. By placing the complex at the center of the huge site (instead, for example, on the edge that most closely abutted the city of Dhaka), and by locating the main building in the middle of a system of lakes, Kahn forged a separate precinct characterized by concentric circles of space surrounding the central parliament building.[32] Calling the resulting complex his "citadel of assembly," he later sought to reinforce the fortified impression with a low pyramidal wall, never executed, that would have surrounded the entire complex at its perimeter.

Describing his concept for the National Assembly complex, Kahn reiterated the objectives that had shaped his initial scheme for the Unitarian Church. A user standing outside the perimeter wall had to decide whether or not to enter the complex. Once inside, she had to again choose her level of participation in a prolonged entry sequence that placed roads, gardens, plazas, a moat, and an ambulatory between city and assembly chamber. In a brochure written in 1965, Kahn emphasized that local citizens could enjoy the grounds alone, employing language that recalled his "wall, garden, arcade, ambulatory, sanctuary" concept for a university chapel, which had informed his plan for the Unitarian Church in Rochester. "As the visitor approaches along the southern boundary of the site," Kahn wrote, "he will have a continuous view of the dominant Assembly Building. . . . [At the entrance] he will see active fountains, garden paths, and elaborate plantings of shrubs and flowers forming alcoves and recesses with garden benches where he may rest and relax."[33] Kahn prolonged the entrance into the

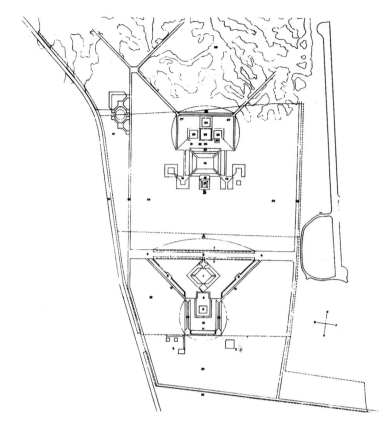

7.2 The second site plan of the National Assembly complex, showing the Citadel of Assembly at the bottom, with the mosque at the south tip of the diamond-shaped National Assembly Building, and the Citadel of Institutions at the top, and residences in upper left, May 1963. From *North Carolina State Student Publication of the School of Design* 14 (May 1964).

building still further with the plinth that nearly surrounds the National Assembly Building, dictating that a user's entrance into the building would be "a gradual approach by means of a long, gradual ramp" (Fig. 7.5).[34]

He extended his conception of concentric rings of space into his early designs for the National Assembly Building itself, a central feature of which was office blocks surrounding a monumental ambulatory that encircled the space of assembly (Fig. 7.6). By employing this conception and by rearranging the elements of the program so that the parliament, mosque, and Supreme Court assembled as the focal point of the design, with the private residences for potentates underplayed, Kahn's early site plans for the National Assembly complex elaborated on, and politicized, the ideal for democratic participation that Kahn had conceived while working on the First Unitarian Church. To get into the assembly chamber, a person would have to penetrate the pyramidal wall, pass through the gardens, ascend the ramp, transverse the South Plaza, enter the office blocks, and process through the ambulatory. As in the early plans for the First Unitarian Church, she would repeatedly be presented with the option to choose her level of engagement with others. Through both site plan and early

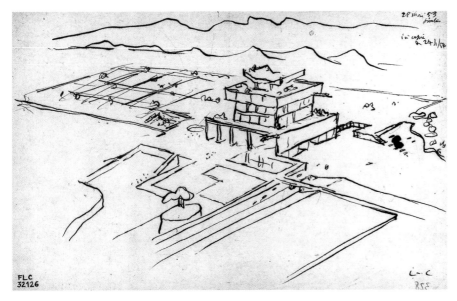

7.3 Le Corbusier, project for Governor's Palace, Chandigarh, India, 1953. From the Fondation Le
Corbusier/© 2000 Artists Rights Society (ARS), New York/ADAGP, Paris/FLC.

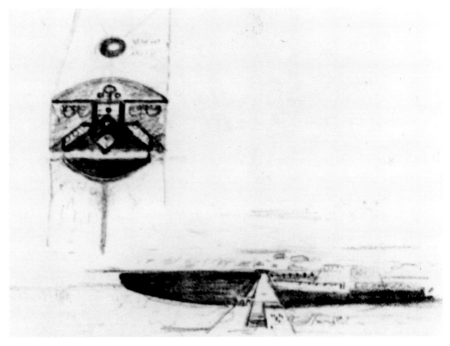

7.4 An early site plan of the Capitol Complex (top) and a perspective of the National Assembly Building
(bottom) with lakes, 1963. From *North Carolina State Student Publication of the School of Design* 14 (May
1964).

7.5 Plinth of the south plaza with the "hollow columns" of the prayer hall at center, Sher-e-Bangla Nagar, Dhaka, Bangladesh, 1962–1983.

National Assembly Building plans, Kahn wanted to nurture each person's freedom while prodding her to join in the chorus of communal enterprise.

EARLY IDEAS FOR THE NATIONAL ASSEMBLY BUILDING: A MONUMENTAL "PEOPLE MARK"

In these early site plans for the National Assembly complex, Kahn transposed ideas he had developed for the Unitarian Church in Rochester into the realm of a political institution. As he worked out the "form-concept" for the parliament building, he unabashedly sought to create a landmark, which, he later asserted, would better be called "social marks, man-marks, people marks, [or] life marks."[35] Such monuments, by virtue of their permanence, their visibility, and their "imageability," would nearly obligate people to view them as material symbols of the political institutions housed within and the societies they served.

To address the needs of Pakistan's eastern capitol, Kahn happily took up a scale on which he had never seriously worked: a site in the hundreds of acres, buildings in the hundreds of thousands of square feet. The prospect of constructing a major governmental complex on such a large site returned him to his interest in monumentality, which had preoccupied him on and off since he had written his essay of 1944.[36] During his design of the Civic Center scheme in 1956–1957, Kahn's thoughts had begun to turn to monumentality once again; he justified the vast scale of his projected buildings by contending that only with enormous projects could architects command city dwellers' attention and reinforce their affiliations to the public realm. He joked to his old friend Isadore

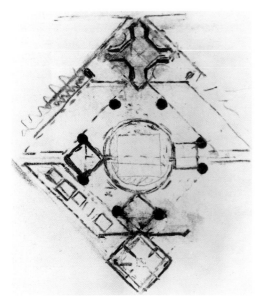

Buten in 1958 that "I have much to talk about even excluding Monumentality," indicating that this was a topic in which Buten believed Kahn was engaged to excess. His renewed preoccupation with monumentality could only have been sparked by discussions in the architectural community, which continued to treat monumentality as a problem yet unsolved. At a conference in which Kahn participated in 1960, Paul Rudolph, José Luis Sert, and Ulrich Franzen shared the view that, as Rudolph put it, "civic architecture is the glaring lack of the twentieth century" and that this lack quashed people's desire to participate in the public realm.[37] In 1961, Kahn wryly wrote to Buten that he planned to deliver a lecture on "an entirely new subject, Monumentality," promising that it would be different from his essay of 1944.[38]

From the moment he took up the commission in Dhaka, monumentality was on Kahn's mind. He insisted that all the important institutions be grouped together, as they were in his Philadelphia Civic Center scheme, placing them in his "citadel of assembly" while relegating the commercial, recreational, and other functions into a separate, distant "citadel of the institutions" (Fig. 7.7). Kahn sequestered the governmental buildings to make them extraordinary, different from the places where the pedestrian activities of everyday life are housed. He believed that anyone who crossed into the special arena of his Capitol Complex, whether government official or common voter, would be transported from the self-interested, small-minded preoccupations of daily life — not to mention the filth and squalor of downtown Dhaka (Fig. 7.8) — to be reminded of her elevated status as a citizen of a polity (Plate 19). Kahn's separation of the National Assembly complex from the city of Dhaka could be interpreted to suggest that he believed government should proceed in haughty sequestration from the people it is elected to represent, but his many statements on the democratic

7.7 Site plan showing the vast distance between the Citadel of Assembly (at bottom, with the diamond of the National Assembly Building at the lower end) and the Citadel of Institutions (top), 1964. From *North Carolina State Student Publication of the School of Design* 14 (May 1964).

nature of his conception indicate that he had no such intention. Nor is the complex perceived that way today: contemporary Bangladeshis regard the complex as a peaceful, majestic place where they can escape the stresses of urban life.

When Kahn turned from the master plan to the design of the National Assembly complex proper, he sought to reinforce the monumentality he had imbued into the site plan by calling on the design techniques of monuments past. Initial sketches for the complex show two grand, Versailles-like axes sweeping toward the climactic capitol, separated from the city and reflected in shallow pools (see Fig. 7.4). As the design proceeded, his ambitions grew ever vaster. He complained to the PWD that he could not finalize the plan with only two hundred acres on which to place the National Assembly Building: "Location (of Assembly Building) not settled because of limited acreage. Doing site studies of 200, 400, 600, 1000 acres. Buildings must be like a good position on a chess board. For its symbolic value no building must be in the wrong place. If I had 1000 acres now I could proceed without delay."[39]

His first perspectives for the National Assembly Building, mosque, and Supreme Court proposed a scale so huge that users appeared as barely more than staccato dots at the bases of the projected buildings (Fig. 7.9). Kahn later

conceded that these visions were more than a little grand: "In the beginning," he joked when lecturing on the project, the National Assembly "was as big as the Hagia Sophia. That was a little bit too much, I think, so we brought it down to something more reasonable."[40] In the end, Kahn's reference point for the scale and the sphere-based interior of the assembly chamber was the Pantheon in Rome, which he often lauded in these years because its interiorized centrality created what he called a "world within a world."[41] With monumental scale and allusions to such august structures, Kahn wished not to overwhelm the user but to ennoble her: often in these years, he praised the psychological effect that extremely large-scale buildings had on a viewer. "If you look at the Baths of Caracalla . . . we all know that we can bathe just as well under an 8-foot ceiling as we can under a 150-foot ceiling." "But," he insisted, "I believe there's something about a 150-foot ceiling that makes a man a different kind of man."[42] If the Capitol Complex at Dhaka were to communicate the nobility of people's aspirations to work with each other—as Kahn put it, "the Majesty of the government of the people working for the common good"[43]—then one of the techniques Kahn had at his disposal, given his own ambitions and the generous and ever-expanding budget, was grandeur.

SITE PLAN DESIGN DEVELOPMENT: CHALLENGING REALITIES, WELCOMING CITIZENS

As Kahn turned from conceptualization of the National Assembly complex to design development, he faced a risk. He wanted nothing more than to attract people to the grounds of the complex and welcome them to the parliament. But his scheme of concentric circles surrounding the National Assembly Building, combined with the imposing scale and monumentality of the building itself, might repel people rather than invite them in. This risk was exacerbated by the client's non-negotiable security provision that access to the assembly building be limited and highly controlled. Not all who voted were welcome inside. Certainly, this was unpropitious for an architect who wished most of all to create an

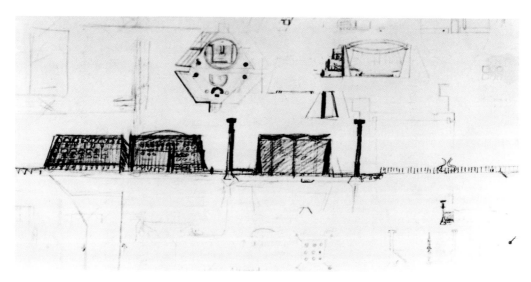

7.9 An early sketch with the National Assembly Building, the mosque (later the prayer hall), and the Supreme Court as three separate, extremely large buildings (the dot between the minaret and the center building indicates a person), 1963. From *North Carolina State Student Publications of the School of Design* 14 (May 1964).

architecture for democracy. Working out the site plan and the design for the National Assembly, Kahn used various programmatic and architectural means to ameliorate the exclusive aura that the complex, in clumsier hands, might have projected, in order to welcome citizens into the complex and psychologically connect them to the building and the institution it housed.

From his earliest site plans, Kahn revealed his hope of enticing even the most retiring of people into his public realm. In his second site plan, which he presented to the client in May 1963, Kahn flipped the orientation of the assembly chamber and lakes, and incorporated the mosque into the body of the building (see Fig. 7.2).[44] He had revised the mosque to make it smaller than the assembly because the PWD felt that such a large religious structure located in a new governmental complex would convey the inaccurate impression that the Pakistani government was dominated by religious fundamentalists.[45] More significantly, he placed the crescent lake at the northern end of the citadel of assembly, away from the city, and the mosque facing Dhaka at the south. Although Carles Vallonrat, Kahn's chief design assistant for the project, maintained that the orientation shifted "because at a certain point it just began to look upside down," other considerations likely played a greater part.[46] The crescent lake, if positioned at the south, would have prevented a direct path linking the National Assembly entrance to Dhaka city, thus isolating the complex too much. Although Kafiluddin instructed Kahn to make the mosque accessible only to those who had business in the National Assembly, Kahn wanted this entrance visible: "Position the entrance of mosque," he directed in a handwritten reminder to himself, "so 'nothing can stand in the way of me (or "one") going there.'"[47] In the end, Kafiluddin and the PWD prevailed, and the entrance of the prayer hall is one flight above the plaza, accessible only from the interior of the building.

As he fleshed out the site plan, Kahn specified two massive plazas to be located at the north and south entrances of the National Assembly Building (Fig. 7.10). Named the South Plaza and the Presidential Square, together they total more than 800,000 square feet of unprogrammed, unrequested, and—in functional terms—unnecessary public space, all abutting the limited-access National Assembly Building. The South Plaza is said to be still the largest paved area in Bangladesh; Kahn envisioned it not only as an axis leading to the National Assembly Building but also, in itself, as a place of gathering.

For the Presidential Square, he designed a massive, one-story plinth in which the roof functions as an amphitheater during outdoor ceremonies. Supporting this plinth are monumental brick arches that create a low, cool, shadowed space dominated by irregular, rhythmic vistas (Fig. 7.11). This is among the most photographed images of the National Assembly Building, equal in sculpted forcefulness to some of the spaces inside. For Kahn it was a place where citizens

7.10 Site plan of the National Assembly Building with relative sizes of the footprint of the south plaza (bottom), the National Assembly Building (center), and the Presidential Plaza (top). From the Public Works Department, Dhaka, Bangladesh.

could always congregate. Adding yet more components to his client's program, he contended that this area "could be used very well as a museum of independence" or "for marshaling ceremonial parades." Most important, he insisted, it should always have "uses which would welcome the general public."[48]

Through his management of the site plan, then, and through his devoted attention to the North and South Plazas, Kahn surrounded the impressively monumental National Assembly Building with open areas that specifically welcomed the nation's people. With such techniques he approached his ideal of an urban complex that ennobled the individual user while making her feel situated in—indeed, responsible for—a larger public realm.

NATIONAL ASSEMBLY BUILDING DESIGN DEVELOPMENT: SITUATING CITIZENS IN LOCAL CULTURE

Kahn's vision for the National Assembly complex, of free individuals freely choosing to participate in the governance of the public realm, and his accompanying "form-concept" of a Western-derived, central plan for parliament, might suggest that he was imposing on an unsuspecting culture a political ideal and a formal structure that was tailored, if not to uniquely American circumstances, then at least to ones foreign to Pakistan. That Kahn employed these conceptions as his datum for the National Assembly Building design indeed reveals a Eurocentric attitude. However, in contrast to the Western sources of these initial ideas, Kahn, as he advanced the design toward his boldest form-giving gestures, exquisitely oriented the siting and the composition of the National Assembly Building and hostels to the place and culture they would serve, sculpting and molding his complex to the climate, and especially to the architectural traditions, of the Indian subcontinent. In doing so, he built in a language that was locally comprehensible while remaining modern, laying the ground for citizens to appropriate the complex as an instantiation of their own highest ideals.[49]

From the time of his Civic Center plan for Philadelphia, and in his subsequently drawn, later versions of the Trenton Jewish Community Center, Kahn alluded to historic precedents in his architecture, both because past monuments offered models for a new monumentality and because such allusions potentially strengthened the ties that bound people into a community by reminding them of their common heritage. In his executed buildings, unlike in some of his conceptual sketches, such allusions were extremely abstract, so much so that they would often barely be discerned. This abstraction occurred because, as he developed a design, Kahn integrated specific images into a compositional system that had its own independent, strong identity. Such was the case with the Salk Institute, in which early site plans resemble Hadrian's Villa, whereas final plans do not. In the National Assembly Building design, Kahn also looked to and abstracted from historical precedents. Because his audience and users were from the Indian subcontinent, he primarily turned to traditions

7.11 Arches under Presidential Square, Sher-e-Bangla Nagar, Dhaka, Bangladesh, 1962–1983.

indigenous to the region, looking specifically to monumental Moghul architecture and the Bengali vernacular. When he did draw on the Western tradition, he devised motifs common to East and West.

Kahn had traveled to India before he received the Dhaka commission, in the summer of 1962, in conjunction with an incipient commission for the Indian Institute of Management in Ahmedabad (1962–1974), in western India.[50] Subsequently, Kahn's sojourns to the subcontinent were frequent, as he assembled commissions for the National Assembly complex in Dhaka, the president's complex in Islamabad, West Pakistan, which was never built (1963–1966), and the Family Planning Services in the northern city of Kathmandu, Nepal, which was partially completed (1970–1975). On some of these trips he traveled extensively. He developed friendships with many Indian architects, most prominent among them Balkrishna Doshi and Mazharul Islam, who recommended Kahn for the Ahmedabad and the Dhaka commissions, respectively. Doshi and Islam introduced Kahn to the architectural heritage of the Indian subcontinent, as well as to a spirituality that was commonplace among intellectuals in India but rare in the American circles in which Kahn had been moving.[51] The cumulative impact of these visits on him was enormous; not only did Kahn's architecture change, but so also did his manner of locution. Increasingly he spoke in the anagogic language for which he remains well known.

Kahn's visits included tours of the architectural monuments of Pakistan and northern India, especially its Moghul palaces, forts, and mausolea. On his first trip to East Pakistan, he visited Moghul monuments in Lahore, where he was much impressed by their siting. He wrote to his wife in Philadelphia, "From Karachi we went to Lahore to see the gardens of the Moghul kings and the architecture of the mosques Palaces Forts Tombs and religious schools. All of it is just superb. Though I shall never get taken by the elemental parts and details the overall effect of the buildings in their courts is strong and forever good."[52] With Vallonrat, he also traveled in India to see the great Moghul complexes in Jaipur, New Delhi, Agra, and Fatehpur Sikri.[53]

When Kahn arrived in Dhaka, he visited its small Moghul palace complex (Fig. 7.12),[54] and he was extensively briefed on local construction techniques and on the sea-level country's hot, wet, unforgiving weather, which included a monsoon season that sometimes lasted up to six months. Wondering how the buildings in Dhaka might "take their place on the land,"[55] Kahn considered the Bengali weather and the Islamic, Moghul mausoleum-gardens that were part of both the Dhaka and the West Pakistani architectural and religious tradition. His initial idea for the overall composition of the National Assembly Building and hostels already echoed Moghul complexes. At the Taj Mahal in Agra, as at the Capitol Complex in Dhaka, a flat precinct is bound by high, red sandstone arcades, with the white principal building, set centrally atop an immense platform, reflected in a pool of water (Figs. 7.13, 7.14, and 7.15). Initially, the PWD objected to the lakes with which Kahn surrounded the National Assembly Building, because, for Bengalis, water unhappily connoted flood and devastation.[56] Kahn argued that the lakes surrounding his National Assembly Building, which recalled French baroque gardens as well as Moghul mausoleums, were not only historically but also climatologically appropriate, as they formed part of the drainage system: "I've chosen to distinguish [the National Assembly Building] from its surroundings by the introduction of a lake. Because it's a delta country, and all important buildings were on mounds. That's the way to protect yourself from flood."[57] Evidently this was not convincing to the client, and in 1964 an employee wrote to the Philadelphia office from Dhaka, "Lou justified the lakes to the [PWD] committee. In the end he said he had the lakes because he wanted them. They were satisfied. But Lou isn't. We need our experts to help us justify lakes."[58] Surely, Kahn wanted pools for their reflective properties, for their moat-like, distancing effects, and for their resonance with the Moghul tradition (Plate 20).

In the early elevations of the National Assembly, Kahn reiterated the motifs of the First Unitarian Church: a blank, uncapped "colonnade" that parted into banks of shadowed windows within (Fig. 7.16), and lightwells projecting above the roof to illuminate a centralized assembly chamber. By mid-1964, this composition disappeared. Kahn dropped the tall lightwells because Kafiluddin and his associates had objected that "The air vents [sic] at the top of the National Assembly building should be connected with each other. . . . if left as they are [they] will give an appearance of chimney stacks sticking out of the building."[59]

7.12 Photo in Kahn's files of the Moghul mausoleum complex in Dhaka. From the Kahn Collection.

The PWD repeatedly proposed that all the lightwells be knit together to suggest a dome, thereby making the building more "Islamic," but Kahn, wishing to avoid overt historical references in his designs, never complied with their request.[60]

He did, however, find ways to allude to the Islamic tradition in a more abstracted manner. As he brought down the height of the lightwells, he also dropped the Rochester-like elevation in favor of a two-walled system that he had invented for the American consulate project at Luanda, a climate also dominated by bright sunlight and tropical rains. For the National Assembly Building, Kahn specified a glass elevation of windowed offices pulled behind a concrete wall carved with great geometric cutouts (Fig. 7.17). He placed courtyards in between. This dual-walled system was a direct response to the thin perforated screens employed in these same years by Rudolph at the Jewett Arts Center in Wellesley and Edward Durrell Stone at the American Embassy in New Delhi; Kahn asserted that his system better shielded peripheral apertures from glare by avoiding the "little pinpoints of glare" of his competitors' designs.[61] Whereas this assertion is contestable, given that the facade's large cutouts permit the sharp Bengali sun to fall in some offices for at least part of the day, the double-walled system did have the same aesthetic advantage as Le Corbusier's *brise soleil*, of releasing the design of the facade from the scale and proportions of individual windows. Kahn pushed his double-walled system to its best advantage as he finalized the design, increasing the gravitas of the facade by editing out the multiple circles that would have made the composition too busy.

In the final design, a rectangular perforation is topped by one in the shape of an elongated triangle (which, in turn, is adjacent to a small circle [Fig. 7.18]).

7.13 View of the National Assembly Building in relation to the hostels, Sher-e-Bangla Nagar, Dhaka, Bangladesh, 1962–1983.

7.14 View of the Taj Mahal in relation to the surrounding cloisters, Agra, Delhi.

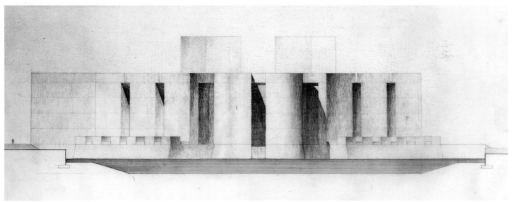

Not only does this two-tiered design create a much-needed vertical emphasis in what had become, by virtue of its mass and its marble banding, an overwhelmingly horizontal building; it also alludes to the double-arched porches of Islamic precedents (Fig. 7.19), reinforcing the connection of the National Assembly Building to the architectural tradition of the people whom it serves. Kahn carried his subtle referencing to the Moghul tradition into even the details: the marble banding of the facade, for example, recalls both his beloved Baptistery in Pisa and the marble inlay on Moghul monuments.[62] Sometimes these allusions are nearly invisible: in the underground and ill-used library, for example, Kahn concentrically arranged the beams supporting the floor of the assembly chamber so that they converge on a single column, an oblique reference to the Diwan-i-kahs at Fatehpur Sikri.

In the design of the hostels, Kahn embraced a different indigenous tradition, that of vernacular building in east Bengal. The PWD stipulated that, for economic reasons, these residences should be brick,[63] a decision that was apparently

7.17 Double-walled facade of the National Assembly Building, Sher-e-Bangla Nagar, Dhaka, Bangladesh, 1962–1983.

agreeable to Kahn, who likely never seriously considered using anything else. Brick was, and remains, the predominant local building material in Bengal—as one local architect joked, in Bangladesh, "all we have is mud." Kahn had used brick before, most prominently in the Yale Art Gallery and the Richards Medical Center; in Dhaka, he shaped the hostels into a dramatic, human-scaled frame for the National Assembly, repeating the arched motifs, double-tiered facades, and two-walled system to create wide, shaded porches and passageways cooled by prevailing winds. Testimony to his extraordinary success in synthesizing the local cultural tradition and modernism, it is on the foundation of these buildings that a modern Bengali architectural idiom has been built.

The kind of regional inflection that Kahn practiced in the National Assembly furthered his aim of finding an architectural idiom that respected, or underscored, the specificity of place. Kahn had initially developed this goal in the 1950s in reaction to the homogenizing explosion of suburbia in the United States. In the early 1960s, Kahn, like other architects, became increasingly sensitive to regional difference as ever more Westerners were hired in developing countries for important public commissions. This was occasioned by three phenomena: decolonialization, economic prosperity in the West, and attempts by the United States to extend its influence in the face of real and perceived threats posed by the imperial ambitions of the Soviet Union. Kahn's work in the subcontinent is one example of the many Western architects practicing in these years in countries profoundly different from home: other such projects include,

7.18 Stacked apertures of the National Assembly Building office blocks, Sher-e-Bangla Nagar, Dhaka, Bangladesh, 1962–1983.

7.19 The Taj Mahal, Agra, Delhi, with stacked porches similar to the stacked apertures of office blocks of the National Assembly Building in Dhaka.

for Baghdad, Frank Lloyd Wright's plans for a cultural center complex, Walter Gropius' schemes for Baghdad University, and Aalto's National Art Gallery (all of 1957–1958); for Islamabad, projects by Stone (1966–1969), Constantin Doxiadis (1959–1963), and Kahn (1963–1966); Le Corbusier's Chandigarh (1950–1965); and ATBAT-Afrique's housing projects in Casablanca, Morocco (1953).

By the mid-1950s, Kahn and many of his colleagues questioned the desirability, and even the possibility, of the "internationalism" that had been a certitude of one dominant strain of the modern movement. Sigfried Giedion recognized the seriousness of this challenge to early modernism: "Forget the International Style," he intoned in 1954: "Western man has now, very slowly, become aware of the harm he has inflicted by his interference [with] . . . other civilizations." In the next decade, Giedion correctly predicted, a new approach would dawn, one that was dominated by "a new hybrid development," which he thought would be "a cross between Western and Eastern."[64]

Kahn, the architect–social engineer, set out to construct a political and symbolic capitol that actualized political values he held to be universal. He eventually did so in a manner that transcended the Eurocentrism of his initial impulses. He developed an idiom that was a genuine "cross between Western and Eastern" in an attempt to make Bengalis aware and proud of their local traditions, encouraging them to adopt the National Assembly Building as a national monument that situated citizens in a polity. Testimony and tribute to his success, the building remains the principal icon of Bengali identity, even though the regime that built the National Assembly has been overthrown, replaced by a new democratic regime of a new country, Bangladesh (Fig. 7.20).

NATIONAL ASSEMBLY BUILDING FINAL DESIGN AND CONSTRUCTION: AUTHENTICITY AND SITUATING THE SELF

Kahn's refusal to defer to his client's request for Islamic imagery, such as a dome, suggests the complexity underlying his use of historically specific imagery in the National Assembly Building design. In making reference to indigenous motifs, Kahn was not aiming at a legibly "contextual" style in the manner of a historicist postmodernist. Doing so would have been antithetical both to his modernist sensibilities, which dictated against ornament and explicit historical reference, and to his pursuit of authenticity, which demanded the eschewal of all forms of rhetoric in the attempt to create objects instantiated with intrinsic meaning and presence. As he had in such previous projects as the Adath Jeshurun synagogue, the Trenton Jewish Community Center, and the First Unitarian Church, in the National Assembly Building Kahn wedded representation to abstraction in a tense, oscillating relationship. He took recourse in comprehensible symbolic imagery—in this case, in motifs drawn from local high and vernacular traditions—in order to create an architecture that a people would appropriate as its own and, in so doing, would be reminded of the traditions its members shared as a commu-

7.20 Rickshaw with a painting of the National Assembly Building.

nity. Having laid the foundation for viewer appropriation of his work, however, Kahn then sought to unsettle each person's unthinking familiarity by reshaping the legible images he adopted into an unfamiliar idiom.

Throughout the 1950s, Kahn had been devising a number of compositional and design techniques that he hoped would force the viewer into an epiphanic awareness of the present, with no illusory recourse to some non-existent higher ideal, in the hope that this would emphasize one's responsibility to live one's life deliberately.[65] He employed simple, imageable forms and tended toward the slightly awkward over the serenely balanced composition, seeking to jolt the viewer into focused awareness. He constructed in masonry, and flaunted his building's weight with uninterrupted passages of walls that invoked a primitivizing heaviness, which he reinforced with enclosed, "constructed rooms" that emanated from the literal structure of the building. The honesty with which Kahn expressed the building's primary materials — no plaster, no veneers — extended into his handling of the principal internal volumes, which he articulated in elevation. In detailing, he made a virtual fetish of expressing the intrinsic properties of his materials and the process by which they had been put together. All these techniques stressed that the building was an object constructed with the human hand and by the human mind, grappling with the stuff of the immediate world.

When Kahn was initially developing his ideas about authenticity while teaching at Yale in the early 1950s, he began to value a quality in design that he called archaic. Later in the decade and in the early 1960s his interest in things primitive flourished, as it was reinforced by such architects and writers as Giedion, James Stirling, Sybil Moholy-Nagy, and Bernard Rudofsky, who, in response to architects' increased exposure to the cultures of developing countries, called for a heightened sensitivity to what Giedion nostalgically called the "natural rhythms of the lives" and the cultural artifacts of "primitive peoples."[66] By the early 1960s, Kahn was insistent in his preference for the primitive over the polished, the authentic over the acculturated: he declared the temples at Paestum, with their "dumpy" proportions and crude details, more beautiful than the stately, elegant Parthenon; he preferred the stiff Kourous to a lithe Kritios.[67] As the International Style became ever more equated with corporate America, Kahn's preoccupation with authenticity became more pronounced: "Here the modern movement is only thirty years old, and we are already polishing and perfecting it," he complained in 1960. Clearly expressing both his affiliation with modernism and his commitment to rethinking it, he continued: "We should be in an archaic phase. Our building should reflect this crudeness."[68]

Kahn brought his aesthetic of authenticity to a climax in the National Assembly Building: by dint of its blunt, individuated presence, the building forces the viewer to reflect on the nature of the institution she faces, and on her role and place within it. An octagonal building of simple geometries and repeating forms, the National Assembly Building is unlike other civic monuments: it is some giant child's set of building blocks, uniquely composed. Massive walls of striated concrete are punctured by monumental, multistoried, non-glazed openings. The emptiness of these apertures exaggerates the heaviness of the facades, making the National Assembly Building seem a hollow, vacant building ready to be appropriated by anyone who approaches it. Both because of its physical size and because of the facade's elementary composition, the National Assembly Building seems to have always occupied this site, primordial and permanent, like the pyramids at Giza or the Pantheon in Rome.

The building's compacted, formal unity is animated by a variety in geometric and volumetric expression that articulates different functions within: the repetitive office blocks bear the triangle-atop-rectangle-next-to-circle motif; to the north are the parted sheer walls of the Presidential Square; to the south, the curving blank towers of the prayer hall; to the east, a spliced oval for the members' lounge; to the west, a cafeteria marked by a great shaded circle cut with concrete swaths. Visibly rising in the center, above all, is a low ring of projecting light shafts that illuminate the assembly chamber, perforated with circles alluding to the centralized configuration of the space below.

This external mapping of internal volumes suggests the presence of a shaper with an almost moralistic attitude to design. Such an approach is completely at odds with Robert Venturi's slightly later, wryly ironic concept of a "decorated shed"; instead it recalls the attitudes of early modernist or of some high Victorian Gothic architects. The National Assembly, in its presentation of multifarious geometric configurations within the tightly bound, centralized whole, holds in dynamic tension the dialectic between rigidity and expressiveness that animates all of Kahn's most successful work.

The insistent honesty with which he approached the overall composition is borne out also in his handling of materials. Inside and outside the building, Kahn, as he had done in all his buildings from the Yale Art Gallery onward, took care to record with what, and by what means, the National Assembly Building was made. Settling on poured, reinforced concrete early in the design, he calculated that construction workers—usually women carrying baskets of wet concrete on their heads—could pour no more than five feet a day. The joint separating one day's pour from the next is recessed, then faced with an inlaid white marble band (Fig. 7.21). The resulting striations, in addition to recalling the inlaid marble ornamentation of Moghul monuments, are the trace marks of the process by which people constructed this enormous building.

Touch is a more primitive sensation than sight, and Kahn took care to appeal to the real or imagined sensations of the hand in his treatment of texture in the National Assembly Building. One is encouraged to think not only about how these surfaces look, but also about how they feel. The banding that marks human scale and the process by which the building was constructed also imparts the impression of the weight of his (already heavy) materials (Fig 7.22).

7.21 Detail of the National Assembly Building facade with alternating flat and raised marble bands at five-foot intervals, Sher-e-Bangla Nagar, Dhaka, Bangladesh, 1962–1983.

7.22 Elevation sketch of the National Assembly Building with marble banding drawn in relation to human figures. From *North Carolina State Student Publication of the School of Design* 14 (May 1964).

7.23 Ground level of the National Assembly Building, showing projecting vertical concrete grooves, a detail that was dropped during construction above the third level. Sher-e-Bangla Nagar, Dhaka, Bangladesh, 1962–1983.

Revising a technique he had used on the facade of the Yale Art Gallery, Kahn alternated flat bands with raised ones, which themselves created texture and, on bright days, the illusion of even greater tactility in the lines of horizontal shadows that they projected on the facade.[69] Kahn wished to reinforce this textural impression with an additional detail that would have significantly altered the appearance of the facade. He specified that the projecting vertical grooves, formed by the joint between two wooden form boards during the pouring of the concrete, should remain raised, and molded into a V-shaped line (Fig. 7.23). He

7.24 A typical plastered building in Dhaka with moldy surfaces.

unsuccessfully tried to get laborers to execute this detail; after unsatisfactory results during the construction of the first two stories, he dropped it. Had this detail been realized, the facade would have been animated and softened by lightly shaded, vertical striations, and its overwhelming horizontality would have been mitigated. As the building is executed, its bottom stories display V-shaped grooves and the remainder do not, forming a potent record in the spirit of authenticity, that human decisions and failings shape the making of even the grandest of monuments.

Kahn's rigorously honest approach to expressing the processes of construction sometimes contravened both common sense and his aspirations to regional sensitivity. For example, he insisted on leaving the concrete of the National Assembly Building exposed inside and out. This defied the building practice in the wet climate of Dhaka, in which plaster protects a building's structure from pervasive greenish-black mold (Fig. 7.24). Although Kahn spread a waterproofing solution over the elevations, it failed to sufficiently protect surfaces from dampness. Today, poor Bangladesh devotes substantial financial resources every year to cleaning black crud off the building's walls.

Although Kahn alluded to historic precedents in various parts of the design of the National Assembly Building, he subverted their referentiality and accentuated abstraction with spatial and compositional techniques that were, in the

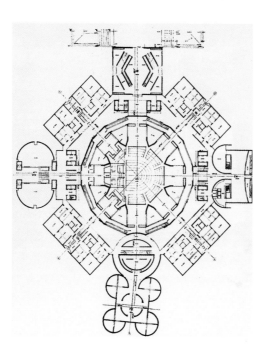

7.25 Final plan of the National Assembly Building, with the prayer hall on the bottom, the Presidential Plaza on the top, and the assembly chamber at the center, surrounded by the ambulatory. From the Kahn Collection.

end, thoroughly modernist.[70] In its centrality and its highly geometricized composition, the National Assembly Building plan recalls such monuments as the Hagia Sophia, the Pantheon, or the Taj Mahal (Fig. 7.25). With this initial idea, however, Kahn elaborated on his early solution for the First Unitarian Church of concentric layers of space surrounding a central meeting area: in the National Assembly Building, six layers of space separate the external perimeter wall from the interior assembly chamber; they include the zone between the double walls of the facade; the zone of offices; the ambulatory, which itself is divided into three zones, a central one that is seven stories high and two peripheral ones leading to offices on either side; and the passageways into the chamber itself. This layering of spaces permitted Kahn to challenge the referentiality of his initial, central plan in a number of ways. In each of the historic monuments mentioned above—take the Pantheon—the entrance is monumentalized to mark the onset of a grand processional, which leads into the central space of worship or commemoration. Kahn, by contrast, undermined the processional sequence into the National Assembly Building chamber, as he had the Beaux-Arts sequences implied in his later plans for the Trenton Jewish Community Center. He consistently underplayed his entrances, whether they led from the South Plaza under the mosque and into the ambulatory, or into the assembly chamber or prayer hall. He also impeded axial movement through the building into the assembly chamber with a lateral spatial pull that he created by layering concentric circles of space. A person standing in the ambulatory of the National Assembly Building looks through a monumental, perforated screen into a different zone, which is also marked by a dramatic shift in scale (Plate 21). Thus did

Kahn challenge the classical principles of hierarchical procession and enclosure.
Instead he introduced multidirectionality, movement, and incompletely bounded
spaces. Such techniques subvert the viewer's initial expectations of bounded,
axial spaces, forcing her to question assumptions about monumental spatial paradigms in a manner that is at the same time authentic and entirely modern.

Kahn employed and combined such compositional techniques as inversion,
disjunction, and repetition. All emphasize the building's abstraction — or at least
its great distance from its many references. Repetition and inversions are evident in Kahn's working and reworking of the circle motif throughout the
National Assembly complex. Here circles, traditionally symbols of unity, stasis,
and purity, are sliced in half, sometimes horizontally, sometimes vertically; flat
circles intersect to intimate a sphere; circles are transgressed with pathways that
shoot through them, sometimes diagonally, sometimes horizontally; circles are
repeated, seemingly ad infinitum (Figs. 7.26 and 7.27). Such a highly
abstracted, formalized handling of the principal geometric motif of the National
Assembly Building suggests the abstract compositional motivations that drove
Kahn's overall approach to the design.

Kahn's affinity for inversion was especially evident in an unexecuted pair of
designs for the mosque and the Presidential Square, located at opposite apexes of
the National Assembly Building. At one point in the design process, Kahn proposed that the mosque be the same truncated pyramid that he had first employed
in his Philadelphia Civic Center plans, a form that, he now claimed, derived from
"the peak of a minaret."[71] As a pendant to the mosque, on the opposite side of the
National Assembly Building, the Presidential Square would be a solid square with
a hollow diamond carved inside: a voided allusion to the footprint of the pyramidal mosque (Fig. 7.28). This inversion vanished in the final scheme, because the
shape of the Presidential Square remained the same, while that of the prayer hall
changed completely. Nevertheless, this inversion demonstrates the formalism of
Kahn's compositional approach, encouraging the viewer to focus on the object
itself and on the means by which it could be, and had been, transformed.

In composing the relationship of the prayer hall to the assembly chamber and
offices, Kahn employed a related compositional technique, which he called
"dichotomous space," of articulating different kinds of spaces differently, making the overall composition ever so slightly yet ever so jarringly disjunctive. The
idea of formal dichotomies came to him when, working on the contemporaneous
Salk Institute, he realized that a research laboratory was "really two buildings,"
a "fireplace and study" kind of building (the offices) and a "microbe and test
tube" kind of building (the laboratories).[72] He decided that these differences
should be exaggerated rather than elided, so he made the Salk Institute's offices
into small, womb-like rooms with shaded interiors in natural woods, and the laboratories long-span, open, white, hygienic-looking spaces edged floor to ceiling
with plate glass (Plate 22). Later he realized that from this *parti* a general princi-

7.26 Repetition of circles in hostels, Sher-e-Bangla Nagar, Dhaka, Bangladesh, 1962–1983.

7.27 Ramp in the ambulatory of the National Assembly Building, Sher-e-Bangla Nagar, Dhaka, Bangladesh, 1962–1983.

ple could be derived. "We must build something that satisfies this, and [something that] satisfies the other," Kahn asserted in 1965. "We must express dichotomous things. We must express them because dichotomous things inspire."[73]

In composing the relationship between the prayer hall and the National Assembly Building, Kahn consistently worked toward expressing the disparate natures of these two institutions by creating "dichotomous space." Initially he drew the mosque as a large separate structure.[74] The client insisted on incorporating the mosque into the body of the National Assembly; in response, Kahn adopted the truncated pyramidal shape to sharply distinguish it from the legislative building to which it was appended. The site plan from May 1963 indi-

7.28 Plan of the National Assembly Building with a voided diamond for the Presidential Square at the top and the pyramidal mosque (later the prayer hall) at the bottom. From the Kahn Collection.

SITUATING THE DEMOCRATIC WAY OF LIFE

cates that he immediately considered cranking the prayer hall off axis as well (see Fig. 7.2). The curvilinear, baroque geometry of late-1964 versions of the staircase was entirely unlike the geometry he used anywhere else in the building: indeed, he had never used such complex geometries before (Fig. 7.29). In the final version (see Fig. 7.25), the inflected axis ostensibly oriented the prayer hall toward Mecca, but Kahn later revealed that a dichotomous relationship between prayer hall and assembly was his real intention. "See, the mosque turns slightly toward the west," he said, excited, in a lecture at Berkeley in 1966. "I purposely did that, I purposely put this building there like that so I could turn the mosque the other way."[75]

Not only in plan, but also in the design of the prayer hall as built, inversion and reversals dominate: solid becomes void, intact becomes perforated, large becomes small. On the exterior, the mosque presents an imposing facade that recalls several fortresses in India and western Europe, Oast houses in Kent, and the Cathedral of St. Cecile at Albi, all of which Kahn saw in these years (Figs. 7.30 and 7.31). Containing no visible apertures, the prayer hall is almost a roofless, curvilinear version of the Trenton Bathhouse, which Kahn had designed a decade earlier. But the massive, heavy exterior walls belie the small, airy interior they create, where daylight streams in through "hollow columns" partitioned by X-shaped concrete walls punctured with circular cutouts (Plate 23). The effect of such reversals is to deflect the viewer's attention away from any specific historicizing reference and onto the abstract play of forms. That is how Kahn described the prayer hall when he, after seemingly endless versions and revisions, finished its design. It was, he wrote, "extremely simple and beautiful. There is a play of large windowless openings in walls of marble and concrete, a different design than that of the other walls of the building."[76]

In the National Assembly Building and hostels, Kahn employed various compositional techniques that convey the impression of unrelenting honesty.

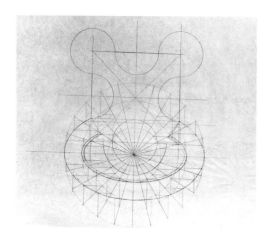

7.29 Intermediate study for the prayer hall. From the Kahn Collection.

7.30 A slide of an Oast House in Kent, from Kahn's collection. From the Kahn Collection.

He expressed both the materials and the processes by which the buildings were made, and organized volumes so that they reflected the internal spaces they housed. He combined this honesty with a primordial awkwardness and a defamiliarizing abstraction, which together promoted an experience of authenticity, which forces the viewer into an awareness of the historical, temporal, and geographical specificity of this building and of her contingent place within it.

THE WAY INTO A WORLD WITHIN A WORLD

Kahn, in conceiving the "Form" of the site plan and the plan for the parliament, first thought through and crystallized his ideals about the institutions of democracy, and worked a strategem he had developed before, in which monumentality facilitated the construction of an active community. In the early site

7.31 Sketch of the Cathedral of St. Cecile, Albi, France, 1959, with cylindrical towers hugging the entrance, similar to the prayer hall of the National Assembly Building in Dhaka. Private collection.

plans and the plans for the National Assembly complex. Kahn developed a conception of a monumental parliament in a communal, garden-like reservation of public buildings. Then, moving from "Form" to "Design" in the site plan and the design for the National Assembly Building, Kahn sometimes accommodated, and sometimes challenged, aspects of the commission in order to make his buildings accord better with his sociopolitical vision of a democracy. As he completed the design for the National Assembly complex, Kahn focused on one component in his situated modernist project, which was to make a building familiar enough to the people it served that they would feel situated in their culture. Finalizing the design and the construction process, Kahn synthesized his political ideals and formal explorations with an idiom that promoted the experience of authenticity.

By its monumentality and its persistent invitation to the common citizen, the National Assembly complex situates its users in the social world; users who amble through the gardens, grounds, and built public spaces of the National Assembly complex are gathered, at least psychologically, into the public realm. By its allusions to local vernacular and monumental architecture, the complex situates its users culturally and encourages them to appropriate its buildings as their national symbol. And through defamiliarization, inversion, repetition, and disjunction, combined with its primordial affect and its insistent materiality, the National Assembly forces the viewer to *concentrate* on the complex and the building, to contemplate it as a discrete, material object in space with which she has a bodily and material relationship. The National Assembly complex generates an insistence of place, a situatedness for which Kahn had been searching for many years, through the course of many projects. Transporting this impression into the realm of the poetic, and furthering the viewer's sense of time and its passing, is Kahn's masterful manipulation of natural light, where dramatic compositions of geometrically drawn shadows, bright circles, or great swathes of light travel across surfaces, transforming the building into a kind of rock sieve, or a gigantic sundial, by which the viewer can track the time of day and season (compare Plate 21 with Plate 24).

Those with business inside, as they pass through the fortress-like border into Kahn's "world within a world,"[77] are encouraged to leave their petty private cares behind, to focus instead on their places in the world and their roles in society. Whether ascending the South Plaza or parking beneath it, one crosses a bridge over a moat to enter into a low, dark space that only accentuates the sublime, monumental sweep of the ambulatory. The entire plan of the National Assembly Building is arranged so that any user, legislator or janitor, passes through the ambulatory several times a day. Through chance meetings and happenstance rejoinders, one is forced into a public role, reminded that the smallest of tasks contributes to the enterprise of democracy. It is in the ambulatory of the National Assembly Building—by conventional standards, a less heraldic space by virtue of its transitional function—that Kahn forged perhaps the greatest space of his career. At a lecture in 1961, he explained: "The institution is truly an inspiring space by reason of the entrance, the galleries of movement, and the harbors leading to the various spaces. This," he insisted, "is the measure of the architect . . . the organization of the connecting spaces. . . . That which gives the man walking through the building outside his specific niche where he works a feeling of the entire sense of the institution—not at his desk, not in his little room, but in the sense of connection between all the rooms and all the functions of this institution."[78]

From overall conception to siting to composition to detail, Louis Kahn in the National Assembly complex struggled with questions that had preoccupied him for more than twenty years. How to create a modernist monumentality? How to make an architecture that conveys the impression of authenticity and brute presence that encourages viewers to feel responsible to themselves? How to make buildings and public spaces that create symbols of communal identity and spatially foster participation in the public realm? To these queries, which continued to engage Kahn for the rest of his life, the National Assembly complex poses his first, and fullest, answers. Here is a proposal about how to make an architecture that is modern and is oriented toward place, the individual, and her community.

LOUIS KAHN'S SITUATED MODERNISM

8

The excavation, analysis, and interpretation of the evolution of Louis Kahn's architecture from his early modernism to his mature situated modernism suggests an image of Kahn, of his architectural agenda, and of the buildings he designed that is quite at odds with received views about him and his work. Kahn was not a lone genius working in the wasteland of early postwar American architecture; he was a lively social animal, a creature of the culture that he inhabited. He was not an apolitical mystic but a highly self-conscious social activist who, based on an understanding of the evolving needs of his and other societies, worked out a complex agenda to fuse the personal experience of self-revelation with the social experience of strengthening one's bonds to the community—experiences that are normally perceived as antithetical but which Kahn saw as complementary. His work presents less the peaceful resolve of Beaux-Arts neo-classicism than the tensions, irresolutions, and dynamism of modern architecture and modern art.

This revised portrayal of Kahn and of the nature of his agenda provides a new foundation for addressing a set of broader questions. What was his contribution to twentieth-century architecture, and how does that contribution fit into the trajectory of architecture in the century, so dominated as it was by the modern movement and attempts to break away from it? What in his life and in his mind brought him to make the contribution that he did? What were the essential features of the architectural agenda that underlay this contribution, and how did he instantiate these ideas in his buildings? Why does Kahn's work still speak to us? What does it say?

In the two decades after World War II, progressive architects watched one dominant strain of the avant-garde, "modern" style, hitherto confined mainly to private homes and a handful of small public buildings, metamorphose into the International Style modernism of corporate skyscrapers, cultural institutions, and governmental seats. At the same time, architects were faced with an emerging social and cultural landscape that posed problems substantially different from those that preoccupied the architects who founded and shaped the early modern movement.[1] It should not be surprising that some members of the avant-garde, such as Le Corbusier, reassessed and altered their own architectural language, while a new generation of architects looked upon the contributions of the early modernists with a critical eye. Some progressive practitioners responded to developments in architectural culture, to the new political and social terrain, and to changing cultural concerns with renewed belief in the relevance of the modern movement as they understood it. Others jettisoned the movement altogether. Still others, like Aalto, Kahn, and various members of Team Ten, reconceptualized the modern architecture of the 1920s. Kahn, in particular, expanded the scope of the modern movement's political, social, and even ethical orientation and, in doing so, further developed critical aspects of its forms. At the same time, he gradually redressed what he came to believe were modernism's deficiencies.

Early modernists believed that the architect was morally bound to identify the Zeitgeist and work with it to build architecture that would transport people toward a better society. Many, including Mies, Le Corbusier, and Gropius, also held that the spirit of their age was defined by industrial technology and the machine. Varying greatly were the practitioners' diagnoses of what aspects of society might be improved, and their assessments of what means might achieve their ends. Still, several highly visible contingents of the modern movement shared the belief that the explosive growth of industrial technology distinguished their century from others, and that from this economic fact stemmed the fundamental social, political, and even psychological phenomena that determined what it meant to be modern.

From these conceptions, of the political and social role of the architect and of the essential features of the age, emerged an array of related stylistic predilections that shaped the distinctive and flexible idiom of early modernism. Industrially manufactured materials were used in imitation, if not execution, of mass production, in order to link this new architecture symbolically to the overriding ethos of the age and to facilitate the production of better housing for the working and middle classes. These materials were manipulated in a manner that revealed, or pretended to reveal, the building's physical structure, which was usually reinforced concrete, steel, or another more conventional material handled to look like one that was industrially produced. In "revealing" the nature of these new materials, architects tended to emphasize transparency, building in volumes rather than in opaque masses. They also tended to separate support systems from the building's skin and to use the open plan. Most early modernists rejected explicit reference to past styles precisely because they believed that the twentieth century differed in kind from centuries past, and so demanded new forms. Instead, they mandated an approach to composition that they claimed ought to be focused on the rational fulfillment of programmatic needs.

Throughout his career, Kahn adhered to and further developed two of the core ideological positions held by the best-known early modernists. The first was their political conviction that architecture should be a force for progressive social change, even if that change was not always pragmatically defined. Kahn believed, like Le Corbusier, whom he considered his mentor from afar, that architecture and urban design should be approached as one practice, and that an explicit social and even political agenda should underlie the making of buildings and public spaces. More, Kahn believed that architecture could, and should, critically contribute to the ethical formation of people's lives. The second core position held by many early modernists was that the architect was obligated to continuously assess his era's principal and changing social, economic, and cultural features in order to ensure that his overall agenda, and the idiom he employed to further it, were suited to his world.

Kahn upheld the central tenets of the modern movement and continued to employ many of its forms. He worked in a restrained, taut aesthetic of simple, abstract volumes and masses that early modernists proposed best expressed their age. He elevated tectonic expression to a central, form-giving feature in his vocabulary, using reinforced concrete as his defining material. He, like his modernist forebears, eschewed applied ornament and rejected direct appropriation of historical motifs or styles as being inappropriate to a language that should strive to accommodate the needs, and express the ethos, of the twentieth century.

Indeed, it was in the spirit of the modernist maxim regarding the dynamism of the world and the concomitant need to adapt architectural form to respond to the times that Kahn, in the years after World War II, jettisoned some of the specific tropes of early modernist practice that the world, by his time, had passed by. He as well as other progressive architects came to believe that the coupling of the twentieth century with industrial technology was no longer tenable, that industrial-technological advances did not constitute the distinguishing characteristic of the postwar age. Many early modernists wished to harness industrial capitalism, seeing in it the potential for progressive ends. Kahn instead challenged capitalism—and, ultimately, the primacy to architects of industrial technology—because of its socially deleterious effects. He began to do so in the 1930s and 1940s together with his colleagues in public housing and city planning, for whom a free market necessarily generated a debased architecture and urban life. When, in the 1950s, the socioeconomic landscape shifted, Kahn decided that the determinative feature of his generation's culture would be not the promise of industrial technology but the integral and destructive linkage of mid-century capitalism with mass consumption and suburbanization. He as well as his colleagues feared that these phenomena would eventually eradicate people's sense that they were a part of, and owed allegiance to, a community and a locale.

Kahn developed the view that a forceful modernist architecture and urbanism for the postwar era would better people's lives by constructing urban spaces and buildings that embodied people's idealized aspirations for their communities and themselves. Such an architecture could not take its forms principally from the objective facts of mass production and industrial technology. Instead, architecture and urbanism had to counteract the socially corrosive effects of mass consumption and suburbanization. They should do so by situating and grounding a building's user, that is to say, by eliciting and reinforcing the social, physical, and psychological distinctiveness of a place.

Initially, Kahn became preoccupied with how to situate people socially while he was working on public housing and urban planning projects in the late 1930s and the 1940s, long before he ever heard the term "mass culture" or considered it a detriment to social well-being. In wartime and in the immediate postwar years, he contemplated the notion of a community individuated by the active participation of its members, and so he used such site planning as in Carver Court and the Jersey Homesteads to encourage users' awareness of the people with whom they lived. Then, in the 1940s, he began to believe that it was through monumentality in civic architecture that he could best manifest the ideal of communal participation and so situate a person in her community. He wrote an essay on monumentality and submitted a competition entry for the most visible American monument of the early postwar era, the Jefferson National Expansion Memorial in St. Louis. Responding to debates among progressive architects on the problem of a modern monumentality, he began to equate the design of a successful modern monumental building or complex with the creation of a vital public realm. In the Jefferson National Expansion Memorial project, Kahn contended that such a building or complex must shape and nurture a community's distinct identity by doing two things: encouraging users spatially to develop connections with the city and its people, and inviting a community to project onto a building or complex an idealized, symbolic image of itself. Only this kind of architecture would spark his user's consciousness of her position as a member of a larger social body, a community that challenged and nurtured her, to which she simultaneously owed loyalty and the obligation to criticize and improve.

In the late 1940s and early 1950s, Kahn began to conceive of "placemaking" not only in its social but also in its geographical, topographical, and phenomenological sense of an architecture oriented around a person's experience of a specific site and unique building. He began to develop this idea while teaching at Yale, where he fell, directly and indirectly, under the influence of the Existentialist ideal of authenticity. With the Yale Art Gallery, which he designed between 1951 and 1954, Kahn began to search for an architectural idiom that might effect an experience consecrated in Existentialist philosophy and aesthetics, an epiphanic, private experience heightening a viewer's consciousness of herself as situated in a given time and place.

As Kahn sought to realize these ideals of situating a person socially, in her community, and situating her personally, temporally, and spatially, he found himself successively casting off various tropes of his early, technologically oriented modernist style. Specifically, he rejected an idiom that celebrated and symbolized the machine, especially mass-produced items that could be manufactured and consumed without regard to a particular community or locale.

Already in the Yale Art Gallery design, Kahn implicitly—perhaps even unconsciously—began to challenge the technological orientation that so dominated an important strain of early modernism. He did so by partially rejecting transparency, one of the stylistic tropes that many early modernists employed in order to express the enormous spatial potential afforded by new materials. He also did so by emphasizing the process of construction in a way that articulated how architecture was made by people, not machines; and after the design of the Richards Medical Center in 1957, in which he and Komendant had used concrete elements that had been pre-cast off-site, Kahn renounced symbols of mass production. At the same time, in schemes for the Trenton Jewish Community Center, he extricated his work from the open plan, which had been devised to express architecture's assimilation of new materials and new techniques drawn from industrial technology. Instead, he began to construct rooms that emerged from the building's structure, offering his users enveloping, static spaces exquisitely scaled to the human body. At the end of the decade, while working on such projects as the First Unitarian Church in Rochester, Kahn eschewed the early modernist emphasis on a functional assessment of the client's stated programmatic needs. He advocated instead that the architect act as a social visionary and engineer, articulating his philosophy of Form and Design, in which the architect's first responsibility was to determine a social vision—a Form—appropriate, perhaps ideal, for every institution that she designed.

With these and many other gestures, Kahn worked toward creating buildings that could become symbolic receptacles for communal identity while fostering agency and individual participation. At the same time, he encouraged in the viewer the impression that the building in which she stood was a *constructed* object, made only for a specific place and in a specific time. With this objective, Kahn reinterpreted humanism by prodding the viewer of his building to make with it a bodily, tactile, phenomenological connection.

Kahn developed a modernism that concentrated on realizing the two practical agendas of situating people socially and personally as the principal means of instantiating his overarching moral agenda that architecture must foster people's ethical formation. People who are anchored in their community, morally obligated and psychologically connected to the people surrounding them, make for better citizens. People who are self-aware are more likely to consider the consequences of their public and private actions. That people should actively participate in the betterment of their community and in assessing their own actions vis-à-vis others was, Kahn believed, a universal moral imperative. In developing this belief he conjoined the political and social vision of early modernism with a philosophico-ethical paradigm drawn from Existentialism and an empirical analysis of the new social and cultural circumstances of the postwar period into a reframed notion of modern architecture dominated by the concept of the situated person, defined in both social and phenomenological terms.[2]

How Kahn, through the 1940s and 1950s, transformed early modernism into a fully realized situated modernism is the story of how he struggled to better conceptualize these practical agendas of situating people socially and personally, to actualize each one in architectural form, and to join them to one another. It was an enormously complex undertaking, which he manifested only piecemeal. Early in his career, he decided to devote himself primarily to institutional buildings that appertained to the public realm: museums, libraries, churches and synagogues, and university facilities. Rarely did he accept a residential or commercial commission. From this foundation Kahn's journey toward situated modernism saw fits and starts, failed directions and incompletely achieved aspirations; at times, design moves that advanced one end thwarted or impeded another. During the design of the Art Gallery at Yale he focused on authenticity at the expense of attending to the problematic of community. While working on the AFL Medical Services and City Tower, he made little progress in finding still better ways to create the experience of authenticity; instead he concentrated on teasing from the techno-organic movement in space frames a monumental urban idiom that might reinvigorate communal identity. In the Adath Jeshurun synagogue commission, Kahn sought to transform the particularistic aspects of a single religion — in this case, Judaism — into a universalizing search for communal identity, an endeavor that forced him to wrestle with the techno-organic language that he at first believed was deeply symbolic but also, he began to suspect, excessively opaque.

While designing the Trenton Jewish Community Center and Bathhouse, Kahn attempted to advance his search for authenticity by introducing into his vocabulary the constructed, tectonically bound room. In doing so, he discovered that in his reinterpretation of the space frame from a spanning into a habitable structure, he had produced an idiom so rigid in its geometry that it created more problems than it solved. He slowly extricated his architecture from a Fulleresque vocabulary. He came to conclude that he might more effectively create monumentality by using an idiom abstracted from architectural precedents, hoping also that in using such allusions, he could directly foster communal sentiment because his users would comprehend or intuit symbolic references to past communal endeavors. But this new symbolic vocabulary had to be abstract because otherwise it would descend into the familiar and comfortable particularism. So Kahn set out to integrate symbolic allusions into, and to merge them with, his existing repertoire of abstract modernist aesthetic devices. Kahn first began to consummate his situated modernism while designing the Unitarian Church in Rochester in 1959–1962, for which he devised a kind of monumentality and a series of planning techniques that began to realize his two practical agendas of situating a person in her society and in herself.

In Rochester, however, Kahn had neither the budget nor, consequently, the creative latitude to fully execute his ideas, and it was only with the completion of the design for the National Assembly complex in Dhaka (and the Salk Institute in La Jolla) that Kahn finally integrated his complex ideas of communal participation and individual responsibility into the situated modernism of his mature architecture. In these buildings, Kahn designed the communal "people marks" to which he had been long aspiring. These monumental buildings draw users in and inspire in them the sense that they belong to a greater social enterprise. At the same time, these buildings force users toward a private, phenomenological experience of that particular constructed object (a parliament building, scientific laboratories) in that unique place on earth (a flat plain below sea level in tropical Bengal, a cliff side overlooking the Pacific Ocean). These buildings' idiom conveys to each individual viewer the sense that the institution in which she stands both lays legitimate claim to universal validity and especially addresses her.

How, then, did Kahn grow? Accounts of the evolution of his work have not fundamentally challenged Vincent Scully's forty-year-old model of Kahn's intellectual development, based on an admixture of assumptions about the origins of a person's thought paradigms which Scully distilled from Freud and Proust: after receiving a Beaux-Arts training under Cret, Kahn supposedly buried that training in order to become a modernist, only to excavate it in a single, epiphanic moment while a fellow at the American Academy at Rome in 1950–1951, when he, with singular heroism and prescience, realized the inadequacies of modernism and the self-evident value of history.[3]

This portrayal of Kahn as the lone genius suffers from three fallacies. First, in heroizing Kahn we ignore the inconsistencies and even contradictions in his ideas; we overlook the dead-end avenues he traveled, and the excessive rigidity in design against which he was constantly, sometimes unsuccessfully, struggling. In a number of buildings, one or another of his practical agendas got the better of him. Kahn made claims for the Yale Art Gallery's and City Tower's tectonic innovativeness, but neither stands the test of even moderately good engineering. His real interests were in authenticity (for the former) and community (for the latter). He designed the laboratories in the Richards Medical Center to reinforce and symbolize group cooperation, but most biologists who work there find the laboratories extremely difficult to adapt to their own cooperative or individual uses. The dormitories at Bryn Mawr are so rigid in their geometric conception that the individual user feels bunkered in. The Performing Arts Center in Fort Wayne and the Ayub Hospital in Dhaka are exorbitantly monumentalizing. The cafeteria at Exeter Academy is a pastiche of excessive symbolism.

Also overlooked in previous models of Kahn's development is the zigzagging movement that eventually got him to his mature architecture. Epiphanies may occur in literature to protagonists like Stephen Dedalus, but it is a fallacy to think that any such pivotal realization came to Kahn. His intellectual development was slow and incremental, with his steps down one path often having been succeeded by steps down another. In the mid-to-late 1940s, he explored, then dropped, Sigfried Giedion's idea of a synthesis of the arts as the means to a new monumentality. In the early to mid-1950s, it was R. Buckminster Fuller's techno-organic movement in space frames which Kahn embraced, only to reject this cellular idiom by the late 1950s, dismissing it in 1961–1962 as just so much "algae."[4]

Third and most important is the fallacy of Kahn as a lone genius, which presents a false view of how a person forms her ideas and praxis. An artist or architect's intellectual development is necessarily embedded in the world she inhabits. The artist is able to frame questions and propose new ideas in reference only to two phenomena. The first is each person's own socially constructed worldview, which Pierre Bourdieu calls the habitus—internalized habits, predispositions, assumptions, and predilections acquired as she lives her individual life in the world.[5] The second phenomenon is the contemporary intellectual discourse in which she participates—what Bourdieu calls the field. Creativity resides in how an individual responds to the discourses in her various, often overlapping fields, how she filters them through her habitus, recombines them, and shapes them into an individual language.

Not every idea is thinkable in every era, and contrary to the conventional, heroizing portrayal of him, Kahn, like most artists, was a thoroughly social and socialized being. He was able to transform early modernism into a situated modernism because he listened, he looked, and he talked. He followed and considered the work of artists, architectural mentors, competitors. He discussed and debated ideas with colleagues and friends, lovers and students. He came up with new ideas by reassessing his own aspirations and style as he grappled with the social and cultural changes in his society, and as he thought through the debates within his intellectual community. He creatively recombined ideas derived from his habitus—impoverished Philadelphian Eastern European Jew, student at the University of Pennsylvania under Cret, painter-*cum*-designer, modernist architect—with ideas emerging in the overlapping fields of his intellectual world: architecture, art, politics, social criticism, and philosophy.

Each step in Kahn's architectural trajectory corresponded with a moment in his personal life when he took in a new set of ideas and formulated his own response to them. He began to contemplate monumentality by entering international debates on the subject that had been fomented by Giedion. When, at fifty years of age, he first made his mark on the American architectural map with his Art Gallery at Yale, he had recently started teaching in the intellectually fecund environment of Yale. He appropriated the language of the techno-organic movement in space frames, which he employed for City Tower and the AFL Medical Services, at the moment that it seemed to many in the architectural community—including many in his own social circle—to hold great promise for a newly invigorated machine-based modernism. When, with the design of the Trenton Jewish Community Center, he rejected that techno-organic idiom and instead became preoccupied, as did so many others, with the social problems caused by "mass culture," consequently turning toward an overt monumentality and abstractly historicizing vocabulary, he was teaching in the highly politicized atmosphere of the Graduate School of Fine Arts at the University of Pennsylvania, and at the School of Architecture at Princeton University, where students and faculty alike routinely uttered the words "history" and "modern" in the same breath. For Kahn, employing allusions to historical motifs, even if abstracted, as a continuing feature of his architecture would have been almost unthinkable before he was exposed to the discourses of the mid-1950s.

Kahn recombined and synthesized some of the philosophical ideas, moral convictions, social critiques, and aesthetic trends of his intellectual community with his preexisting modernist views, especially views about ethical responsibility in the practice of architecture. From this he generated a vocabulary that was timely, singular, and powerful. To reveal the mechanics of how he worked within these discourses is not to diminish his creativity, because every artist thinks within the bounds of her own time. Nor does revealing the situated nature of his intellectual formation deny the singularity of his achievement. It is hard to think of another body of buildings produced in the decades after World War II that remain more powerfully present in the contemporary architectural imagination than do those by Kahn. It is doubly important, then—important from a historical point of view and important from a contemporary point of view—that his architecture, and the nature of the agenda that drove it, be reassessed.

My own studies of modernism, the social functions of architecture, monumentality, and phenomenology have enabled me to see these dimensions in Kahn's architecture and therefore—from his sketches, paintings, writings, letters, and journal entries—to evaluate more precisely the evolution of his architecture. This investigation is more than an exercise in historical clarification or in revealing previously unacknowledged aspects of Kahn's work, however. If one believes that an artist's or architect's intentions are a crucial factor, though not the only factor, in determining the meaning of the work he produces, then tracking the precise course of the maturation of Kahn's intentions helps to unlock central meanings in his forms.

Tracing the evolution of Kahn's intentions and practice reveals that he was, for years, preoccupied with creating two social-architectural relationships. He wished to strengthen communal sentiment in his users and believed that one of the principal means for doing so was to create the impression of monumentality. He also wanted to spark his users' cognizance of themselves, and he believed that this could best be achieved in a building that offered the experience of authenticity. He hoped that this communal sentiment, when combined with self-awareness, would encourage individual social responsibility. With the National Assembly complex and the Salk Institute, Kahn forged these complex ambitions into a mature design vocabulary, a lexicon of design techniques that gave architectural form to his practical agendas of situating a person socially and personally through their principal means, monumentality and authenticity. These techniques were integral to his best projects, not only the buildings in Dhaka and La Jolla but also the Kimbell Art Museum (1966–1972), the Exeter library (1965–1972), and the Yale Center for British Art (1969–1974) as well as such unbuilt projects as the Mikveh Israel synagogue for Philadelphia (1961–1972), the Hurva synagogue for Jerusalem (1967–1974), and the Holocaust Memorial for New York City (1966–1972). The complex and fluid interrelationships among Kahn's practical agendas to situate people, and the internally manifold phenomena of monumentality and authenticity, are central to understanding his work and his contribution to twentieth-century architecture.

Kahn instantiated these ideas through identifiable, specific design techniques that he had developed over twenty years, and which appear in all his major buildings. The principal means by which Kahn anchors his user in her social world is monumentality, an intricate phenomenon that is often inaccurately assumed to reside mainly in a building's large scale. Monumentality creates the sense of social cohesion that is central to the consolidation of a community by impressing upon people the importance and power of a thing or a person whose name is the repository of larger social aspirations or achievements. Central to this impression of social power is the sense of long-lastingness; the perception that this city, building, institution, or artwork — and the values it represents — will last through generations, societies, time.

Kahn achieves monumentality by employing a number of carefully considered compositional techniques. Of these, large scale is certainly the most obvious. All his public buildings appear to be, indeed usually are, big. Kahn perceptually intensifies the actual massiveness of his buildings with several devices. He designs relatively unbroken surface fields, as in the travertine lateral facades of the Kimbell, the gridded slate elevations of the Yale Center for British Art, and the concrete perimeter facades of the Salk Institute. He also exaggerates the impression of physical weight by making his masonry walls lie densely on the ground. Apertures do not make Kahn's facades seem airier: often unglazed, as in the shadowy, empty holes of the Indian Institute of Management in Ahmedabad or the unbuilt Mikveh Israel synagogue, they paradoxically reinforce the sense of the building's mass. A building by Kahn looks heavy, here to stay.

An architectural work can be massive and weighty without conveying to viewers and users that the institution it houses is important and central to their public well-being. Monumentality also relies on distinctiveness, which contributes to the quality Kevin Lynch calls imageability, for anything that is noticeably unlike the things that surround it sticks more readily in the mind. Kahn plans all of his mature buildings with simple geometric figures, either singly or in combination; then, from the figure's periphery, he creates heavily bounded walls. These simple geometries differentiate his buildings from their surroundings and, in doing so, enhance their imageability: the Exeter library, surrounded by a village-like panoply of small haphazard structures, is a cube-like prism, large, tall, and controlled; the Yale Center for British Art, on a street in New Haven clotted with the visual noise and incident typical of a mid-sized city, bears a rectangular gridded facade that is taut, restrained, and blank.

Buildings as different as the Exeter library and the Yale Center for British Art, the Indian Institute of Management and the Kimbell Art Museum, rely on these devices, revealing Kahn's intention to make "an architecture of institutions": his buildings are consequential, singular, and lasting parts of the social landscape, homes to institutions on which a community's health and vibrancy depend. The monumental imageability of Kahn's buildings, together with the public nature of the institutions they house, nearly insist that members of a community appropriate them as symbols. They stand as physical embodiments of the social values—what Kahn called "the way of life"—that their institutions represent. People *remember* buildings by Kahn, even when they know nothing of the man who designed them.

It is partly by means of highly abstracted allusions to historical monuments that Kahn encourages a community to transform a building from a landmark into what he called a "people mark," an architectural vehicle that situates people in their community. The techniques he uses to create a sense of monumentality are not unique to his work. The historical precedents to which he repeatedly alludes in drawings or when speaking to students and friends—the Pantheon in Rome, the Cathedral at Albi, the Baptistery at Pisa, castles in Scotland, the Pyramids at Giza—depend on the same devices that Kahn's buildings do although, in style, each of these monuments differs from the next. At times, Kahn also alludes to, and radically abstracts from, specific monuments, as in the National Assembly complex in Dhaka, which recalls the Taj Mahal, and in the Hurva synagogue in Jerusalem, which evokes the Western Wall. By drawing on devices abstracted from the legacy of monumental architecture, Kahn's buildings become receptacles for communal identification partly by provoking viewers' associative memories—embodied history, internalized as second nature and so forgotten as history. Viewers recognize (if only with a feeling that what they see is somehow familiar), and thereby tend to identify with, the building and therefore, by association, with the institution housed within. Viewers appropriate these vast new constructions as a modern continuation of a preexisting communal heritage.

Kahn's buildings also usually include monumental spaces that facilitate the nourishment of an active community. Many of his projects—the unbuilt meeting house at the Salk Institute and the Hurva and Mikveh Israel synagogues as well as the completed National Assembly complex in Dhaka, the library at Exeter, and the Yale Center for British Art—contain either ambulatories, grand central cores, or both, oriented around a multistory void. These light-filled, stately spaces exist even when, as in the library at Exeter and the Yale Center for

British Art, they are programmatically unnecessary. In such spaces users gather themselves into a community. For example, the library for Exeter Academy, a small, elite preparatory school, is the site of regularly scheduled concerts and theatrical performances attended by local townspeople. Even on the rare occasion when Kahn was designing a public building that was not a communal or a civic institution, such as in his project for a commercial skyscraper in Kansas City of 1966–1973, he lavished his attention on the bottom stories, seeking to open the private building to the citizens of the city in which it stood.

Monumentality in political and religious buildings has often been a weapon to bludgeon the viewer into a sense of fearful awe, in which her insignificance and powerlessness are spatialized by her smallness in the face of institutional grandeur. Kahn, by contrast, tries in his buildings to monumentalize democratic participation: he intends not to exert power over his viewer but rather to induce her to take responsibility for herself as a person and a citizen. This he does by balancing his communal aspirations with the particularity of individual experience. With a variety of different compositional techniques, Kahn situates each viewer personally in order to heighten her consciousness of herself as an active agent who is appropriating a specific monumental work in a highly particularized social world. Taken together, these techniques engage the viewer visually, cognitively, and phenomenologically.

Kahn's work situates the user personally partly by means of tensions, or even irresolutions, that emerge as a by-product of his quest for authenticity, because this quest sometimes produces strategies and conceptual agendas that conflict with his practical aim of situating the user in her community. In addition to the tension produced by the juxtaposition of monumentality with authenticity, Kahn's buildings demand that their users negotiate the shifting terrain between restraint and expressiveness, and between representation and abstraction.

The most obvious tension in his architecture pits restraint against expressiveness: on the one hand is Kahn's penchant for simple geometric forms; on the other, his luxurious treatment of materials and picturesque inflections.[6] Be it the cool concrete, marble, and slate of the Yale Center for British Art or the warm brick and wood of the Indian Institute of Management, Kahn from these palettes elicits a sensual richness that pulsates against the rigid framework of his geometries. Similarly, he inflects his geometries—which by definition are neutral, universalizing, and abstract—in a picturesque manner in order to accommodate what he called Design, namely, the functional exigencies demanded by individual users. The result is an architecture not unlike the more expressive strain of minimalist art in which a nearly romantic impulse to sensuality emanates, even vibrates, from a rigid, often geometrically defined structure of restraint.

This visual tension between restraint and expression is paralleled by a more cognitively elicited tension between, or irresolution of, representation and abstraction. In the years he was developing his mature idiom, Kahn adopted two symbolic vocabularies in succession: the techno-organic language of space frames and then an idiom loosely evocative of the monuments of history. He chose each of these vocabularies in part because he believed that they contained a symbolic dimension that would advance his vision of an architecture of community. At the same time, he employed devices drawn from the tradition of modernist art and architecture to mitigate his buildings' representational qualities and make them overwhelmingly abstract.

Kahn forces the user to focus on the compositional rather than representational aspects of his buildings by employing four specific formal devices, which heighten his work's abstraction and draw the viewer in conceptually. These devices are the subversion of expectations, visual disjuncture, the use of simple forms, and their repetition and variation. The subversion of expectations is immediately evident in the Trenton Bathhouse, the Salk Institute, and the Exeter library; the viewer approaches all these buildings searching in vain, sometimes for minutes, for clues to the location of the entrance. This device of pulling the viewer up short is extended in the Exeter library and employed in the Yale Center for British Art, where she perceives a grid, that canonical modernist trope of neutrality and abstraction, only to notice that the grid's vertical elements are progressively narrowed from bottom to top in a gesture that is doubly disorienting. First it frustrates the viewer's expectation of regularity, determined by the use of the grid. In short order the viewer develops an explanation for this irregularity, presuming that it must represent a structural reality in the dynamics of compression. This presumption is also quickly undermined when the viewer enters the building to find a supporting frame of reinforced concrete, which obviates the necessity to reduce loads near the building's crown. The result is a surprising formal element that visually alludes to a non-existent structural condition—a complex moment indeed. At the Kimbell Art Museum, a similar device, also related to structure, appears: the principal unit of organization is a concrete, cycloid vault that is shaped like a barrel vault but which rests not on walls, as the viewer might expect, but on four points. Voids of light occupy the space where the trained eye demands mass.

Visual disjuncture also makes the viewer stop to focus on Kahn's compositional moves. In the Yale Center for British Art, for example, one enters a light-filled, airy, woody atrium, the apotheosis of stasis and calm. This establishes the viewer's expectations for the building. But when she passes into the second internal courtyard, she discovers it aggressively invaded by a silo of blank concrete. Disjuncture is similarly evident at the Salk Institute, between the laboratories and the private offices—the laboratories, a blank, silent monumental expanse of projection and recession; the offices, homey, wooded, individuated cells. Here is what Kahn calls "dichotomous space," a composition that resists the classical, unified whole.

A reliance on simple forms is the third formal device with which Kahn challenges the viewer out of complacent reception. The prayer hall at the National Assembly complex in Dhaka alludes to precedents that would be variously familiar to Kahn's audience: to his colleagues in the West, castles in Scotland and Carcassonne in France; to his users, viewers, and colleagues in the East, forts in northern India and Pakistan. Yet it refers overtly to no specific precedent. Kahn made the prayer hall in Dhaka, like many of his buildings, an overwhelmingly abstract composition. However much the prayer hall might remind the viewer of a building she has seen before, what she sees before her is four cylinders and four walls: a geometric composition.

Kahn repeats the elements of this composition, with minor and subtle differences, in the plan, the elevations, and the section of the National Assembly Building to which the prayer hall is appended. His use of this fourth technique, repetition and variation, which he also employs in such buildings as the Salk Institute, the Kimbell Art Museum, and the Mikveh and Hurva synagogue projects, extricates from their referents those forms that might have alluded to historic precedent. Emphasis instead is thrown onto geometries. The viewer focuses not on specific allusions but on the formal aspects of the building, the abstract compositional elements that it employs.

Through these devices of abstracting the representational, Kahn gets the viewer to *focus* in a way that she might not in buildings that employed an effortlessly legible, familiar visual language. In semiotic terms, the viewer is surprised by certain formal, conceptual, or narrative inconsistencies in what she sees, and so is compelled to "enter" the composition as she strives to make of it a conceptually unified whole. She becomes engaged in the attempt to reconcile contradictory elements and conflicting forces.[7]

Kahn wrests his users out of complacency and into active, focused appropriation. In doing so, he creates an experience that more closely resembles the normal condition for the appropriation of painting or sculpture, which, as Walter Benjamin theorizes, is not perceived in the distracted and somewhat passive state that architecture usually is.[8] It is all but impossible to enter one of Kahn's buildings and not to notice it, not to inspect it or look intently at it. Kahn's insistence on the compositional aspects of his forms obliges the viewer to perceive them abstractly, seeing in them multiple and shifting allusions rather than a stable, identifiable referent. This idiom—representational on the one hand, abstract on the other—offers Kahn a latitude that he could not have achieved had he used either language purely and in isolation. A non-representational vocabulary excludes viewers who are unaccustomed to engaging with such unfamiliar forms. An overtly representational vocabulary, such as historicism, limits reception to audiences schooled in the forms employed. By holding abstraction and representation in balance, Kahn expands his field of reception.

At the same time, by holding abstraction and representation in tension, he captures his viewer's focused attention. These devices make the viewer aware of the process by which she is appropriating this discrete, constructed object. In becoming meta-aware—aware of her awareness—the viewer's consciousness of herself as an active, perceiving agent is heightened. This meta-awareness constitutes part of the experience of authenticity to which Kahn, in his architecture, aspired.

In addition to engaging the viewer on the more conceptual levels established by the tensions between monumentality and authenticity, expression and restraint, representation and abstraction, Kahn enhances the viewer's chances for the experience of authenticity by inviting her to psychologically appropriate his monumental buildings. He does so by lavishing attention on the phenomenological in a way that gives new meaning to the old Renaissance concept of humanism. He closely manages scale and space, and expresses materials and the processes of construction. Rooms are vigorously shaped and, even when large in scale, proportioned to the body. Once a viewer is inside the "constructed rooms" of the Trenton Bathhouse, the offices at the Salk Institute, the art galleries at the Yale Center for British Art, she senses not the dynamism and spatial flow of early modernism but a static, almost primal equilibrium. Kahn's spaces envelop the viewer and slow her down. Even when he uses an open plan, as in the Kimbell Art Museum, he avoids a loft-like atmosphere by using low-slung, cycloid vaults that both bring the roofline close to the user and disaggregate the building into smaller cells that are more related to the scale of the human body.

Thus whether it be the massive ambulatory of the National Assembly Building or the intimate offices of the Salk Institute, the viewer is constantly reminded of her bodily relationship to the building. This reminder is reinforced by his expression of the construction process, with materials left uncovered and clear signs indicating how they were brought together—a product of his insistence that the architect must demonstrate that a building is a series of human decisions, "a struggle, not a miracle." Reinforced concrete, manipulated as a handmade medium, is imprinted with the memory of its making with trace marks from the formwork; wood is installed to show that it is laid by hand. The effect of Kahn's approach to construction is that the user senses that the building is not an object foreign to her, but is of her or of people like her. Thoughts turn to individuals and the processes by which this particular structure was built. By insisting that his building is an object constructed by one group of human beings for another, Kahn effectuates a connection between user and building that feels deeply personal.

He situates the user, moreover, not only in relation to the constructed object but also personally in relation to the site, thereby enhancing her sense of place. Early in his most productive years, Kahn deliberately avoided materials that smacked only of the man-made world: he stopped using visible steel after the completion of the Yale Art Gallery; even large sheets of plate glass rarely appear. Instead he routinely employed materials that are, in one sense or another, drawn from nature: wood, slate, brick, marble. Even reinforced concrete is not exploited for its potential plasticity but handled as if it were a stronger and more tensile form of rock. In managing these materials, he expresses their origins and their unique properties, leaving them uncovered, underscoring differences in color temperature, hue, and texture. After 1958, Kahn treats natural light as itself another constructive material in his palette. In the Kimbell Art Museum, he teases the sharp Texas sunshine into a soft, silvery sheen; in the unbuilt, darkened Hurva synagogue, he transforms a blazing sun into sharp-edged yellow swathes. As a result of his use of natural light and his particular choices and expression of materials, nature's presence—sometimes gentle, sometimes stark—suffuses this architecture without ever becoming the singular or overt focus of the design.

The result of Kahn's sensitivity to scale, his vigorous shaping of spaces, his expression of materials, of the processes of construction, and of the predictable ephemerality of natural light, is that the user, over time, witnesses the continuously changing spectacle of nature from the bedrock of an anchored location. Combined with his use of the modernist devices that compel the viewer to appropriate the building actively and dynamically rather than move through it complacently, and with his insistence that a building be what it appears to be— that interior volumes relate to exterior masses, that what holds the building up remain unmasked—these techniques help to create the perception of immediacy and presence that is one of the hallmarks of his architecture. The user, already aware of the communal nature of the building when experiencing its monumentality, becomes conscious of her situatedness in that—only that— place. She perceives a profound connection with the natural world from which the building came, the building itself, the people who made it, and those who move around and through it.

Kahn's architecture is modern, then, in many senses. His architectural agenda originated in, and addressed, the principal questions asked by architects in the modern movement in the immediate postwar years: his preoccupation with strengthening community stemmed from debates among American architects in the 1930s and 1940s on the suitability of the International Style to the project of creating good public housing; his wish to create monumentality originated in the debates on monumentality in CIAM in the 1940s and 1950s; his quest for authenticity was inspired by reassessments of modernism in art and architecture in the early 1950s. Kahn's architecture is also modern in the sense that, throughout, it employs compositional devices drawn from the modern movement: simple forms, abstraction, tectonic expression, the grid. It also draws from techniques that modern architecture shares with modern literature and art, such as the subversion of expectations and visual disjuncture—techniques that Kahn, like James Joyce in *Ulysses* and Pablo Picasso in the *Demoi-*

selles d'Avignon, used to challenge the viewer out of complacency and force her to question assumptions and perceive things anew. Most important, Kahn's architecture is modern in the more profound sense that it emanates from the cultural, political, and social aspirations and aims of early modernism. Kahn's architecture is, first of all, founded on an ethical vision: he was convinced that his buildings and public spaces could make a better social, even a better political, world. Unlike the work of Venturi and Moore—with which he is sometimes linked, being portrayed as the father of historicist postmodernism—Kahn's work is insistently, self-consciously heroic. It contains not a trace of the over-acculturated angst, the ironic distance, and comedic sense of play that are the canonical features of postmodernism.

Louis Kahn reconceptualized early modernism in light of the modernist premise that architecture must dynamically respond to changing cultural and social conditions, which he applied to the postwar years to make this powerful architectural movement relevant to the postwar era. Kahn reshaped his early, machine-oriented modernism into a fully realized, situated modernism, an idiom that locates people socially, geographically, within their communities, and inside and outside themselves while sustaining the modern movement's ethical stance and universalizing aspirations. The world to which Kahn responded by creating a situated modernism should not seem unfamiliar. In the years since his death, we have become ever more worried that the world is so fragmented, so dissociated, as to admit of no coherent, ethically founded agenda. We remain fearful that global capitalism and the continuing annihilation of the urban center will eradicate social and cultural identities and differences. We remain anxious that in an overmediated culture an authentic experience of ourselves, each other, and our physical world may be impossible. We remain alarmed that we are losing profound, integrated social connections with those who people our daily lives, and that a public realm vital to the governance of democracies is either dying or dead.

These are among our era's dominant cultural, social, and political preoccupations. Kahn's architecture still has aesthetic power and social force, then, for many reasons. It creates an engaged, active, and constantly changing relationship between building and viewer. It forces us to confront the age-old dilemma of balancing personal fulfillment with communal responsibility. It encourages us, by its synthesis of authenticity with monumentality, to be better people and better citizens, and to envision a more noble public realm. It reminds people that they at once are bounded by their locales and cultures and also transcend them by their common humanity. It proposes one man's solutions to problems that are our own.

NOTES

INTRODUCTION

1. See, for example, William Curtis, "Authenticity, Abstraction and the Ancient Sense: Le Corbusier and Louis Kahn's Ideas of Parliament," *Perspecta* 20 (1983): 191–194.

2. Kahn in an interview with WFIL-TV, p. 3 of transcript, 19 September 1962, "Lectures," Box 115, Louis I. Kahn Collection, University of Pennsylvania and Pennsylvania Historical Commission, Philadelphia (hereafter abbreviated as Kahn Collection).

3. David Brownlee and David DeLong, *Louis I. Kahn: In the Realm of Architecture* (New York: Rizzoli, 1993); Patricia Cummings Loud, *The Art Museums of Louis I. Kahn* (Durham: Duke University Press, 1989); Peter Reed, "Toward Form: Louis I. Kahn's Urban Designs for Philadelphia, 1939-1962" (Ph.D. diss., University of Pennsylvania, 1989); Susan Solomon, *Louis I. Kahn's Trenton Jewish Community Center* (New York: Princeton Architectural Press, 2000); Eugene J. Johnson and Michael Lewis, *Drawn from the Source: The Travel Sketches of Louis I. Kahn* (Williamstown, Mass.: Williams College Museum of Art, 1996).

4. Kahn, in "Marin City Redevelopment," *Progressive Architecture* 41 (November 1960): 151.

5. Kahn, lecture at the University of California at Berkeley (November 1968), Getty Center for the Study of Art and Humanities.

6. Michel Foucault, "The Discourse on Language," in *The Archaeology of Knowledge and the Discourse on Language*, trans. A. M. Sheridan Smith (New York: Pantheon, 1972), 215–237; Pierre Bourdieu, "The Intellectual Field: A World Apart," in *In Other Words: Essays Towards a Reflexive Sociology*, trans. Matthew Adamson (1987; Stanford, Calif.: Stanford University Press, 1990), 140–149.

7. Bourdieu, "The Intellectual Field," 147.

8. Foucault, "The Discourse on Language," 227; Bourdieu, *Working Papers and Proceedings of the Center for Psychosocial Studies* 14 (Chicago: Center for Psychosocial Studies, 1987). Thanks to Hélène Lipstadt for the Bourdieu reference.

9. See Sarah Williams Goldhagen and Réjean Legault, eds., *Anxious Modernisms: Experimental Postwar Architecture* (Cambridge, Mass., and Montreal: MIT Press and Canadian Centre for Architecture, 2000), especially my essay "Reconceptualizing the Modern," 301–323.

10. Giorgio Ciucci, "Il mito Movimento Moderno e le vicende dei Ciam," *Casabella* 44 (November–December 1980): 28–35, 118. On Le Corbusier's political inclinations, see Mary Caroline McLeod, "Urbanism and Utopia: Le Corbusier from Regional Syndicalism to Vichy" (Ph.D. diss., Princeton University, 1985); and Danilo Udovicki-Selb, "The Elusive Faces of Modernity: The Invention of the 1937 Paris Exhibition and the Temps Nouveaux Pavilion" (Ph.D. diss., Massachusetts Institute of Technology, 1994). On Mies's political inclinations, see Richard Pommer, "Mies van der Rohe and the Political Ideology of the Modern Movement," in *Mies van der Rohe: Critical Essays* (New York: Museum of Modern Art, 1989), 96–145. On the attitudes of various modern architects toward structure and material, see Edward Ford, *The Details of Modern Architecture*, vols. 1–2 (Cambridge: MIT Press, 1990–1996). For attempts to expand the definition of the modern movement, see Colin St. John Wilson, *The Other Tradition in Modern Archi-*

tecture (London: Academy Editions, 1995); Peter Blundell Jones, *Hugo Häring: The Organic Versus the Geometric* (Stuttgart: Axel Menges, 1999); Neil Levine, *The Architecture of Frank Lloyd Wright* (Princeton: Princeton University Press, 1996); Anthony Alofsin, *Frank Lloyd Wright–The Lost Years, 1910–1922: A Study of Influence* (Chicago: University of Chicago Press, 1993).

11. William J. R. Curtis, *Modern Architecture since 1900*, 3rd ed. (London: Phaidon, 1996); Kenneth Frampton, *Modern Architecture: A Critical History*, 3rd ed. (London: Thames and Hudson, 1992). Joan Ockman, in *Architecture Culture, 1943–1968: A Documentary Anthology* (New York: Rizzoli, 1993), documents the heterogeneity of the period while asserting its teleological evolution.

CHAPTER 1: KAHN AND AMERICAN MODERNISM

1. On the PSFS building see William Jordy, *American Buildings and Their Architects: The Impact of European Modernism in the Mid-Twentieth Century* (Anchor: Garden City, N.Y., 1972), 87–164.

2. Pierre Bourdieu, *The Logic of Practice*, trans. Richard Nice (1980; Stanford: Stanford University Press, 1990), 57–58.

3. David Brownlee in Brownlee and David DeLong, *Louis I. Kahn: In the Realm of Architecture* (New York: Rizzoli, 1993), 20; hereafter cited as Brownlee and DeLong, *In the Realm*. For more on the cooperative spirit in immigrant communities, see Irene E. Ayad, "Louis I. Kahn and Neighborhood Design: *The Mill Creek Redevelopment Area Plan*, 1951–1954" (Ph.D. diss., Cornell University, 1995).

4. On Philadelphia as a friendly place: Esther Kahn (widow of Louis Kahn), interview with the author, 1992; remembrances of his father: Kahn, journal entry from approximately 1972, collection of Sue Ann Kahn.

5. Kahn, journal entry from approximately 1972, collection of Sue Ann Kahn.

6. Esther Kahn, interview with the author, 1992.

7. Gregariousness is reported by many interviewees in Richard Saul Wurman's *What Will Be Has Always Been: The Words of Louis I. Kahn* (New York: Access Press and Rizzoli, 1986), 265–304 passim; see, for example, the interview of Jack MacAllister, 289–292.

8. For example, in 1959 when Kahn was working on the Unitarian Church in Rochester, he noted his ideas and then wrote that he wanted to consult Philip Johnson and Arthur Drexler about them (noted on a drawing in the collection of the Unitarian Church, Rochester).

9. Kahn in an interview with WFIL-TV, p. 3 of transcript, 19 September 1962, "Lectures," box 115, Louis I. Kahn Collection, University of Pennsylvania and Pennsylvania Historical and Museum Commission, Philadelphia (hereafter referred to as Kahn Collection).

10. On the coming of the modern movement to Philadelphia, see Robert A. M. Stern, *George Howe* (New Haven: Yale University Press, 1975), 196.

11. Ibid., 149.

12. Brownlee, in Brownlee and DeLong, *In the Realm*, 25–26.

13. On the Jersey Homesteads see ibid., 26–27; Ralph H. Danof, "Jersey Homesteads," in *A Place on Earth: A Critical Appraisal of Subsistence Homesteads*, ed. Russell Lord and Paul H. Johnstone (Washington, D.C.: U.S. Department of Agriculture, 1942), 131–161; Paul Conklin, *Tomorrow a New World: The New Deal Community Program* (Ithaca: Cornell University Press, 1959), 256–276.

14. Clipping (unidentified) in file 11, box 45, Alfred Kastner Collection, American Heritage Center, Laramie, Wyo. (hereafter cited as Kastner Collection).

15. "Tugwell Hands Out $1,800,000 for N.J. 'Commune,'" *Philadelphia Inquirer*, 7 May 1936, 1, cited by Brownlee in Brownlee and DeLong, *In the Realm*, 26.

16. Memo by Kahn, "Outline Report on Jersey Homesteads," 16–22 February 1936, p. 2, box 45, Kastner Collection.

17. The most comprehensive treatment of Oscar Stonorov remains the special issue on him in *L'architettura: Cronache e storia* 18 (June 1972), especially the following articles: Bruno Zevi, "Design as Political Action," 18; Edmund Bacon, "Oscar Stonorov and the City," 116; and Frederick Gutheim, "The Social Architecture of Oscar Stonorov," 77–107. Stonorov biography is from Gutheim, 77.

18. Stonorov, quoted in Bacon, "Stonorov and the City," 116; see also Eric J. Sandeen, "The Design of Public Housing in the New Deal: Oscar Stonorov and the Carl Mackley Houses," *American Quarterly* 37 (Winter 1985): 647–667.

19. Catherine Bauer, *Modern Housing* (Boston: Houghton Mifflin, 1934); see also Bauer, "The Current Change in Civic Hopes and Attitudes," *Housing and Town and Country Planning Bulletin* 1 (Lake Success, N.Y.: United Nations, n.d.): 35–37; Bauer, "Architectural Opportunities in Public Housing," *Architectural Record* 85 (January 1939): 65–68; and Catherine Bauer Wurster, "The Social Front of Modern Architecture," *Journal of the Society of Architectural Historians* 24 (March 1965): 48–52. On Bauer, see Mary Susan Cole, "Catherine Bauer and the Public Housing Movement, 1926–1937" (Ph.D. diss., George Washington University, 1975); and Cole, *Tributes for Catherine Bauer Wurster* (Berkeley: University of California Press, 1964).

20. Cole, "Catherine Bauer," 214.

21. Ibid., 256.

22. Brownlee, in Brownlee and DeLong, *In the Realm*, 29.

23. On Bauer and Mumford see Cole, "Catherine Bauer," 116–118, 206–214.

24. Bauer, "Change in Civic Hopes," 35.

25. Lewis Mumford, "Patriotism and Its Consequences," *Dial* 66 (19 April 1919): 406, quoted in Casey Nelson Blake, *Beloved Community: The Cultural Criticism of Randolph Bourne, Van Wyck Brooks, Waldo Frank, and Lewis Mumford* (Chapel Hill: University of North Carolina Press, 1990), 188.

26. "Collectivism" is the term used by historians, as in Richard Pells, *Radical Visions and American Dreams* (New York: Harper and Row, 1973), 105–118. Mumford's preferred term was "communism," although he took care to distinguish his ideal from the communism of the Soviet Republics. See Mumford, *Technics and Civilization* (New York: Harcourt Brace, 1934), 400–409. In 1939, Mumford had written: "Our communities present a true picture of the economic institutions that produce them. They are chaotic because capitalism is chaotic; they are socially misplanned and economically disorganized because capitalism is misplanned and disorganized; they do not sustain human values because capitalism puts pecuniary values first." Mumford, "Social Imperatives," in *Public Housing in America*, ed. Morris B. Schnapper (New York: Wilson, 1939), quoted in Sandeen, "Design of Public Housing," 664. The literature on Mumford is vast: see the collection of essays edited by Thomas P. Hughes and Agatha C. Hughes, *Lewis Mumford: Public Intellectual* (New York: Oxford University Press, 1990); and Robert Wojtowicz, *Lewis Mumford and American Modernism* (New York: Cambridge University Press, 1996).

27. In "Change in Civic Hopes," 36, Bauer argued that school buildings and community centers should serve as focal points for new neighborhoods; she also quoted Mumford in *The Culture of Cities* (New York: Harcourt Brace, 1938), 475, who argued for strong local institutions "framed to the human scale."

28. Stonorov, "Address to the Housing Course of the Pennsylvania School of Social Work," 28 March 1939, in "Speeches 1932–1939," box 28, Stonorov papers, American Heritage Center, Laramie, Wyo., hereafter cited as Stonorov papers.

29. Bauer Wurster, "The Social Front of Modern Architecture," 49–50. Bauer Wurster specifically mentions the Siemensstadt in Berlin as an example of the kind of public housing development that her work and that of her American colleagues was meant to critique.

30. On the Mackley Houses and Stonorov's relationship to Mumford and Bauer, see Sandeen, "Design of Public Housing"; and Richard Pommer, "The Architecture of Urban Housing in the United States During the Early 1930s," *Journal of the Society of Architectural Historians* 37 (December 1978): 235–264.

31. On Mumford and other intellectuals' response to the Great Depression, see Pells, *Radical Visions*, chapter 3 ("The Search for Community"), 96–150.

32. As reported in the minutes (1947) of the American chapter of CIAM, in "International Congress for Modern Architecture," box 5, Stonorov papers. On CIAM after the Athens Charter and on Sert more specifically, see Eric Mumford, *The CIAM Discourse on Urbanism* (Cambridge, Mass.: MIT Press, 2000); and Jos Bosman, "CIAM after the War: A Balance of the Modern Movement," *Rassegna* 52 (December 1992): 6–21.

33. Paul and Percival Goodman, *Communitas: Means of Livelihood and Ways of Life* (Chicago: University of Chicago Press, 1947). Although *Communitas* appeared after the war, in 1947, it was written in the early 1940s, and the Goodmans had published several articles in the wartime years sketching out their principal ideas: Paul and Percival Goodman, "Architecture in Wartime," *New Republic* 109 (20 December 1943): 878–892; Goodman and Goodman, "Architectural Form," *Chicago Review* 3 (May 1949): 1, 6. Kahn had attended architectural school with Percival Goodman at the University of Pennsylvania, and although the two were never close friends, they did remain in touch from time to time. See Kahn to Goodman, in "Louis I. Kahn, Lectures, 1958 Only," box 64, Kahn Collection.

34. Michael Walzer describes this tension between "the lively longing for personal pleasure" and "the lively sense of oneself as participant in a free state, concerned for the common good" in *Obligations* (Cambridge: Harvard University Press, 1970), 91–92; Robert B. Westbrook connects Walzer's ideas to social critiques in the 1940s in "Fighting for the American Family: Private Interest and Political Obligation in World War II," in *The Power of Culture: Critical Essays in American History*, ed. Richard Wightman Fox and T. J. Jackson Lears (Chicago: University of Chicago Press, 1993), 194–221.

35. On Dewey, see Robert Westbrook, *John Dewey and American Democracy* (Ithaca: Cornell University Press, 1991). For more on communitarianism, see Paul Rosenberg, "Liberal Neutralism and the Social-Democratic Project," in *Critical Review*, special issue, *Communitarianism* 8 (Spring 1994): 223–224. On Mumford's thought as an antecedent to more recent ideas of communitarianism, see Casey Blake, "The Perils of Personality: Lewis Mumford and Politics after Liberalism," in *Mumford: Public Intellectual*, 283–300, and Blake, *Beloved Community*.

36. On Paul Goodman's political philosophy, see Lewis Fried, "The Kingdom of *The Empire City*: Paul Goodman's Regional Labor," in *Artist of the Actual: Essays on Paul Goodman*, ed. Peter Parisi (Methuchen, N.J.: Scarecrow Press, 1986), 59–79; and Kingsley Widmer, *Paul Goodman* (Boston: Twayne, 1980), 42.

37. See, for example, Mumford in *The Culture of Cities*, 33, 140–141.

38. Goodman and Goodman, *Communitas*, 50. A later example of an author who equated the values of the New England village and Periclean Greece was Paul Zucker, in *Town and Square from the Agora to the Village Green* (New York: Columbia University Press, 1959).

39. See, for example, Seyla Ben-Habib, "Models of Public Space: Hannah Arendt, the Liberal Tradition, and Jurgen Habermas," in *Habermas and the Public Sphere*, ed. Craig Calhoun (Cambridge: MIT Press, 1992), 75.

40. Brownlee, in Brownlee and DeLong (*In the Realm*, 32), suggests that Stonorov was "in

charge of most" of the work on the pamphlets that they prepared for Revere Copper and Brass, discussed below. Although it is always difficult to parse out responsibility on collaborative projects, the manuscript for a film based on the ideas in *You and Your Neighborhood: A Primer for Neighborhood Planning* is in Kahn's handwriting alone; "Can Neighborhoods Exist?" box 33, Stonorov papers. This suggests that Kahn and Stonorov were equally engaged by these ideas.

41. Kahn quoted in Bacon, "Stonorov and the City," 116.

42. See also "A.S.P.A.," box 63, Kahn Collection; and Brownlee in Brownlee and DeLong, *In the Realm*, 34. The ASPA held preliminary meetings in 1944. For a detailed discussion of the organizations to which Kahn belonged in the 1940s, see Brownlee, in Brownlee and DeLong, *In the Realm*, 34–35.

43. The Carver Court project is described in "Carver Court," *Architectural Forum* 81 (December 1944): 109–116; Elizabeth Mock, *Built in the U.S.A., 1932–1944* (New York: Museum of Modern Art, 1944); Brownlee, "Adventures," 30; Stern, *Howe*, 197–198.

44. George Howe, Oscar Stonorov, and Louis I. Kahn, "'Standards' Versus Essential Space: Comments on Unit Plans for War Housing," *Architectural Forum* 76 (May 1942): 308–311, reprinted in *Louis I. Kahn: Writings, Lectures, Interviews*, ed. Alessandra Latour (New York: Rizzoli, 1993), 14–17.

45. Lewis Mumford, *Faith for Living* (New York: Harcourt Brace, 1940).

46. This quotation and those in this and the following paragraph are from *You and Your Neighborhood*, which is unpaginated.

47. Stonorov to Meyers, 2 February 1944, "Correspondence January–March 1944," box 50, Stonorov papers.

48. The history of Philadelphia's Citizen's Council on City Planning is briefly outlined in John F. Barman, "Visions of a Post-War City: A Perspective on Urban Planning in Philadelphia and the Nation, 1942–1945," in *Introduction to Planning History in the United States*, ed. Donald A. Krueckeberg (New Brunswick, N.J.: Center for Urban Policy Research, 1983), 175.

49. Stonorov to Howard Meyers, p. 2, 2 February 1944, "Correspondence January–March 1944," box 50, Stonorov papers.

50. On city planners' solicitations of citizen participation, see, for example, W. Pope Barney and Edmund Krimmel, Report of the Philadelphia Chapter, A.I.A. Committee on the Development of the "Triangle," "A.I.A. Triangle Committee," box 60, Kahn Collection.

51. "New Buildings for 194X," *Architectural Forum* 78 (May 1943): 74–79.

52. Stonorov and Kahn, "Hotel," in ibid., 74.

53. Mies van der Rohe, "Museum for a Small City," in "New Buildings," 84–85.

54. Paul Zucker, ed., *New Architecture and City Planning* (New York: Philosophical Library, 1944), 577–588.

55. Lewis Mumford wrote on monumentality in *The Culture of Cities*, 433–440; and in "Monumentalism, Symbolism, and Style," *Architectural Review* 105 (April 1949): 173–180.

56. For a general discussion of the history of monumentality in modern architecture, which includes an excellent bibliography, see Christiane C. Collins and George R. Collins, "Monumentality: A Critical Matter in Modern Architecture," *Harvard Architecture Review: Monumentality and the City* 4 (Spring 1984): 15–35. For Howe, see George Howe, "Monuments, Memorials, and Modern Design—An Exchange of Letters," *Magazine of Art* 37 (October 1944): 202–207. For Giedion, see Sigfried Giedion, José Luis Sert, and Fernand Léger, "Nine Points on Monumentality," in *architecture you and me: the diary of a development* (Cambridge: Harvard University Press, 1958, reprinted in *Harvard Architecture Review: Monumentality and the City* 4 (Spring 1984); and Giedion, "The Need for a New Monumentality," in Zucker, *New Architecture and City*

Planning (hereafter cited as Zucker symposium). For Mock, see Elizabeth Mock, introduction to *Built in the U.S.A., 1932–1944*, ed. Elizabeth Mock (New York: Museum of Modern Art, 1945). For Johnson, see Philip Johnson, "War Memorials: What Price Aesthetic Glory?" *ArtNews* 44 (September 1945), 8–10, 24–25, and a similar article in *Progressive Architecture* 30 (February 1949): 8, 10, 12. For Labatut, see Jean Labatut, "Monuments and Memorials," in *Forms and Functions of Twentieth-Century Architecture*, ed. Talbot Hamlin, vol. 3 (New York: Columbia University Press, 1952), 523–533. For Hudnut, see Joseph Hudnut, "The Monument Does Not Remember," *Atlantic Monthly* 176 (September 1945): 55–59.

57. *The Architectural Review*, "In Search of a New Monumentality: A Symposium," *Architectural Review* 104 (September 1948): 117–129, with contributions by Gregor Paulsson, H. R. Hitchcock, William Holford, Sigfried Giedion, Walter Gropius, Lucio Costa, and Alfred Roth. The title of the 1947 CIAM conference was "The Synthesis of the Arts," recalling a proposal for a new monumentality advanced by Giedion, Léger, and Sert. The 1951 conference was entitled "The Core of the City," and the topic was monumentality and public space. The proceedings of the 1951 conference were published in International Conference of Modern Architects, *The Heart of the City: Toward the Humanization of Public Life*, ed. J. Tyrwhitt, J. L. Sert, et al. (New York: Pelligrini and Cudahy, 1952).

58. For a general discussion on war memorials and living memorials, see Mary McLeod, "The Battle for the Monument: The Vietnam Veteran's Memorial," in *The Experimental Tradition: Essays on Competition in Architecture*, ed. Hélène Lipstadt (New York: Architectural League and Princeton Architectural Press, 1989), 115–116.

59. On living memorials constructed at the end of World War I, see James Mayo, *War Memorials as Political Landscape* (New York: Praeger, 1988); see also "War Memorials," *The American City* 59 (January 1944): 35, in which the author wrote that after the *American City*'s plea for living memorials at the end of World War I, "from one end of our country to the other a new spirit of commemoration found expression."

60. Quotations are from "War Memorials," 35–36. Other articles on living memorials from the same periodical are "Public Libraries as War Memorials," *The American City* 58 (December 1943): 79; "Municipal Forests for Post-War," 59 (January 1944): 44; "Planning Memorial Community Buildings," 59 (June 1944): 113–115; "War Memorials That Further Practical Democracy," 59 (October 1944): 72–75; "'Community Institutes' as War Memorials," 59 (November 1944): 77–78; "What Type Memorial?" 60 (February 1945): 63–65; "When the Boys and Girls Come Home," 58 (August 1943): cover.

61. Hudnut, "Monument," 59.

62. "In Search," *Architectural Review*," 117.

63. Ibid.

64. Sigfried Giedion alludes to the fact that adherence to the doctrine of functionalism was more important in the United States than in Europe because the modern movement was younger there, in "Need," Zucker symposium. As late as 1944, George Nelson mused that "only seven years ago" magazines could not find enough good modernist work to fill one issue (Nelson, "Stylistic Trends," Zucker symposium, 570). As late as 1950, when George Howe was appointed dean of the School of Architecture at Yale, Howe felt compelled to justify his modernist predilections, explaining that whereas traditional programs focused "solely on problems of aesthetics and monumentality," his at Yale would "bring all the departments together in the study of more material related to industry, business organization and mass manufacturing processes, sociology and economics." Press release, 23 February 1950, p. 2, in "Howe–Rob't Stern correspondence," box 2, Howe Collection, Avery Library, Columbia University.

65. Nelson, "Stylistic Trends," Zucker symposium, 572.

66. See, for example, Bates Lowrey, *Building a National Image: Architectural Drawings for the American Democracy, 1789–1912* (Washington, D.C.: National Building Museum, 1985).

67. Mumford, *The Culture of Cities*, 138.

68. George Howe, "Two Years of Architecture," book review, *Yale Review* 27 (September 1937): 204–206, and Howe, "Monuments, Memorials, and Modern Design"; Mock, introduction to *Built in the U.S.A.*

69. Giedion, "Need," Zucker symposium, 556.

70. "Collective consciousness" is from "In Search," *Architectural Review*, 117; see also unsigned book review of Zucker's *New Architecture and City Planning* in *Architectural Forum* 82 (February 1945): 164.

71. Walter Curt Behrendt, *Modern Building: Its Nature, Problems, and Forms* (New York: Harcourt Brace, 1937), 180–181; Hitchcock, "In Search," *Architectural Review*, 124.

72. Giedion, "Need," Zucker symposium, 565.

73. Ibid., 556.

74. Giedion et al., "Nine Points," 50.

75. On Le Corbusier's ideas on a synthesis of the arts, see Christopher Pearson, "Integrations of Art and Architecture in the Work of Le Corbusier: Theory and Practice from Ornamentalism to the 'Synthesis of the Major Arts'" (Ph.D. diss., Stanford University, 1995).

76. Giedion, "Nine Points," 51.

77. Bruno Taut, *Alpine Architecture*, ed. Dennis Sharp, trans. Shirley Palmer (1919; reprint, New York: Praeger, 1972); Sigfried Giedion, *Space, Time, and Architecture: The Growth of a New Tradition* (Cambridge: Harvard University Press, 1943), 481–483.

78. Giedion, "Need," Zucker symposium, 562–563.

79. One thing is nearly certain, that Zucker did not initially solicit Kahn's contribution, as he had Jean Labatut's on the suggestion of Sigfried Giedion (Labatut declined). According to Zucker's bibliographer, Harold Markowitz, Zucker destroyed much correspondence during his lifetime. What he saved became the possession of Zucker's companion, Lotte Eggers, when Zucker died. In turn, Eggers passed it along to Markowitz, who now lives in Philadelphia. Markowitz has only a few items unrelated to the 1944 book. The Paul Zucker collection, Avery Library, Columbia University, has no documentation relating to the symposium. Similarly, there is no documentation in Kahn's papers, and neither Esther Kahn nor Anne Tyng recollects how Kahn came to write the essay. It seems likely that Zucker also solicited the contributions of the other participants in the section. Zucker's early list of projected participants in the symposium lists "Oscar Stonorov and Louis I. Kahn, Associated Architects," suggesting that Zucker knew of Kahn simply through his partnership with Stonorov. It seems possible that Zucker had asked George Howe to write an essay, knowing of Howe's developing interest in monumentality, and that Howe passed along the duty to Kahn. My thanks to Eric Mumford of Washington University in St. Louis for discussing this issue with me.

80. Kahn's essay, long and long-winded, has been narrowly interpreted as a prolegomenon for a later practice of structural rationalism. See Kenneth Frampton, *Studies in Tectonic Culture* (Cambridge: MIT Press, 1996), 209–246, hereafter cited as *Tectonic Culture*, and Joan Ockman's introduction to Kahn's essay on monumentality in Ockman, ed., *Architecture Culture, 1943–1968* (New York: Rizzoli, 1993), 47.

81. The source of transmission may have been Jean Labatut, to whom Giedion sent a copy of his essay late in 1943. A draft of Giedion's "Nine Points," from approximately November 1943 (based on surrounding correspondence), is in Labatut's papers, box 68, Firestone Library, Princeton University. Labatut had known Kahn since 1928, stating, "I found him stimulating for the students and he found me stimulating also. We were always in

good contact with each other." Labatut, interview with Michael Wurmfeld, in Wurmfeld, ed., *Princeton's Beaux-Arts and Its New Academicism from Labatut to the Program of Geddes: An Exhibition of Original Drawings over Fifty Years* (Princeton, n.d.).

82. Hudnut offered Kahn a teaching post at Harvard University in 1946; Hudnut to Kahn, "U.N.O.," box 63, Kahn Collection; see also Brownlee, in Brownlee and DeLong, *In the Realm*, 34. Brownlee reports that Kahn and Mock corresponded in 1944 regarding the possible making of a film; p. 48, n. 72.

83. Kahn, "Monumentality," Zucker symposium, 577.

84. Ibid.

85. Ibid.

86. Ibid., 582.

87. Ibid., 584–585.

88. Ibid., 585.

89. Ibid., 586, 578.

90. Ibid., 587.

91. Kenneth Frampton has most consistently propounded Kahn's place as the inheritor of the French structural rationalist tradition. See his "Kahn and the French Connection," *Oppositions* 22 (Fall 1980): 21–53; Frampton, "Louis I. Kahn and the New Monumentality, 1944–1972," *Design Book Review* 28 (Spring 1993): 6–13; and *Tectonic Culture*, 209–246. Brownlee (in Brownlee and DeLong, *In the Realm*, 43) also notes Kahn's debt to Cret. In *Tectonic Culture*, Frampton argues that Kahn's essay on monumentality exemplifies his tectonic approach to architecture, which is later to be seen in Kahn's Art Gallery addition (discussed in Chapter 2 of this book) and his proposal for a new City Hall (discussed in Chapter 3). Frampton explicitly defines the tectonic approach as the expression not only of structure and construction but also of statical forces and resistance, and contends that Kahn's interest in structural expression, first declared in the essay on monumentality, "established the basic thematic of his work," and that he had inherited Viollet-le-Duc's ideas from Cret, who had written an article on Viollet's greatest student, Anatole de Baudot (*Tectonic Culture*, 51, 209, 213). Frampton's characterization of Kahn's attitude to structure is inaccurate, so also are the lines of transmission he traces (Viollet-le-Duc to de Baudot to Cret to Kahn), for he neglects to mention that Cret's article on de Baudot is unmitigatedly derogatory. Cret writes: "But in the enthusiasm that many of us feel for the austere and logical forms which are developed by mechanical mathematics, and in the reaction against the mawkish, the illogical, the senselessly elaborated and meaningless architecture that has been developed out of a feeble sentiment . . . we must guard against a tendency to make a fetish of the rigid forms that are produced by pure mechanics. . . . Foolish people, while they are avoiding one vice, rush upon its opposite!" Cret, "The Architect as Collaborator of the Engineer," reprinted in *Paul Philippe Cret: Architect and Teacher*, ed. Theo B. White (Philadelphia: Art Alliance Press, 1973), 63. A more immediate and powerful source of transmission for Kahn's ideas regarding structural rationalism came from Le Corbusier. Kahn's extremely worn and well-used copy of Le Corbusier's *Vers une architecture* is currently in the collection of Sue Ann Kahn; according to his widow, Esther Kahn, Kahn read the book in French as soon as he got his hands on it (interview with the author, 1992).

92. This is what Bourdieu would define as the "intellectual field." Bourdieu, "The Intellectual Field: A World Apart," in *In Other Words: Essays Towards a Reflexive Sociology*, trans. Matthew Adamson (1987; reprint, Stanford: Stanford University Press, 1990), 140–149.

93. Roland Marchand, in "Visions of Classlessness, Quests for Dominion," describes the immediate postwar years as one of great promise in which Americans expected a "technologically wondrous future for all;" in *Reshaping America: Society and Institutions*,

1945–1960, ed. Robert H. Bremner and Gary W. Reichard (Columbus: Ohio State University Press, 1982), 163. American optimism regarding the promise of technology is also discussed by Joseph Corn in his introduction and his conclusion to *Imagining Tomorrow: History, Technology, and the American Future*, ed. Joseph Corn (Cambridge: MIT Press, 1986). Discussion of technological progress during the war and in the immediate postwar era is in William Chafe, *The Unfinished Journey: America since World War II*, 2nd ed. (New York: Oxford University Press, 1991), 7–11; 112–117.

94. See Mumford in *Technics and Civilization*.

95. "New Era in Plastics," *Newsweek* 21 (17 May 1943): 42; "Plastics: A Way to a Better More Carefree Life," *House Beautiful* 89 (October 1947): 123, 141; both quoted in Jeffrey Meikle, "Plastic, Material of a Thousand Uses," in Corn, *Imagining Tomorrow*, 93. Between 1939 and 1949 the plastics industry expanded considerably; see Meikle, "Materials and Metaphors: Plastics in American Culture," in *New Perspectives on Technology and American Culture*, ed. Bruce Sinclair (Philadelphia: American Philosophical Society, 1986), 39. In the 1950s, the U.S. government sponsored many research studies on plastics; see Chafe, *The Unfinished Journey*, 113.

96. Kahn's notes on the "Idea Center for Plastics" studio are in "Yale University – Professorship," box 61, and in "Yale University 1948–49," box 60, Kahn Collection. This will be further discussed in Chapter 2.

97. Kahn, "Monumentality," Zucker symposium, 581.

98. Ibid., 580.

99. Kahn to Eero Saarinen, October 1947, cited in Rumiko Handa, "Design Through Drawing: Eero Saarinen's Design in the Jefferson National Expansion Memorial Competition" (Ph.D. diss., University of Pennsylvania, 1992), 104. My thanks to Hélène Lipstadt for pointing me to this source.

100. Facts on the JNEM competition are in "Competition: Jefferson National Expansion Memorial," *Progressive Architecture* 27 (May 1948): 51–73; and in George Howe, "Jefferson National Expansion Memorial Competition," *Architectural Forum* 88 (March 1948): 14–18. See also Hélène Lipstadt, "In the Shadow of the Tribune Tower: American Architecture Competitions, 1922–1960," in Lipstadt, *The Experimental Tradition*, 79–94. I am grateful to Professor Lipstadt for sharing her research with me on this project, including her copy of George Howe's competition prospectus, *Architectural Competition for the Jefferson National Expansion Memorial, Program* (St. Louis, Mo., 1947).

101. *Architectural Competition* program, 15.

102. Kahn to Saarinen, 21 October 1947, quoted in Handa, "Design Through Drawing," 104.

103. Kahn, journal entry, collection of Sue Ann Kahn.

104. Thanks to Mary McLeod, Columbia University, for initially pointing out this similarity to me. Elizabeth Mock of the Museum of Modern Art (New York) wrote Stonorov with praise for Le Corbusier's St. Dié on 22 October 1945, "Correspondence October–December 1945," box 50, Stonorov papers.

105. See Alberto Sato, "The Thresholds of Carlos Raúl Villanueva: The University City of Caracas" (delivered at "The New Inside the New: Latin American Architecture and the Crisis of the International Style, 1937–1954" [19–20 April 1996]), Harvard University.

106. This and subsequent citations are taken from the competition board that Kahn submitted for the JNEM competition.

107. All information regarding this Yale studio problem is from Advanced Architectural Design Problem III, "Yale Professor 1950," box 61, Kahn Collection.

108. Kahn's name was apparently given as a potential consultant to the project, should the U.N. officials decide that the complex would be built in Philadelphia, as was considered during the early months of 1947 (see Lawrence Vale's essay in *Mumford: Public Intel-*

lectual). Kahn asked Howard Myers, then editor of *Architectural Forum*, for an introduction to Harrison and a recommendation; this Myers did, sending Kahn a copy of the letter he wrote to Harrison (Howard Myers to Wallace Harrison, 14 January 1947, carbon copy in "Beaux-Arts Institute of Design," box 61, Kahn Collection; see also Kahn to Howard Myers, 14 May 1947, unmarked file, box 61, Kahn Collection). The following month, Kahn received a request from Thomas Creighton, editor of *Progressive Architecture*, to sign a public petition against Harrison's control of the U.N. project. The petition questioned "whether [Harrison's] selection was for political expediency rather than his recognized abilities" (Creighton to Kahn, 11 February 1947, unmarked file, box 61, Kahn Collection).

109. An issue of the *World Government News* 5 (New York City; published by the United World Federalists, March 1947) is in "World Government," box 63, Kahn Collection; on p. 8, the text calls for a world republic with a headquarters based in Evanston, Ill. Mumford was also at least flirting with the idea of world government: see pp. 266–276 of Lawrence Vale's essay "Designing Global Harmony: Lewis Mumford and the United Nations Headquarters," in *Mumford: Public Intellectual*. In the *World Government News* brochure that Kahn kept, Mumford was listed as a member of the editorial board.

110. Correspondence between Kahn and various members of the Progressive Citizens of America is in "Progressive Citizens of America PCA," box 62, Kahn Collection. Background on Henry Wallace in general and the Progressive Citizens of America in particular can be found in John Morton Blum, *V Was for Victory: Politics and Culture During World War II* (New York: Harcourt Brace Jovanovich, 1976), 279–292; Blum, ed., *The Price of Vision: The Diary of Henry A. Wallace, 1942–1946* (Boston: Houghton Mifflin, 1973); and in Richard Pells, *The Liberal Mind in a Conservative Age*, 2nd ed. (Middletown, Conn.: Wesleyan University Press, 1989), 69–71, 109.

111. Pells, *The Liberal Mind*, 69–71. William Chafe, in *The Unfinished Journey*, 31, writes that while in 1945 nearly 80 percent of Americans endorsed the United Nations, by 1948 such optimism was already diminished in the heat of the Cold War.

112. Pells, *The Liberal Mind*, 69–71.

113. See correspondence between Kahn and various members of the PCA in "Progressive Citizens of America PCA," box 62, Kahn Collection, on 3 April, 15 October, 20 September, and 23 December, among others.

CHAPTER 2: THE QUEST FOR AUTHENTICITY

1. Kahn's Yale Art Gallery addition was reviewed in (among other places) *Architectural Forum* 97 (November 1952): 148–149; *Perspecta* 3 (1955): 59–61; *New York Herald Tribune* (28 November 1953): 10; *Progressive Architecture* 5 (May 1952): 22–24; *New York Times* (1 November 1953); *Architectural Review* 118 (December 1955): 355–361.

2. It was not the first academic post he had been offered: the previous year, Joseph Hudnut tried to convince him to come teach at Harvard. This opportunity Kahn declined, writing, "I am only now finding time to develop some sociological, construction, and aesthetic ideas which have been at the back of my mind for some time"; given his acceptance of the Yale position the following year it seems more likely that Hudnut's invitation did not appeal because Cambridge was too long a commute from Philadelphia, and Kahn never had the slightest inclination to move out of his hometown. Kahn to Hudnut, 15 May 1946, "U.N.O.," box 63, Kahn Collection. Brownlee (in Brownlee and DeLong, *In the Realm*), 44, also suggests this as the reason Kahn turned Hudnut's offer down. It was probably for this reason that Kahn declined an invitation from Walter Gropius in 1952 to take over Mies van der Rohe's program at the Illinois Institute of Technology in Chicago upon Mies's retirement—a move that would have significantly advanced his career. The

original letter is in Kahn's copy of Gropius' *Architecture and Design in the Age of Science* (New York: Spiral Press, 1952) in Kahn's personal library, collection of Sue Ann Kahn. Kahn responded in March 1953, writing, "Your letter came as a warm friend." Kahn to Gropius, "Louis I. Kahn (personal) – 1953," box 60, Kahn Collection.

3. See Peter Reed, "Toward Form: Louis I. Kahn's Urban Designs for Philadelphia, 1939–1962" (Ph.D. diss., University of Pennsylvania, 1989), 138–145; Brownlee, in Brownlee and DeLong, *In the Realm*, 44–46. David Rothstein, in an interview with Richard Saul Wurman, commented that "the most interesting times in the office were when he started at Yale . . . he would come back from Yale quite stimulated." Archive of Richard Saul Wurman, tape 108, Newport, Rhode Island.

4. Robert A. M. Stern, "Yale, 1950–1965," *Oppositions* 4 (October 1974): 36. Jack West, a student of architecture from 1945 to 1948, now an architect in Sarasota, Florida, described his surprise when expected to perform Beaux-Arts schemes one year, modernist ones the next. West, interview with the author, March 1992. For general descriptions of architectural education that include this period and discuss Yale, see Stern, "Yale"; Kenneth Frampton and Alessandra Latour, "Notes on American Architectural Education from the End of the Nineteenth Century until the 1970s," *Lotus* 27 (1980): 5–40; Spiro Kostof, "The Shape of Time at Yale, circa 1960," in *The History of History in American Schools of Architecture, 1865–1975*, ed. Gwendolyn Wright and Janet Parks (New York: Buell Center, 1990).

5. Sawyer described the program he established at Yale in "The Arts at Yale," *Yale Alumni Magazine* 13 (April 1950): 3–7. As director of the Worcester Museum of Fine Arts, Sawyer had organized an exhibition of the most advanced American painting: the catalogue was *A Decade of American Painting, 1930–1940* (Worcester, Mass.: Worcester Art Museum, 1942).

6. On the program at Harvard under Gropius, see, among others, Winfried Nerdinger, "From Bauhaus to Harvard. . . ," in Wright and Parks, *The History of History*, 89–99; and William Jordy, "The Aftermath of the Bauhaus in America," in *The Intellectual Migration*, ed. Bernard Bailyn and Donald Fleming (Cambridge: Harvard University Press, 1969), 485–543. Yale's program is described in a letter by Charles Sawyer (9 February 1974) to Robert Stern, "Howe-Rob't Stern Correspondence," box 2, Howe Collection, Avery Library, Columbia University. For curriculum committee recommendations, see, for example, the memo "A Basic Curriculum," written by Leslie Cheek, Jr., April 1948, box 60, "Yale University, 1948–1949," Kahn Collection.

7. On Albers at Black Mountain, see Martin Duberman, *Black Mountain: An Exploration in Community* (New York: Dutton, 1972).

8. Esther Kahn, interview with the author, May 1991. Albers' appreciation of Kahn is indicated in a letter he wrote to Sawyer in 1949: "I am looking forward very much to hearing from you again and from Louis Kahn." Albers to Sawyer, 23 July 1949. Sawyer forwarded the letter on to Kahn, and it is in "Yale University, 1948–1949," box 60, Kahn Collection. It is unclear how Albers and Kahn met, but Kahn may have known of Albers' work through an exhibition in 1947 at the Philadelphia Art Alliance, an organization in which Kahn was an active member. See exhibition notice of show entitled *Five American Printmakers* (Philadelphia Art Alliance, 11 February–16 March 1947), box 12, folder 109, Josef Albers papers, Yale University Manuscripts and Archives.

9. The Gestalt movement was not new, for it had been influential in Germany since the 1930s. But it had only recently become known to intellectuals in the United States, as American psychologists, accustomed to a more pragmatic methodology, did not embrace the movement's ideas until the late 1940s. The history of the reception of Gestalt psychology in America is discussed in Jean Matler Mandler and George Man-

dler, "The Diaspora of Experimental Psychology: The Gestaltists and Others," in Bailyn and Fleming, *The Intellectual Migration*, 371–419, esp. 396–400.

10. Cheek, "A Basic Curriculum." The memo reads "The purpose of the curriculum would be to develop an understanding of the visual media by free manipulation of their basic materials and tools. No artistic formulas, present or past, would be presented for the student to copy."

11. Memo by Albers, January 1949, box 22, folder 193, Josef Albers papers, Yale University Manuscripts and Archives.

12. Josef Albers, "The Educational Value of Manual Work and Handicraft in Relation to Architecture," in *New Architecture and City Planning*, ed. Paul Zucker (New York: Philosophical Library, 1944), 688–694.

13. Ibid., 688.

14. Ibid., 689.

15. Albers, memo describing his painting techniques for the "Homage to the Square" series, box 22, folder 192, Josef Albers papers, Yale University Manuscripts and Archives.

16. Josef Albers, "Abstract—Presentational," in *American Abstract Artists* (New York: RAM Press, 1946), n.p.

17. Charles Sawyer, ed., *"Intrinsic Significance" in Modern Art*, with essays by Katherine Dreier, James Johnson Sweeney, and Naum Gabo (New York: Philosophical Library, 1949).

18. Clement Greenberg, review of Albers show at the Janis Gallery, *The Nation* (19 February 1949).

19. Albers quoted in Elaine de Kooning, "Albers Paints a Picture," *Art News* 49 (November 1950): 40.

20. Albers quoted in ibid., 41.

21. Ibid., 58.

22. Thomas B. Hess, *Willem de Kooning* (New York: Museum of Modern Art, 1968), 72–73.

23. Hess, in "De Kooning Paints a Picture" (*Art News* 52 [March 1953]: 30–34, 64–67), emphasizes struggle and the creative process as determinative in creating de Kooning's aesthetic.

24. Ibid., 33.

25. Irving Sandler, in his essay for *20 Artists: Yale School of Art, 1950–1970* (New Haven: Yale University Press, 1981), claims that connections between New Haven and the New York art world were limited in the 1950s, but his conclusion was not based on archival sources. Albers' papers suggest a different story.

26. Henry-Russell Hitchcock, *Painting Toward Architecture* (Meriden, Conn.: Miller Company, 1948). For a review see Aline Loucheim, "Abstraction on the Assembly Line," *Art News* 46 (December 1947): 25–27.

27. See Yale University Art Gallery, *The Société Anonyme and the Dreier Bequest at Yale University: A Catalogue Raisonné*, ed. Robert L. Herbert, Eleanor S. Apter, and Elise K. Kenney (New Haven: Yale University Art Gallery and Yale University Press, 1984).

28. Monographs on these artists are in Kahn's library, and are listed in the bibliography of Kahn's library prepared by Joseph Burton of Clemson University. My thanks to Professor Burton for sharing this document with me. Color transparencies and an exhibition catalogue of a Dubuffet exhibition at a New York gallery are in the file marked "personal" in the clippings files at the Kahn Collection.

29. The show was held at the Dubin Galleries: a notice is in "Louis I. Kahn (Personal) no. 4 (1951) & 52," box 60, Kahn Collection. Anne Griswold Tyng, whose work was also represented in the exhibit, reports that another exhibition of a similar nature was held in 1955 (Tyng, interview with the author, January 1992).

30. Kahn to Hauf, 8 January 1948, "Yale University, 1948–1949," box 60, Kahn Collection.

31. Kahn received an overdue notice from the Yale Library for the *Royal Institute of British Architects Journal* 44, 3rd ser., no. 5; the only article in the volume that could have interested him was on collaborations between artists and architects: "Modern Art and Architecture" (9 January 1937): 209–219.

32. See notes and memos in "The National Center of UNESCO," box 61, and "Yale Professor–1950," box 61, Kahn Collection.

33. Kahn sketchbook pages in "Yale University, 1948–1949," box 60, Kahn Collection. Information on this studio project can also be found in "Yale Professor–1950" and "Yale University–Professorship," box 61, Kahn Collection.

34. See Noyes memo "Modern Design: The Search for Appropriate Form," in file folder "Lectures Art Gallery 1946–47," YRG 16, series 2, box 17, Yale University Manuscripts and Archives.

35. Reed, in "Toward Form," 138–141, argues that Kahn's move toward greater abstraction came from the influence of George Howe and Eugene Nalle's course in basic design, developed after Howe arrived to replace Harold Hauf in fall 1950. Reed writes: "There is a remarkable similarity between many of his own drawings and the detailed notes outlining the course. It almost seems that Kahn assumed the role of the pupil" ("Toward Form," 140). But plates 318–320 in Jan Hochstim's monograph *The Paintings and Sketches of Louis I. Kahn* (New York: Rizzoli, 1991), demonstrate that many of Kahn's abstract drawings predate Nalle and Howe's arrival at Yale.

36. Joseph Amisano, interview with Richard Saul Wurman, 1974, Archive of Richard Saul Wurman, Newport, Rhode Island.

37. 2 February 1951, "Letters to Louis I. Kahn," box 60, Kahn Collection.

38. Kahn to David Wisdom, Anne Tyng, and "Alice, Bill, and Armstrong," 6 December 1950, in "Letters to LI Kahn," box 60, Kahn Collection.

39. George Howe to Kahn, 22 January 1951, in "Correspondence with YALE UNIVERSITY YALE ART GALLERY," box 107, Kahn Collection.

40. The building had previously been commissioned to Philip Goodwin (co-designer with Edward Durrell Stone of New York's Museum of Modern Art), but Goodwin had resigned early in 1951 owing to a sudden illness. Goodwin proposed that Philip Johnson replace him, but Johnson suggested Kahn, and the recommendation was seconded by George Howe. For a complete description of the hiring and design process for the Yale Art Gallery, see Patricia Cummings Loud, *The Art Museums of Louis I. Kahn* (Durham: Duke University Press, 1989), 52–96; and Loud, "Yale University Art Gallery," in Brownlee and DeLong, *In the Realm*, 417–420.

41. Tyng and Kahn's joint interest in the ideas of Fuller are discussed at length in Chapter 3 of this book. Tyng had been working in Kahn's office since 1946, after graduating from Harvard University's Graduate School of Design. Her autobiography is in Anne Griswold Tyng, "Architecture Is My Touchstone," *Radcliffe Quarterly* 70 (September 1984): 5–7. Kahn described Tyng in 1951 as "one of the most outstanding designers . . . [with] extraordinary vision and courage." Kahn to E. Krimmel, 28 December 1951, recommending Tyng for the Municipal Improvements Committee, "AIA Municipal Improvements Committee," box 63, Kahn Collection. Tyng fell under the influence of Fuller in 1949 or 1950 when he was lecturing to publicize what he called his "geodesic dome revolution." She described Fuller's influence on her work in an interview with the author, March 1992, and in her "Louis Kahn's 'Order' in the Creative Process," in Alessandra Latour's interview with her in *Louis I. Kahn: L'uomo, il maestro*, ed. Alessandra Latour (Rome: Edizioni Kappa, 1986), 285.

42. Kahn was so uninterested in the expression of structural forces that even as the tetrahedrons of the Yale Art Gallery ceiling were being poured in November 1952, he exhib-

ited a fundamental misunderstanding of a space frame's basic structural principles. Reacting to galleys of an article by Vernon Read, in which he was taken to task for configuring beam and joist construction to suggest a space frame, Kahn objected to the elementary assertion that a true space frame, unlike his design, was "supported by a minimum of three columns, and so framed that it could be picked up at any point without falling apart." Bracketing the line, he scrawled a huge question mark above it, and wrote a query to Tyng, "Is this true[?]." Read's manuscript, with Kahn's comments, are in "Yale Art Gallery," box 107, Kahn Collection.

43. Read, the author of the earliest critique of the Yale Art Gallery, published in *Architectural Forum*, pointed out with some consternation that by specifying a "space frame" of concrete Kahn had designed a ceiling far heavier than it needed to be. See "Building Engineering, 1: Tetrahedral Floor System: Yale's New Design Laboratory Conceals Lighting and Ductwork with a 31-Inch Deep Floor Structure," *Architectural Forum* 97 (November 1952): 149–150. Moreover, although the Art Gallery ceiling looked like a space frame, it acted, structurally, like a simple slab-and-beam structure; the tetrahedrons that created such an aggressive pattern completely obscured the ceiling's statics (Loud, in *The Art Museums of Louis I. Kahn*, 72–73).

44. Kahn, "North Carolina State College," box 56, Kahn Collection.

45. In addition to the jury, Haskell and Kahn served together on the Architect's Advisory Committee of the Public Housing Administration from 1951 to 1954; "PHA Advisory Committee," box 61, Kahn Collection. For the jury in May 1951, see "Yale Professor–1951," box 61, Kahn Collection. Correspondence between Haskell and Kahn indicates that they were friendly, if not close friends: Kahn to Haskell, 21 April 1951; Haskell to Kahn, 27 June 1951, both in "Louis T. Kahn (Personal) No. 4 (1951) and 52," box 60, Kahn Collection. Haskell certainly knew of the Smithsons' work, as it had been widely discussed in the British architectural community. A notice that the Smithsons had won the competition was published in the British *Architect's Journal* 111 (4 May 1950): 541; a very schematic set of plans, with no details, was published in the same journal the following week: 111 (11 May 1950): 576–577. Subsequent articles came out only in 1953–1954. One month after he and Kahn served on the jury at Yale together, Haskell expressed in print thoughts similar to those subsequently embraced by Kahn. He scornfully dismissed what he called "art architects," to whom "the very idea of heating engineers or other mechanical engineers, with their pipes, ducts, and statistical tables, is abhorrent." Arguing that by paying services their due the architect could find a vocabulary that best expressed the spirit of the era, Haskell argued that "the science of heating and lighting and acoustic . . . are a grand new achievement of the twentieth century, needing only *imagination* to convert them into art." "D.H." [Douglas Haskell], "The Crystal Ball," *Architectural Forum* 94 (June 1951): 200.

46. Kahn, "Toward a Plan for Midtown Philadelphia," *Perspecta* 2 (1953): 23.

47. Kahn, 28 February 1953, North Carolina State conference, transcript in "North Carolina State College," box 56, Kahn Collection; later printed as "How to Develop New Methods of Construction," *Architectural Forum* 101 (November 1954): 157.

48. Interview with Kahn, in "The New Art Gallery and Design Center," special dedication issue, *Yale Daily News* (6 November 1953): 2.

49. Kahn in Henry S. F. Cooper, "The Architect Speaks," *Yale Daily News* (6 November 1953): 2.

50. Kahn, 28 February 1953, North Carolina State conference, transcript in "North Carolina State College," box 56, Kahn Collection.

51. Kahn first discussed the concept of beauty at this lecture at Tulane; it was published as "A Lecture by Louis Kahn" in the *Student Publication of the School of Architecture*,

Tulane University 1 (1955): n.p., and is reprinted in *Louis I. Kahn: Writings, Lectures, Interviews*, ed. Alessandra Latour (New York: Rizzoli, 1991), 62–64. He also discussed beauty in the nearly contemporaneous poem "Order Is," which was published in *Perspecta* 3 (1955): 59, and in November 1955 in his review of Rachel Wischnitzer's book on synagogue design in the United States, filed in "LIK Miscellaneous 1954–56," box 65, Kahn Collection.

52. Quoted in Walter McQuade, "The Building Years of a Yale Man," *Architectural Forum* 118 (June 1969): 88.

53. Reyner Banham, "The New Brutalism," *Architectural Review* 118 (December 1955): 355–361; and Banham, *The New Brutalism: Ethic or Aesthetic?* (Stuttgart: Karl Kramer, 1966).

54. Banham, *The New Brutalism*, 16.

55. See Nigel Whitley, "Banham and '*Otherness*': Reyner Banham (1922–1988) and His Quest for an *architecture autre*," *Architectural History* 33 (1990): 188–221.

56. For the impact of Existentialist ideas on Le Corbusier, see Mary McLeod, "Alger: L'appel de la Méditerranée," in *Le Corbusier, une encyclopédie* (Paris: Centre Georges Pompidou, 1987), 26–32; on the Smithsons, see Sarah Williams Goldhagen, "Freedom's Domiciles: Three Proposals by Alison and Peter Smithson," in *Anxious Modernisms: Experimental Postwar Architecture*, ed. Sarah Williams Goldhagen and Réjean Legault (Cambridge, Mass: MIT Press, 2000), 75–95.

57. *No Exit* was reviewed in *The Nation* 163 (14 December 1946): 708; *New Republic* 115 (9 December 1946): 764; *New Yorker* 22 (7 December 1946): 69; *Newsweek* (9 December 1946): 92. As for Sartre's other works, *L'âtre et le néant* (Paris: Gallimard, 1943) was published in translation in 1956 as *Being and Nothingness: A Phenomenological Essay on Ontology*, trans. Hazel E. Barnes (New York: Philosophical Library), and *La nausée* (Paris: Gallimard, 1938) was published in translation as *Nausea*, trans. Lloyd Alexander (Norfolk, Conn.: New Directions, 1949).

58. "Existentialist," *New Yorker* 22 (16 March 1946): 24–25; and Edmund Wilson, profile on Sartre, *New Yorker* 23 (2 August 1947): 58 ff.; J. C. Brown, "Chief Prophet of the Existentialists," *New York Times Magazine* (2 February 1947): 20–22; and "Sartre Enters a New Phase," *New York Times Magazine* (30 January 1949): 12, 18–19; "Existentialism," *Time* (28 January 1946): 28–29; Sigfried Kracauer, "Consciousness, Free and Spontaneous," *Saturday Review of Literature* 31 (26 June 1948): 22–23. Hayden Carruth, in his introduction to the 1964 English translation of *Nausea* published by New Directions, wrote that Existentialism was well-established among American intellectuals by 1946–1947 (facetiously, he asserts that "everyone knew what it meant"); this new philosophy was, he continues, "virtually the only exportable commodity that prostrate Europe could offer" (v–vi).

59. For a recent example see Jonathan Fineberg, *Art since 1940: Strategies of Being* (New York: Abrams, 1995). Michael Leja, in *Reframing Abstract Expressionism: Subjectivity and Painting in the 1940s* (New Haven: Yale University Press, 1993), contests this long-standing characterization of Abstract Expressionism. In drawing distinctions between his "Modern Man" discourse and Existentialism, however, Leja does not explain why artists could not have been drawing from both wellsprings of ideas.

60. "Archaic" from Vincent Scully, "Art Gallery and Design Center, Yale University," *Museum* 9 (1956): 113; "without rhetoric" from Scully, "Archetype and Order in Recent American Architecture," *American Institute of Architects Journal* 42 (December 1954): 251.

61. Sigfried Giedion, "The Humanization of Urban Life," *Architectural Record* 111 (April 1952): 123.

62. Weiss discussed "an existentialist term, authenticity," in "On the Responsibility of the

Architect," *Perspecta* 2 (1953): 44–47, which printed transcribed excerpts from the studio discussions. Howe, "[Untitled talk. Delivered before the students of the Graduate School of Design, Harvard University, 1954]," box 1, Howe Archive, Avery Library, Columbia University.

63. On authenticity, see William Smoot, "The Concept of Authenticity in Sartre," *Man and World* 7 (May 1974): 135–149 (thanks to Charissa Terranova for this reference); Marjorie Grene, "Authenticity: An Existential Virtue," *Ethics* 62 (July 1952): 266–274; Ronald Santoni, *Bad Faith, Good Faith and Authenticity in Sartre's Early Philosophy* (Philadelphia: Temple University Press, 1995); and Lionel Trilling, *Sincerity and Authenticity* (Cambridge: Harvard University Press, 1972). On Heidegger and authenticity, see Karsten Harries, "Authenticity, Poetry, God," in *From Phenomenology to Thought, Errancy, and Desire: Essays in Honor of William J. Richardson, S.J.*, ed. Babette E. Babich (Dordrecht: Kluwer Academic, 1995).

64. It was this point in particular that became the foundation for the Frankfurt School theorists' critique of authenticity; see especially Theodor Adorno's *The Jargon of Authenticity*, trans. Knut Tarnowski and Frederick Will (Evanston: Northwestern University Press, 1973).

65. Sartre, *Nausea*.

66. See Sartre in the posthumously published *The War Diaries*, trans. Q. Hoare (New York: Pantheon, 1984); and Santoni, *Bad Faith*, 54, 94–96.

67. Sartre, *Nausea*, 17.

68. On Sartre's delegitimation of the optical, see Martin Jay, *Downcast Eyes: The Denigration of Vision in Twentieth-Century French Thought* (Berkeley: University of California Press, 1993), 263–298.

69. Sartre, *Nausea*, 11.

70. Ibid., 19.

71. Kahn wrote a self-critique of the Art Gallery soon after it was completed, stating, "Now that the Gallery is finished, I find that the order could have been more developed to include a vertical control system integrated with the column system." He goes on to describe his design for the Adath Jeshurun synagogue, in which such a problem is addressed; this design is discussed in Chapter 4 of this book. "Notes on the Yale University Art Gallery and Design Center," 7 August 1954, in "Louis I. Kahn/Department of State," box 34, Kahn Collection.

CHAPTER 3: TECHNO-ORGANIC SYMBOLS OF COMMUNITY

1. Kahn, "On the Responsibility of the Architect," *Perspecta* 2 (1953): 50.

2. Patricia Cummings Loud, in *The Art Museums of Louis I. Kahn* (Durham: Duke University Press, 1989), 58, asserts that Kahn probably decided to use a space frame for the Art Gallery ceiling between May and August 1951. See Chapter 2, n. 42, on Kahn's lack of understanding of the space frame's structural principles as late as November 1952.

3. When Fuller was editing the Philadelphia-based *Shelter* magazine, he and Kahn became friendly enough that Esther Kahn remembers Fuller arriving at their house in a model Dymaxion car to take Louis for a ride (Esther Kahn, interview with the author, May 1991). On Fuller, see "Bucky Fuller Starts 'The Only Architectural Revolution,'" *Architectural Forum* 95 (August 1951): 144–151; and "D.H." [Douglas Haskell], "The Crystal Ball," *Architectural Forum* 94 (June 1951): 198–200. Articles by Fuller from this period include "The Ninety Percent Automotive Factor," *North Carolina State* 2 (Spring 1952): 30–33; "4D Timelock, Chapters 10–12," *North Carolina State* 2 (Spring 1952): 11–21; "Architect and Agriculture," *North Carolina State* 3 (Fall 1952): 15–19; "Architecture from the Scientific Viewpoint," *North Carolina State* 3 (Spring 1953):

6–9; "No More Second-Hand God," *North Carolina State* 4 (Fall 1953): 16–24; "Fluid Geography," *North Carolina State* 4 (Winter 1954): 41–47. Biographical information on Fuller can be found in Robert Marks, ed., *Buckminster Fuller, Ideas and Integrities: A Spontaneous Autobiographical Disclosure* (Englewood Cliffs, N.J.: Prentice-Hall, 1963); John McHale, "Buckminster Fuller," *Architectural Review* 120 (July 1956): 13–20; and John McHale, *R. Buckminster Fuller* (New York: Braziller, 1961).

4. Fuller to John Entenza, letter of recommendation for Tyng, 5 April 1965, "Fuller, R. Buckminster. Correspondence 1965," box 55, Kahn Collection. Fuller repeated the story in his interview with Richard Saul Wurman, 1974 (Archive of Richard Saul Wurman, Newport, R.I.), claiming (incorrectly, for the chronology is wrong) that although Kahn refused to acknowledge it, it was from these Metro-North train rides that the idea for the Art Gallery ceiling had sprung.

5. Fuller taught at Yale in the academic year 1951–1952; the cardboard geodesic is published in *Perspecta* 2 (1953): 28–35.

6. William Huff graduated from Yale in 1952. He has written extensively on his relationship with Kahn, in "Kahn and Yale," reprinted in *Louis I. Kahn: L'uomo, il maestro,* ed. Alessandra Latour (Rome: Edizioni Kappa, 1986). See also Huff, "Louis Kahn: Sorted Recollections and Lapses in Familiarities," *Little Journal Society of Architectural Historians, Western New York Chapter* 5 (September 1981). He also described their relationship in an interview with the author, July 1992. Years later, Kahn recounted his relationship with Huff in a letter of recommendation for him: "You know he was a student at Yale at the time I was critic of the thesis class. I was then groping to express my belief in the importance of the orders of spaces and orders in nature as related to design. The class rapport and his relentlessly questioning mind helped him to made a remarkable design statement. I gained immeasurably by the exchange of our forum—teacher and student." Kahn to Norman Rice, March 1970, "William Huff Pittsburgh 1970," box 69, Kahn Collection.

7. Geodesic domes were built under Fuller's instruction at Cornell University, MIT, North Carolina State, Princeton, and Yale. Reference to Fuller's dome at Cornell is in the newsletter "Aspen Conference on Design" (June 1951), a copy of which is in Kahn's papers, "Aspen Conf Colo," box 63, Kahn Collection. Reference to the dome at MIT is in "Bucky Starts," *Architectural Forum* 100 (February 1954): 147. North Carolina State was so well-regarded in the early 1950s that Holmes Perkins, then dean of the School of Architecture at the University of Pennsylvania, reported that whenever he needed a new faculty member, his first instinct would be to "raid North Carolina." Perkins, interview with the author, March 1991. Fuller visited at North Carolina State in the fall semester 1953; reference is in "Marines Test a Flying Bucky Fuller Barracks," *Architectural Forum* 100 (March 1954): 37. He visited at Princeton sometime in 1953; reference is in *Architectural Forum* 100 (February 1954): 163. Kahn participated in a conference at North Carolina State on architectural illumination in February 1953; the text of Kahn's lecture is in "North Carolina State College—LIK," box 56, Kahn Collection; his comments were later printed as "How to Develop New Methods of Construction," *Architectural Forum* 101 (November 1954): 157. He spoke at Princeton at a conference entitled "Architecture and the University," held in December 1953 ("Princeton University—correspondence, December, 1953–February, 1958," box 55, Kahn Collection). The proceedings of the conference were later published as *Architecture and the University: Proceedings of a Conference Held at Princeton University, December Eleventh and Twelfth Nineteen Hundred and Fifty Three* (Princeton: Princeton University Press, 1954).

8. Tyng, interview with the author, March 1992.

9. See, for example, Le Ricolais, letter to the editor in response to a previous article on Buckminster Fuller, *Architectural Forum* 111 (September 1959): 98.

10. On 3 March 1953, John Fitzgibbon, who had been a fellow at the Fuller Research Foundation and was based at North Carolina State, wrote to Kahn, promising to send along a paper he had recently received from Le Ricolais. "North Carolina State College—LIK," box 56, Kahn Collection. In December of that year, Kahn sent Le Ricolais his schemes for City Tower, and Le Ricolais wrote back, "I am delighted with this fascinating document received yesterday on which I am going to pay great attention." Le Ricolais to Kahn, 13 December 1953, Tyng Collection, Philadelphia. Kahn and Le Ricolais finally met in March 1954. "Le Ricolais, R.—Paris, France," box 62, Kahn Collection. Subsequently, Le Ricolais moved to the University of Pennsylvania, where he and Kahn co-taught the Master's Studio; they developed a lifelong friendship, becoming, as Le Ricolais described it, "indestructible." Le Ricolais to Kahn, 11 May 1965, "Le Ricolais," box 56, Kahn Collection. On Le Ricolais, see Peter McLeary, "Some Principles of Structure Exemplified in the World of R. Le Ricolais," *Zodiac* 22 (1973): 1–69; Tim Vreeland, "Robert Le Ricolais," *Architectural Design* 30 (October 1960): 412–416; Z. S. Makowski, *Architectural Association Journal* 76 (March 1961): 218–238.

11. Samuely described his design for the Pavilion of Transport in "Space Frames and Stressed Skin Construction," *Royal Institute of British Architects Journal* 59 (March 1952): 166–173.

12. Kahn, in a letter to Tyng, 15 April 1954, described presenting his ideas to Samuely when he came to Yale to lecture. The letter is reprinted in Alexandra Tyng, *Beginnings: Louis I. Kahn's Philosophy of Architecture* (New York: Wiley, 1984), 66. Tyng reports that Kahn was instrumental in getting Samuely invited to speak at Yale, where Kahn hosted him. Tyng, interview with the author, March 1992. Samuely also visited Kahn's office on 24 April 1954. Chronology, Kahn Collection.

13. Fuller's popularity among students of architecture is noted by Douglas Haskell in "The Crystal Ball"; this popularity is apparent in the issues of *North Carolina State* in the years 1951–1955.

14. Ibid.

15. Samuely, from "Is This Tomorrow's Structure? Space Frame Enthusiasts Marshal Many Reasons for Predicting It Is," *Architectural Forum* 98 (February 1953): 152. Kahn received a copy of Samuely's text in early 1952, with a request from Vernon Read that he reply with comments. He never replied. "Louis I. Kahn (personal) 1953," box 60, Kahn Collection.

16. Ibid.

17. Fuller explored the possibilities of a geodesic house in "New Directions: Buckminster Fuller," *Perspecta* 1 (Summer 1952): 29–34.

18. "Only architectural revolution" is from "Bucky Fuller Starts 'The Only Architectural Revolution,'" 144; Fuller, "transcendental world plan," describing ideas developed in previous years, is from Marks, *Ideas and Integrities*, 25. Le Ricolais, more circumspect by nature, also foresaw revolutionary potential in these forms, remarking that the "structural facts" on which they were based "nonplus our present knowledge of the science of building." Le Ricolais, December 1952, draft of a response to a paper by Felix Samuely for *Architectural Forum*, in Le Ricolais Collection, UE VII, 149, Architectural Archives, University of Pennsylvania. The Haskell quotation is from "The Crystal Ball," 198 and 200.

19. George Howe acerbically noted that not until 1953 did New York City's conservative Architectural League sponsor its annual exhibition of new architecture containing only modernist work. Howe, "Some Observations of an Elderly Architect," *Perspecta* 2 (1953): 3. Joseph Hudnut, "The Three Lamps of Modern Architecture, 1: The Lamp of Progress," *Architectural Record* 113 (March 1953): 138–143; Sert and Rudolph from

"The Changing Philosophy of Architecture," with excerpts from statements given at the recent conference for the American Institute of Architects, *Architectural Record* 116 (August 1954): 180 (Rudolph) and 181 (Sert).

20. Matthew Nowicki's Livestock Judging Pavilion in North Carolina, for example, was published three times in *Architectural Forum* in the early 1950s: in October 1952 ("Parabolic Pavilion," 134–140), in June 1953 ("Parabolic Cable Roof," 98, 170–171), and in April 1954 ("The Great Livestock Pavilion Complete," 130–134). The work of Catalano, Torroja, and Nowicki was published often in *North Carolina State*, and Holmes Perkins, former dean of the School of Fine Arts at the University of Pennsylvania, reports that he was negotiating to get Nowicki to teach at Penn because his accomplishments were so highly regarded. (When Nowicki died unexpectedly in 1951, Perkins hired Nowicki's wife, Stanislawa Nowicki, instead.) Perkins, interview with the author, April 1992.

21. Hitchcock, *The Crystal Palace: Its Structure, Its Antecedents, and Its Immediate Progeny* (Northampton, Mass.: Smith College of Art, 1951). A copy still exists in Kahn's personal library, which is in the collection of Sue Ann Kahn.

22. Dwight D. Eisenhower, "Atoms for Peace," reprinted in *The Annals of America*, vol. 17, *1950–1960: Cold War in the Nuclear Age* (Chicago: Encyclopedia Brittanica, 1968), 211–214; discussed in Paul Carter, *Another Part of the Fifties* (New York: Columbia University, 1983), 262–265.

23. Fuller, "No More Second-Hand God," 22.

24. Haskell, "Crystal Ball," 198–200.

25. That space frames were being perceived as the shot in the arm that modernism needed is apparent in Rudolph's refutation of them: immediately after he complained of modern architecture's poverty of symbolic form (in the statement quoted earlier), he continued, "We have the structural exhibitionists. Exciting as Buckminster Fuller's domes may be, or the latest space frame, they are merely a means to an end and not architecture." Rudolph, "The Changing Philosophy of Architecture," *Architectural Record* 116 (August 1954): 180.

26. Roland Marchand, "Visions of Classlessness, Quests for Dominion: American Popular Culture, 1945–1960," in *Reshaping America: Society and Institutions, 1945–1960*, ed. Robert H. Bremner and Gary W. Richard (Columbus: Ohio State University Press, 1982), 163.

27. The exhibition catalogue was *Aspects of Form: A Symposium on Form in Nature and Art*, ed. Lancelot Law Whyte (London: Percy Lund Humphries, 1951). Tyng bought a copy of the ICA catalogue as soon as it was available in the United States, around 1952. Tyng, interview with the author, March 1992.

28. Ernst von Haeckel, "Report of the Scientific Results of the Voyage of the H.M.S. *Challenger* During the Years 1873–1874," of which a plate appears on the cover of the *North Carolina State College Student Publication of the School of Design* 3 (Spring 1953), a special issue devoted to the work of Le Ricolais. "Stupendous" quotation appears on p. 1 of Le Ricolais' "Contribution to Space Structures" in the same issue. Tyng discussed her interest in Haeckel's studies in the early 1950s in an interview with the author, 1991, and mentioned them in her doctoral dissertation, Tyng, "Speed Spiral" (Ph.D. diss., University of Pennsylvania, 1975), 151–161.

29. Kepes finished the manuscript that accompanied his exhibition *The New Landscape in Art and Science* in 1952, although the exhibition appeared in 1953. The manuscript was not published in book form until 1956 (*The New Landscape in Art and Science* [Chicago: Paul Theobald, 1956]). The schedule for spring semester final review (Department of Architecture, 1951, "Yale—Professor 1950," box 61, Kahn Collection) indicates that Kahn and Kepes served together on a jury.

30. This exhibition was first held at MIT, then traveled to the Aspen Institute for the conference that summer. Information on Kepes' exhibition, suggesting that Kahn saw the show, is in "Aspen Conf. Colo.," box 63, Kahn Collection.

31. Fuller, "No More Second-Hand God," 23.

32. Kepes, *The New Landscape*, 19–20.

33. The thoughts of Tyng, who was the person closest to Kahn in these years, are important. Evidence of Tyng's thought in these years exists mainly in Kahn's writings (her letters to him when she was in Rome in 1953–1954 were probably destroyed). For her own retrospective account, see her later writings. In 1962 Tyng received a grant from the Graham Foundation to write up the ideas she had been working on for the past decade. The manuscript is still in her possession; in it, her attraction to the idea that these discoveries reveal an almost mystical order is apparent. Tyng, in an interview with the author, confirmed that she had held this notion since the early 1950s.

34. Tyng reports that she was profoundly influenced by Whyte in these years (interview with the author, March 1991); Kepes cites Whyte in *The New Landscape*, 173 ff.

35. Kahn's landscape consultant, Dan Kiley, sent him a copy of *The Next Development in Man* (1944; reprint, New York: Henry Holt, 1948) the year it was published, asking for comments; the copy still exists in Kahn's personal library, in the possession of Sue Ann Kahn. Kiley to Kahn, 3 May 1948, in "American Institute of Architects 1947," box 60, Kahn Collection. Kahn may have spent some time with the book, because he held the man who sent it in high regard: he described Kiley in 1951 as a man of "wide imagination," "deep insight," "wide experience and invincible integrity"; Kahn, letter of recommendation for Kiley, 23 August 1951, "Louis I. Kahn (personal) No. 4 (1951) & 52," box 60, Kahn Collection. Another colleague recommended *Next Development* again in 1953, writing, "I like the book very much. It adds to the new optimism about the future that I connect first with Fuller." "Ted" (last name unknown) to Kahn, 24 September 1953, letter from "Bry Ted Diana" in Madras, India, to Kahn and Tyng, in "Louis I. Kahn (personal)–1953," box 60, Kahn Collection.

36. Fuller first used the phrase "one-town community" in conjunction with his Dymaxion World Map; it is quoted in Robert Marks, *The Dymaxion World of Buckminster Fuller* (New York: Reinhold, 1960), 39. He later expanded it to refer to the potential of technology in general, which "has shrunken the world to a one-town community" (Marks, *Dymaxion World*, 61). Tyng's ideas on the structure of human culture and its relation to organic principles are best expressed in her "Geometric Extensions of Consciousness," *Zodiac* 19 (1969): 130–162. Fuller also used the phrase "from microcosm to macrocosm."

37. Whyte, *Next Development*: "world community" is from p. vii; "contemporary man" is from p. 10.

38. Esther Kahn reports that Kahn became "very interested" in crystallography in the early 1950s. Although it is impossible to ascertain when Kahn bought certain books, it does seem likely that Kahn purchased the books that exist in his personal library (in the possession of Sue Ann Kahn) on these topics in the early 1950s. Among them are Roderick Impey Murchison, *Siluria: The History of the Oldest Fossiliferous Rocks and Their Foundations* (London: John Murray, 1859); and Louis Figuier, *The Vegetable World: Being a History of Plants with Their Structures and Peculiar Properties* (London, n.d.).

39. A transcript of Kahn's lecture at North Carolina State (February 1953) is in "North Carolina State College–LIK," box 56, Kahn Collection. A transcript of his lecture at Princeton is in "Princeton University–correspondence, December, 1953–February, 1958," box 55, Kahn Collection. Kahn, "Toward a Plan for Midtown Philadelphia," *Perspecta* 2 (August 1953): 10–27.

40. From Kahn, "Toward a Plan," 23.

41. Kahn to Tyng, 18 December 1953, reprinted in Tyng, *Beginnings*, 65–66.

42. Kahn wrote to Howard Spitznagel, an old classmate and an architect in Sioux Falls, South Dakota, "I have been struggling with the differentiation between 'order' and 'design.'" Kahn to Spitznagel, 16 December 1953, "Louis I. Kahn (personal) – 1953," box 60, Kahn Collection. Kahn spoke of order as consistent and design as circumstantial at the Princeton conference on 11 December 1953, "Architecture and the University," pp. 54–55 of transcript, "Princeton University – correspondence, December, 1953–February, 1958," box 55, Kahn Collection. Kahn's concept of order is close to that of Kepes' in *The New Landscape*, 19, and Whyte's in *The Next Development*, viii. My argument, that Kahn's concept of order is based on geometric structure found in nature, differs from that of many other scholars who interpret this notion as a Platonic archetype that also encompasses historical references (see Peter Reed, "Toward Form: Louis I. Kahn's Urban Designs for Philadelphia, 1939–1962" [Ph.D. diss., University of Pennsylvania, 1989], 94; Francesco Tentori, "Order and Form in the Work of Louis Kahn," reprinted in Latour, *L'uomo, il maestro*). Closest to the argument I present here is that (perhaps not surprisingly) of Kahn and Tyng's daughter, Alexandra Tyng, in *Beginnings*, 162, in which she argues, "Order is the harmony of all laws of nature working together."

43. Telegram including Kahn's rewrite of the last paragraph of his North Carolina address of February 1953, 22 July 1953, "North Carolina State College – LIK," box 56, Kahn Collection.

44. Robert Le Ricolais, "Space Partition and Architecture," Le Ricolais Collection, UE VII, 149, Architectural Archives, University of Pennsylvania.

45. Typescript, "Architecture and the University" conference, "Princeton University – correspondence, December, 1953–February, 1958," box 55, Kahn Collection.

46. Ibid.

47. The quotation is from "Toward a Plan for Midtown Philadelphia," *Perspecta* 2 (August 1953): 23, which was written in the summer of 1953, but Kahn had stated the same idea less articulately at the conference on architectural illumination at North Carolina State in February of that year. See "North Carolina State College – LIK," box 56, Kahn Collection. Kahn derived his comparison of space frames to gothic vaulting systems from Felix Samuely, who had written in an article published two months earlier, "In medieval times, the tendency to use structural members in only one plane was not so apparent." Samuely, "Is This Tomorrow's Structure?" 152.

48. That Kahn equated structures of "hollow stones" with space frames is clear in his rewrite of his statement at North Carolina State, in which he explicitly equated the two terms. "North Carolina State College – LIK," box 56, Kahn Collection. Robert Le Ricolais, in "Contributions to Space Structures," *North Carolina State* 3 (Spring 1953), wrote that "the geodesic systems of [the type used by] Mr. Buckminster Fuller . . . display all the structural knowledge we have. . . . Most of these skeletons . . . are made with hollow siliceous tubes," the material that constitutes a radiolarian.

49. Given City Tower's apparently speculative nature, it is not surprising that Kahn scholars have paid it little attention. See DeLong in Brownlee and DeLong, *In the Realm*, 56.

50. Tyng reports that the hexagons were Kahn's idea. Tyng, interview with the author, March 1991. Le Ricolais advocated hexagonal plans in multistoried buildings in a paper he sent Kahn the month before, arguing that they had the additional advantage of demanding fewer supports per square foot of usable space. Tyng claims that Le Ricolais "had nothing to do with" City Tower, but she also says that it was Kahn, not her, who had the idea to change the plan into three hexagons. Tyng, interview with the author, March 1991. Le Ricolais sent Kahn a paper on what he called "Hexacore" high-rise structures in early April 1953; "Le Ricolais," box 56, Kahn Collection.

51. For a history of thought on how to integrate Philadelphia's city hall into the postwar urban fabric, see John Maass, "Philadelphia City Hall: Monster or Masterpiece?" *Journal of the American Institute of Architects* 43 (February 1965): 23–30. Some suggested demolishing the city hall's offices but keeping the tower, arguing that it had become a local symbol; Edmund Bacon, head of the City Planning Commission, favored complete demolition and the construction of a new civic center on a Schuylkill River site; others wanted to retain the old building and construct an annex across the street, on Reyburn Plaza. In box 31, Kahn Collection, is a report by Clarke, Rapuano, and Holleran, consulting engineers and landscape architects to the Philadelphia City Planning Commission, dated February 1947, that recommends demolishing the offices and retaining the tower but adds that the building has "nothing to recommend it as a monument" (p. 3). By 1951, the Philadelphia City Planning Commission had named Reyburn Plaza as the site for a new city hall; *Penn Center Redevelopment Area Plan* (Philadelphia, 1952). The plans to replace or augment Philadelphia's old city hall are covered very well in Reed, "Toward Form," 129–130, and in James F. O'Gorman, *Drawing Toward Building: Philadelphia Architectural Graphics, 1782–1986* (Philadelphia: Pennsylvania Academy of Fine Arts and University of Pennsylvania Press, 1986), 132–134 and 208–209. Finally it was decided to retain the city hall and build an annex. See memo announcing a luncheon meeting of the Citizen's Council on City Planning, in which the topic was "Should City Hall Be Demolished or Rehabilitated?" in "Citizen's Council on City Planning. Memos," box 65, Kahn Collection. At a meeting of the Philadelphia chapter of the AIA on 1 May 1957, the organization advised the city to retain the old city hall. "American Institute of Architects–NATL," box 63, Kahn Collection.

52. This project is reproduced in Peter Reed, "Toward Form"; it is also discussed in his essay on Philadelphia's urban plans in Brownlee and DeLong, *In the Realm*, 307. I am grateful to Peter Reed for assisting my research on this topic.

53. Edmund Krimmel, head of the Committee on Municipal Improvements, expressed the same concern for democratic participation that Kahn and Stonorov had advocated in their city-planning booklets of the late 1940s, arguing that there was inadequate transportation to and from the site and that "the decentralizing of the civic center in Los Angeles was said to have resulted in a marked fall off in citizen visits to City Hall." Minutes of the Committee on Municipal Improvements, December 1951, "AIA Municipal Improvements Committee," box 63, Kahn Collection.

54. Tyng, in an interview with the author, March 1991, identified the six-sided polygonal plans (reproduced as Kahn's work in *The Louis I. Kahn Archive: Personal Drawings* [New York: Garland, 1987]) as her own, and the earliest manifestations of the project. It is unlikely that Tyng is claiming credit where credit is not due, since the drawing style is hers, not Kahn's.

55. A memorandum to the Committee on Municipal Improvements, January 1952, reports that in spite of the committee's opposition, Bacon strongly supported the idea of a new civic center "giving stimulus to a new area." "AIA Municipal Improvements Committee," box 63, Kahn Collection.

56. Tyng was living in Europe, and Kahn wrote to her to report that the selection of an architect for a new city hall was imminent. "I cannot allow the grass to grow under my feet. . . . Some say, Lou, you should be caught dead doing a building on the Reyburn Plaza. But how long must I wait?" Kahn asked, conscious that he was still largely unknown and now more than fifty years old. "If a building must go there, who could do better?" With Tyng's encouragement, Kahn wrote to major city officials, including Bacon and Mayor Joseph Clark, asking them to consider hiring him as architect for the city hall annex. Kahn to Tyng, 24 January 1954, Tyng Collection. These letters were

published after the research for this book was done in Louis Kahn, *Louis Kahn to Anne Tyng: The Rome Letters, 1953–1954*, ed. Anne Griswold Tyng (New York: Rizzoli, 1987). Tyng's encouragement is clear in Kahn to Tyng, 12 February 1954: "Tonight I have also composed a letter to the mayor and to Bacon and to [Charles] Sawyer. I stressed my previous work and knowledge and the other points you suggested in your lovely letter. Maybe you can come in tonight and type them for me. " Tyng Collection. Charles Sawyer was the managing director of the City of Philadelphia. Kahn also wrote to Frances Lamner, the head of the Philadelphia Redevelopment Authority; all are in "City Hall & Office Building," box 59, Kahn Collection. To some, Kahn suggested a competition for the project; Bacon he asked directly to be considered for the commission. "You know of my great interest in the project and the thought I have already given it," Kahn wrote, referring to his and Tyng's ideas for City Tower. Privately he admitted that despite revealing to city officials his "own ambition in the matter," he didn't think he had "a ghost of a chance" (Kahn to Tyng, 30 January 1954, Tyng Collection, Philadelphia).

57. Kahn to Tyng, 12 February 1954, Tyng Collection; Kahn to Tyng, 7 March 1954, Tyng Collection.

58. Kahn to Tyng, 7 March 1954, Tyng Collection.

59. The phrase "nondirectional space" appears on one drawing Kahn sent to Tyng that remains in Tyng's collection; it also appears on a drawing of City Tower in the Kahn Collection.

60. Tyng, in an interview with the author, December 1993, reports that Kahn's early ideas for the structure of the Adath Jeshurun synagogue were also a direct response to criticisms of the Art Gallery at Yale. The quotation is from Kahn, letter to the Foreign Buildings Office of the State Department in response to an inquiry for a portfolio, approximately 30 June 1954, "Louis I. Kahn *State Department*," box 34, Kahn Collection.

61. From the original draft of "Toward a Plan," it is clear that the wind-stress argument was Kahn's idea. "Perspecta 4," box 64, Kahn Collection.

62. Professor Anthony Webster of Columbia University, and Professor Peter McLeary of the University of Pennsylvania independently asserted that Kahn and Tyng's wind-stress argument regarding City Tower was incorrect. Webster and McLeary, interviews with the author, spring 1992. Tyng claims that Nick Gianopolus, Kahn's structural engineer for many projects in the 1950s, understood and sanctioned the project's structure. But Gianopolus claims that neither Tyng nor Kahn asked his opinion of the project. Had they, he continued, he would have told them that it was not efficient as far as wind stresses were concerned and was, moreover, virtually unbuildable. Tyng and Gianopolus, interviews with the author, 1992.

63. Kahn, "This Business of Architecture," in *The Student Publication of the School of Architecture of Tulane University*, reprinted in *Louis I. Kahn: Writings, Lectures, Interviews*, ed. Alessandra Latour (New York: Rizzoli, 1993), 62–64.

64. Kahn, "Toward a Plan for Midtown Philadelphia," draft in "Perspecta 4," box 64, Kahn Collection.

65. Information on the AFL Medical Services building can be found in Heinz Ronner and Sharad Jhaveri, *Louis I. Kahn: The Complete Works, 1935–74* (Boulder, Colo.: Westview Press, 1977); "Dedication," *Philadelphia Inquirer* (17 February 1957): A14; "Demolition," *Philadelphia Inquirer* (27 August 1973): B3; Victoria Donohue, "Downtown Philadelphia Loses Its Only Kahn Building," *Progressive Architecture* 54 (November 1973): 23, 26; and "Kahn Finds Lessons in Ruins of His Work," *Philadelphia Inquirer* (27 August 1973): B3.

66. "Kahn Finds Lessons."

67. Ibid.

68. Tim Vreeland, interview with the author, February 1994.

69. A. Vierendeel, "Théorie générale des poutres Vierendeel," in *Mémoires de la Société des Ingenieurs Civils de France* (Paris, 1900); see L. C. Maugh, *The Analysis of Vierendeel Trusses by Successive Approximations* (Zurich, 1935).

70. A notable exception was Luigi Figini and Mario Ridolfi's Chiesa della Madonna dei Poveri in Milan, 1952–1954, published in *Casabella* 208 (1955).

71. See Chapter 2 of this book for a full discussion of authenticity.

CHAPTER 4: GATHERING PEOPLE INTO A COMMUNITY

1. Kahn, "This Business of Architecture," *Student Publication of the School of Architecture of Tulane University*, reprinted in *Louis I. Kahn: Writings, Lectures, Interviews*, ed. Alessandra Latour (New York: Rizzoli, 1991), 64.

2. Gallup and *Ladies' Home Journal* polls cited in Robert Wuthnow, *The Restructuring of American Religion: Society and Faith since World War II* (Princeton: Princeton University Press, 1988), 15–16.

3. Cited in Elaine Tyler May, *Homeward Bound: American Families in the Cold War Era* (New York: Basic Books, 1988), 26.

4. Wuthnow, *Restructuring*, 36.

5. Ibid., 36–37.

6. Will Herberg, *Protestant–Catholic–Jew* (Garden City, N.J.: Doubleday, 1955); see also the discussion of Herberg in Mark Silk, *Spiritual Politics: Religion and America since World War II* (New York: Simon and Schuster, 1988), 17.

7. William Lee Miller, "Religion, Politics, and the Great Crusade," *Reporter* (7 July 1953); quoted in Paul Carter, *Another Part of the Fifties* (New York: Columbia University Press, 1983), 124. Eisenhower's comment is quoted in Carter, *Another Part*, and published originally in the *New York Times*, 23 December 1952.

8. William H. Whyte, *The Organization Man* (New York: Simon and Schuster, 1956; reprint, Garden City, N.J.: Doubleday, n.d.), 417. Much of the information in these paragraphs paraphrases Whyte's findings, presented in the chapter "The Church of Suburbia," 404–422.

9. Ibid.; Wuthnow makes much the same point in *Restructuring*, 58.

10. See Carter, *Another Part*, chaps. 5 and 6, 114–140, and 141–167; quotation is from Wuthnow, *Restructuring*, 66.

11. Lewis H. Heilbron, "Center and Synagogue: Roles in Serving American Jewry," *National JWB [Jewish Welfare Board] Circle* (New York City, 1955): 11, copy in the files of the Trenton Jewish Community Center, Trenton, New Jersey.

12. Wuthnow, *Restructuring*, 54–58.

13. *Architectural Forum* published monthly statistics on actual construction activity and forecasts of future construction activity. The figure from 1953 comes from the construction report of August 1953, p. 44. For a discussion of the rise in religious construction see also Wuthnow, *Restructuring*, 26–36.

14. "Forecast 1958," *Architectural Forum* 107 (October 1957): 37, forecasts that religious construction from 1956 to 1957 would rise by 21 percent.

15. See, for example, Gregor Paulsson and Henry-Russell Hitchcock's entries in the *Architectural Review* symposium "In Search of a New Monumentality," 104 (September 1943): 122–125.

16. "Saarinen Challenges the Rectangle," *Architectural Forum* 98 (January 1953): 133.

17. "Philip Johnson," *Architectural Review* 117 (April 1955): 246.

18. As DeLong points out in Brownlee and DeLong, *In The Realm*, 79–93.

19. Much of the information in the paragraph is drawn from several interviews with Mrs. Esther Kahn, now deceased, in the years from 1990 to 1992. On the tensions in Philadelphia (as elsewhere) between Jewish immigrants from Eastern Europe and those from Germany, see Murray Friedman, "The Making of a National Jewish Community," in *Jewish Life in Philadelphia, 1830–1940*, ed. Murray Friedman (Philadelphia: ISHI Public, 1983), 1–25 passim. For more on Kahn's lack of strong identification with his Jewish heritage, see Susan G. Solomon, "Secular and Spiritual Humanism: Louis I. Kahn's Work for the Jewish Community in the 1950s and 1960s" (Ph.D. diss, University of Pennsylvania, 1997).

20. Kahn's comment to Komendant is quoted in Auguste Komendant, *Eighteen Years with Architect Louis I. Kahn* (Englewood, N.J.: Aloray Publishers, 1975), 190.

21. One of Sue Ann Kahn's Christmas carols is in "Rome 1951," box 60, Kahn Collection. Signed "Lou, Esther, and Sue Ann," the words to the carol were: "Once a babe lay resting in a stable far. Peace and love go with him, peace and love go with him. Guiding them to their king, three wise men then saw a star. Peace and love go with him, peace and love go with him. Jesus Christ our loving king is born."

22. Esther Kahn, interview with the author, September 1992.

23. "National Jewish Welfare Board," box 61, Kahn Collection; for more on Kahn's trip to Israel, see Solomon, "Secular and Spiritual Humanism," 7–91.

24. Kahn's attitude to his religious ethnicity was not unusual for intellectuals of his generation, many of whom prided themselves on valuing the ideal of cosmopolitanism over their specifically Jewish identity. Famous exemplars of this culture were the New York writers Alfred Kazin and Irving Howe, but similar ideals were also held by Jewish intellectuals based in other East Coast cities, such as the sociologist David Riesman, who came from a prominent Jewish family in Philadelphia. For a description of the Jewish cosmopolitan ideal of the 1940s and 1950s, see David Hollinger, "Ethnic Diversity, Cosmopolitanism, and the Emergence of the American Liberal Intelligentsia," in *In the American Province: Studies in the History and Historiography of Ideas* (Baltimore: Johns Hopkins University Press, 1985), 56–73. Thanks to Gwendolyn Wright of Columbia University for this reference.

25. For a more comprehensive history of the Adath Jeshurun congregation, see Solomon, "Secular and Spiritual Humanism," 106–120.

26. Reasons for the Adath Jeshurun congregation's move are cited in the minutes of the meetings of the Board of Directors, 11 June 1951 and 18 June 1954, Archive of the Adath Jeshurun Synagogue, Elkins Park, and confirmed by Rabbi Morris Dembrowitz of the Ner Zedek Ezrath Israel synagogue in Philadelphia, in an interview with the author, September 1993. Dembrowitz was a young rabbi at the Adath Jeshurun in the mid-1950s, and a member of the building committee that initially hired Kahn.

27. Rabbi Dembrowitz and another member of the Adath Jeshurun congregation in the early 1950s, Morton Goren of Elkins Park, independently characterized the congregation as "liberal Conservative" in interviews with the author, September 1993.

28. In "Synagogue and School Building–Congregation/Adath Jeshurun," box 60, Kahn Collection, is a clipping reproducing Wright's design, quoting Wright's comments on the project. The date of the article, June 1954, is approximately the same time that Kahn started working on his schemes for the Adath Jeshurun. The earliest date for the Adath Jeshurun is May 1954, when Rabbi Dembrowitz and Ben Weiss, the head of the building committee, contacted Kahn (Weiss to Kahn, "Synagogue and School Building–Congregation/Adath Jeshurun," box 60, Kahn Collection). Dembrowitz, in an interview with the author, Sep-

tember 1993, reported that competition with Beth Shalom was a major consideration in the decision-making process of the Adath Jeshurun building committee.

29. Minutes of the meetings of the Board of Directors, 13 December 1955, Archive of the Adath Jeshurun Synagogue, Elkins Park.

30. Quotations and the background for the commission are from Rabbi Dembrowitz, interview with the author, September 1993. Additional background information is from minutes of the meetings of the Board of Directors of the Adath Jeshurun, now located at a different site in Elkins Park, in a structure designed by Percival Goodman.

31. Solomon ("Secular and Spiritual Humanism," 120–143) has a different interpretation of the events, arguing that a schism in the building committee led Weiss to suggest to Kahn that he had secured the commission, when in fact Weiss had no authority to hire Kahn. As my account of the events makes clear, I disagree. But, for an understanding of the principal issues the Adath Jeshurun raises, the difference between Solomon's account and my own is not important. We agree that Kahn clearly believed he was on his way to designing his first major synagogue.

32. The inquiry is in "Synagogue and School Building–Congregation/Adath Jeshurun," box 60, Kahn Collection.

33. Tyng, interview with the author, December 1993.

34. Between April and July 1954, Kahn wrote to the State Department in Washington, D.C.: "The [Yale Art] Gallery is finished, [and] I find that the order could have been more developed to include a vertical control system integrated with the column system. The cantilever possibilities of the deep construction combined with the wider shear head of a hollow column would create a system of fewer columns. Each column would carry the air supply and return and other utilities thereby distributing service at the column points and giving better zone control. I am now applying this idea to a religious building for Philadelphia." "Louis I. Kahn/Department of State," box 34, Kahn Collection.

35. Kahn to Tyng, 25 April 1954, reprinted in Alexandra Tyng, *Beginnings: Louis I. Kahn's Philosophy of Architecture* (New York: John Wiley and Sons, 1984), 66.

36. Kahn, "A Synagogue: Adath Jeshurun of Philadelphia," *Perspecta* 3 (1955): 62–63. The date is probably between October 1954 and February 1955, based on a letter from Kahn to Benjamin Weiss in May 1955, saying that the Adath Jeshurun scheme had been published in *Perspecta*. "LIK–Miscellaneous 1954–56," box 65, Kahn Collection.

37. Kahn, "A Synagogue"; Rabbi Morris Dembrowitz, interview with the author, September 1993.

38. Kahn, review of *Synagogue Architecture in the U.S.*, by Rachel Wischnitzer (Philadelphia: Jewish Publication Society of America, 1954), for the Jewish Publication Society of America, "LIK–Miscellaneous 1954–56," box 65, written between September and November of 1955 (hereafter cited as Wischnitzer review). That Kahn, in the Wischnitzer review, was referring to his ideas for Adath Jeshurun is apparent in the repetition of his ideas on synagogues generally when he published his second scheme for the Adath Jeshurun in *Perspecta*.

39. Paul Thiry, Richard Bennett, and Henry Kamphoefner, *Churches and Temples* (New York: Progressive Architecture Library/Van Nostrand Reinhold, 1953). This book, which is inscribed LIK 54, remains in Kahn's personal library, currently in the possession of Sue Ann Kahn of New York City. Kahn studied the book extensively, as evidenced by the many bookmarks still marking various plates.

40. Thiry et al., *Churches and Temples*, 3J.

41. Kahn, "A Synagogue."

42. Thiry et al., *Churches and Temples*, 6J.

43. Kahn, "This Business of Architecture," in Latour, *Louis I. Kahn*, 64.

44. Kahn to Tyng, reprinted in Tyng, *Beginnings*, 67–68.

45. Kahn, letter to State Department, 1954, in "Louis I. Kahn/Department of State," box 34, Kahn Collection.

46. The program for the Adath Jeshurun is in "Synagogue and School Building–Congregation/Adath Jeshurun," box 60, Kahn Collection.

47. Kahn projected the total cost of the first scheme as $1.1 million, according to correspondence with the building committee in "Synagogue and School Building–Congregation/ Adath Jeshurun," box 60, Kahn Collection.

48. Tyng reports that Kahn shifted to circular columns in the interest of practicality; the quotation is from Kahn, "A Synagogue," 62–63.

49. Kahn to Adath Jeshurun Building Committee, 16 August 1954, "Synagogue and School Building–Congregation/Adath Jeshurun," box 60, Kahn Collection.

50. Minutes of the Adath Jeshurun Executive Committee, 13 September 1954, Archive of the Adath Jeshurun Synagogue, Elkins Park.

51. Minutes of the meetings of the Board of Directors, 10 January 1955, Archive of the Adath Jeshurun Synagogue, Elkins Park.

52. Weiss to Kahn, 29 April 1955, "LIK–Miscellaneous 1956–56," box 65, Kahn Collection.

53. Ben Weiss to Kahn, 29 April 1955, "LIK Miscellaneous 1954–56," box 65, Kahn Collection; and Rabbi Dembrowitz, interview with the author, September 1993.

54. Tyng, interview with the author, December 1993.

55. Dembrowitz, interview with the author, September 1993.

56. Kahn to Adath Jeshurun Building Committee, 16 August 1954, "Synagogue and School Building–Congregation/Adath Jeshurun," box 60, Kahn Collection.

57. This was first suggested by Marcello Angrisani in "Louis Kahn e la storia," *Edilizia Moderna* 86 (1965): 83–93, and has been subsequently repeated by Kenneth Frampton in "Louis Kahn and the French Connection," *Oppositions* 22 (Fall 1980): 21–53, and most recently by DeLong, in Brownlee and DeLong, *In the Realm*, 55.

58. Collection of Sue Ann Kahn, New York City.

59. Peter Reed, "Toward Form: Louis I. Kahn's Urban Designs for Philadelphia, 1939–1962" (Ph.D. diss., University of Pennsylvania, 1989), 175. DeLong repeats the observation in Brownlee and DeLong, *In the Realm*, 55.

60. See Chapter 5 for a discussion of Kahn's turn toward history in the mid-to-late 1950s.

61. Kahn, Wischnitzer review.

62. Ibid.

CHAPTER 5: STRUGGLING FOR A NEW IDIOM

1. Although the Richards Medical Center was Kahn's most recognized project of the mid-1950s, and the only one of the major projects that was constructed, the technological issues that dominated its design were profoundly influenced by Kahn's collaborator and structural engineer, Auguste Komendant. Kahn's lectures, journal entries, and correspondence indicate that his preoccupation with the technical issues of the sort that the Richards Medical Center raised did not extend into other projects or deeply shape his ideas in these years. Therefore the Richards Medical Center provides a less clear indication of how Kahn's ideas were evolving in the mid-1950s than does the unbuilt, and less resolved, Trenton Jewish Community Center project.

2. The most extensive discussions of the Jewish Community Center (JCC) and Bathhouse are Susan Solomon, *Louis I. Kahn's Trenton Jewish Community Center* (New York: Princeton Architectural Press, 2000); Solomon, "Jewish Community Center," in Brownlee and DeLong, *In the Realm*, 318–323; and Solomon, "Beginnings," *Progressive Architecture* 65 (December 1984): 68–73. The most complete analysis of the various phases of design for

the Trenton JCC is in Heinz Ronner and Sharad Jhaveri, *Louis I. Kahn: Complete Work, 1935–1974,* 2nd ed. (Basel: Birkhauser, 1987), 82–91; Kahn collaborated on the first edition of this publication. In "Beginnings," p. 68, Solomon writes that "there are no extant records" at the JCC; in fact, correspondence there indicates that Kahn's main competitor for the commission was the New York–based Percival Goodman. See, for example, "Minutes of the Construction Committee of the Jewish Community Center of Trenton," 6 May and 30 September 1954; Percival Goodman to Harvey Saaz, 13 September 1954, JCC files, Trenton, New Jersey (hereafter JCC files). I am indebted to Jerome Mellman, the current director of the Trenton JCC, for allowing me to use these documents. Jack MacAllister (a former employee in Kahn's office) and Anne Tyng both reported, in interviews with the author in August 1993, that Douglas Haskell had recommended Kahn for the commission.

3. On the history of Jewish community centers in America generally, see Louis Kraft, *A Century of the Jewish Community Center Movement* (Philadelphia: Jewish Publication Society of America, 1962); Louis Kraft and Charles S. Bernheimer, eds., *Aspects of the Jewish Community Center, Benjamin Rabinowitz Memorial Volume* (Philadelphia: Maurice Jacobs Press with National Association of Jewish Center Workers, 1954); James Yaffee, *The American Jews* (New York: Random House, 1968), 207–210.

4. "Supplementary Report of Jewish Community Center Program Committee," JCC files.

5. Nathan Kramer, in his unpublished manuscript "A History of Jews in Trenton," reports that in 1927 foreign-born Jews constituted 34 percent of Jews in the Trenton vicinity, but this number had declined to 24 percent by 1949; of that 24 percent, Kramer continued, more than half "neither spoke nor read Yiddish." A copy of Kramer's manuscript is in the JCC files.

6. On the changed role of Jewish community centers after World War II, see Irving Brodsky, "The New Role of the Community Center," in *The Social Welfare Forum, 1964* (New York: Columbia University Press, 1964), 200–216; Nathan Kramer, untitled article in *The Jewish Community Center Reporter* 3 (15 February 1950): 1; Herbert Millman, "The Concerns of the Jewish Community Center," *American Rabbi* (November 1961), copy in JCC files; Louis H. Heilbron, "Center and Synagogue: Roles in Serving American Jewry," *Jewish Welfare Board Circle*: 11, 13, 14, copy in JCC files.

7. The divisiveness of Zionism is often discussed in literature on Jewish community centers after the war, for example in Heilbron, "Center and Synagogue," 12. A discussion of the issue from the point of view of one prominent participant can be found in Elizabeth Young-Bruehl, *Hannah Arendt: For the Love of the World* (New Haven: Yale University Press, 1982), 222–224, 361–362.

8. "Supplementary Report of Jewish Community Center Program Committee," JCC files.

9. Kramer, "A History of Jews in Trenton."

10. Both Marshall Meyers, who came to work in Kahn's office in 1957, and Jack MacAllister, who worked on the Trenton Jewish Community Center from 1955 to 1958, reported that class differences within the organization contributed in large part to a lack of institutional identity. Interviews with the author, January 1994.

11. There is no discussion regarding the nature of a Jewish community center in any of the minutes of the board of directors or of the building committee in the years 1955–1957 beyond those general observations discussed in the "Supplementary Report of Jewish Community Center Program Committee," JCC files, of 1954. This is particularly striking in contrast with the constant self-analysis of the Unitarian congregation in Rochester, discussed in Chapter 6. The program of the Jewish Community Center changed numerous times over a four-year period. For one of the earliest statements of the program, see "John M. Hirsch/Stanley R. Dube} Associated Architects, 1% of fee," box 35, Kahn Collection.

12. Kahn, "Monumentality," in *New Architecture and City Planning*, ed. Paul Zucker (New

York: Philosophical Library, 1944), reprinted in *Architecture Culture, 1943–1968*, ed. Joan Ockman (New York: Rizzoli, 1993), 48.

13. Correspondence between Louis Kaplan, George Warren, and Harold Kramer, February–March 1955, JCC files, indicates that the decision to build the Bathhouse first was a controversial one.

14. David DeLong, in "The Mind Opens to Realizations" (in Brownlee and DeLong, *In the Realm*, 58), states that the Greek cross plan for the Bathhouse was complete in February 1955; however, drawings from March indicate that the square scheme was still the prevailing idea. The first surviving drawing (a blueprint) of the Bathhouse in its final form is dated April 28.

15. Anne Tyng has often claimed that she designed the Trenton Bathhouse, and she made the same claim to this author in an interview in March 1993.

16. Vreeland, interview with the author, January 1994. Vreeland's version of the story strongly supports Tyng's story. I did not prompt him to any disclosure; in fact, I had not asked about the Bathhouse at all. The original drawings for the Bathhouse have been lost. Tyng went so far as to intimate that Kahn had destroyed them in order to obscure the importance of her contribution (Tyng's drawing style is recognizably different from Kahn's). However unpalatable the idea, it is plausible, as Tyng wrote Kahn numerous letters from Rome in 1953–54, and all have disappeared, presumably destroyed by Kahn after their relationship fell apart. Hence, although Kahn saved virtually every piece of paper that crossed the transom of his office entrance (including, for example, notices to lectures he could not possibly have attended), it seems likely that he did also destroy documents selectively.

17. As Peter Reed has noted in "Toward Form" (Ph.D. diss.: Louis I. Kahn's Urban Designs for Philadelphia, 1939–1962, University of Pennsylvania, 1989), 96, Kahn's first description of served and servant spaces is in his book review of Rachel Wischnitzer, *Synagogue Architecture in the United States* (Philadelphia: Jewish Publication Society of America, 1955), published in the *Jewish Review and Observer* (Cleveland) on 17 February 1956. Drafts of the manuscript, in "Descriptions of Buildings," box 54, Kahn Collection, indicate that the text was written sometime between September and December 1955. The final text is in "LIK Miscellaneous 1954–56," box 65, Kahn Collection.

18. Kahn, interview with John Peter, Philadelphia, 1961, in *The Oral History of Modern Architecture: Interviews with the Greatest Architects of the Twentieth Century* (New York: Harry N. Abrams, 1994), 214, also quoted in Susan Solomon, "Secular and Spiritual Humanism: Louis I. Kahn's Work for the Jewish Community in the 1950s and 1960s" (Ph.D. diss, University of Pennsylvania, 1997), 180 n. 75.

19. Tyng, interview with the author, 1993.

20. Kahn, journal entry, 1955–ca. 1962, Kahn Collection. The sentence "space made by a dome" is probably a reference to Eero Saarinen's Kresge Auditorium at MIT, completed in 1955.

21. Arthur Drexler, "Buildings for Business and Government in America," *Zodiac* 1 (1957): 137. For an account of the International Style's role and place in postwar modernism, see my concluding essay, "Reconceptualizing the Modern," in *Anxious Modernisms: Experimental Postwar Architecture*, ed. Sarah Williams Goldhagen and Réjean Legault (Cambridge, Mass: MIT Press, 2000).

22. Vincent Scully, "Archetype and Order in Recent American Architecture," *Art in America* 42 (December 1954): 251.

23. Paul Rudolph, in "The Changing Philosophy of Architecture," *Architectural Record* 116 (August 1954): 180.

24. Colin Rowe, "Neo-'Classicism' and Modern Architecture, II," in *The Mathematics of the*

Ideal Villa (Cambridge: MIT Press, 1982), 152. According to their author, although these essays were published in 1982, they were written in the mid-1950s. Rowe came to the United States in 1951 to study with Henry-Russell Hitchcock and Christopher Tunnard at Yale; Rowe, letter to the author, January 1994.

25. For example, Rudolph's Sanderling Beach Club was published in *Architectural Record* 114 (October 1953): 150–155, and the house at Siesta Key was published in *House and Home* and reproduced in *The Architect's Journal* 118 (27 August 1953): 254–255. A survey of Rudolph's architecture of the period may be found in Paul Rudolph, *The Architecture of Paul Rudolph*, ed. Sibyl Moholy-Nagy (London: Thames and Hudson, 1970).

26. Johnson's house project of 1953 is published in *Philip Johnson: Architecture, 1949–1965*, 2nd ed. (London: Thames and Hudson, 1967), 25.

27. Kahn himself discussed his attentiveness to Le Corbusier's work in "How'm I Doing, Corbusier? An Interview with Louis Kahn," *Pennsylvania Gazette* (Philadelphia) 71 (December 1972): 18–26. William Huff, in "Louis Kahn: Sorted Recollections and Lapses in Familiarities," *Little Journal* (Society of Architectural Historians, Western New York Chapter) 5 (September 1981): 3, discusses the influence of Philip Johnson at Yale in the early 1950s. By the mid-1950s, Johnson and Kahn were friends, showing each other projects and asking for critiques: Tim Vreeland reported, in an interview with the author, January 1994, that Johnson would come into Kahn's office in the mid-1950s and offer suggestions on Kahn's work. One of Kahn's drawings for the First Unitarian Church in Rochester (in the collection of the church) notes that he had shown the scheme to Johnson, who had liked the idea.

28. For an excellent description of the relation of the Trenton Bathhouse to the projects for the Adler and De Vore houses, see DeLong, "The Mind Opens," 57–58.

29. "Prototype Elementary School," *Progressive Architecture* 35 (October 1954): 127–132. For a discussion of the Gropius and Clauss plans, see also my dissertation, "Changing Symbols of Public Life: Louis Kahn's Religious and Civic Projects, 1944–1966" (Ph.D. diss., Columbia University, 1995).

30. "Design Award: Home for the Indigent," *Progressive Architecture* 36 (January 1955): 90–91.

31. Kahn, journal entry, 1955–ca. 1962, Kahn Collection.

32. For the most recent example, see DeLong, "The Mind Opens," 79–80. Neil Levine suggests that the octahedral scheme looks like a drawing by Francesco di Giorgio published in Rudolph Wittkower's *Architectural Principles in the Age of Humanism*, first published as a book in 1949. Colin Rowe did send Kahn a copy of the Wittkower book in 1955, but *after* Kahn and Tyng had finalized their plan for the Bathhouse. Most of Kahn's historical sources are easily traceable to projects he either kept slides of, or marked in books from his personal library.

33. Tyng, interview with the author, February 1994. She added that she later picked up on this scheme when she started working for the design of the Bryn Mawr dormitories several years later. For a description of Tyng's designs for Bryn Mawr, see Michael J. Lewis, "Eleanor Donnelley Erdman Hall, Bryn Mawr College," in Brownlee and DeLong, *In the Realm*, 352–357.

34. Kahn delivered this lecture on 21 September 1955, at the Poor Richard Club, Philadelphia, for the opening meeting of the Philadelphia Art Directors Club. A notice for his lecture is in "LIK Lectures 1946–1956," box 64, Kahn Collection.

35. Robert Slutsky and Colin Rowe, interviews with the author in October 1993 and January 1994, respectively; Rowe to Kahn, 7 February 1955, in "Correspondence from University's [*sic*] and Colleges," box 65, Kahn Collection; Slutsky to Kahn, 28 January 1956, "LIK Miscellaneous 1954–56," box 65, Kahn Collection.

36. A notice of the June meeting remains in the JCC files, indicating that Kahn would present "drawings and photographs" of the project and the Greenacres County Club in Trenton.

37. "Spaces of a variety of dimension and character supported by their space order needs lend themselves to the development of meaningful form by space distinctions in a more complex hierarchy of spaces." "Perspecta 4," box 62, Kahn Collection.

38. Tyng, interview with the author, March 1993.

39. Selected drawings of this scheme were published in Louis Kahn, "Order in Architecture," *Perspecta* 4 (1957): 60–61. The most complete documentation of this project is in Ronner and Jhaveri, *Louis I. Kahn*, 34–35, and in Louis Kahn, *The Louis I. Kahn Personal Archive: Personal Drawings* (New York: Garland, 1987), vol. 1, 428–439. Drawings published in the Ronner collection include those in the collection of the Museum of Modern Art, New York, which are not published in the Garland volume. For a description of Kahn's Civic Center scheme, see Peter Reed, "Toward Form," 202–235, and Reed, "Philadelphia Urban Design," in Brownlee and DeLong, *In the Realm*, 417.

40. Reed, in "Toward Form," 203 n.3, cites the PCPC's *Pilot Plan* (Philadelphia, 1957) and asserts that the PCPC was studying this area under the designation Market East by at least the end of 1956.

41. Kahn first mentioned giving a civic center as a studio problem at a lecture at Tulane University. Kahn visited Tulane twice in 1955, once in January and once in May; however, the visit in May was for only two days, so perhaps the lecture he delivered there was on his first visit rather than his second. Information on his first visit is in "LIK–Lectures–1946–1956," box 64, Kahn Collection; information on his second is in "Louis I. Kahn–Personal 1955–56," box 65, Kahn Collection. One example of Kahn's assigning the problem to his students is the studio at Penn that Kahn taught with Robert Le Ricolais in 1956, in which they assigned an "Arena for the City of Philadelphia." "Pennsylvania, University of," box 62, Kahn Collection.

42. International Conference of Modern Architects, *The Heart of the City: Toward the Humanization of Urban Life*, ed. J. Tyrwhitt, J. L. Sert, and Ernesto Rogers (New York: Pelligrini and Cudahy, 1952).

43. Kahn, journal entry, sometime before June 1955, Kahn Collection.

44. Kahn, journal entry, 1955, Kahn Collection. The similarity of such a system to Alison and Peter Smithson's Berlin Hauptstadt plan of 1958 cannot be overlooked, although the Smithsons were also very influenced by Le Corbusier.

45. Kahn, "Perspecta 4," box 62, Kahn Collection.

46. This structure was compared to a lampshade in "Louis Kahn and the Living City," *Architectural Forum* 108 (March 1958): 117.

47. In the first edition of Ronner and Jhaveri (1974), *Louis I. Kahn*, 37.

48. "Order in Architecture," 61.

49. "Perspecta 4," box 62, Kahn Collection. It should be noted that the phrase is not written in Kahn's handwriting. But it sounds enough like Kahn, and is filed with Kahn's notes for the article "Order in Architecture," so I hypothesize that the sheet contains someone else's transcriptions of Kahn's dictation.

50. This project is discussed by Meredith Clausen in *Pietro Belluschi: Modern American Architect* (Cambridge: MIT Press, 1994), 251–254.

51. Kahn, "City Planning for the Year 2000," lecture at the Cooper Union, 9 January 1956, tape in Department of Audio-Visual Resources, Cooper Union, New York.

52. For general sources on the 1950s see William H. Chafe, *The Unfinished Journey: America Since World War II*, 2nd ed. (New York: Oxford University Press, 1991); William L. O'Neill, *American High: The Years of Confidence, 1945–1960* (New York: Free Press, 1986); Godfrey Hodgson, *America in Our Time: From World War II to Nixon, What Hap-*

pened and Why (New York: Vintage, 1976); Editors of Fortune, *U.S.A.: The Permanent Revolution* (New York: Prentice-Hall, 1951); David Halberstam, *The Fifties* (New York: Villard Books, 1993).

53. Chafe, *The Unfinished Journey*, 112.

54. Ibid.

55. Chafe (ibid., 117) argues that suburban housing developments "came to symbolize the middle class lifestyle."

56. John C. Keats, *The Crack in the Picture Window* (Cambridge, Mass.: Riverside Press, 1956), xi.

57. Chafe, *The Unfinished Journey*, 112.

58. Ibid., 117.

59. Warren Susman, with the assistance of Edward Griffin, "Did Success Spoil the United States? Dual Representations in Postwar America," in *Recasting America: Culture and Politics in the Age of Cold War* (Chicago: University of Chicago Press, 1989), 24. See also T. J. Jackson Lears's essay, pp. 38–57 of the same volume, entitled "A Matter of Taste: Corporate Cultural Hegemony in a Mass-Consumption Society"—especially p. 48, in which Lears writes that "across the political spectrum, celebrants and doubters alike accepted the same basic assumption that postwar America was a homogeneous mass-consumption society."

60. Keats, *Crack in the Picture Window*, xv.

61. Whyte had been known in architectural circles at least since the early 1950s because of his chapters on suburbia in *The Organization Man* (New York: Simon and Schuster, 1956; reprint, Garden City, N.J.: Doubleday, n.d.), 295–435; for example, he spoke at the Citizen's Council on City Planning in Philadelphia in 1955. A notice is in "Citizen's Council on Planning," box 65, Kahn Collection. See Whyte's article "Urban Sprawl," *Fortune* (January 1958): 103–111, 194, 198.

62. Mary Mix Foley, "The Debacle of Popular Taste," *Architectural Forum* 106 (February 1957): 140.

63. Keats, *Crack in the Picture Window*, xi.

64. "The brutal empire of the masses" is from José Ortega y Gasset, *The Revolt of the Masses* (1930; New York: Norton, 1957), 19; "barbarism" is from ibid., 72. On Ortega y Gasset in particular and the history of critiques of mass culture in general, see Patrick Brantlinger's extremely provocative *Bread and Circuses: Theories of Mass Culture as Social Decay* (Ithaca: Cornell University Press, 1983).

65. Information on Linn and McHarg is in Ann L. Strong and George Thomas, *The Book of the School: One Hundred Years, The Graduate School of Fine Arts at the University of Pennsylvania* (Philadelphia: Graduate School of Fine Arts, 1990), 139 ff. An invoice in "Martin Research Labs," box 31, Kahn Collection, indicates that McHarg was the landscape architect of record for that project. Harriet Pattison reported that Linn worked on one project with Kahn in the early 1960s; moreover, the two were friends, as is indicated by correspondence between them in, among other places, "Karl Linn," box 56, Kahn Collection. Kahn supported Linn for a promotion at Penn; see Kahn to Holmes Perkins, January 1963, box 56, Kahn Collection.

66. My characterization of the issues much discussed at Penn in these years is partly based on my interviews with Holmes Perkins, Romaldo Giurgola, Denise Scott Brown, Richard Saul Wurman, and David Rothstein, 1991–1993. See also Denise Scott Brown, "Between Three Stools," *Architectural Design* special issue "Urban Concepts" (London: Academy Editions, 1990), 8–20; and Scott Brown, "A Worm's Eye View of Recent Architectural History," *Architectural Record* 172 (February 1984): 69–81; and descriptions of the various courses offered in these years in the *University of Pennsylvania Bulletin*.

67. McHarg, *University of Pennsylvania Bulletin* 52, no. 24 (9 May 1952): 9–13; see also Strong and Thomas, *The Book of the School*, 139–140.

68. Strong and Thomas, *The Book of the School*, 139–140.

69. From a speech by Holmes Perkins at a planning conference at Carnegie Mellon University, 17 October 1958, "Dean Perkins' Speeches and Articles 1959–1960," UPB 8.41, box 9, University of Pennsylvania Archives.

70. Paul and Percival Goodman, *Communitas: Means of Livelihood and Ways of Life* (Chicago: University of Chicago Press, 1947). Paul Goodman spoke at Penn in 1956; David Rothstein (who worked in Kahn's office) was on the committee that invited him. "Committee: Program of the School of Fine Arts, 1955–56," UPB 8.4, box 94, University of Pennsylvania Archives. *Communitas* appears on syllabi for courses taught by Blanche Lemco, Tim Vreeland, Robert Geddes, and Holmes Perkins, in, among other places, "Architectural Problems Fall 1956–57," UPB 8.4, box 96, University of Pennsylvania Archives, and "Dean Perkins' Speeches & Articles 1958–59," UPB 8.41, box 9, University of Pennsylvania Archives.

71. Kahn, "Order in Architecture," original manuscript in "Perspecta 4," box 62, Kahn Collection. "A city street is not . . . a machine for traffic to pass through but a square for people to remain within"; Goodman and Goodman, *Communitas*, 49.

72. Lynch, *The Image of the City* (Cambridge: MIT Press, 1960).

73. Lynch, "The Form of Cities," *Scientific American* 190 (April 1954): 55–63; Lynch, "Some Childhood Memories of the City," *Journal of the American Institute of Planners* 22 (1956): 144–152.

74. Lynch's impact on Kahn can be discerned through correspondence between Kahn and Pietro Belluschi. Belluschi wrote to Kahn in July 1955, asking him if he had "given any further thought" to his project, the aim of which was to design "a new synthetic arrangement of the automobile-pedestrian apparatus in American cities" (unmarked file, box 122, Kahn Collection). Kahn must have drafted a reply almost immediately, and the draft is in his journal, K12.22 (1955). Kevin Lynch and Gyorgy Kepes had written to Kahn in August 1954 , asking him if he would review their manuscript; Kahn replied that December that he would be "delighted and honored" to do so (unmarked file, box 66, Kahn Collection). Kahn did not receive the manuscript until 11 August 1955 (after he replied to Belluschi); the manuscript, "The Perceptual Form of the City," is in "Massachusetts Institute of Technology," box 62, Kahn Collection. In much revised form, this text was later published by Lynch alone as *The Image of the City*. By 16 August 1955, Kahn had drafted a new letter to Belluschi; a copy is in "Massachusetts Institute of Technology," box 62, and in an unmarked file, box 122, Kahn Collection. Kahn commented on Lynch and Kepes' manuscript, lauding those passages advocating "communication" in the city, by which Lynch meant not only signs but also "shapes, colors and textures," such as church spires and monuments, all of which combined to connect urban dwellers to their environment by creating a sense of place. A second, revised letter to Belluschi reflects the impact of Lynch's and Kepes' ideas: Kahn wrote that he believed that the civic center could be the "creative center of communication," or what he called "the cathedral of the city." Lynch's impact on Kahn's ideas on monumentality and place making was reinforced in the late 1950s, because Lynch became a ubiquitous honorary presence at Penn, with Perkins enthusiastically supporting his work. Holmes Perkins asked Lynch to speak at a symposium he was chairing at the Association of Collegiate Schools of Architecture in June 1954: "A.S.C.A. Convention, Program Committee," UPB 8.4, box 90, University of Pennsylvania Archives. The following year Perkins recommended Lynch to teach a course in town planning, writing, "I know of no one better." Perkins to H. H. Madbill, "Dean Perkins' Letters of Recom-

mendation, 1954–55," UPB 8.41, box 9, University of Pennsylvania Archives. Perkins assigned Lynch's writings in his required course, entitled Civic Design, and invited him to speak both on panels that he organized and in his class. A copy of Lynch's course syllabus, "The Perceptual Form of the City," is in Perkins' file, "Architectural Problems Fall 1956–57," UPB 8.4, box 96, University of Pennsylvania Archives, and Lynch came to speak in Perkins' class in 1957 (Perkins, thank-you note to Lynch, March 1957, "Visiting Lecturers 1956–57," UPB 8.4, box 98, University of Pennsylvania Archives). The Lynch-Kepes manuscript appears on Perkins' course syllabi in the 1950s; see "Courses: Architecture 1956–1957," UPB 8.4, box 96, University of Pennsylvania Archives. Perkins invited Lynch to speak on a panel he chaired at a conference of the Association of Collegiate Schools of Architecture (Perkins to Lynch, 2 June 1954, "A.C.S.A. Convention, Program Committee," UPB 8.4, box 90, University of Pennsylvania Archives) and in his class (Perkins to Lynch, 19 March 1957, "Visiting Lecturers 1956–1957," UPB 8.4, box 98, University of Pennsylvania Archives). Although Kahn and Perkins were not especially close friends, Perkins' students went on to study with Kahn, and with them they carried Lynch's ideas. For example, a thesis by Louis Sauer on street design, which Kahn directed in the fall term of 1958, discusses landmarks, nodes, foci, edges, and paths—all Lynch's terms—and the impact of Lynch's philosophy is everywhere apparent. Louis Sauer, "The Idea and Image of Destinations in Relation to Movement Systems, or, How to Design Streets so that a Man Knows Where He's Going," in "University of Pennsylvania–Problems, 1958," box 63, Kahn Collection.

75. Holmes Perkins, lecture of November 1952 to the Architects' Society of Ohio, in Perkins' papers, the Architectural Archives, University of Pennsylvania.

76. Anderson in "The Sixties: A P/A Symposium on the State of Architecture, Part I," *Progressive Architecture* 42 (March 1961): 128.

77. Philip Johnson, "The Seven Crutches of Modern Architecture," reprinted in Ockman, *Architecture Culture*, 191.

78. Tyng, in an interview with the author, 1993, reported that Kahn subscribed to *Architectural Forum*, although there is no guarantee that he read the article in question.

79. An offprint of Whyte's article is in Kahn's papers: "Misc. F," box 68, Kahn Collection; Kahn to Whyte, December 1957, box 68, Kahn Collection.

80. Whyte spoke at the Philadelphia chapter of the Citizen's Council on City Planning on 2 May 1955; Keats spoke on 29 March 1957, "Citizen's Council on City Planning," box 65, Kahn Collection.

81. The best sources for information on the Graduate School of Fine Arts at Penn are Strong and Thomas, *The Book of the School*, and the GSFA Archive at the University of Pennsylvania. Also important are Scott Brown, "A Worm's Eye View," 69–81; and Brown, "Between Three Stools," 9–20. Other sources include Joseph Esherick, "Architectural Education in the Thirties and the Seventies," in *The Architect: Chapters in the History of the Profession*, ed. Spiro Castoff (New York: Oxford University Press, 1977), 238–279. Earlier, somewhat misguided attempts to characterize the architecture program include Jan Rowan, "Wanting to Be: The Philadelphia School," *Progressive Architecture* 42 (April 1961): 131–163; and Mimi and John Lobell, "The Philadelphia School: An Architectural Philosophy," in *Louis I. Kahn: L'uomo, il maestro*, ed. Alessandra Latour (Rome: Edizioni Kappa, 1986), 381–395.

82. Kahn, "Order in Architecture," in "Perspecta 4," box 62, Kahn Collection.

83. Kahn, in Walter McQuade, "Architect Louis I. Kahn and His Strong-Boned Structures," *Architectural Forum* 107 (October 1957): 136.

84. Kahn's statement on manufactured buildings appeared in his answer to a questionnaire sent to him by Ian MacAllum, an editor of the *Architectural Review*, December 1956,

"Architecture Review," box 65, Kahn Collection. Peter Blake's statement comes from "The Vanishing American House," *Zodiac* 1 (October 1957): 90. A slightly later article on the same topic is Jules Langsner, "Neo Classicism? Ornamented Modern? The Quest for Ornament in American Architecture," *Zodiac* 4 (1959): 70–71. Critics of mass culture had been skeptical of the technologizing of domesticity for many years; Ortega y Gasset had argued in 1930 that his vilified "mass man" had been born in the nineteenth century, conceived in the wake of rapid progress in science and industry. Brantlinger, *Bread and Circuses*, 193.

85. Kahn, "Monumentality," 581.

86. For an elaboration on the early modern movement's position on tradition and the use of historical precedents, see my "Reconceptualizing the Modern."

87. See Eugene Johnson, in *International Handbook of Contemporary Developments in Architecture* (Westport, Conn.: Greenwood Press, 1981), 507.

88. Johnson's thinking was inspired by Emil Kaufmann's *Von Ledoux bis Le Corbusier: Ursprung und Entwicklung der Autonomen-Architektur*; see Franz Schulze, *Philip Johnson: Life and Work* (New York: Alfred A. Knopf, 1994), 1958.

89. Philip Johnson, "House at New Canaan," *Architectural Review* 108 (September 1950): 152–159.

90. A number of contemporary critics were quick to point out these themes; among them was William Jordy in "The Formal Image," *Architectural Review* 124 (December 1958): 157–165; and Colin Rowe, "Neo-'Classicism' and Modern Architecture, I and II," both in *The Mathematics of the Ideal Villa* (Cambridge: MIT Press, 1982), 119–158.

91. Johnson, "Style and International Style," in *Philip Johnson: Writings* (New York: Oxford University Press, 1979), 73.

92. Ibid., 79.

93. Howe, "Training," *Perspecta* 1 (1952): 5.

94. Editorial, "Building a Civilized Society," *Architectural Forum* 110 (1959): 67.

95. For a discussion of this sense of cultural supremacy in the field of painting see Serge Guilbaut, *How New York Stole the Idea of Modern Art: Abstract Expressionism, Freedom, and the Cold War* (Chicago: University of Chicago Press, 1983).

96. The consensus of American intellectuals that the country's economic and political institutions were basically beneficent has been discussed by many historians of the era. See especially Hodgson, *America in Our Time*, chapter 4, "The Ideology of Liberal Consensus," 67–98; Richard Pells, *The Liberal Mind in a Conservative Age: American Intellectuals in the 1940s and 1950s*, 2nd ed. (Middletown, Conn.: Wesleyan University Press, 1989), chapter 2, "The Shattered Peace," 52–116; Chafe, *The Unfinished Journey*, 141; Elaine Tyler May, *Homeward Bound: American Families in the Cold War Era* (New York: Basic Books, 1988), passim.

97. Schulze, *Philip Johnson*, 145. Johnson was describing his thoughts in the 1930s, but presumably this would also apply to later years. The article to which Johnson referred was by John Carey and appeared in the *Times Literary Supplement* of 12–18 January 1990.

98. Charles Moore reported that Kahn took over Labatut's studio in 1956, in Michael Wurmfeld, ed., *Princeton's Beaux-Arts and Its New Academicism from Labatut to the Program of Geddes: An Exhibition of Original Drawings over Fifty Years* (Princeton, 1976), 23–25. In 1958 a group of Princeton students carted their projects to Philadelphia once a week to receive Kahn's critiques; Moore reported on travels to Philadelphia with his peers in an interview with Richard Saul Wurman, tape in archive of Richard Saul Wurman, Newport, R.I. Travels to Philadelphia in 1958 by Charles Moore, Jeremiah Ford, and Charles Bellingrath were also reported by Ford, in a letter to the author, 1990.

99. Unlike at Yale or Penn, students at Princeton earned their architecture degrees in con-

junction with the University's Department of Art History and Archaeology, where they studied under the tutelage of Donald Drew Egbert. Labatut's program at Princeton has been described on a number of occasions. The most important are the series of interviews and personal statements by Charles Moore, Robert Venturi, Heath Licklidder, Emilio Ambasz, Jean Labatut, and others in Wurmfeld, *Princeton's Beaux-Arts*. Robert Venturi and Denise Scott Brown wrote on the approach that they had developed to architecture while in Princeton in a letter to Ada Louise Huxtable; a copy is in Labatut's papers, box 48, Firestone Library, Princeton University (this letter was later published as "Learning the Right Lessons from the Beaux-Arts," *Architectural Design* 49 [1979]: 23–31). Egbert's lectures on the Ecole des Beaux-Arts were edited by David van Zanten and published in *The Beaux-Arts Tradition in French Architecture Illustrated by the Grands Prix de Rome* (Princeton: Princeton University Press, 1980). Van Zanten also wrote a history of the earlier period of Princeton's School of Architecture, in "The 'Princeton System' and the Founding of the School of Architecture, 1915–1920," in *The Architecture of Robert Venturi*, ed. Christopher Mead (Albuquerque: University of New Mexico Press, 1989), 34–44. Gwendolyn Wright discusses the program at Princeton in "History for Architects," in *The History of History in American Schools of Architecture, 1865–1975*, ed. Gwendolyn Wright and Janet Parks (New York: Buell Center, 1990), 39–41.

100. Kahn had been friends with Labatut since the 1940s, but in the mid-1950s the two men became closer by serving together on a Committee on the Allied Arts, sponsored by the American Institute of Architects. When Labatut had to travel to Europe for several months in 1953, it was Louis Kahn whom he asked to take over his responsibilities as chair of that committee. Correspondence between Labatut and Kahn on this committee is in "Committee on Allied Arts," box 63, Kahn Collection.

101. Jean Labatut, "The Advanced Study of Architecture," May 1941, p. 24, in box 38, Labatut Papers, Firestone Library, Princeton University.

102. Stanislaus von Moos, *Venturi, Rauch and Scott Brown: Buildings and Projects* (New York: Rizzoli, 1987), 23.

103. See the response to Peressutti's presentation of the Torre Velasca in Oscar Newman, ed., *CIAM '59 in Otterlo* (Stuttgart: Karl Kramer Verlag, 1961).

104. "Recent Work of the BBPR Studio," *Architectural Record* 128 (September 1960): 187; this is a quotation from the BBPR studio (exact source not cited); the next quotation is the writer's summation of BBPR's philosophy. See also Leonard Fiori and Massimo Prizzon, eds., *BBPR: Le Torre Velasca* (Milan: Editrice Abitare Segesta, 1982).

105. In a lecture delivered at Penn, Peressutti entitled his talk "Past and Present in Architecture: Our Responsibilities." Notice of the lecture is in UPB 8.4, "Exhibitions 1955–56," box 94, University of Pennsylvania Archives.

106. In Wurmfeld, *Princeton's Beaux-Arts*, Moore reported that he was Kahn's teaching assistant for the academic year 1955–1956 and also told of traveling to the Yucatan. Evidence of the Yucatan trip is also in the box marked "Faculty and Courses prior to 1968," Archives of the School of Architecture, Princeton University.

107. T. S. Eliot, "Tradition and the Individual Talent," in *Selected Essays* (New York: Harcourt Brace and Company, 1950). The following quotations are from pp. 3–5.

108. Kahn was juror for two studios in 1955, in which three theses dealt with issues of monumentality and history. In January 1955, William H. Roehl presented a thesis entitled "Monumentality in Civic Architecture in the United States," and Philemon Sturges presented one on the redevelopment of Fairmount Park in Philadelphia. That June, Kahn was again on a jury in which the studio projects addressed similar themes; one that survives is George A. Hartman's "An Analysis of the Language of Architecture." The boards for these theses are in the Archive of the School of Architecture, Princeton Uni-

versity; transcripts of Kahn's and other jurors' comments are filed in folders labeled with the students' names.

109. Aldo Rossi, *The Architecture of the City*, trans. Diane Ghirardo and Joan Ockman (Cambridge: MIT Press, 1982), 33.

110. Kahn, "Closing Remarks," in Newman, *CIAM '59 in Otterlo*, 211.

111. The new scheme is in Ian MacAllum, "Genetrix: Personal Contributions to American Architecture," *Architectural Review* 121 (May 1957): 344–345. See Solomon, "Jewish Community Center," 321.

112. See, for example, Rowe's "Neo-'Classicism' II," 152–156.

113. Rowe and Slutsky met with Kahn in December 1955; according to Slutsky, Rowe pointed out to Kahn the "Palladian" qualities inherent in such projects as the second scheme of the JCC. Subsequently, Rowe sent Kahn a copy of Rudolph Wittkower's *Architectural Principles in the Age of Humanism* "as a token of gratitude and as a sort of memorial to the subsequent dialectics." Kahn, perhaps after his meeting with Rowe (as DeLong has suggested in Brownlee and DeLong, *In the Realm*, 59), wrote a journal entry on "The Palladian Plan," quoted earlier. Kahn's cellular rooms, in their rejection of the modern movement's separation of structure and skin, shared much with Rowe's "neo-p," bay-system plans (Rowe had included a tracing of an ideal plan by Palladio in his letter).

114. Kahn, in "Description of the Spaces and Functions of the Community Building," dated 21 May 1957, file folder "Trenton J.C.C.–MacAllister," box 108, Kahn Collection.

115. None of the members of Kahn's office that I interviewed remembered whether or not Komendant had been consulted in conjunction with the JCC, but Komendant, in an interview with Richard Saul Wurman before Komendant died, said that he had worked on the project with Kahn. Archive of Richard Saul Wurman, Newport, R.I.

116. Transcript of a lecture from May 1957, "LIK Lectures," box 53, Kahn Collection.

117. Kahn, in "Description of the Spaces and Functions of the Community Building," dated 21 May 1957, "Trenton J.C.C.–MacAllister," box 108, Kahn Collection.

118. Ibid. This solution foreshadows Komendant's 1960 roof design for the sanctuary of the Unitarian Church at Rochester, and was almost certainly prepared with his collaboration.

119. Minutes of one of the meetings with the NJWB, dated 19 December 1957, are in the JCC files. This is the memo that is quoted below.

120. Kahn to Gianopolus, "Trenton Jewish Community Center/Keast & Hood, Structural Engineers," box 108, Kahn Collection.

121. Solomon, "Jewish Community Center," 322.

122. George Warren, interview with the author, summer 1993.

CHAPTER 6: RETHINKING MODERNISM

1. Auguste Komendant told Holmes Perkins that the First Unitarian Church in Rochester was "the best Kahn had made yet." Komendant, *Eighteen Years with Architect Louis I. Kahn* (Englewood, N.J.: Aloray, 1975), 40.

2. From a note on Kahn's drawing 525.31, Kahn Collection.

3. Information on Rochester's urban redevelopment project appeared in "Renaissance on the Genesee," *Architectural Forum* 111 (July 1959): 104–109.

4. The figure of half a million dollars comes from Robert Jonas, a member of the original building committee, in an interview with the author, summer 1991, and is confirmed in a press release by the New York State Council on the Arts, "UCRNY I–New York State Council Arts, May 8, 1967," box 14, Kahn Collection. Information on the history of the Unitarian congregation is drawn from "Architectural and Building Committee Reminiscences,

First Unitarian Church, Rochester, New York," a series of audio tapes compiled by Jean France and other original members of the selection and building committees in 1979 (hereafter "Reminiscences"); from Nancy J. Salzer, "Covenant for Freedom: A History of the First Unitarian Congregational Society of Rochester, New York, 1829–1975"; and from "Fact Finding on Four Courses of Action," a memo dated December 1958. All are in the files of the First Unitarian Church in Rochester. Interviews with two members of the original building committee have also been very useful: interview with Jean France, November 1991; interview with Jim Cunningham, May 1993. Jean France's lecture "Louis Kahn and the First Unitarian Church of Rochester, New York: A Client's Eye View," delivered to the Society of Architectural Historians in 1992, has provided additional insights, and I would like to thank Mrs. France for her warm support and assistance. See also Robin Williams, "First Unitarian Church and School," in Brownlee and DeLong, *In the Realm*, 340–345; and Williams, "An Architectural Myth: The Design Evolution of Louis Kahn's First Unitarian Church," master's thesis, University of Pennsylvania, 1990. Both of Williams' writings give a carefully documented history of the building's design development.

5. "An Interim Report on the Church Property from the Board of Trustees," memo, files of the First Unitarian Church. All subsequent synopses and quotations of David Williams' statements in this paragraph are from the same document.

6. The standard history of the Unitarian religion is David Robinson, *The Unitarians and the Universalists* (Westport, Conn.: Greenwood, 1985); "dignity rather than depravity" is from p. 3.

7. The quotation is from Jim Cunningham, interview with the author, May 1993.

8. An influential doctrine released in the 1930s by Unitarian authorities declared that a "religion that does not express itself through action in human society is not in any sense a religion at all." Robinson, *Unitarians*, 14.

9. Salzer, "Covenant for Freedom," 8–10.

10. Jean France's story of how she joined the Unitarian Church makes this clear. Having moved to Rochester, she attended services at a more conservative Protestant congregation, where she "was told to vote Republican while my son heard about death in Sunday School." Volunteering for John F. Kennedy's presidential campaign, she asked there for a more suitable congregation and was sent to the First Unitarian church. France, interview with the author, November 1991.

11. "Building Committee Correspondence–Roche/April 1959 through December 1960," box 15, Kahn Collection.

12. France, "Louis Kahn," 3.

13. Cunningham to Kahn, 7 April 1959; Kahn to Cunningham, April 9, 1959; both in "Building Committee Correspondence–Roche/April 1959 through December 1960," box 15, Kahn Collection.

14. Quotation is from France, "Louis Kahn," 1–3. Jim Cunningham, in "Reminiscences," suggested that perhaps Kahn consulted with a Unitarian minister in Philadelphia before they arrived for their interview. Komendant, in *Eighteen Years*, 35, also reported that Kahn "studied very thoroughly this religion and had several meetings with their ministers. He also talked with other ministers." I have found no documentation of Kahn's visits with any Unitarian ministers.

15. Kahn received, on 3 June 1959, a document entitled "Report to the Congregation from the Fact Finding Committee on Church Architecture," containing findings and statistics from the First Unitarian Church's surveys. "Building Committee Correspondence–Roche/April 1959 through December 1960," box 15, Kahn Collection.

16. One copy of the program is in "Building Committee Correspondence–Roche/April 1959 through December 1960," box 15, Kahn Collection.

17. On 15 July 1959, Kahn wrote to Robert Jonas, chairman of the board of trustees of the church, saying, "I have begun studies of the basic forms and spaces which I will be able to talk against your finding of needs." "Building Committee Correspondence–Roche / April 1959 through December 1960," box 15, Kahn Collection. This would suggest that these first sketches were drawn in mid-summer 1959. But two days later he wrote to Margaret Squire, an editor at *Progressive Architecture*, saying, "I have a good idea for the Unitarian Church but nothing down on paper yet." "Master File April 1 thru October 30 '59," box 9, Kahn Collection.

18. The presentation drawings, including site plans and sections, are in the collection of the Rochester Unitarian Church, and their existence was not known to previous scholars. The month of Kahn's visit to meet the members of the congregation is in correspondence between Kahn and William Neuman (chair of the church's board of directors), "Building Committee Correspondence–Roche/April 1959 through December 1960," box 15, Kahn Collection.

19. Unidentified voice from "Building Committee Reminiscences," First Unitarian Church, Rochester.

20. Ibid.

21. Jim Cunningham, interview with the author, May 1993.

22. Kahn, "Closing Remarks," in *CIAM '59 in Otterlo*, ed. Oscar Newman (Stuttgart: Karl Kramer Verlag, 1961), 208.

23. A copy of the 1956 studio program is in "Courses–Architecture 1956–57," UPB 8.4, box 96, University of Pennsylvania Archives; Kahn gave the problem again in the spring semester of 1957; the program is in "University of Penna: Miscellaneous Correspondence," box 63, Kahn Collection.

24. Kahn must have been referring to the time that he was a fellow at the American Academy in Rome, for after that he did not start traveling again until 1958, when he went to Israel in May and stopped in Paris and in London. Chronology, Kahn Collection.

25. Kahn, "Spaces Order and Architecture," *Royal Architectural Institute of Canada* 34 (October 1957): 375–376.

26. John Keats, *The Crack in the Picture Window* (Boston: Houghton Mifflin, 1957), xi.

27. David Riesman, *The Lonely Crowd: A Study in the Changing American Character* (1950; reprint, New Haven: Yale University Press, 1961); William H. Whyte, *The Organization Man* (New York: Simon and Schuster, 1956); C. Wright Mills, *The Power Elite* (New York: Oxford University Press, 1956). My understanding of the prominence of these themes in the 1950s has been aided by Warren Susman, "Did Success Spoil the United States? Dual Representations in Postwar America," in *Recasting America: Culture and Politics in the Age of the Cold War* (Chicago: University of Chicago Press, 1989), 19–37, and, in the same collection, Jackson Lears, "A Matter of Taste: Corporate Cultural Hegemony in a Mass-Consumption Society," 38–60; also Paul Carter, *Another Part of the Fifties* (New York: Columbia University Press, 1983); and T. B. Bottomore, *Critics of Society* (New York: Pantheon, 1966).

28. Eric Hoffer, *The True Believer: Thoughts on the Nature of Mass Movements* (New York: Harper and Row, 1951); Hannah Arendt, *The Origins of Totalitarianism* (New York: Harcourt Brace, 1951) and *The Human Condition* (Chicago: University of Chicago Press, 1958).

29. Paul Nelson, "Design for Tomorrow," *Perspecta* 5 (1956): 59.

30. Scully in "Architecture–Fitting and Befitting," *Architectural Forum* 114 (June 1961): 87.

31. Linn and McHarg complained that consumerism evaporated people's sense of public duty, with Linn arguing that Penn's faculty should instill in students a sense of civic responsibility that would extricate them from the manipulative solipsism of Madison Avenue. Linn,

memo to the university, January 1960; a copy is filed in "Misc. 1961," box 64, Kahn Collection. Aldo Giurgola was very close to Kahn from the mid-1950s onward. Later he wrote a book on Kahn's architecture with Jaimini Mehta, entitled *Louis I. Kahn* (Boulder, Colo.: Westview Press, 1975). Tim Vreeland worked in Kahn's office for many years.

32. Studio problem for Architecture 200, "Architectural Problems Fall 1956–1957," UPB 8.4, box 96, University of Pennsylvania Archives.

33. Vreeland's design brief for a courthouse stresses that the courtroom should "be ample in its proportions and totally in keeping with its solemn purpose" ("Design Problems 1957–58," UPB 8.4, box 100, University of Pennsylvania Archives); Giurgola's brief demands that "the character of the architecture of the courthouse may be synthesized with this consideration: in the United States the majesty of the law is represented by the judge; his task is to preserve social order" ("Design Problems," UPB 8.4, box 112, University of Pennsylvania Archives). The work of Kahn's students employed similar language and explored similar themes; one student in a project for a civic center for Philadelphia argued that "the civic center should provide opportunities, in an impartial way, for spontaneous manifestation of social life, the relation of individuals with one another and the relations of individuals with the community." Erich Sulke, "Program for the Design of a Civic Center of the New Town," in "Courses–Arch 600," UPB 8.4, box 100, University of Pennsylvania archives. Such themes were also being addressed by students at Princeton; see the thesis of Jeremiah Ford entitled "The Center" in the Archives of the School of Architecture, Princeton University (Kahn was Ford's thesis adviser).

34. On their debt to, and their departures from, Le Corbusier, see Alison and Peter Smithson, "Banham's Bumper Book on Brutalism, Discussed by Alison and Peter Smithson," *Architect's Journal* (28 December 1966): 1590–1591.

35. The Smithsons presented these ideas in "The Built World: Urban Re-Identification," *Architectural Design* (June 1955), reprinted in *Ordinariness and Light: Urban Theories, 1952–1960, and Their Application in a Building Project, 1963–1970* (Tokyo: Shokokusa Publishing, 1979), 107–110. Literature both by and on the Smithsons is vast; the most important sources are Alison Smithson, ed., *Team 10 Primer* (London: Whitefriar's Press, 1965); Alison and Peter Smithson, eds., *Team 10 Meetings* (New York: Rizzoli, 1991); *A + P Smithson: Pensieri, progetti e frammenti fino al 1990*, ed. Marco Vidotto (Genoa: Sagep Editrice, 1991); David Robbins, ed., *The Independent Group: Postwar Britain and the Aesthetics of Plenty* (Cambridge: MIT Press, 1990); Reyner Banham, *The New Brutalism: Ethic or Aesthetic?* (New York: Reinhold, 1966); and the unpublished bibliography of their writings, prepared by Alison Smithson. Peter Smithson wrote about his trip to the United States in "Letter to America," *Architectural Design* 28 (March 1958): 93–102; together the Smithsons wrote "Louis Kahn," *Architect's Yearbook* 9 (1960): 102–118. Robin Middleton wrote on the impact of Kahn's urban-planning ideas on the Smithsons in "The New Brutalism or a Clean, Well-Lighted Place," *Architectural Design* 37 (January 1967): 7–8.

36. Wurman, interview with the author, April 1992. The writer who has most emphasized relations between Team 10 and the GSFA at Penn is Denise Scott Brown, in "Between Three Stools: A Personal View of Urban Design Pedagogy," in *Urban Concepts*, special issue, *Architectural Design* 38 (London: Academy Editions, 1990), 9–20; and Brown, "A Worm's Eye View of Recent Architectural History," *Architectural Record* 172 (February 1984): 69–81.

37. Perkins, "Urban Form," dated 1961 for the symposium on Metropolitan Planning, published in the *Proceedings of the American Philosophical Society* 106 (June 1962): 190.

38. The exhibition was brought to Penn by faculty member Blanche Lemco, who later mar-

ried Dutch Team Ten member Sandy von Ginkel. It took place from March 18 to April 5 and showed work presented at CIAM X in Dubrovnik; "Committees: Exhibitions 1956–57," UPB 8.4, box 96, University of Pennsylvania Archives.

39. Peter Smithson visited the United States in September–October 1957; this was recounted to the author in an interview with Smithson (October 1991) and confirmed by a letter from John Johanson to Holmes Perkins in which Johanson offered to have Smithson give a lecture at Penn. "Visiting Lecturers 1957–58," UPB 8.4, box 102, University of Pennsylvania Archives. Smithson recounted that he and Kahn became fast friends; this is confirmed by, for example, Kahn to Smithson, "Master File Correspondence October thru December 1957," box 9, Kahn Collection. In 1960 Kahn convinced Holmes Perkins to invite Peter Smithson to the GSFA to teach (see "Prospective Teachers Arch. & F. A. 1961–62," UPB 8.4, box 108), but Smithson declined. In October 1959, the Smithsons were included in an exhibition at the GSFA, "Work of Three English Architects" (there were actually four architects; the other two were James Stirling and William Howell); see "Committee: Exhibitions 1958–59," UPB 8.4, box 104, University of Pennsylvania Archives. On Kahn's invitation to Otterlo, see J. Bakema to Kahn, June 1959 ("from Smithson in London we heard of your interest in attending Otterlo"), "CIAM," box 115, Kahn Collection.

40. For evidence of the Smithsons' previous interest in popular culture, see "But Today We Collect Ads," *Ark* 18 (November 1956), reprinted in Robbins, *The Independent Group*, 185–186. Indeed, Mills's definition of the differences between "a mass" and "a public" read like an articulation of the ideas toward which many of the architects and urban planners at Penn were inarticulately groping. See, for example, Mills, *The Power Elite*, 300–305. However, as far as I can tell, Mills's work was not widely known at the GSFA at Penn until the mid-1960s.

41. Transcript, Kahn's lecture on WFIL-TV, "Lectures," box 115, Kahn Collection.

42. Notes on Kahn speaking, in an unidentified hand, unmarked file, box 122, Kahn Collection.

43. Kahn in "The New Art of Urban Design—Are We Equipped?" in "Louis I. Kahn—Architectural League," box 61, Kahn Collection.

44. Kahn's rising interest in using and transforming historical precedents in design is discussed in Chapter 5 of this book. The plan is reproduced in Jean Paul Richter, ed., *The Literary Works of Leonardo da Vinci* (1883), plates 88 and 89. Kahn owned a copy of this book, which is now in the collection of Sue Ann Kahn, New York. A similar plate appears in Rudolph Wittkower's *Architectural Principles in the Age of Humanism*, which was widely available in its second edition (London: Alec Tiranti, 1952) and popular at Yale's school of architecture when Kahn was teaching there. There was also a well-publicized exhibition of Leonardo's architectural drawings at Penn in 1958. A notice of the exhibition (held from 3 to 17 October 1958) is in "Committee: Program—Films School of Fine Arts—Lectures," UPB 8.4, box 104, University of Pennsylvania Archives.

45. Scully, "Modern Architecture: Toward a Redefinition of Style," *Perspecta* 4 (1957): 10.

46. Jordy, "The Formal Image," *Architectural Review* 127 (March 1960): 159.

47. Banham, in his article "1960: Stocktaking," in *Architectural Review* 127 (February 1960): 94, writes that in the return to "tradition" and the Italian Renaissance among architects of the decade, "its symbol was the Vitruvian Man, its slogan 'Divina Proporzione,' its hero Palladio, its prophet—quite coincidentally—Rudolf Wittkower." See Wittkower, *Architectural Principles*.

48. Saarinen, "The Changing Philosophy of Architecture," *Architectural Record* 116 (August 1954): 182.

49. Scully, "Modern Architecture," 8–9.

50. "Nature of art," Kahn, "Closing Remarks," 216. "Nature will only laugh," William

Huff, notes on a lecture by Kahn, in the Archive of Richard Saul Wurman, Newport, Rhode Island.

51. Kahn to Arthur Drexler, July 1960, box 9, Kahn Collection.

52. Kahn to Maurice van Horn (chair of the building committee), July 1961, "Rochester Unitarian Some Expenses Reimbur.?" box 81, Kahn Collection.

53. Statements regarding a "question" are from Kahn, "On Form and Design," *Journal of Architectural Education* 15 (Fall 1960): 65; lecture delivered at the conference of Association of Collegiate Schools of Architecture in April 1960; the statement regarding the inseparability of school and sanctuary is from "Louis Kahn," transcript of a dialogue in Kahn's office, printed in *Perspecta* 7 (1961): 14. Williams correctly notes that the "form concept" drawing postdated Kahn's sketches for the church and was in fact drawn in 1960, as he was working on his "form and design" ideas. However, it was not the idea for an *ambulatory* that Kahn added that October, but rather the idea of the sanctuary as a "question." See Williams, "An Architectural Myth," 12 and 42 n. 24.

54. Kahn, "Closing Remarks," 207.

55. Kahn to Alison and Peter Smithson, 5 March 1959, box 9, Kahn Collection.

56. Kahn to Allan Rae, 16 July 1959, unmarked file, box 66, Kahn Collection.

57. Most previous interpretations of Kahn's philosophy have characterized his ideas as mystical and Platonic: Manfredo Tafuri condemns Kahn's "Myth of Order" and "neo-platonic mysticism" that "resolves oppositions in messianic appeasement." *Theories and History of Architecture*, trans. Giorgio Verrecchia (New York: Harper and Row, 1979), 7. DeLong writes, "Until he discovered the Platonic image for any given problem, questions of material and site remained of secondary importance," quoting Kahn's statement from Otterlo that "the realization of what an auditorium is is absolutely beyond the problem of whether it is in the Sudan, or in Rio de Janeiro" (DeLong, "The Mind Opens . . ." in Brownlee and DeLong, *In the Realm*, 72). Given that many other statements and writings contradict the apparent Platonism underlying this passage, it is likely that Kahn's contention that the form of an auditorium is not place-specific was an expression of his conception of music as a trans-cultural language, not of his design philosophy as a whole.

58. Kahn, untitled lecture at Princeton, February 1960, p. 9, in "Faculty and Courses Prior to 1968," Archives of the School of Architecture, Princeton University.

59. Kahn, "Form and Design," reprinted in *Louis I. Kahn: Writings, Lectures, Interviews*, ed. Alessandra Latour (New York: Rizzoli, 1991), 113.

60. Kahn to Allan Rae, 16 July 1959, unmarked file, box 66, Kahn Collection.

61. Kahn, lecture at the School of Architecture at the University of California at Berkeley, 1966, Special Collections, Getty Center for the History of Art and Humanities.

62. For the extenuated design process that Kahn's "Form and Design" lecture recounts, see chapter five of my doctoral dissertation, "Changing Symbols of Public Life: Louis Kahn's Religious and Civic Institutions, 1944–1966, and Architectural Culture at the End of the Modern Movement" (Ph.D. diss., Columbia University, 1995).

63. Kahn, "Form and Design," 116.

64. Minutes of the building committee, 27 March 1960, files of the First Unitarian Church.

65. Kahn, "Form and Design," 116.

66. Van Horn to Kahn, 2 April 1960, "Building Committee Correspondence – Roche/April 1959 through December 1960," box 15, Kahn Collection.

67. Kahn, "Form and Design," 113.

68. The Goldenberg House commission began in January and terminated in August 1959; "Goldenberg House," box 80, Kahn Collection. Kahn described the designs for the Goldenberg House in "Louis Kahn," transcript of a dialogue in Kahn's office, printed in *Perspecta* 7 (1961): 94.

69. This point is discussed at length in Chapter 5.

70. First is Kahn to class of Jeremiah Ford, 1959, at the School of Architecture, Princeton University; second is Kahn in a class at Penn, according to notes taken by Tim Vreeland, filed in an unmarked file, box 122, Kahn Collection.

71. Vreeland notes, unmarked file, box 122, Kahn Collection.

72. Sigfried Giedion, "Forget the 'International Style': The State of Contemporary Architecture, 1: The Regional Approach," *Architectural Record* 115 (January 1954): 135; James Bailey, "Louis I. Kahn in India: An Old Order at a New Scale," *Architectural Forum* 125 (July–August 1966): 63–67.

73. Heinz Ronner and Shared Jhaveri, in *Louis I. Kahn: Complete Work, 1935–1974*, 2nd ed. (Basel: Birkhauser, 1987), describe this early dome as a "fishbelly lattice truss" dome. What this means exactly is unclear, but in any case it is, according to William Huff (who worked on the charette for this project and actually built this model), incorrect. Huff, interview with the author, May 1994.

74. William Huff, in an interview with the author, May 1994, told of Kahn's visit to the churches at Albi and Ronchamp during the time of his trip to Otterlo in September 1959.

75. "Memo on Preplanning for the Worship Area," dated 18 July 1959, files of the First Unitarian Church.

76. Kahn's interest in natural light was also apparent in his design for the Weiss House, 1948–1950, in which he designed for the living room a series of panels that could be moved to change the way light fell to the interior.

77. The comment was Kahn's dismissal of Paul Rudolph and Edward Durrell Stone's use of light screens, quoted in Mary Huntington Hall, "Salk's Ambitious Castle," *San Diego* (February 1962): 41. This issue is further discussed in Chapter 7.

78. Kahn first talked about glare in the same lecture where he introduced his "form and design" ideas, "The Difference Between Form and Design" (January 1960), transcript in "LIK Lectures," box 15, Kahn Collection. Kahn went to Luanda on the first, and left on the thirteenth, of January 1960, "Miscellaneous 1959," box 64, Kahn Collection. I am grateful to Tim Vreeland for pointing out to me, in an interview with the author (January 1994), the importance of Kahn's trip to Luanda for later versions of the Unitarian Church.

79. Kahn in "Louis Kahn," transcript of a dialogue in Kahn's office, printed in *Perspecta* 7 (1961): 14.

80. Ibid.

81. Kahn, lecture at Princeton, p. 7, copy in "Faculty and Courses Prior to 1968," Archives of the School of Architecture, Princeton University.

82. Kahn, quoted in Jules Prown, *The Architecture of the Yale Center for British Art*, 2nd ed. (New Haven: Yale University Press, 1982), 43.

83. The description refers to a later scheme for the roof of the lounge, but it relays Kahn's aspirations for the whole. Minutes of the building committee, June 1960, files of the First Unitarian Church.

84. Komendant, *Eighteen Years*, 37.

85. See memo, Bill Porter to contractor, August 1961, "Master File–August 1–61 through 9/28/62," box 9, Kahn Collection.

86. Porter, interview with the author, July 1993.

87. Kahn in Henry S. F. Cooper, "The Architect Speaks," *Yale Daily News* (6 November 1953): 2.

88. Kahn had become interested in woodwork after his visit to England in 1959, where, with the Smithsons, he visited Elizabethan manor houses. Liking the cabinetry in these interiors, he began checking out books on British manor houses from the GSFA library

shortly after his return, and collecting books on the topic for his own library. He also wanted to use wood for the sanctuary floor, which would have made a much warmer interior than the poured concrete slab the building committee eventually settled on for budgetary reasons. Huff, in an interview with author, June 1994, reported that Kahn had been much impressed by the woodwork in Elizabethan manor houses when he came back from Otterlo. Alison and Peter Smithson, in an interview with the author in 1992, reported their visits with Kahn to Elizabethan manors. See Kahn, note to Maurice van Horn, July 1961, "Rochester Unitarian Some Expenses Reimbur?," and reply, "Contract and Contract Correspond./First Unitarian Society/Rochester, New York," box 81, Kahn Collection. See overdue notice to Kahn from Penn librarian, which includes the title "English Homes," "Misc. 1961," box 64, Kahn Collection, and books in Kahn's library, which includes, among others, Charles Lathan, *In English Homes* (London, 1909); Thomas Rickman, *Styles of Architecture in England: From the Conquest to the Reformation* (London, 1881).

89. See Duncan Buell to Wheeling Steel Corporation (October 1961), "October November Master File 1962," box 9, Kahn Collection; Buell to W. H. Maze Company (August 1962), "August Master 1962," box 9, Kahn Collection.

90. Komendant, *Eighteen Years*, 40.

CHAPTER 7: SITUATING THE DEMOCRATIC WAY OF LIFE

1. For an excellent narrative account of the design development of the National Assembly and Hostels, see Peter Reed, "Sher-e-Bangla Nagar, Capital of Bangladesh," in Brownlee and DeLong, *In the Realm*, 374–383.

2. During the 1950s and early 1960s, this problem was termed one of "disparity" between the two halves of the country. It is discussed in Karl von Vorys, *Political Development in Pakistan* (Princeton: Princeton University Press, 1965), and in Charles Peter O'Donnell, *Bangladesh: Biography of a Muslim Nation* (Boulder: Westview Press, 1984), 58–65. In his autobiography, Ayub Khan also mentions the problem: Mohammad Ayub Khan, *Friends Not Masters: A Political Autobiography* (New York: Oxford University Press, 1967), 222–224. That tensions between East and West Pakistan were generally felt was confirmed in interviews conducted with Carles Vallonrat, Kahn's chief assistant on the project in its early stages of design, and with Mazharul Islam, the Bengali architect responsible for suggesting Kahn for the commission. Interview with Vallonrat, November 1991; interview with Islam, January 1991.

3. Information on Ayub Khan that Kahn would have known is from "Introduction to Pakistan," a brochure in "Pakistan Literature," box 119, Kahn Collection; Moshin Ali, "Basic Democracies," *Christian Science Monitor* (November 1, 1960); and from a booklet on U.S. aid to Pakistan published by the Morgan Guaranty Bank, a copy of which is in "AC–Post Report–Karachi, W.P.," box 119, Kahn Collection.

4. Khan described his aspirations for Pakistan in his autobiography; also see Lawrence Zirig, *The Ayub Khan Era: Politics in Pakistan, 1958–1969* (Syracuse: Syracuse University Press, 1971), 2–10.

5. Ali, "Basic Democracies."

6. Jack MacAllister, who was working in Kahn's office at the time, later said that "the whole project . . . was to mollify the East Pakistani . . . to build a multi-million dollar project for that seemed insane." MacAllister, interview with Richard Saul Wurman, Archive of Richard Saul Wurman, Newport, Rhode Island.

7. Information for this and the subsequent paragraph is from the author's interview with Mazharul Islam, January 1991.

8. Duncan Buell to Kahn, November 1963, unmarked file, box 116, Kahn Collection.

9. Roy Vollmer to Kahn, November 1964, "PACCAP Vollmer Reports," box 122, Kahn Collection.

10. Information is from interviews with Mazharul Islam and previous and former members of the PWD in Dhaka, including Amir Hossein and Abdul Wazid (January 1991). Ayub Khan's autobiography is *Friends Not Masters*.

11. On the State Department's Embassy-building program, see Jane C. Loeffler, *The Architecture of Diplomacy: Building America's Embassies* (New York: Princeton Architectural Press, 1998); Loeffler, "The Architecture of Diplomacy: Heyday of the United States Embassy-Building Program, 1954–1960," *Journal of the Society of Architectural Historians* 49 (September 1990): 251–278; and Ron Robin, *Enclaves of America: The Rhetoric of American Political Architecture Abroad, 1900–1965* (Princeton: Princeton University Press, 1992), especially part 2, pp. 91–179.

12. Memo, Sweeley to Johnstone, August 1960, on the history of the proposed Luanda project. The documents remain in the files of the State Department, Washington, D.C. I am indebted to Jane Loeffler of Washington, D.C., for sharing with me both these documents and her extensive knowledge on the building of U.S. embassies in the 1950s and 1960s.

13. See Sweeley to Kahn, March 1960, and Robert Hughes to Kahn, April 1960, both in "Communications and Correspondence AFRICA Dept. of State – Off. of Foreign Buildings," box 34, Kahn Collection; memo, Sweeley to Johnstone on a history of the Luanda project, August 1960, in the files of the State Department, Washington, D.C.

14. Kahn to Irving Litvag, director of Special Events, Washington University, April 1964. "Louis I. Kahn, Lectures, 1959," box 59, Kahn Collection. During the years that Kahn was designing and constructing the National Assembly complex, the spelling of the city's name was the same as it had been in the days when Bengal was a British colony. Subsequent to establishment of the country of Bangladesh, the transliterated name of the city was changed to Dhaka to better reflect its Muslim heritage.

15. Copies of pertinent documents are in box 65, "General Electric"; box 80, "General Electric Co/ L.I. Kahn Consultant"; and box 9, "October 16, 1957–September 7, 1958, LN Letters from 8/22–9/7," all of the Kahn Collection.

16. Linn, memo to the University of Pennsylvania, n.p., 1 November 1960, in "Misc. 1961," box 64, Kahn Collection.

17. Hitchcock to Kahn, April 1960, "Voice of America – Louis I. Kahn Recorded November 19, 1960," box 55, Kahn Collection.

18. In a meeting of a board on the value of public art, Kahn lauded recent public spaces in New York, saying, "It builds patriotism and good feelings about your city." "One and one-half percent committee (Peacock Changed to Ordinance Committee)," box 62, Kahn Collection.

19. Kahn, lecture in June 1961, "Cranbrook Speech – 1961–to be edited," box 54, Kahn Collection. When William H. Whyte sent Kahn in 1957 a copy of his article "Urban Sprawl," Kahn wrote back, "It arouses a spirit of home beyond one's own. It arouses a spirit of patriotism and civic responsibility." Kahn to Whyte, December 1957, in "F. Misc.," box 68, Kahn Collection.

20. Kahn, lecture at Pratt Institute, November 1959, transcript in "Lectures," box 115, Kahn Collection. At Otterlo that September, Kahn had similarly said, "Suppose you want to meet here, upholding certain cultural, social, or other interests of our democracy, you now have no place to meet." Kahn, "Closing Remarks," in *CIAM '59 in Otterlo*, ed. Oscar Newman (Stuttgart: Karl Kramer Verlag, 1961), 207.

21. For example, Roy Vollmer wrote to Kahn in November 1964, just before the elections, that "Miss Jinnah [Khan's opponent] is winning. I have it on best authority. If she gets in it will be absolute chaos. Ayub still has until March to buy off the basic democrats."

"PAKCAP — Correspondence to/from ROYGUS October 8, 1964 thru June 30, 1965," box 117, Kahn Collection.

22. Khan, reprint of speech in "AC — Post Report — Karachi, W.D.," box 119, Kahn Collection.

23. Kahn's notes to himself to negotiate with the PWD, November 1963, in unmarked file, box 116, Kahn Collection.

24. "Second Capital — Pakistan 62–63 Pakistan Public Works Department (Ahmad, Farqui, Qureshim, Hasan, etc.)," box 117, Kahn Collection. Previous uses of the site were told to the author in interviews with Mazharul Islam (January 1991), Henry Wilcots (January 1992), and Carles Vallonrat (November 1991).

25. The provision for a separate mosque was later dropped, and only the prayer hall was built. The original program is in "Second Capital — Pakistan 62–63 Pakistan Public Works Department (Ahmad, Farqui, Qureshim, Hasan, etc.)," and cable from Kafiluddin to Kahn from January 1963 in "PAC — Cablegrams to/from Addl Chief/ 2 years 1966–67," both in box 117, Kahn Collection.

26. Kafiluddin to Kahn from January 1963 in "PAC — Cablegrams to/from Addl Chief/ 2 years 1966–67," box 117, Kahn Collection.

27. Kahn, draft of the statement for *North Carolina State College*, "North Carolina," box 56, Kahn Collection. The final draft reads a little differently; see "The Development by Louis I. Kahn of the Design for the Second Capital of Pakistan at Dacca," *Student Publication of the School of Design, North Carolina State College, Raleigh* 14 (May 1964). For commentary on the differences between the two drafts, see my article under the name Sarah Williams Ksiazek, "Architectural Culture in the Fifties: Louis Kahn and the National Assembly Complex in Dhaka," *Journal of the Society of Architectural Historians* 52 (December 1993): 416–435.

28. Mary Caroline McLeod, "Urbanism and Utopia: Le Corbusier from Regional Syndicalism to Vichy" (Ph.D. diss., Princeton University, 1985).

29. First draft of Kahn's statements for the publication of his drawings for the Capitol Complex, "North Carolina," box 56, Kahn Collection.

30. Kahn, lecture at the School of Architecture at the University of California, Berkeley, 1966, published in *Perspecta* 28 (1997). The tape is in Special Collections, Getty Center for the History of Art and Humanities.

31. Notes taken by Duncan Buell while Kahn was dictating, in "Pakistan Cablegrams dictated rapidly by Lou to DPW w/CEV on Thursday 11-7-63 but not sent," box 117, Kahn Collection.

32. In October 1964, Vollmer wrote to the Chair of the East Pakistan Water and Power Development Authority, saying, "It is our intention to have a wall surrounding the entire capital site. The wall would be a pyramid shape in section and contain all the utility services to the site." Drawings for the wall exist in the (uncatalogued) office drawings of the Kahn Collection. "PAKCAP — Correspondence to/from ROYGUS October 8, 1964 thru June 30, 1965," box 117, Kahn Collection. Anant Raje, an architect who was working in Kahn's office during the design development of the complex at Dhaka (who later took over and completed Kahn's project in Ahmedabad), reported that Kahn told him that the site plan was much influenced by Pisa. Raje, interview with the author, March 1991. This idea recalled not only Kahn's concept for a university chapel but also Le Corbusier's Capitol Complex at Chandigarh, which was placed not in the center of the city but at its edge, and which was isolated by a large berm of earth. Kahn had visited Chandigarh on an early trip to the Indian subcontinent and declared the governmental complex there "not one bit less than magnificent" (Vallonrat, interview with the author, November 1991). At the top of the notes taken by Duncan Buell while Kahn was dictating, Buell wrote "Chandigarh MARG Dec. 61 issue," clearly a notation to look at a recent

publication on Le Corbusier's complex to substantiate Kahn's point regarding the importance of distance between the governmental buildings and the city (notes taken by Duncan Buell while Kahn was dictating, in "Pakistan Cablegrams dictated rapidly by Lou to DPW w/CEV on Thursday 11-7-63 but not sent," box 117, Kahn Collection).

33. Kahn, in "PAC Progress Brochure" (June 1965), box 122, Kahn Collection.

34. Ibid.

35. Kahn, p. 8 of transcript of conversation with Karl Linn, 14 May 1965, "Linn, Karl," box 58, Kahn Collection.

36. For more on the debates on, and Kahn's interest in, monumentality in the 1940s, see Chapter 1.

37. "The New Art of Urban Design—Are We Equipped?" Transcript of a conference held at the Architectural League in New York with Kahn, Sert, Franzen, Rudolph, Vincent Scully, and others, 1960, in "Louis I. Kahn—Architectural League," box 61, Kahn Collection. This was later published in *Architectural Forum* 114 (June 1961): 88–89.

38. Kahn to Isadore (Mish) Buten, August 1958, "Oct. 16, 1957–Sept. 7, 1958 ltrs from 8/22–9/7," box 9, Kahn Collection. See also Kahn to Buten, August 1961, "Misc. Corresp. Ap–July 1960," box 64, Kahn Collection, in which he writes, "I have decided because of my mental development in these twelve years to speak on an entirely new subject, 'Monumentality.' Undoubtably you are surprised . . . but I have the favor of the Fates and the good fortune to have been directed much to my expectations and find myself in a developed state of mind ready to change from 'monumentality' to 'monumentality.'" Kahn gave the lecture on 27 October 1961 at their club, according to correspondence with Buten: the letter is in "Misc. Corresp. Ap–July 1960," box 64, Kahn Collection.

39. Telegraph, Kahn to Kafiluddin, 22 January 1964, "PAC—Cablegrams to/from ADDLCHIEF 1964," box 117, Kahn Collection, also quoted by Reed in "Sher-e-Bangla Nagar," 377.

40. Kahn, lecture at the School of Architecture at the University of California, Berkeley, 1966, Special Collections, Getty Center for the History of Art and Humanities.

41. For a discussion of the relationship of Kahn's assembly to the Pantheon in Rome, see Florindo Fusaro, *Il Parlamento e la nuova capitale a Dacca di Louis I. Kahn, 1962/1974* (Rome: Officina edizioni, 1985), 76.

42. Kahn in "Marin City Redevelopment," *Progressive Architecture* 41 (November 1960): 153.

43. Kahn, draft of a text for a booklet describing progress on the Second Capital in Pakistan, June 1965; "PAC Progress Booklet," box 122, Kahn Collection.

44. Reed, in "Sher-e-Bangla Nagar," 376, has also noted that this second plan also reduced the site to six hundred acres and brought the two citadels closer together in response to governmental capacity to procure acreage.

45. Carles Vallonrat reported that it was the client's concern for Pakistan's opportunities to secure Western funding that motivated the changes in the scale of the mosque. Vallonrat, interview with the author, November 1991.

46. Vallonrat, interview with the author, November 1991.

47. Kahn, handwritten note to himself, July 1964, "Program—Building Area Take-off LIK PAK," box 122, Kahn Collection. Several months earlier, Kafiluddin had instructed Kahn that the entrance to the mosque should be raised one floor and that it "should not be for the general public"; "Lou's notes 5-20-64," box 122, Kahn Collection; a related memo is Kafiluddin to Kahn (26 May 1964), "Second Capital—Pakistan/Public Works Department—Correspondence—1964," box 117, Kahn Collection. The issue of public access was discussed in, among others, Roy Vollmer's notes of January 1965, "PAKCAP—Correspondence to/from ROYGUS October 8, 1964 thru June 30, 1965," box 117, Kahn Collection.

48. The first quotation is from September 1964, in "Second Capital—Pakistan—Cable-

grams to/from Kafiluddin Ahmad August 27, 1962–November 26, 1963," box 117, Kahn Collection; the second is from Kahn's notes for the "PAC Progress Booklet" (October 1964), in "PAKCAP–Correspondence to/from ROYGUS October 8, 1964–June 30, 1965," box 117, Kahn Collection.

49. This is one reason that Bangladeshis proudly claim the National Assembly Complex in Dhaka as their national monument–painting portraits of it on stamps and scarves, rickshaws and teacups–whereas Le Corbusier's Capitol Complex in Chandigarh, which equals Kahn's complex in monumentality but neither in cultural sensitivity nor in phenomenological finesse, stands majestic but rejected and underused.

50. Kathleen James, "Indian Institute of Management, Ahmedabad, India, 1962–74," in Brownlee and DeLong, *In the Realm*, 368; and Gautaum Sarabhai to Kahn, 4 April 1962, "National Institute of Design," box 113, Kahn Collection.

51. Kahn's contacts with Indian culture began in 1958, when he met and befriended the Indian architect Balkrishna V. Doshi in Philadelphia in October 1958, when Doshi was in the United States on a grant from the Graham Foundation. Doshi, interview with Richard Saul Wurman, Archive of Richard Saul Wurman, Newport, R.I. By 1960, perhaps at Doshi's encouragement but perhaps through some other channel, Kahn had become a member of the Tagore Society of Philadelphia, a literary club devoted to studying the poetry of Sir Rabindranath Tagore, a Hindu Bengali poet (notices of meetings are in "Holzborg," box 64, Kahn Collection).

52. Kahn to Mrs. Esther I. Kahn, undated, in the collection of Sue Ann Kahn, New York. He was also bemused in a vaguely superior way by this foreign culture, continuing: "[It was very] hot–greeted by the whole DPW [PWD]–about 30 engineers all with their dark brown faces open colored shirts and white trousers sandaled shoes all except the bearded ones looked quite alike."

53. Kahn and Carles Vallonrat visited the Taj Mahal in Agra, Fatehpur Sikri, and the Moghul monuments in Delhi on one of their earliest trips to India (Vallonrat, interview with the author, September 1991). According to Kahn's calendars, this would have been in either November 1962 or July 1963, when Kahn was in India in conjunction with his project in Ahmedabad. "LIK Calendars," box 121, Kahn Collection.

54. Kahn visited a small Moghul mausoleum-garden in Dhaka, but it is not nearly as impressive as those he saw in India and West Pakistan. Hence it is likely that he would have taken inspiration from those far more monumental sites. Komendant also discussed Kahn's itinerary in *Eighteen Years with Architect Louis I. Kahn* (Englewood, N.J.: Aloray Publishers, 1975), 82.

55. Kahn, quoted in Heinz Ronner and Sharad Jhaveri, *Louis I. Kahn: Complete Work, 1935–1974*, 2nd ed. (Basel: Birkhauser, 1987), 234.

56. David Wisdom, in an interview with Alessandra Latour, discussed the Pakistani reaction to Kahn's lakes, in *Louis I. Kahn: L'uomo, il maestro*, ed. Alessandra Latour (Rome: Edizioni Kappa, 1986), 117.

57. Kahn, draft of "Remarks" (eventually published in *Perspecta* 9–10 [1965]), p. 5, in "Yale Speech for *Perspecta* 9 LIK," box 54 (speech given in October 1963), Kahn Collection.

58. "Lou's notes 5-20-64," box 122, Kahn Collection.

59. "Second Capital–Pakistan Public Works Department–Correspondence–1964," box 117, Kahn Collection.

60. Kafiluddin to Kahn, 26 May 1964, "Second Capital–Pakistan–Pakistan Public Works Department Correspondence–1964," box 117, Kahn Collection. Carles Vallonrat reports that the PWD asked Kahn many times to make the building more Islamic, and that Kahn always prevaricated in his replies and then ignored their requests. Vallonrat, interview with the author, 6 December 1991.

61. Kahn, "The Difference Between Form and Design" (October 1961), in "LIK Lectures," box 15, Kahn Collection. He made virtually the same statements in Jan Rowan, "Wanting to Be: The Philadelphia School," *Progressive Architecture* 42 (April 1961): 137–141. Kahn made similarly nasty comments about Stone's screens in Mary Huntington Hall, "Salk's Ambitious Castle," *San Diego* (February 1962): 41 (he also used the two-screen system for the Salk Institute's meeting house design).

62. Roy Vollmer sent Kahn a telegram in October 1964: "*marble* excellent concept for higher category buildings. Traditionally used in the great palaces and gardens of the Moghuls." "PACCAP Vollmer Reports," box 122, Kahn Collection.

63. On the client's decision to use brick, see Reed, "Sher-e-Bangla Nagar," 379.

64. Sigfried Giedion, "Forget the 'International Style': The State of Contemporary Architecture, 1: The Regional Approach," *Architectural Record* 115 (January 1954): 135.

65. For a full account of the aesthetic of authenticity and its relationship to Existentialist philosophy, see Chapter 2.

66. See Stirling, "Regionalism in Modern Architecture," *Architect's Year Book* 7 (1957): 62–68; Moholy-Nagy, "Environment and Anonymous Architecture," *Perspecta* 3 (1955): 3–8; Moholy-Nagy, *Native Genius in Anonymous Architecture* (New York: Horizon Press, 1957); Rudofsky, *Architecture Without Architects* (New York: Museum of Modern Art, 1964); Giedion, "Forget the 'International Style.'"

67. Kahn, November 1959, lecture at the Pratt Institute in New York City, in "Lectures," box 115, Kahn Collection, with the exception of "dumpy," which comes from a different iteration of the same idea, quoted in Christian Devillers, "The Indian Institute of Management by Louis I. Kahn, 1962–1974, Ahmedabad," *Casabella* 571 (September 1990): 62.

68. Kahn, quoted in William Jordy, "The Formal Image: U.S.A.," *Architectural Review* 127 (March 1960): 160. For more on primitivizing impulses in the postwar period, see the introduction and conclusion, and the articles on Bernard Rudofsky (by Felicity Scott) and the Italian Neo-Realists (by Maristella Casciato), all in Sarah Williams Goldhagen and Réjean Legault, *Anxious Modernisms: Experimental Postwar Architecture* (Cambridge: MIT Press, 2000).

69. His office claimed that these raised striations, similar to the concrete string courses of the Art Gallery at Yale, had a practical function in that they would serve as drip courses to throw water off the facade, although Kahn probably knew that in Dhaka they would not perform this function, for in October 1964 an assistant, Roy Volmer, wrote to Kahn from Dhaka that because of strong winds, rain in east Bengal falls horizontally as often as vertically: "Rains come from the north and south (supposedly equally) blowing horizontal rain at 45 degrees to 30 degrees from level." "PAKCAP Correspondence to/from ROYGUS October 8, 1964 thru June 30, 1965," box 117, Kahn Collection.

70. For similar readings of Kahn's buildings, see Devillers, "Indian Institute," 30–38, 59–63; Michael Benedikt, *Deconstructing the Kimbell* (New York: Sites Books, 1991).

71. Kahn, in *North Carolina State Student Publication of the School of Design* 14 (May 1964).

72. "Really two buildings" is from notes on Kahn's descriptions of the Salk center in unmarked file, box 122, Kahn Collection.

73. May 1965, in "Karl Linn," box 58, Kahn Collection. Kahn repeated the idea in April 1966 in his lecture to the Boston Society of Architects, "Boston Society of Architects," box 57, Kahn Collection.

74. The mosque may have been included at least at one point in the design process, but at another the client was also directing that it be dropped. In June 1963, Kafiluddin Ahmed noted that the speaker was now saying that attached to the assembly chamber "should be a proper mosque and not a prayer hall." "W-CAP-3/ACE I, 1963/4," in files of Public Works Department, Dhaka, Bangladesh. Similarly, a letter from J. Huq to

Kahn of the year before directed Kahn that the assembly chamber "should have a mosque adjoining it instead of a prayer hall." "PAC-Cablegrams to/from ADDLCHIEF/ 2 years 1966–67," box 117, Kahn Collection. By contrast, correspondence of October 1964 mentions both a prayer hall and a mosque: Z. A. K. Baqai, "Second Capital/Pakistan/Pakistan Public Works Department/Correspondence–1964," box 117, Kahn Collection.

75. Kahn, lecture at the School of Architecture at the University of California at Berkeley, 1966, Special Collections, Getty Center for the History of Art and Humanities.

76. Kahn to Vollmer, 25 August 1965, "PAKCAP–Correspondence to/from ROYGUS October 8, 1964 thru June 30, 1965," box 117, Kahn Collection.

77. Kahn, in a lecture on 29 May 1963 (p. 24, transcript of lecture to the American Institute of Interior Designers, "AID Speech–Liturgical Conference," box 68, Kahn Collection), described the National Assembly Building as a "world within a world," which is the same phrase he used to describe the Pantheon in Rome at a lecture in Princeton on 22 November 1961 ("Lectures," box 115, Kahn Collection) and at a lecture in Aspen on 27 June 1962 ("Aspen Conference–June 1962," box 59, Kahn Collection).

78. Kahn, lecture at Princeton, "Princeton 1961," Box 65, Kahn Collection.

CHAPTER 8: LOUIS KAHN'S SITUATED MODERNISM

1. For a more extensive consideration of the modern movement, its various strains, and their trajectories in the postwar period, see Sarah Williams Goldhagen, "Reconceptualizing the Modern," in *Anxious Modernisms: Experimental Postwar Architecture*, ed. Sarah Williams Goldhagen and Réjean Legault (Cambridge: MIT Press, 2000).

2. Other modernist architects—for example, Alvar Aalto, Eileen Gray, Bruno Taut—had developed their own, very different versions of situated modernism before Kahn came to his. It is highly unlikely, however, that Kahn drew ideas from these predecessors. He is said to have criticized Aalto's work (see Robin Evans, *The Projective Cast: Architecture and Its Three Geometries* [Cambridge: MIT Press, 1995], 74), and no evidence survives that he even knew of the architecture of Gray or Taut. We must, then, in light of the earlier situated modernists, and in light of the account of his intellectual development presented here, consider situated modernism a continuous tradition within modernism which Kahn reinvented for himself. For an account of situated modernism as one of several continuous strains of the modern movement, see Goldhagen, "Reconceptualizing the Modern," where much that is written here about the character of modernism in architecture and its development during the twentieth century is laid out in greater depth.

3. Vincent Scully, *Louis I. Kahn* (New York: Braziller, 1961).

4. Quoted in Michael J. Lewis, "Eleanor Donnelly Erdman Hall, Bryn Mawr College," in Brownlee and DeLong, *In the Realm*, 354.

5. Pierre Bourdieu, *The Logic of Practice*, trans. Richard Nice (1980; Stanford: Stanford University Press, 1990), 57–58.

6. On the artistic power in a tense relationship between restraint and expressiveness, see Sean Scully, in "The Beauty of the Real: H.-M. Herzog Interviews Sean Scully," in *Sean Scully: The Catherine Paintings*, ed. Hans-Michael Herzog (Ostfildern: Cantz Verlag, 1995), 73.

7. This is why Kahn's work has been, and will continue to be, subject to multiple and opposing interpretations. Witness, to name but one example, the opposition between critics and writers who see in his architecture a precursor to historicist postmodernism and those who see in it an abstract minimalism or abstract expressionism. Examples of the first camp include Scully, *Louis I. Kahn*; Brownlee and DeLong, *In the Realm*; and Peter Reed, "Toward Form: Louis I. Kahn's Urban Designs for Philadelphia,

1939–1962" (Ph.D. diss., University of Pennsylvania, 1989); examples of the second camp include Michael Benedikt, *Deconstructing the Kimbell: An Essay on Meaning in Architecture* (New York: Sites Books, 1991); Christian Devillers, "L'Indian Institute à Ahmedabad," *Casabella* 54 (September 1990): 36–58, and, to some extent, William Jordy in *American Buildings and Their Architects, IV: The Impact of European Modernism in the Mid-Twentieth Century* (Garden City, N.J.: Doubleday/Anchor, 1970), 361–426. On the notion of an "open" work that is continuously accessible over time by virtue of "gaps" built into it, see Umberto Eco, *The Open Work*, trans. Anna Cancogni (Cambridge: Harvard University Press), 1989); Wolfgang Iser, *The Implied Reader: Patterns of Communication in Prose Fiction from Bunyan to Beckett* (Baltimore: Johns Hopkins University Press, 1974). For a description of an interpreter's expectations, and how those expectations shape her reception of a work of art, see Hans-Georg Gadamer, *Truth and Method* (1975; New York: Crossroad, 1982), especially 235–238.

8. Walter Benjamin, in "The Work of Art in the Age of Mechanical Reproduction," writes: "Architecture has always represented the prototype of a work the reception of which is consummated in a state of distraction." In *Iluminations*, ed. Hannah Arendt, trans. Harry Zohn (New York: Schocken Books, 1968), 239.

ACKNOWLEDGMENTS

Through the many years of working on this project, I have often thought that my sensitivity to the importance of community comes in part from my finding of a home in the community of academia. Many have contributed to the evolution of this book, which is so embedded in my intellectual formation. Bill Jordy, my teacher at Brown University, discussed Louis Kahn's architecture with me long before I thought of writing this book. He supported my work for many years; I admired him, and I feel sad that he did not live to see this final product. Some of the ideas in this book were first developed at Columbia University in a doctoral dissertation written in the Department of Art History and Archaeology under the devoted guidance and direction of Mary McLeod and Robin Middleton, with intellectual and personal support also offered by Barry Bergdoll, Richard Brilliant, Kenneth Frampton, and Gwendolyn Wright.

Thoughtful and important comments on later versions of various chapters were offered by George Baird, David B. Brownlee, Daniel Jonah Goldhagen, K. Michael Hays, Alice Jarrard, and Neil Levine. Francesco Passanti gave the manuscript an especially careful reading, suggesting breaking one chapter into two and expanding them both. This improved the structure of the entire book and its argument. I am grateful to all these colleagues and friends for their friendship, for their wisdom, and for generously sharing their time and ideas.

Many people who cared for Kahn and his architecture spent precious time to help me get things right. Among them, I am especially grateful to Anne Griswold Tyng, who showed me, at a time when she would share them with no one else, the letters Kahn had written her while she was in Rome. Over a period of eighteen months I spoke on the phone with her, and visited her at her home in Philadelphia, numerous times. I am also thankful for the help and support of Sue Ann Kahn and Esther Kahn, Rabbi Morris Dembrowitz, Jeremiah Ford, Jean France, Robert Geddes, William Huff, Philip Johnson, Blanche Lemco van Ginkel, Marshall Meyers, Harriet Pattison, G. Holmes Perkins, David Rothstein, Colin Rowe, Denise Scott Brown, Robert Slutsky, Alison Smithson, Peter Smithson, Carles Vallonrat, Tim Vreeland, Henry Wilcots, and Richard Saul Wurman. At the Architectural Archives in Philadelphia, which houses the collections of Kahn, Robert Le Ricolais, G. Holmes Perkins, and others, Julia Converse, Matt Pisarski, and Bill Whittaker provided timely and professional assistance in response to all manner of requests.

In Bangladesh, a number of architects who esteem Kahn's work there did their best to help me with access to needed materials and information. I fondly thank Kazi Khaled Ashraf, Hasina Chowdhury, Mazharul Islam, Uttam Saha, and Abdul Wazid. In Ahmedabad, Balkrishna Doshi and Anant Raje offered many insights into Kahn's Indian Institute of Management.

Many additional archivists at, and tenders to, various collections were extremely helpful and are too numerous to name here. I thank the archivists at the following collections: the University of Pennsylvania Archives; the School of Architecture, Princeton University, and the Jean Labatut papers, Firestone Library, Princeton University; the Alfred Kastner and Oscar Stonorov Collections at the American Heritage Center, Laramie, Wyoming; and the Kahn documents at the Getty Center for the History of Art and Humanities. At Columbia University, I used the George Howe and Paul Zucker collections at the Avery Architectural Library; at Yale University, I consulted the Josef Albers collection and the Yale University Art Gallery collection at Sterling Library. Kind thanks as well to the many people who helped me at the Public Works Department in Dhaka, Bangladesh, and to Kevin Keim at the Charles Moore Foundation in Austin, Texas.

Columbia University's Department of Art History and Archaeology provided the much-needed initial funding for my trip to Bangladesh and for other research. I received a Mike Hogg grant from the School of Architecture at the University of Texas at Austin during my happy year teaching there. These and other funds helped me hire a small parade of research assistants, all of them good-humored, who contributed to the completion of various stages of the manuscript. These include Laura Briggs, John Maier, John McMorrough, and Lan-Ying Ip. Patricia Fidler, Mary Mayer, and Jenya Weinreb of Yale University Press made the task of preparing the manuscript for publication a nearly pleasurable one.

Danny Goldhagen rightly insisted that I write the final chapter of this book when I wanted nothing more than to be done with it. His love and good humor, his interest in and enthusiasm for my ideas helped me through the final drafts of this book. I am immensely grateful to my sister, Joan Williams, for her love, wisdom, and guidance on many matters professional and personal. My mother, Jeanne Williams, nurtured my independence of mind with good-humored warmth and love, and made part of the early stages of research memorable with a joint trip to the Salk Institute. The ever-generous Norma Goldhagen offered and provided loving care for Veronica at critical moments during the completion of the manuscript, and Veronica has waited patiently, and long enough, for Mommy to be done with her book. Gideon sat, good-naturedly, in my lap while I put in the final edits.

My father, Norman Williams, Jr., died, without me by his side, during the first
year that I taught at Harvard, when this project and my life were still a shapeless
mass of untapped potential. A city planner, intellectual, and activist for social
justice, he taught me to look at cities, to see politics and history in the built
environment, and to believe that a better future is made by women and men. He
taught me so much more, and I shall always miss him. This book is dedicated to
his memory.

INDEX